Special Price

£1-99

BOOKS THAT HAVE CHANGED MAN'S THINKING

THE LIFE OF SAMUEL JOHNSON LL. D.

Boswell (right) and Dr. Johnson set off on a tour of Scotland

JAMES BOSWELL

THE LIFE OF SAMUEL JOHNSON LL. D.

Selected and abridged
by
EDMUND FULLER

With an Introduction
and Appreciation
by
COLIN BELL

Distributed by
HERON BOOKS

CONTENTS

LIST OF ILLUSTRATIONS

EDITOR'S FOREWORD

James Boswell's The Life of Samuel Johnson, LL.D. *is an inevitable choice for our series on* BOOKS THAT HAVE CHANGED MAN'S THINKING. *Almost from the time of its publication in 1791 it has generally been referred to as the first and best of biographies in English, and in subsequent centuries it exerted an incalculable influence upon the way writers have looked upon and appraised our great men. The* Life, *which we present in a masterly, one-volume abridgement by Edmund Fuller, came to be written through a happy conjunction of a time, a place, and of two remarkable people. The time was the eighteenth century, the place the vigorous literary world of England, and the two people, whose fateful partnership as chronicler and subject brought far greater fame to both than either would have had alone, were of course Boswell and Johnson.*

The Life *was the first real biography in the sense that before Boswell's time very few if any full-scale efforts of the kind had been written that showed the subject in all honesty " with all his warts on ". As for its being the best of biographies, we may refer not only to the judgement of posterity but to Boswell himself. Never a modest man, he knew exactly what he was doing, and explained it to his readers at length in the opening pages of his book. " Indeed I cannot conceive a more perfect mode of writing any man's life," he wrote, " than not only relating all the most important events of it in their order, but interweaving what he privately wrote, and said, and thought; by which mankind are enabled as it were to see him live." Boswell was correct in stating that the chief merit of his book was " the quantity it contains of Johnson's conversation."*

1

That he deliberately chose Dr. Johnson, with his " wonderful powers of mind " and "store of wit and wisdom " as his subject is in itself very much to Boswell's credit. Moreover he took pains to sketch his hero in his every aspect, " the shade as well as light."

Boswell knew he was pioneering a novel literary form, and he was not reticent about the difficulties he faced: " I must be allowed to suggest, that the nature of the work, ... as it consists of innumerable detached particulars, all of which, even the most minute, I have spared no pains to ascertain with a scrupulous authenticity, has occasioned a degree of trouble far beyond that of any other species of composition." His success was gratifying. " I have Johnsonised the land " he boasted after the book had appeared.

Who was Dr. Johnson? Undoubtedly a brilliant man, and the literary arbiter of his day, he nevertheless would have been forgotten by all but scholars had it not been for Boswell's Life. *His literary works, the innovating* Dictionary of the English Language *and a quantity of heavily-written essays, poems, tragedies, biographies and criticism, have now been largely forgotten. And who was Boswell? A Scottish lawyer with an incurable literary bent, he too achieved some reputation in his day with two travel books and even more with his* Life, *but until recent years he was generally regarded as a minor figure who had acquired fame by climbing onto the coat tails of Dr. Johnson. Then in the 1920's a vast hoard of his papers came to light, in particular his voluminous private journals; and their continuing publication, as Colin Bell describes so well in his Appreciation, has entirely altered our estimate of the man. As Boswell's reputation rises, that of Dr. Johnson is changed. More than ever he is now remembered simply as the principal character in Boswell's rich repertory.*

COURTLANDT CANBY
EDITOR OF THE SERIES

INTRODUCTION

It is all too easy for books to die from a surfeit of reputation. There comes a point, after a generation or more of reverence, when half the population won't read a man on the assumption that the classics are boring, and the other half read with such expectation that they must be disappointed. Boswell's Johnson *has so often been described as " the best biography in English " that the phrase might almost be part of the title; it holds its place in our culture not because so many read it, but because everyone thinks they ought to have read it. Since it has also fallen into the hands of those arch-enemies of literature, the Schools Examination Boards, it is even more difficult to come to the book itself fresh, eager and unprejudiced.*

Accordingly, to introduce it in the awed tones and unreal language of the academic critic, would be to it yet further disservice. It is perfectly true to say that no biography written before can match it, and that none since has any merit that does not incorporate Boswell's technical discoveries; but it is not a historic monument, it is a book. Without it, Johnson himself would be a minor figure in the English past, and Boswell effectively unknown; but books are to be read, not put on show like rusting artefacts, grubbed triumphantly from the muckheaps of the dead.

There are indeed few books in the language better able to survive on their own merits. It is not necessary to know that Boswell was the first biographer to reveal both his subject and himself in uncensored detail to appreciate the honesty and the accuracy of his record. The mere fact that Boswell introduced the dramatic method into biography isn't as important as its actual use—giving a pace, excitement and authenticity that mere narrative could never achieve. It certainly isn't necessary to have to struggle through the turgid wastes of earlier " official lives " in order to enjoy the splendours of Boswell. The most arid, least satisfying, approach to this book is that of grim cultural duty; it deserves far better than to be opened as one might race through the Cathedrals of Europe—merely in order to have done with it. The finest recommendation one might give this new edition is simply that it is new — and thus the volume itself does not already look and smell like the furthest shelves of the dullest library.

It is of course an old and honourable practice to skip from time to time the minutiae of Johnson's career in search of what has been called " the Glory of the Life "—Johnson's conversation. Since biographer and subject did not meet until 1763, and met most often in the 'seventies, it is in the later part of the book that most of Johnson's talk is to be found. As Boswell says, Johnson " talked for victory," and would take that part in any argument most likely to provoke a battle. Consequently the record of his talk has drama, history, literature, fact—and dogmatic fiction—interwoven. It gives at times a contradictory impression of his views (mere consistency is no virtue in any case), but a splendid picture of the man.

Johnson has 336 entries in the Oxford Dictionary of Quotations, *many of them now so rooted in our language that they form part of everyman's vocabulary. Yet although Johnson was a prolific writer, of gigantic contemporary repute (" the Great Cham " he was called, and held an honorary Doctorate and State pension), it is significant that 227 of those quotations are drawn, not from his own published works, but from Boswell's faithful record. Without his biographer, we should know merely that his contemporaries thought Johnson an unparalleled conversationalist—but we should not have the evidence to judge for ourselves; we should know his literary style, often pompous and archaic, but not his natural talking style, incisive, measured and robust. Where Johnson on paper was concerned to escape the vernacular for the complexities of the High Classical,*

4

Boswell's only concern was to purge his own writings of the Scotticisms that he unfortunately felt lacked respectability. Johnson fled English for the dead languages; Boswell merely purged his English of its native colouration.

It is from Boswell that we learn Johnson's own view of biography: " Nobody can write the life of a man, but those who have eat and drunk and lived in social intercourse with him ". Johnson's own Life of Savage *has that merit—as of course most of his* Lives of the Poets *do not—but Boswell's* Johnson *is itself a monument to the principle. As a student, Boswell had heard Adam Smith point out that we " are glad to know the minutest detail about a great man ", and that too is borne out by Boswell's own application of the rule. Boswell ate, and drank, and lived in social intercourse with his subject —and understood that it was at least as important to record the private Johnson as the public man.*

Boswell had in fact resolved to write the Life *long before Johnson's death, and many of their friends understood that this was effectively agreed between the two: Johnson supplied copies of his correspondence, and details of his youth and early work, in a manner which makes clear not only Boswell's determination, but Johnson's consent. On Johnson's death, Boswell would probably have begun work even had he not received an instantaneous commission. Johnson died on December 13, 1784—and by January 21, 1785 Boswell was already hard at work collecting materials and anecdotes. Even so, the book did not finally appear until May 16, 1791—long after the first flush of public interest in the subject, and at the extremely high price for the day of two guineas. Despite this, and despite the fact that Boswell had been beaten to the press by two rivals, within two months of publication 1200 of the 1700 copies printed had been sold: a good sale on a substantial print-order, in a country where literacy of any sort was far from universal, even among the ruling class.*

Two years later, the second edition appeared. Malone, who had helped Boswell with the original, advising, editing, proof-reading, produced four more editions between Boswell's death (May 19, 1795) and 1811. The Life *was, from the very start, both a classic—and a best-seller. One may buy it still because it is a classic—but to read it, remember only that it was, and is, a book that sells; not furniture for the well-appointed home, but a delight for the lively mind.*

COLIN BELL

DEDICATION TO
SIR JOSHUA REYNOLDS

MY DEAR SIR,

Every liberal motive that can actuate an Authour in the dedication of his labours, concurs in directing me to you, as the person to whom the following Work should be inscribed.

If there be a pleasure in celebrating the distinguished merit of a contemporary, mixed with a certain degree of vanity not altogether inexcusable, in appearing fully sensible of it, where can I find one, in complimenting whom I can with more general approbation gratify those feelings? Your excellence not only in the Art over which you have long presided with unrivalled fame, but also in Philosophy and elegant Literature, is well known to the present, and will continue to be the admiration of future ages. Your equal and placid temper, your variety of conversation, your true politeness, by which you are so amiable in private society, and that enlarged hospitality which has long made your house a common centre of union for the great, the accomplished, the learned, and the ingenious; all these qualities I can, in perfect confidence of not being accused of flattery, ascribe to you.

If a man may indulge an honest pride, in having it known to the world, that he has been thought worthy of particular attention by a person of the first eminence in the age in which he lived, whose company has been universally courted, I am justified in availing myself of the usual privilege of a Dedication, when I mention that there has been a long and uninterrupted friendship between us.

If gratitude should be acknowledged for favours received, I have this opportunity, my dear Sir, most sincerely to thank you for the many happy hours which I owe to your kindness,—for the cordiality with which you have at all times been pleased to welcome me,—for the number of valuable acquaintances to whom you have introduced me,— for the *noctes cœnœque Deûm,* which I have enjoyed under your roof.

If a work should be inscribed to one who is master of the subject of it, and whose approbation, therefore, must ensure it credit and success, the life of Dr. Johnson is, with the greatest propriety, dedicated to Sir Joshua Reynolds, who was the intimate and beloved friend of that great man; the friend, whom he declared to be "the most invulnerable man he knew; whom, if he should quarrel with him, he should find the most difficulty how to abuse." You, my dear Sir, studied him, and knew him well: you venerated and admired him. Yet, luminous as he was upon the whole, you perceived all the shades which mingled in the grand composition; all the little peculiarities and slight blemishes which marked the literary Colossus. Your very warm commendation of the specimen which I gave in my "Journal of a Tour to the Hebrides," of my being able to preserve his conversation in an authentick and lively manner, which opinion the Publick has confirmed, was the best encouragement for me to persevere in my purpose of producing the whole of my stores.

In one respect, this Work will, in some passages, be different from the former. In my "Tour," I was almost unboundedly open in my communications, and from my eagerness to display the wonderful fertility and readiness of Johnson's wit, freely shewed to the world its dexterity, even when I was myself the object of it. I trusted that I should be liberally understood, as knowing very well what I was about, and by no means as simply unconscious of the pointed effects of the satire. I own, indeed, that I was arrogant enough to suppose that the tenour of the rest of the book would sufficiently guard me against such a strange imputation. But it seems I judged too well of the world; for, though I could scarcely believe it, I have been undoubtedly informed, that many persons, especially in distant quarters, not penetrating enough into Johnson's character, so as to understand his mode of treating his friends, have arraigned my judgement, instead of seeing that I was sensible of all that they could observe.

8

It is related of the great Dr. Clarke, that when in one of his leisure hours he was unbending himself with a few friends in the most playful and frolicksome manner, he observed Beau Nash approaching; upon which he suddenly stopped;—"My boys, (said he,) let us be grave: here comes a fool." The world, my friend, I have found to be a great fool, as to that particular on which it has become necessary to speak very plainly. I have, therefore, in this Work been more reserved; and though I tell nothing but the truth, I have still kept in my mind that the whole truth is not always to be exposed. This, however, I have managed so as to occasion no diminution of the pleasure which my book should afford; though malignity may sometimes be disappointed of its gratifications.

I am,
My dear Sir,
Your much obliged friend,
And faithful humble servant,
JAMES BOSWELL.

London,
April 20, 1791.

I at last deliver to the world a Work which I have long promised, and of which, I am afraid, too high expectations have been raised. The delay of its publication must be imputed, in a considerable degree, to the extraordinary zeal which has been shewn by distinguished persons in all quarters to supply me with additional information concerning its illustrious subject; resembling in this the grateful tribes of ancient nations, of which every individual was eager to throw a stone upon the grave of a departed Hero, and thus to share in the pious office of erecting an honourable monument to his memory.

The labour and anxious attention with which I have collected and arranged the materials of which these volumes are composed, will hardly be conceived by those who read them with careless facility. The stretch of mind and prompt assiduity by which so many conversations were preserved, I myself, at some distance or time, contemplate with wonder; and I must be allowed to suggest, that the nature of the work, in other respects, as it consists of innumerable detached particulars, all which, even the most minute, I have spared no pains to ascertain with a scrupulous authenticity, has occasioned a degree of trouble far beyond that of any other species of composition. Were I to detail the books which I have consulted, and the inquiries which I have found it necessary to make by various channels, I should probably be thought ridiculously ostentatious. Let me only observe, as a specimen of my trouble, that I have sometimes been obliged to run half over London, in order to fix a date correctly; which, when I had accomplished, I well knew would obtain me no praise, though a failure would have been to my discredit. And after all, perhaps, hard as it may be, I shall not be surprised if omissions or mistakes be pointed out with invidious severity. I have also been extremely careful as to the exactness of my quotations; holding that there is a respect due to the publick, which should oblige every Authour to attend to this, and never to presume to introduce them with,—"I think I have read;"—or —"If I remember right;" when the originals may be examined.

I beg leave to express my warmest thanks to those who have been pleased to favour me with communications and advice in the conduct of my Work. But I cannot sufficiently acknowledge my obligations to my friend Mr. MALONE, who was so good as to allow me to read to him almost the whole of my manuscript, and made such remarks as were greatly for the advantage of the Work; though it is but fair to him to mention, that upon many occasions I differed from him, and followed my own judgement.

It is painful to me to think, that while I was carrying on this Work, several of those to whom it would have been most interesting have died. Such melancholy disappointments we know to be incident to humanity; but we do not feel them the less. Let me particularly lament the Reverend THOMAS WARTON, and the Reverend Dr. ADAMS. Mr. WARTON, amidst his variety of genius and learning, was an excellent Biographer. His contributions to my Collection are highly estimable; and as he had a true relish of my "Tour to the Hebrides," I trust I should now have been gratified with a larger share of his kind approbation. Dr. ADAMS, eminent as the Head of a College, as a writer, and as a most amiable man, had known JOHNSON from his early years, and was his friend through life. What reason had I to hope for the countenance of that venerable Gentleman to this Work, will appear from what he wrote to me upon a former occasion from Oxford, November 17, 1785:—"Dear Sir, I hazard this letter, not knowing where it will find you, to thank you for your very agreeable 'Tour,' which I found here on my return from the country, and in which you have depicted our friend so perfectly to my fancy, in every attitude, every scene and situation, that I have thought myself in the company, and of the party almost throughout. It has given very general satisfaction; and those who have found most fault with a passage here and there, have agreed that they could not help going through, and being

11

entertained with the whole. I wish, indeed, some few gross expressions had been softened, and a few of our hero's foibles had been a little more shaded; but it is useful to see the weaknesses incident to great minds; and you have given us Dr. Johnson's authority that in history all ought to be told."

Such a sanction to my faculty of giving a just representation of Dr. JOHNSON I could not conceal. Nor will I suppress my satisfaction in the consciousness, that by recording so considerable a portion of the wisdom and wit of "the brightest ornament of the eighteenth century," I have largely provided for the instruction and entertainment of mankind.

London, April 20, 1791.

ADVERTISEMENT
TO THE SECOND EDITION

That I was anxious for the success of a work which had employed much of my time and labour, I do not wish to conceal: but whatever doubts I at any time entertained, have been entirely removed by the very favourable reception with which it has been honoured. That reception has excited my best exertions to render my Book more perfect; and in this endeavour I have had the assistance not only of some of my particular friends, but of many other learned and ingenious men, by which I have been enabled to rectify some mistakes, and to enrich the Work with many valuable additions.

In the strangely mixed scenes of human existence, our feelings are often at once pleasing and painful. Of this truth, the progress of the present Work furnishes a striking instance. It was highly gratifying to me that my friend, Sir JOSHUA REYNOLDS, to whom it is inscribed, lived to peruse it, and to give the strongest testimony to its fidelity; but before a second edition, which he contributed to improve, could be finished, the world has been deprived of that most valuable man; a loss of which the regret will be deep, and

12

lasting, and extensive, proportionate to the felicity which he diffused through a wide circle of admirers and friends.

In reflecting that the illustrious subject of this Work, by being more extensively and intimately known, however elevated before, has risen in the veneration and love of mankind, I feel a satisfaction beyond what fame can afford. We cannot, indeed, too much or too often admire his wonderful powers of mind, when we consider that the principal store of wit and wisdom which this Work contains, was not a particular selection from his general conversation, but was merely his occasional talk at such times as I had the good fortune to be in his company; and, without doubt, if his discourse at other periods had been collected with the same attention, the whole tenor of what he uttered would have been found equally excellent.

His strong, clear, and animated enforcement of religion, morality, loyalty, and subordination, while it delights and improves the wise and the good, will, I trust, prove an effectual antidote to that detestable sophistry which has been lately imported from France, under the false name of *Philosophy*, and with a malignant industry has been employed against the peace, good order, and happiness of society, in our free and prosperous country; but, thanks be to God, without producing the pernicious effects which were hoped for by its propagators.

It seems to me, in my moments of self-complacency, that this extensive biographical work, however inferior in its nature, may in one respect be assimilated to the *Odyssey*. Amidst a thousand entertaining and instructive episodes the *Hero* is never long out of sight; for they are all in some degree connected with him; and He, in the whole course of the History, is exhibited by the Authour for the best advantage of his readers:

—Quid virtus et quid sapientia possit,
Utile proposuit nobis examplar Ulyssen.

Should there be any cold-blooded and morose mortals who really dislike this Book, I will give them a story to apply. When the great Duke of Marlborough, accompanied

13

by Lord Cadogan, was one day reconnoitering the army in Flanders, a heavy rain came on, and they both called for their cloaks. Lord Cadogan's servant, a good humoured alert lad, brought his Lordship's in a minute. The Duke's servant, a lazy sulky dog, was so sluggish, that his Grace being wet to the skin, reproved him, and had for answer with a grunt, "I came as fast as I could;" upon which the Duke calmly said,—"Cadogan, I would not for a thousand pounds have that fellow's temper."

There are some men, I believe, who have, or think they have, a very small share of vanity. Such may speak of their literary fame in a decorous style of diffidence. But I confess, that I am so formed by nature and by habit, that to restrain the effusion of delight, on having obtained such fame, to me would be truly painful. Why then should I suppress it? Why "out of the abundance of the heart" should I not speak? Let me then mention with a warm, but not insolent exultation, that I have been regaled with spontaneous praise of my work by many and various persons eminent for their rank, learning, talents, and accomplishments; much of which praise I have under their hands to be reposited in my archives at Auchinleck. An honourable and reverend friend speaking of the favourable reception of my volumes, even in the circles of fashion and elegance, said to me, "you have made them all talk Johnson."—Yes, I may add, I have Johnsonised the land; and I trust they will not only talk, but think, Johnson.

To enumerate those to whom I have been thus indebted, would be tediously ostentatious. I cannot however but name one whose praise is truly valuable, not only on account of his knowledge and abilities, but on account of the magnificent, yet dangerous embassy, in which he is now employed, which makes every thing that relates to him peculiarly interesting. Lord Macartney favoured me with his own copy of my book, with a number of notes, of which I have availed myself. On the first leaf I found in his Lordship's handwriting, an inscription of such high commendation, that even I, vain as I am, cannot prevail on myself to publish it.

[July 1, 1793.]

The Life of
Samuel Johnson, LL.D.

To write the Life of him who excelled all mankind in writing the lives of others, and who, whether we consider his extraordinary endowments, or his various works, has been equalled by few in any age, is an arduous, and may be reckoned in me a presumptuous task.

Had Dr. Johnson written his own Life, in conformity with the opinion which he has given, that every man's life may be best written by himself; had he employed in the preservation of his own history, that clearness of narration and elegance of language in which he has embalmed so many eminent persons, the world would probably have had the most perfect example of biography that was ever exhibited. But although he at different times, in a desultory manner, committed to writing many particulars of the progress of his mind and fortunes, he never had persevering diligence enough to form them into a regular composition. Of these memorials a few have been preserved; but the greater part was consigned by him to the flames, a few days before his death.

As I had the honour and happiness of enjoying his friendship for upwards of twenty years; as I had the scheme of writing his life constantly in view; as he was well apprised of this circumstance, and from time to time obligingly satisfied my enquiries, by communicating to me the incidents of his early years; as I acquired a facility in recollecting, and was very assiduous in recording, his conversation, of which the extraordinary vigour and vivacity constituted one of the first features of his character; and as I have spared no pains in obtaining materials concerning him, from every quarter where I could discover that they were to be found, and have been favoured with the most liberal communications by his friends; I flatter myself that few biographers have entered upon such a work as this, with more advantages; independent of literary abilities, in which I am not vain enough to compare myself with some great names who have gone before me in this kind of writing.

Instead of melting down my materials into one mass, and constantly speaking in my own person, by which I might have appeared to have more merit in the execution of the work, I have resolved to adopt and enlarge upon the excellent plan of Mr. Mason, in his Memoirs of Gray. Wherever narrative is necessary to explain, connect, and supply, I furnish it to the best of my abilities; but in the chronological series of Johnson's life, which I trace as distinctly as I can, year by year, I produce, wherever it is in my power, his own minutes, letters, or conversation, being convinced that this mode is more lively, and will make my readers better acquainted with him, than even most of those were who actually knew him, but could know him only partially; whereas there is here an accumulation of intelligence from various points, by which his character is more fully understood and illustrated.

Indeed I cannot conceive a more perfect mode of writing any man's life, than not only relating all the most important events of it in their order, but interweaving what he privately wrote, and said, and thought; by which mankind are enabled as it were to see him live, and to "live o'er each scene" with him, as he actually advanced through the several stages of his life. Had his other friends been as diligent and ardent as I was, he might have been almost entirely preserved. As it is, I will venture to say that he will be seen in this work more completely than any man who has ever yet lived.

And he will be seen as he really was; for I profess to write, not his panegyrick, which must be all praise, but his Life; which, great and good as he was, must not be supposed to be entirely perfect. To be as he was, is indeed subject of panegyrick enough to any man in this state of being; but in every picture there should be shade as well as light.

16

and when I delineate him without reserve, I do what he himself recommended, both by his precept and his example.

"If the biographer writes from personal knowledge, and makes haste to gratify the publick curiosity, there is danger lest his interest, his fear, his gratitude, or his tenderness, overpower his fidelity, and tempt him to conceal, if not to invent. There are many who think it an act of piety to hide the faults or failings of their friends, even when they can no longer suffer by their detection; we therefore see whole ranks of characters adorned with uniform panegyrick, and not to be known from one another but by extrinsick and casual circumstances. 'Let me remember, (says Hale,) when I find myself inclined to pity a criminal, that there is likewise a pity due to the country.' If we owe regard to the memory of the dead, there is yet more respect to be paid to knowledge, to virtue, and to truth."

What I consider as the peculiar value of the following work, is, the quantity it contains of Johnson's conversation; which is universally acknowledged to have been eminently instructive and entertaining; and of which the specimens that I have given upon a former occasion, have been received with so much approbation, that I have good grounds for supposing that the world will not be indifferent to more ample communications of a similar nature.

That the conversation of a celebrated man, if his talents have been exerted in conversation, will best display his character, is, I trust, too well established in the judgement of mankind, to be at all shaken.

If authority be required let us appeal to Plutarch, the prince of ancient biographers. "Nor is it always in the most distinguished achievements that men's virtues or vices may be best discerned; but very often an action of small note, a short saying, or a jest, shall distinguish a person's real character more than the greatest sieges, or the most important battles."

I am fully aware of the objections which may be made to the minuteness on some occasions of my detail of Johnson's conversation, and how happily it is adapted for the petty exercise of ridicule, by men of superficial understanding, and ludicrous fancy; but I remain firm and confident in my opinion, that minute particulars are frequently characteristick, and always amusing, when they relate to a distinguished man. I am therefore exceedingly unwilling that any thing, however slight, which my illustrious friend thought it worth his while to express, with any degree of point, should perish. For this almost superstitious reverence, I have found very old and venerable authority, quoted by our great modern prelate, Secker, in whose tenth sermon there is the following passage:

"*Rabbi David Kimchi,* a noted Jewish Commentator, who lived about five hundred years ago, explains that passage in the first Psalm, *His leaf also shall not wither,* from Rabbins yet older than himself, thus: That *even the idle talk,* so he expresses it, *of a good man ought to be regarded;* the most superfluous things he saith are always of some value. And other ancient authours have the same phrase, nearly in the same sense."

Having said thus much by way of introduction, I commit the following pages to the candour of the Publick.

SAMUEL JOHNSON was born in Lichfield, in Staffordshire, on the 18th of September, N.S. 1709; and his initiation into the Christian church was not delayed; for his baptism is recorded in the register of St. Mary's parish in that city, to have been performed on the day of his birth. His father was Michael Johnson, a native of Derbyshire, of obscure extraction, who settled in Lichfield as a bookseller and stationer. His mother was Sarah Ford, descended of an ancient race of substantial yeomanry in Warwickshire. They were well advanced in years when they married, and never had more than two children, both sons, Samuel, their first-born, who lived to be the illustrious character whose various excellence I am to endeavour to record, and Nathanael, who died in his twenty-fifth year.

Mr. Michael Johnson was a man of a large and robust body, and of a strong and active mind; yet, as in the most solid rocks, veins of unsound substance are often discovered, there was in him a mixture of that disease, the nature of which eludes the most minute enquiry, though the effects are well known to be a weariness of life, an unconcern about those things which agitate the greater part of mankind, and a general sensation of gloomy wretchedness. From him then his son inherited, with some other qualities, "a vile melancholy," which in his too strong expression of any disturbance of mind, "made him mad all his life, at least not sober." Michael was, however, forced by the narrowness of his circumstances to be very diligent in business, not only in his shop, but by occasionally resorting to several towns in the neighbourhood, some of which were at a considerable distance from Lichfield. At that time booksellers' shops in the provincial towns of England were very rare, so that there was not one even in Birmingham, in which town old Mr. Johnson used to open a shop every market-day. He was a pretty good Latin scholar, and a citizen so creditable as to be made one of the magistrates of Lichfield; and, being a man of good sense, and skill in his trade, he acquired a reasonable share of wealth, of which however he afterwards lost the greatest part, by engaging unsuccessfully in a manufacture of parchment.

Johnson's mother was a woman of distinguished understanding. I asked his old school-fellow, Mr. Hector, surgeon, of Birmingham, if she was not vain of her son. He said, "she had too much good sense to be vain, but she knew her son's value." Her piety was not inferiour to her understanding; and to her must be ascribed those early impressions of religion upon the mind of her son, from which the world afterwards derived so much benefit.

Of the power of his memory, for which he was all his life eminent to a degree almost incredible, the following early instance was told me in his presence at Lichfield, in 1776, by his step-daughter, Mrs. Lucy Porter, as related to her by his mother. When he was a child in petticoats, and had learnt to read, Mrs. Johnson one morning put the common prayer-book into his hands, pointed to the collect for the day, and said, "Sam, you must get this by heart." She went up stairs, leaving him to study it: but by the time she had reached the second floor, she heard him following her.

"What's the matter?" said she. "I can say it," he replied; and repeated it distinctly, though he could not have read it more than twice.

Young Johnson had the misfortune to be much afflicted with the scrophula, or king's-evil, which disfigured a countenance naturally well formed, and hurt his visual nerves so much, that he did not see at all with one of his eyes, though its appearance was little different from that of the other. There is amongst his prayers, one inscribed *"When my* EYE *was restored to its use,"* which ascertains a defect that many of his friends knew he had, though I never perceived it. I supposed him to be only near-sighted; and indeed I must observe, that in no other respect could I discern any defect in his vision; on the contrary, the force of his attention and perceptive quickness made him see and distinguish all manner of objects, whether of nature or of art, with a nicety that is rarely to be found. When he and I were travelling in the Highlands of Scotland, and I pointed out to him a mountain which I observed resembled a cone, he corrected my inaccuracy, by shewing me, that it was indeed pointed at the top, but that one side of it was larger than the other. And the ladies with whom he was acquainted agree, that no man was more nicely and minutely critical in the elegance of female dress. When I found that he saw the romantick beauties of Islam, in Derbyshire, much better than I did, I told him that he resembled an able performer upon a bad instrument. It has been said, that he contracted this grievous malady from his nurse. His mother, yielding to the superstitious notion, which, it is wonderful to think, prevailed so long in this country, as to the virtue of the regal touch; a notion, which our kings encouraged, and to which a man of such enquiry and such judgement as Carte could give credit; carried him to London, where he was actually touched by Queen Anne. Mrs. Johnson indeed, as Mr. Hector informed me, acted by the advice of the celebrated Sir John Floyer, then a physician in Lichfield. Johnson used to talk of this very frankly; and Mrs. Piozzi has preserved his very picturesque description of the scene, as it remained upon his fancy. Being asked if he could remember Queen Anne,—"He had (he said) a confused, but somehow a sort of solemn recollection of a lady in diamonds, and a long black hood." This touch, however, was without any effect. I ventured to say to him, in allusion to the political principles in which he was educated, and of which he ever retained some odour, that "his mother had not carried him far enough; she should have taken him to ROME."

He was first taught to read English by Dame Oliver, a widow, who kept a school for young children in Lichfield. He told me she could read the black letter, and asked him to borrow for her, from his father, a bible in that character. When he was going to Oxford, she came to take leave of him, brought him, in the simplicity of her kindness, a present of gingerbread, and said he was the best scholar she ever had. He delighted in mentioning this early compliment: adding, with smile, that "this was as high a proof of his merit as he could conceive." His next instructor in English was a master, whom, when he spoke of him to me, he familiarly called Tom Brown, who, said he, "published a spelling-book, and dedicated it to the UNIVERSE; but, I fear, no copy of it can now be had."

He began to learn Latin with Mr. Hawkins, usher, or undermaster of Lichfield school, "a man (said he) very skilful in his little way." With him he continued two years, and then rose to be under the care of Mr. Hunter, the headmaster, who, according to his account, "was very severe, and wrong-headedly severe. He used (said he) to beat us unmercifully; and he did not distinguish between ignorance and negligence; for he would beat a boy equally for not knowing a thing, as for neglecting to know it. He would ask a boy a question, and if he did not answer it, he would beat him, without considering whether he had an opportunity of knowing how to answer it. For instance, he would call up a boy and ask him Latin for a candlestick, which the boy could not expect to be asked. Now, Sir, if a boy could answer every question, there would be no need of a master to teach him."

Johnson was very sensible how much he owed to Mr. Hunter. Mr. Langton one day asked him how he had acquired so accurate a knowledge of Latin, in which, I believe, he was exceeded by no man of his time; he said, "My master whipt me very well. Without that, Sir, I should have done nothing." He told Mr. Langton, that while Hunter was flogging his boys unmercifully, he used to say, "And this I do to save you from the gallows." Johnson, upon all occasions, expressed his approbation of enforcing instruction by means of the rod. "I would rather (said he) have the rod to be the general terrour to all, to make them learn, than tell a child, if you do thus, or thus, you will be more esteemed than your brothers or sisters. The rod produces an effect which terminates in itself. A child is afraid of being whipped, and gets his task, and there's an end on't; whereas, by exciting emulation and comparisons of superiority, you lay the foundation of lasting mischief; you make brothers and sisters hate each other."

That superiority over his fellows, which he maintained with so much dignity in his march through life, was not assumed from vanity and ostentation, but was the natural and constant effect of those extraordinary powers of mind, of which he could not but be conscious by comparison; the intellectual difference, which in other cases of comparison of characters, is often a matter of undecided contest, being as clear in his case as the superiority of stature in some men above others. Johnson did not strut or stand on tip-toe; he only did not stoop. From his earliest years, his superiority was perceived and acknowledged. He was from the beginning a king of men. His schoolfellow, Mr. Hector, has obligingly furnished me with many particulars of his boyish days; and assured me that he never knew him corrected at school, but for talking and diverting other boys from their business. He seemed to learn by intuition; for though indolence and procrastination were inherent in his constitution, whenever he made an exertion he did more than any one else. In short, he is a memorable instance of what has been often observed, that the boy is the man in miniature: and that the distinguishing characteristicks of each individual are the same, through the whole course of life. His favourites used to receive very liberal assistance from him; and such was the submission and deference with which he was treated, such the desire to obtain his regard,

1
James Boswell, a portrait by Sir Joshua Reynolds.

that three of the boys, of whom Mr. Hector was sometimes one, used to come in the morning as his humble attendants, and carry him to school. One in the middle stooped, while he sat upon his back, and one on each side supported him; and thus he was borne triumphant. Such a proof of the early predominance of intellectual vigour is very remarkable, and does honour to human nature.—Talking to me once himself of his being much distinguished at school, he told me, "they never thought to raise me by comparing me to any one; they never said, Johnson is as good a scholar as such a one; but such a one is as good a scholar as Johnson; and this was said but of one, but of Lowe; and I do not think he was as good a scholar."

He discovered a great ambition to excel, which roused him to counteract his indolence. He was uncommonly inquisitive; and his memory was so tenacious, that he never forgot anything that he either heard or read. Mr. Hector remembers having recited to him eighteen verses, which, after a little pause, he repeated *verbatim*, varying only one epithet, by which he improved the line.

He never joined with the other boys in their ordinary diversions: his only amusement was in winter, when he took a pleasure in being drawn up on the ice by a boy barefooted, who pulled him along by a garter fixed around him; no very easy operation, as his size was remarkably large. His defective sight, indeed, prevented him from enjoying the common sports; and he once pleasantly remarked to me, "how wonderfully well he had contrived to be idle without them." Lord Chesterfield, however, has justly observed in one of his letters, when earnestly cautioning a friend against the pernicious effects of idleness, that active sports are not to be reckoned idleness in young people; and that the listless torpor of doing nothing alone deserves that name. Of this dismal inertness of disposition, Johnson had all his life too great a share. Mr. Hector relates, that "he could not oblige him more than by sauntering away the hours of vacation in the fields, during which he was more engaged in talking to himself than to his companion."

After having resided for some time at the house of his uncle, Cornelius Ford, Johnson was, at the age of fifteen, removed to the school of Stourbridge, in Worcestershire, of which Mr. Wentworth was then master. This step was taken by the advice of his cousin, the Rev. Mr. Ford, a man in whom both talents and good dispositions were disgraced by licentiousness, but who was a very able judge of what was right. At this school he did not receive so much benefit as was expected. It has been said, that he acted in the capacity of an assistant to Mr. Wentworth, in teaching the younger boys. "Mr. Wentworth (he told me) was a very able man, but an idle man, and to me very severe; but I cannot blame him much. I was then a big boy; he saw I did not reverence him; and that he should get no honour by me. I had brought enough with me, to carry me through; and all I should get at his school would be ascribed to my own labour, or to my former master. Yet he taught me a great deal."

He thus discriminated, to Dr. Percy, Bishop of Dromore, his progress at his two grammar-schools. "At one, I learned much in the school, but little from the master; in the other, I learnt much from the master, but little in the school."

The two years which he spent at home, after his return from Stourbridge, he passed in what he thought idleness, and was scolded by his father for his want of steady application. He had no settled plan of life, nor looked forward at all, but merely lived from day to day. Yet he read a great deal in a desultory manner, without any scheme of study, as chance threw books in his ways, and inclination directed him through them. He used to mention one curious instance of his casual reading, when but a boy. Having imagined that his brother had hid some apples behind a large folio upon an upper shelf in his father's shop, he climbed up to search for them. There were no apples; but the large folio proved to be Petrarch, whom he had seen mentioned, in some preface, as one of the restorers of learning. His curiosity having been thus excited, he sat down with avidity, and read a great part of the book. What he read during these two years, he told me, was not works of mere amusement, "not voyages and travels, but all literature, Sir, all ancient writers, all manly: though but little Greek, only some of Anacreon and Hesiod: but in this irregular manner (added he) I had looked into a great many books, which were not commonly known at the Universities, where they seldom read any books but what are put into their hands by their tutors; so that when I came to Oxford, Dr. Adams, now master of Pembroke College, told me, I was the best qualified for the University that he had ever known come there."

In estimating the progress of his mind during these two years, as well as in future periods of his life, we must not regard his own hasty confession of idleness; for we see, when he explains himself, that he was acquiring various stores; and, indeed he himself concluded the account, with saying, "I would not have you think I was doing nothing then." He might, perhaps, have studied more assiduously; but it may be doubted, whether such a mind as his was not more enriched by roaming at large in the fields of literature, than if it had been confined to any single spot.

He went to Oxford, and was entered a Commoner of Pembroke College, on the 31st of October, 1728, being then in his nineteenth year.

The Reverend Dr. Adams, who afterwards presided over Pembroke College with universal esteem, told me he was present, and gave me some account of what passed on the night of Johnson's arrival at Oxford. On that evening, his father, who had anxiously accompanied him, found means to have him introduced to Mr. Jorden, who was to be his tutor. His being put under any tutor, reminds us of what Wood says of Robert Burton, authour of the "Anatomy of Melancholy," when elected student of Christ Church; "for form's sake, *though he wanted not a tutor*, he was put under the tuition of Dr. John Bancroft, afterwards Bishop of Oxon."

His father seemed very full of the merits of his son, and told the company he was a good scholar, and a poet, and wrote Latin verses. His figure and manner appeared strange to them; but he behaved modestly, and sat silent, till upon something which occurred in the course of conversation, he

suddenly struck in and quoted Macrobius; and thus he gave
the first impression of that more extensive reading in which
he had indulged himself.

His tutor, Mr. Jorden, fellow of Pembroke, was not, it
seems, a man of such abilities as we should conceive requisite for the instructor of Samuel Johnson, who gave me the
following account of him. "He was a very worthy man, but
a heavy man, and I did not profit much by his instructions.
Indeed, I did not attend him much. The first day after I
came to college, I waited upon him, and then staid away
four. On the sixth, Mr. Jorden asked me why I had not attended. I answered, I had been sliding in Christ-Church
meadow. And this I said with as much *nonchalance* as I
am now talking to you. I had no notion that I was wrong or
irreverent to my tutor." BOSWELL. "That, Sir, was great
fortitude of mind." JOHNSON. "No, Sir, stark insensibility."

He had a love and respect for Jorden, not for his literature, but for his worth. "Whenever (said he) a young man
becomes Jorden's pupil, he becomes his son."

The "morbid melancholy," which was lurking in his constitution, and to which we may ascribe those particularities,
and that aversion to regular life, which, at a very early period, marked his character, gathered such strength in his
twentieth year, as to afflict him in a dreadful manner. While
he was at Lichfield, in the college vacation of the year 1729,
he felt himself overwhelmed with an horrible hypochondria,
with perpetual irritation, fretfulness, and impatience; and
with a dejection, gloom, and despair, which made existence
misery. From this dismal malady he never afterwards was
perfectly relieved; and all his labours, and all his enjoyments, were but temporary interruptions of its baleful influence. How wonderful, how unsearchable are the ways of
God! Johnson, who was blest with all the powers of genius
and understanding in a degree far above the ordinary state
of human nature, was at the same time visited with a disorder so afflictive, that they who know it by dire experience,
will not envy his exalted endowments. That it was, in some
degree, occasioned by a defect in his nervous system, that
inexplicable part of our frame, appears highly probable. He
told Mr. Paradise that he was sometimes so languid and

inefficient, that he could not distinguish the hour upon the town-clock.

Johnson, upon the first violent attack of this disorder, strove to overcome it by forcible exertions. He frequently walked to Birmingham and back again, and tried many other expedients, but all in vain. His expression concerning it to me was "I did not then know how to manage it."

But let not little men triumph upon knowing that Johnson was an HYPOCHONDRIACK, was subject to what the learned, philosophical, and pious Dr. Cheyne has so well treated under the title of "The English Malady." Though he suffered severely from it, he was not therefore degraded. The powers of his great mind might be troubled, and their full exercise suspended at times; but the mind itself was ever entire. I am aware that he himself was too ready to call such a complaint by the name of *madness;* in conformity with which notion, he has traced its gradations, with exquisite nicety, in one of the chapters of his RASSELAS. But there is surely a clear distinction between a disorder which affects only the imagination and spirits, while the judgement is sound, and a disorder by which the judgement itself is impaired.

It is a common effect of low spirits or melancholy, to make those who are afflicted with it imagine that they are actually suffering those evils which happen to be most strongly presented to their minds. Some have fancied themselves to be deprived of the use of their limbs, some to labour under acute diseases, others to be in extreme poverty; when, in truth, there was not the least reality in any of the suppositions; so that when the vapours were dispelled, they were convinced of the delusion. To Johnson, whose supreme enjoyment was the exercise of his reason, the disturbance or obscuration of that faculty was the evil most to be dreaded. Insanity, therefore, was the object of his most dismal apprehension; and he fancied himself seized by it, or approaching to it, at the very time when he was giving proofs of a more than ordinary soundness and vigour of judgement. That his own diseased imagination should have so far deceived him, is strange; but it is stranger still that some of his friends should have given credit to his groundless opinion, when they had such undoubted proofs that it was totally fallacious; though it is by no means surprising that those who wish to depreciate him, should, since his death, have laid hold of this circumstance, and insisted upon it with very unfair aggravation.

The history of his mind as to religion is an important article. I have mentioned the early impressions made upon his tender imagination by his mother, who continued her pious cares with assiduity, but, in his opinion, not with judgement. "Sunday (said he) was a heavy day to me when I was a boy. My mother confined me on that day, and made me read 'The Whole Duty of Man,' from a great part of which I could derive no instruction. When, for instance, I had read the chapter on theft, which from my infancy I had been taught was wrong, I was no more convinced that theft was wrong than before; so there was no accession of knowledge. A boy should be introduced to such books by having his attention directed to the arrangement, to the style, and other excellencies of composition; that the mind being thus engaged by an amusing variety of objects may not grow weary."

He communicated to me the following particulars upon the subject of his religious progress. "I fell into an inattention to religion, or an indifference about it, in my ninth year. The church at Lichfield, in which we had a seat, wanted reparation, so I was to go and find a seat in other churches; and having bad eyes, and being awkward about this, I used to go and read in the fields on Sunday. This habit continued till my fourteenth year; and still I find a great reluctance to go to church. I then became a sort of lax *talker* against religion, for I did not much *think* against it; and this lasted till I went to Oxford, where it would not be *suffered*. When at Oxford, I took up Law's 'Serious Call to a Holy Life,' expecting to find it a dull book, (as such books generally are,) and perhaps to laugh at it. But I found Law quite an overmatch for me; and this was the first occasion of my thinking in earnest of religion, after I became capable of rational enquiry." From this time forward religion was the predominant object of his thoughts; though, with the just sentiments of a conscientious christian, he lamented

28

that his practice of its duties fell far short of what it ought to be.

The particular course of his reading while at Oxford, and during the time of vacation which he passed at home, cannot be traced. Enough has been said of his irregular mode of study. He told me, that from his earliest years he loved to read poetry, but hardly ever read any poem to an end; that he read Shakspeare at a period so early, that the speech of the Ghost in Hamlet terrified him when he was alone; that Horace's Odes were the compositions in which he took most delight, and it was long before he liked his Epistles and Satires. He told me what he read *solidly* at Oxford was Greek; not the Grecian historians, but Homer and Euripides, and now and then a little Epigram; that the study of which he was the most fond was Metaphysicks, but he had not read much, even in that way. I always thought that he did himself injustice in his account of what he had read, and that he must have been speaking with reference to the vast portion of study which is possible, and to which a few scholars in the whole history of literature have attained; for when I once asked him whether a person whose name I have now forgotten, studied hard, he answered, "No, Sir. I do not believe he studied hard. I never knew a man who studied hard." Trying him by that criterion upon which he formed his judgement of others, we may be absolutely certain, both from his writings and his conversation, that his reading was very extensive. Dr. Adam Smith, than whom few were better judges on this subject, once observed to me, that "Johnson knew more books than any man alive." He had a peculiar facility in seizing at once what was valuable in any book, without submitting to the labour of perusing it from beginning to end. He had, from the irritability of his constitution, at all times, an impatience and hurry when he either read or wrote. A certain apprehension arising from novelty, made him write his first exercise at College twice over; but he never took that trouble with any other composition: and we shall see that his most excellent works were struck off at a heat, with rapid exertion.

Dr. Adams told me that Johnson, while he was at Pembroke College, "was caressed and loved by all about him,

29

was a gay and frolicksome fellow, and passed there the happiest part of his life." But this is a striking proof of the fallacy of appearances, and how little any of us know of the real internal state even of those whom we see most frequently; for the truth is, that he was then depressed by poverty, and irritated by disease. When I mentioned to him this account as given me by Dr. Adams, he said, "Ah, Sir, I was mad and violent. It was bitterness which they mistook for frolick. I was miserably poor, and I thought to fight my way by my literature and my wit; so I disregarded all power and all authority."

The Bishop of Dromore observes in a letter to me, "The pleasure he took in vexing the tutors and fellows has been often mentioned. But I have heard him say, what ought to be recorded to the honour of the present venerable master of that College, the Reverend William Adams, D.D., who was then very young, and one of the junior fellows; that the mild but judicious expostulations of this worthy man, whose virtue awed him, and whose learning he revered, made him really ashamed of himself, 'though I fear (said he) I was too proud to own it.'

"I have heard from some of his contemporaries that he was generally seen lounging at the College gate, with a circle of young students round him, whom he was entertaining with wit, and keeping from their studies, if not spiriting them up to rebellion against the College discipline, which in his maturer years he so much extolled."

I do not find that he formed any close intimacies with his fellow-collegians. But Dr. Adams told me, that he contracted a love and regard for Pembroke College, which he retained to the last. He was not, however, blind to what he thought the defects of his own college: and I have, from the information of Dr. Taylor, a very strong instance of that rigid honesty which he ever inflexibly preserved. Taylor had obtained his father's consent to be entered of Pembroke, that he might be with his schoolfellow Johnson, with whom, though some years older than himself, he was very intimate. This would have been a great comfort to Johnson. But he fairly told Taylor that he could not, in conscience, suffer him to enter where he knew he could not have an able tutor. He then made enquiry all round the University, and having found that Mr. Bateman, of Christ-Church, was the tutor of highest reputation, Taylor was entered of that College. Mr. Bateman's lectures were so excellent, that Johnson used to come and get them at second-hand from Taylor, till his poverty being so extreme, that his shoes were worn out, and his feet appeared through them, he saw that this humiliating circumstance was perceived by the Christ-Church men, and he came no more. He was too proud to accept of money, and somebody having set a pair of new shoes at his door, he threw them away with indignation. How must we feel when we read such an anecdote of Samuel Johnson!

The *res angusta domi* prevented him from having the advantage of a complete academical education. The friend to whom he had trusted for support had deceived him. His debts in College, though not great, were increasing; and his scanty remittances from Lichfield, which had all along been made with great difficulty, could be supplied no longer, his father having fallen into a state of insolvency. Compelled, therefore, by irresistible necessity, he left the College in autumn, 1731, without a degree, having been a member of it little more than three years.

Dr. Adams, the worthy and respectable master of Pembroke College, has generally had the reputation of being Johnson's tutor. The fact, however, is, that in 1731, Mr. Jorden quitted the College, and his pupils were transferred to Dr. Adams; so that had Johnson returned, Dr. Adams *would have been his tutor*. It is to be wished, that this connection had taken place. His equal temper, mild disposition, and politeness of manner, might have insensibly softened the harshness of Johnson, and infused into him those more delicate charities, those *petites morales,* in which, it must be confessed, our great moralist was more deficient than his best friends could fully justify. Dr. Adams paid Johnson this high compliment. He said to me at Oxford, in 1776, "I was his nominal tutor; but he was above my mark." When I repeated it to Johnson, his eyes flashed with grateful satisfaction, and he exclaimed, "That was liberal and noble."

And now (I had almost said *poor*) Samuel Johnson returned to his native city, destitute, and not knowing how he should gain even a decent livelihood. His father's misfortunes in trade rendered him unable to support his son; and for some time there appeared no means by which he could maintain himself. In the December of this year his father died.

The state of poverty in which he died, appears from a note in one of Johnson's little diaries of the following year, which strongly displays his spirit and virtuous dignity of mind. "I layed by eleven guineas on this day, when I received twenty pounds, being all that I have reason to hope for out of my father's effects, previous to the death of my mother; an event which I pray GOD may be very remote. I now therefore see that I must make my own fortune. Meanwhile, let me take care that the powers of my mind be not debilitated by poverty, and that indigence do not force me into any criminal act."

Johnson was so far fortunate, that the respectable character of his parents, and his own merit, had, from his earliest years secured him a kind reception in the best families at Lichfield. Among these I can mention Mr. Howard, Dr. Swinfen, Mr. Simpson, Mr. Levett, Captain Garrick, father of the great ornament of the British stage; but above all, Mr. Gilbert Walmsley, Registrar of the Ecclesiastical Court of Lichfield.

In these families he passed much time in his early years. In most of them, he was in the company of ladies, particularly at Mr. Walmsley's, whose wife and sisters-in-law, of the name of Aston, and daughters of a Baronet, were remarkable for good breeding; so that the notion which has been industriously circulated and believed, that he never was in good company till late in life, and consequently had been confirmed in coarse and ferocious manners by long habits, is wholly without foundation. Some of the ladies have assured me, they recollected him well when a young man, as distinguished for his complaisance.

In the forlorn state of his circumstances, he accepted of an offer to be employed as usher in the school of Market-Bosworth, in Leicestershire. This employment was very irksome to him in every respect, and he complained grievously of it in his letters to his friend, Mr. Hector, who was now settled as a surgeon at Birmingham. The letters are lost; but Mr. Hector recollects his writing "that the poet had described the dull sameness of his existence in these words, *'Vitam continet una dies'* (one day contains the whole of my life); that it was unvaried as the note of the cuckow; and that he did not know whether it was more disagreeable for him to teach, or the boys to learn, the grammar rules." His general aversion to this painful drudgery was greatly enhanced by a disagreement between him and Sir Wolstan Dixie, the patron of the school, in whose house, I have been told, he officiated as a kind of domestick chaplain, so far, at least, as to say grace at table, but was treated with what he represented as intolerable harshness; and, after suffering for a few months such complicated misery, he relinquished a situation which all his life afterwards he recollected with the strongest aversion, and even a degree of horror.

Being now again totally unoccupied, he was invited by Mr. Hector to pass some time with him at Birmingham, as his guest, at the house of Mr. Warren, with whom Mr. Hector lodged and boarded. He continued to live as Mr. Hector's guest for about six months, and then hired lodgings in another part of the town, finding himself as well situated at Birmingham as he supposed he could be any where, while he had no settled plan of life, and very scanty means of subsistence. He made some valuable acquaintances there, amongst whom were Mr. Porter, a mercer, whose widow he afterwards married, and Mr. Taylor, who by his ingenuity in mechanical inventions, and his success in trade, acquired an immense fortune. But the comfort of being near Mr. Hector, his old schoolfellow and intimate friend, was Johnson's chief inducement to continue here.

In what manner he employed his pen at this period, or whether he derived from it any pecuniary advantage, I have not been able to ascertain. He probably got a little money from Mr. Warren; and we are certain, that he executed here one piece of literary labour, of which Mr. Hector has favoured me with a minute account. Having mentioned that he had read at Pembroke College a Voyage to Abyssinia, by Lobo, a Portuguese Jesuit, and that he thought an abridge-

33

ment and translation of it from the French into English might be an useful and profitable publication, Mr. Warren and Mr. Hector joined in urging him to undertake it. He accordingly agreed; and the book not being to be found in Birmingham, he borrowed it of Pembroke College. A part of the work being very soon done, one Osborn, who was Mr. Warren's printer, was set to work with what was ready, and Johnson engaged to supply the press with copy as it should be wanted; but his constitutional indolence soon prevailed, and the work was at a stand. Mr. Hector, who knew that a motive of humanity would be the most prevailing argument with his friend, went to Johnson, and represented to him that the printer could have no other employment till his undertaking was finished, and that the poor man and his family were suffering. Johnson upon this exerted the powers of his mind, though his body was relaxed. He lay in bed with the book, which was a quarto, before him, and dictated while Hector wrote. Mr. Hector carried the sheets to the press, and corrected almost all the proof sheets, very few of which were even seen by Johnson. In this manner, with the aid of Mr. Hector's active friendship, the book was completed, and was published in 1735, with London upon the title-page, though it was in reality printed at Birmingham, a device too common with provincial publishers. For this work he had from Mr. Warren only the sum of five guineas.

Johnson had, from his early youth, been sensible to the influence of female charms. When at Stourbridge school, he was much enamoured of Olivia Lloyd, a young quaker, to whom he wrote a copy of verses, which I have not been able to recover. His juvenile attachments to the fair sex were, however, very transient: and it is certain, that he formed no criminal connection whatsoever. Mr. Hector, who lived with him in his younger days in the utmost intimacy and social freedom, has assured me, that even at that ardent season his conduct was strictly virtuous in that respect; and that though he loved to exhilarate himself with wine, he never knew him intoxicated but once.

In a man whom religious education has secured from licentious indulgences, the passion of love, when once it has

34

seized him, is exceedingly strong; being unimpaired by dissipation, and totally concentrated in one object. This was experienced by Johnson, when he became the fervent admirer of Mrs. Porter, after her first husband's death. Miss Porter told me, that when he was first introduced to her mother, his appearance was very forbidding: he was then lean and lank, so that his immense structure of bones was hideously striking to the eye, and the scars of the scrophula were deeply visible. He also wore his hair, which was straight and stiff, and separated behind: and he often had, seemingly, convulsive starts and odd gesticulations, which tended to excite at once surprise and ridicule. Mrs. Porter was so much engaged by his conversation that she overlooked all these external disadvantages, and said to her daughter, "this is the most sensible man that I ever saw in my life."

Though Mrs. Porter was double the age of Johnson, and her person and manner, as described to me by the late Mr. Garrick, were by no means pleasing to others, she must have had a superiority of understanding and talents as she certainly inspired him with a more than ordinary passion; and she having signified her willingness to accept of his hand, he went to Lichfield to ask his mother's consent to the marriage; which he could not but be conscious was a very imprudent scheme, both on account of their disparity of years, and her want of fortune. But Mrs. Johnson knew too well the ardour of her son's temper, and was too tender a parent to oppose his inclinations.

I know not for what reason the marriage ceremony was not performed at Birmingham; but a resolution was taken that it should be at Derby, for which place the bride and bridegroom set out on horseback, I suppose in very good humour. But though Mr. Topham Beauclerk used archly to mention Johnson's having told him with much gravity, "Sir, it was a love marriage on both sides," I have had from my illustrious friend the following curious account of their journey to church upon the nuptial morn:—"Sir, she had read the old romances, and had got into her head the fantastical notion that a woman of spirit should use her lover like a dog. So, Sir, at first she told me that I rode too fast, and she could not keep up with me: and, when I rode a little slower, she passed me, and complained that I lagged behind. I was not to be made the slave of caprice; and I resolved to begin as I meant to end. I therefore pushed on briskly, till I was fairly out of her sight. The road lay between two hedges, so I was sure she could not miss it; and I contrived that she should soon come up with me. When she did, I observed her to be in tears."

This, it must be allowed, was a singular beginning of connubial felicity; but there is no doubt that Johnson, though he thus shewed a manly firmness, proved a most affectionate and indulgent husband to the last moment of Mrs. Johnson's life: and in his "Prayers and Meditations," we find very remarkable evidence that his regard and fondness for her never ceased, even after her death.

He now set up a private academy, for which purpose he hired a large house, well situated near his native city. In the Gentleman's Magazine for 1736, there is the following advertisement: "At Edial, near Lichfield, in Staffordshire, young gentlemen are boarded and taught the Latin and Greek Languages, by SAMUEL JOHNSON." But the only pupils that were put under his care were the celebrated David Garrick and his brother George, and a Mr. Offely, a young gentleman of good fortune who died early. As yet, his name had nothing of that celebrity which afterwards commanded the highest attention and respect of mankind. Had such an advertisement appeared after the publication of his LONDON, or his RAMBLER, or his DICTIONARY, how would it have burst upon the world! with what eagerness would the great and the wealthy have embraced an opportunity of putting their sons under the learned tuition of SAMUEL JOHNSON. The truth, however, is, that he was not so well qualified for being a teacher of elements, and a conductor in learning by regular gradations, as men of inferiour powers of mind. His own acquisitions had been made by fits and starts, by violent irruptions into the regions of knowledge; and it could not be expected that his impatience would be subdued, and his impetuosity restrained, so as to fit him for a quiet guide to novices.

Johnson was not more satisfied with his situation as the master of an academy, than with that of the usher of a school; we need not wonder, therefore, that he did not keep his academy above a year and a half. From Mr. Garrick's account he did not appear to have been profoundly reverenced by his pupils. His oddities of manner, and uncouth gesticulations, could not but be the subject of merriment to them; and in particular, the young rogues used to listen at the door of his bed-chamber, and peep through the key-hole, that they might turn into ridicule his tumultuous and awkward fondness for Mrs. Johnson, whom he used to name by the familiar appellation of *Tetty* or *Tetsey,* which, like *Betty* or *Betsey,* is provincially used as a contraction for *Elizabeth,* her christian name, but which to us seems ludicrous, when applied to a woman of her age and appearance. Mr. Garrick described her to me as very fat, with a bosom of more than ordinary protuberance, with swelled cheeks, of a florid red, produced by thick painting, and increased by the liberal use of cordials; flaring and fantastick in her dress, and affected both in her speech and her general behaviour. I have seen Garrick exhibit her, by his exquisite talent of mimickry, so as to excite the heartiest burst of laughter; but he, probably, as is the case in all such representations, considerably aggravated the picture.

While Johnson kept his academy, there can be no doubt that he was insensibly furnishing his mind with various knowledge; but I have not discovered that he wrote any thing except a great part of his tragedy of IRENE. Mr. Peter Garrick, the elder brother of David, told me that he remembered Johnson's borrowing the Turkish History of him, in order to form his play from it. When he had finished some part of it, he read what he had done to Mr. Walmsley, who objected to his having already brought his heroine into great distress, and asked him, "how can you possibly contrive to plunge her into deeper calamity!" Johnson, in sly allusion to the supposed oppressive proceedings of the court of which Mr. Walmsley was registrar, replied, "Sir, I can put her into the Spiritual Court!"

Johnson now thought of trying his fortune in London, the great field of genius and exertion, where talents of every kind have the fullest scope, and the highest encouragement. It is a memorable circumstance that his pupil David Garrick went thither at the same time,[1] with intent to complete his education, and follow the profession of the law, from which he was soon diverted by his decided preference for the stage.

How he employed himself upon his first coming to London is not particularly known. He had a little money and he knew how he could live in the cheapest manner. His first lodgings were at the house of Mr. Norris, a staymaker, in Exeter-street, adjoining Catharine-street, in the Strand. "I dined (said he) very well for eight-pence, with very good company, at the Pine-Apple in New-street, just by. Several of them had travelled. They expected to meet every day; but did not know one another's names. It used to cost the rest a shilling, for they drank wine; but I had a cut of meat for six-pence, and bread for a penny, and gave the waiter a penny; so that I was quite well served, nay, better than the rest, for they gave the waiter nothing."

His OFELLUS in the *Art of Living in London*, I have heard him relate, was an Irish painter, whom he knew at Birmingham, and who had practiced his own precepts of economy for several years in the British capital. He assured Johnson, who, I suppose, was then meditating to try his fortune in London, but was apprehensive of the expence, "that thirty pounds a year was enough to enable a man to live there without being contemptible. He allowed ten pounds for cloaths and linen. He said a man might live in a garret at eighteen-pence a week; few people would inquire where he lodged; and if they did, it was easy to say, 'Sir, I am to be found at such a place.' By spending three-pence in a coffee-house, he might be for some hours every day in very good company; he might dine for six-pence, breakfast on bread and milk for a penny, and do without

---

[1] Both of them used to talk pleasantly of this their first journey to London. Garrick, evidently meaning to embellish a little, said one day in my hearing, 'we rode and tied.' And the Bishop of Killaloe [Dr. Barnard] informed me, that at another time, when Johnson and Garrick were dining together in a pretty large company, Johnson humorously ascertaining the chronology of something, expressed himself thus: "that was the year when I came to London with two-pence half-penny in my pocket." Garrick overhearing him, exclaimed, "eh? what do you say? with two-pence half-penny in your pocket?"—JOHNSON. "Why, yes; when I came with two-pence half-penny in *my* pocket, and thou, Davy, with three half-pence in thine."

supper. On *clean-shirt* day he went abroad, and paid visits."
I have heard him more than once talk of his frugal friend,
whom he recollected with esteem and kindness, and did not
like to have one smile at the recital. "This man (said he,
gravely) was a very sensible man, who perfectly understood
common affairs: a man of a great deal of knowledge of the
world, fresh from life, not strained through books."

Amidst this cold obscurity, there was one brilliant circumstance to cheer him; he was well acquainted with Mr.
Henry Hervey, one of the branches of the noble family of
that name, who had been quartered at Lichfield as an officer
of the army, and had at this time a house in London, where
Johnson was frequently entertained, and had an opportunity
of meeting genteel company. Not very long before his
death, he mentioned this, among other particulars of his
life, which he was kindly communicating to me; and he described this early friend "Harry Hervey," thus: "He was a
vicious man, but very kind to me. If you call a dog HERVEY,
I shall love him."

He told me he had now written only three acts of his
IRENE, and that he retired for some time to lodgings at
Greenwich, where he proceeded in it somewhat further,
and used to compose, walking in the Park; but did not stay
long enough at that place to finish it.

In the course of the summer he returned to Lichfield,
where he had left Mrs. Johnson, and there he at last finished
his tragedy, which was not executed with his rapidity of
composition upon other occasions, but was slowly and
painfully elaborated.

Johnson's residence at Lichfield, on his return to it at
this time, was only for three months, and as he had as yet
seen but a small part of the wonders of the Metropolis, he
had little to tell his townsmen. He now removed to London
with Mrs. Johnson; but her daughter, who had lived with
them at Edial, was left with her relations in the country.
His lodgings were for some time in Woodstock-street, near
Hanover-square, and afterwards in Castle-street, near Cav-
endish-square.

His tragedy being by this time, as he thought, completely
finished and fit for the stage, he was very desirous that it

should be brought forward. Mr. Peter Garrick told me, that Johnson and he went together to the Fountain Tavern, and read it over, and that he afterwards solicited Mr. Fleetwood, the patentee of Drury-lane theatre, to have it acted at his house; but Mr. Fleetwood would not accept it, probably because it was not patronized by some man of high rank; and it was not acted till 1749, when his friend David Garrick was manager of that theatre.

The GENTLEMAN'S MAGAZINE, begun and carried on by Mr. Edward Cave, under the name of SYLVANUS URBAN, had attracted the notice and esteem of Johnson, in an eminent degree, before he came to London as an adventurer in literature. He told me, that when he first saw St. John's Gate, the place where that deservedly popular miscellany was originally printed, he "beheld it with reverence."

Though Johnson was often solicited by his friends to make a complete list of his writings, and talked of doing it, I believe with a serious intention that they should all be collected on his own account, he put it off from year to year, and at last died without having done it perfectly. I have one in his own hand-writing, which contains a certain number; I indeed doubt if he could have remembered every one of them, as they were so numerous, so various, and scattered in such a multiplicity of unconnected publications; nay, several of them published under the names of other persons, to whom he liberally contributed from the abundance of his mind. We must, therefore, be content to discover them, partly from occasional information given by him to his friends, and partly from internal evidence.[1]

His first performance in the Gentleman's Magazine, which for many years was his principal source for employment and support, was a copy of Latin verses, in March, 1738, addressed to the editor in so happy a style of compliment, that Cave must have been destitute both of taste and sensibility, had he not felt himself highly gratified.

---

[1] While in the course of my narrative I enumerate his writings, I shall take care that my readers shall not be left to waver in doubt, between certainty and conjecture, with regard to their authenticity; and, for that purpose, shall mark with an *asterisk* (*) those which he acknowledged to his friends, and with a *dagger* (†) those which are ascertained to be his by internal evidence. When any other pieces are ascribed to him, I shall give my reasons.

It appears that he was now enlisted by Mr. Cave as a regular coadjutor in his magazine, by which he probably obtained a tolerable livelihood. At what time, or by what means, he had acquired a competent knowledge both of French and Italian, I do not know; but he was so well skilled in them, as to be sufficiently qualified for a translator. That part of his labour which consisted in emendation and improvement of the productions of other contributors, like that employed in levelling ground, can be perceived only by those who had an opportunity of comparing the original with the altered copy. What we certainly know to have been done by him in this way, was the Debates in both houses of Parliament, under the name of "The Senate of Lilliput," sometimes with feigned denominations of the several speakers, sometimes with denominations formed of the letters of their real names, in the manner of what is called anagram, so that they might easily be decyphered. Parliament then kept the press in a kind of mysterious awe, which made it necessary to have recourse to such devices. In our time it has acquired an unrestrained freedom, so that the people in all parts of the kingdom have a fair, open, and exact report of the actual proceedings of their representatives and legislators, which in our constitution is highly to be valued; though, unquestionably, there has of late been too much reason to complain of the petulance with which obscure scribblers have presumed to treat men of the most respectable character and situation.

Thus was Johnson employed during some of the best years of his life, as a mere literary labourer "for gain, not glory," solely to obtain an honest support.

But what first displayed his transcendent powers, and "gave the world assurance of the MAN," was his "LONDON, a Poem, in Imitation of the Third Satire of Juvenal;" which came out in May this year, and burst forth with a splendour, the rays of which will for ever encircle his name. Boileau had imitated the same satire with great success, applying it to Paris: but an attentive comparison will satisfy every reader, that he is much excelled by the English Juvenal. Oldham had also imitated it, and applied it to London: all which performances concur to prove, that

41

great cities, in every age, and every country, will furnish similar topicks of satire. Whether Johnson had previously read Oldham's imitation, I do not know; but it is not a little remarkable, that there is scarcely any coincidence found between the two performances, though upon the very same subject.

The particulars which Oldham has collected, both as exhibiting the horrours of London, and of the times, contrasted with better days, are different from those of Johnson, and in general well chosen, and well exprest.[1]

Where, or in what manner this poem was composed, I am sorry that I neglected to ascertain with precision, from Johnson's own authority. He has marked upon his corrected copy of the first edition of it, "Written in 1738;" and, as it was published in the month of May in that year, it is evident that much time was not employed in preparing it for the press. The history of its publication I am enabled to give in a very satisfactory manner.

We may be certain, though it is not expressly named in the following letters to Mr. Cave, in 1738, that they all relate to it:

"TO MR. CAVE.
"Castle-street, Wednesday Morning.
"SIR,   [*No date.*   1738.]
"When I took the liberty of writing to you a few days ago, I did not expect a repetition of the same pleasure so soon; for a pleasure I shall always think it, to converse in any manner with an ingenuous and candid man; but having the inclosed poem in my hands to dispose of for the benefit of the authour, (of whose abilities I shall say nothing, since I send you his performance,) I believed I could not procure more advantageous terms from any person than from you,

---

[1] I own it pleased me to find amongst them one trait of the manners of the age in London, in the last century, to shield from the sneer of English ridicule, what was some time ago too common a practice in my native city of Edinburgh!
"If what I've said can't from the town affright
Consider other *dangers of the night;*
When brickbats are from upper stories thrown,
And *emptied chamber-pots come pouring down
From garret windows.*"

42

who have so much distinguished yourself by your generous encouragement of poetry; and whose judgement of that art nothing but your commendation of my trifle can give me any occasion to call in question. I do not doubt you will look over this poem with another eye, and reward it in a different manner from a mercenary bookseller, who counts the lines he is to purchase, and considers nothing but the bulk. I cannot help taking notice, that besides what the authour may hope for on account of his abilities, he has likewise another claim to your regard, as he lies at present under very disadvantageous circumstances of fortune. I beg, therefore, that you will favour me with a letter to-morrow, that I may know what you can afford to allow him, that he may either part with it to you, or find out, (which I do not expect,) some other way more to his satisfaction.

"I have only to add, that as I am sensible I have transcribed it very coarsely, which, after having altered it, I was obliged to do, I will, if you please to transmit the sheets from the press, correct it for you; and take the trouble of altering any stroke of satire which you may dislike.

"By exerting on this occasion your usual generosity, you will not only encourage learning, and relieve distress, but (though it be in comparison of the other motives of very small account) oblige in a very sensible manner, Sir,

"Your very humble Servant,
"SAM. JOHNSON."

"To MR. CAVE.
"SIR,   "Monday, No. 6, Castle-street.

"I am to return you thanks for the present you were so kind as to send by me, and to intreat that you will be pleased to inform me by the penny-post, whether you resolve to print the poem. If you please to send it me by the post, with a note to Dodsley, I will go and read the lines to him, that we may have his consent to put his name in the title-page. As to the printing, if it can be set immediately about, I will be so much the authour's friend, as not to content myself with mere solicitations in his favour. I propose, if my calculation be near the truth, to engage for the reimbursement of all that you shall lose by an impression of

500; provided, as you very generously propose, that the profit, if any, be set aside for the authour's use, excepting the present you made, which, if he be a gainer, it is fit he should repay. I beg that you will let one of your servants write an exact account of the expense of such an impression, and send it with the poem, that I may know what I engage for. I am very sensible, from your generosity on this occasion, of your regard to learning, even in its unhappiest state; and cannot but think such a temper deserving of the gratitude of those who suffer so often from a contrary disposition. I am, Sir,

"Your most humble Servant,
"SAM. JOHNSON."

To us who have long known the manly force, bold spirit, and masterly versification of this poem, it is a matter of curiosity to observe the diffidence with which its authour brought it forward into publick notice, while he is so cautious as not to avow it to be his own production; and with what humility he offers to allow the printer to "alter any stroke of satire which he might dislike." That any such alteration was made, we do not know. If we did, we could but feel an indignant regret; but how painful is it to see that a writer of such vigorous powers of mind was actually in such distress, that the small profit which so short a poem, however excellent, could yield, was courted as a "relief."

Johnson's "London" was published in May, 1738; and it is remarkable, that it came out on the same morning with Pope's satire, entitled "1738;" so that England had at once its Juvenal and Horace as poetical monitors. The Reverend Dr. Douglas, now Bishop of Salisbury, to whom I am indebted for some obliging communications, was then a student at Oxford, and remembers well the effect which "London" produced. Every body was delighted with it; and there being no name to it, the first buz of the literary circle was, "here is an unknown poet, greater even than Pope." And it is recorded in the Gentleman's Magazine of that year, that it "got to the second edition in the course of a week."

POPE, who then filled the poetical throne without a rival,

2
Samuel Johnson, after a portrait by Sir Joshua Reynolds.

it may reasonably be presumed, must have been particularly struck by the sudden appearance of such a poet; and, to his credit, let it be remembered, that his feelings and conduct on the occasion were candid and liberal. He requested Mr. Richardson, son of the painter, to endeavour to find out who this new authour was. Mr. Richardson, after some inquiry, having informed him that he had discovered only that his name was Johnson, and that he was some obscure man, Pope said, "He will soon be *déterré*." We shall presently see, from a note written by Pope, that he was himself afterwards more successful in his inquiries than his friend.

Though thus elevated into fame, and conscious of uncommon powers, he had not that bustling confidence, or, I may rather say, that animated ambition, which one might have supposed would have urged him to endeavour at rising in life. But such was his inflexible dignity of character, that he could not stoop to court the great; without which hardly any man has made his way to a high station. He could not expect to produce many such works as his "LONDON," and he felt the hardships of writing for bread; he was, therefore, willing to resume the office of a schoolmaster, so as to have a sure, though moderate income for his life; and an offer being made to him of the mastership of a school, provided he could obtain the degree of Master of Arts, Dr. Adams was applied to, by a common friend, to know whether that could be granted him as a favour from the University of Oxford. But though he had made such a figure in the literary world, it was then thought too great a favour to be asked.

Pope, without any knowledge of him but from his "London," recommended him to Earl Gower, who endeavoured to procure for him a degree from Dublin, by the following letter to a friend of Dean Swift:

"SIR,

"Mr. Samuel Johnson (author of LONDON, a satire, and some other poetical pieces) is a native of this country, and much respected by some worthy gentlemen in his neighbourhood, who are trustees of a charity-school now vacant; the certain salary is sixty pounds a year, of which they are desirous to make him master; but, unfortunately, he is not capable of receiving their bounty, which *would make him happy for life,* by not being *a Master of Arts;* which, by the statutes of this school, the master of it must be.

"Now these gentlemen do me the honour to think that I have interest enough in you, to prevail upon you to write to Dean Swift, to persuade the University of Dublin to send a diploma to me, constituting this poor man Master of Arts in their University. They highly extol the man's learning and probity; and will not be persuaded that the University will make any difficulty of conferring such a favour upon a stranger, if he is recommended by the Dean. They say, he is not afraid of the strictest examination, though he is of so long a journey; and will venture it, if the Dean thinks it necessary; choosing rather to die upon the road, *than be starved to death in translating for booksellers;* which has been his only subsistence for some time past.

"I fear there is more difficulty in this affair, than those good-natured gentlemen apprehended; especially as their election cannot be delayed longer than the 11th of next month. If you see this matter in the same light that it appears to me, I hope you will burn this, and pardon me for giving you so much trouble about an impracticable thing; but, if you think there is a probability of obtaining the favour asked, I am sure your humanity, and propensity to relieve merit in distress, will incline you to serve the poor man, without my adding any more to the trouble I have already given you, than assuring you that I am, with great truth, Sir,

"Your faithful servant,
"GOWER."
"Trentham, Aug. 1, 1739."

It was, perhaps, no small disappointment to Johnson that this respectable application had not the desired effect; yet how much reason has there been, both for himself and his country, to rejoice that it did not succeed, as he might probably have wasted in obscurity those hours in which he afterwards produced his incomparable works.

In 1739 his separate publications were, "A Complete

Vindication of the Licensers of the Stage, from the malicious and scandalous Aspersions of Mr. Brooke, Authour of Gustavus Vasa," * being an ironical attack upon them for their Suppression of that Tragedy; and, "Marmor Norfolciense; or an Essay on an ancient prophetical Inscription, in monkish Rhyme, lately discovered near Lynne in Norfolk, by PROBUS BRITANNICUS." * In this performance, he, in a feigned inscription, supposed to have been found in Norfolk, the county of Sir Robert Walpole, then the obnoxious prime minister of this country, inveighs against the Brunswick succession, and the measures of government consequent upon it. To this supposed prophecy he added a Commentary, making each expression apply to the times, with warm Anti-Hanoverian zeal.

"Marmor Norfolciense" became exceedingly scarce, so that I for many years endeavoured in vain to procure a copy of it. At last I was indebted to the malice of one of Johnson's numerous petty adversaries, who, in 1775, published a new edition of it, "with Notes and a Dedication to SAMUEL JOHNSON, LL.D. by TRIBUNUS;" in which some puny scribbler invidiously attempted to found upon it a charge of inconsistency against its author, because he had accepted of a pension from his present Majesty and had written in support of the measures of government. As a mortification to such impotent malice, of which there are so many instances towards men of eminence, I am happy to relate, that this *telum imbelle* did not reach its exalted object, till about a year after it thus appeared, when I mentioned it to him, supposing that he knew of the republication. To my surprise he had not yet heard of it. He requested me to go directly and get it for him, which I did. He looked at it and laughed, and seemed to be much diverted with the feeble efforts of his unknown adversary, who, I hope, is alive to read this account. "Now (said he) here is somebody who thinks he has vexed me sadly; yet, if it had not been for you, you rogue, I should probably never have seen it."

As Mr. Pope's note concerning Johnson, alluded to in a former page, refers both to his "London," and his "Marmor Norfolciense," I have deferred inserting it till now. I am indebted for it to Dr. Percy, the Bishop of Dromore,

who permitted me to copy it from the original in his possession. It was presented to his Lordship by Sir Joshua Reynolds, to whom it was given by the son of Mr. Richardson
the painter, the person to whom it is addressed. I have transcribed it with minute exactness, that the peculiar mode of
writing, and imperfect spelling of that celebrated poet, may
be exhibited to the curious in literature. It justifies Swift's
epithet of "papersparing Pope," for it is written on a slip
no larger than a common message-card, and was sent to Mr.
Richardson, along with the imitation of Juvenal.

"This is imitated by one Johnson who put in for a Pub-
lick-school in Shropshire, but was disappointed. He has an
infirmity of the convulsive kind, that attacks him sometimes,
so as to make Him a sad Spectacle. Mr. P. from the Merit
of This Work which was all the knowledge he had of Him
endeavour'd to serve Him without his own application; &
wrote to my L^d. gore, but he did not succeed. Mr. Johnson
published afterw^{ds} another Poem in Latin with Notes the
whole very Humerous call'd the Norfolk Prophecy.

"P."

Johnson had been told of this note; and Sir Joshua Reynolds informed him of the compliment which it contained,
but, from delicacy, avoided shewing him the paper itself.
When Sir Joshua observed to Johnson that he seemed very
desirous to see Pope's note, he answered, "Who would not
be proud to have such a man as Pope so solicitous in enquiring about him?"

The infirmity to which Mr. Pope alludes, appeared to me
also, to be of the convulsive kind, and of the nature of that
distemper called St. Vitus's dance; and in this opinion I am
confirmed by the description which Sydenham gives of that
disease. "This disorder is a kind of convulsion. It manifests
itself by halting or unsteadiness of one of the legs, which
the patient draws after him like an ideot. If the hand of the
same side be applied to the breast, or any other part of the
body, he cannot keep it a moment in the same posture, but
it will be drawn into a different one by a convulsion, notwithstanding all his efforts to the contrary." Sir Joshua

Reynolds, however, was of a different opinion, and favoured me with the following paper.

"Those motions or tricks of Dr. Johnson are improperly called convulsions. He could sit motionless, when he was told to do so, as well as any other man. My opinion is, that it proceeded from a habit which he had indulged himself in, of accompanying his thoughts with certain untoward actions, and those actions always appeared to me as if they were meant to reprobate some part of his past conduct. Whenever he was not engaged in conversation, such thoughts were sure to rush into his mind; and, for this reason, any company, any employment whatever, he preferred to being alone. The great business of his life (he said) was to escape from himself; this disposition he considered as the disease of his mind, which nothing cured but company.

"One instance of his absence of mind and particularity, as it is characteristick of the man, may be worth relating. When he and I took a journey together into the West, we visited the late Mr. Banks, of Dorsetshire; the conversation turning upon pictures, which Johnson could not well see, he retired to a corner of the room, stretching out his right leg as far as he could reach before him, then bringing up his left leg, and stretching his right still further on. The old gentleman observing him, went up to him, and in a very courteous manner assured him, though it was not a new house, the flooring was perfectly safe. The Doctor started from his reverie like a person waked out of his sleep, but spoke not a word."

While we are on this subject, my readers may not be displeased with another anecdote, communicated to me by the same friend, from the relation of Mr. Hogarth.

Johnson used to be a pretty frequent visitor at the house of Mr. Richardson, author of Clarissa, and other novels of extensive reputation. Mr. Hogarth came one day to see Richardson, soon after the execution of Dr. Cameron, for having taken arms for the house of Stuart in 1745-6; and being a warm partisan of George the Second, he observed to Richardson, that certainly there must have been some very unfavourable circumstances lately discovered in this particular case, which had induced the King to approve of an execution for rebellion so long after the time when it was committed, as this had the appearance of putting a man to death in cold blood, and was very unlike his Majesty's usual clemency. While he was talking, he perceived a person standing at a window in the room, shaking his head, and rolling himself about in a strange ridiculous manner. He concluded that he was an ideot, whom his relations had put under the care of Mr. Richardson, as a very good man. To his great surprize, however, this figure stalked forwards to where he and Mr. Richardson were sitting, and all at once took up the argument, and burst out into an invective against George the Second, as one, who, upon all occasions, was unrelenting and barbarous; mentioning many instances, particularly, that when an officer of high rank had been acquitted by a Court Martial, George the Second had with his own hand struck his name off the list. In short, he displayed such a power of eloquence, that Hogarth looked at him with astonishment, and actually imagined that this ideot had been at the moment inspired. Neither Hogarth nor Johnson were made known to each other at this interview.

He produced one work this year [1744] fully sufficient to maintain the high reputation which he had acquired. This was "THE LIFE OF RICHARD SAVAGE," * a man, of whom it is difficult to speak impartially, without wondering that he was for some time the intimate companion of Johnson; for his character was marked by profligacy, insolence, and ingratitude: yet, as he undoubtedly had a warm and vigorous, though unregulated mind, had seen life in all its varieties, and been much in the company of the statesmen and wits of his time, he could communicate to Johnson an abundant supply of such materials as his philosophical curiosity most eagerly desired; and as Savage's misfortunes and misconduct had reduced him to the lowest state of wretchedness as a writer for bread, his visits to St. John's Gate naturally brought Johnson and him together.

It is melancholy to reflect, that Johnson and Savage were sometimes in such extreme indigence, that they could not pay for a lodging; so that they have wandered together whole nights in the streets. Yet in these almost incredible scenes of distress, we may suppose that Savage mentioned many of the anecdotes with which Johnson afterwards enriched the life of his unhappy companion, and those of other Poets.

He told Sir Joshua Reynolds, that one night in particular, when Savage and he walked round St. James's-square for want of a lodging, they were not at all depressed by their situation; but in high spirits and brimful of patriotism, traversed the square for several hours, inveighed against the minister, and "resolved they would *stand by their country*."

I am afraid, however, that by associating with Savage, who was habituated to the dissipation and licentiousness of the town, Johnson, though his good principles remained steady, did not entirely preserve that conduct, for which, in days of greater simplicity, he was remarked by his friend Mr. Hector; but was imperceptibly led into some indulgences which occasioned much distress to his virtuous mind.

That Johnson was anxious that an authentick and favourable account of his extraordinary friend should first get possession of the publick attention, is evident from a letter which he wrote in the Gentleman's Magazine for August of the year preceding its publication.

"MR. URBAN,

"As your collections show how often you have owed the ornaments of your poetical pages to the correspondence of the unfortunate and ingenious Mr. Savage, I doubt not but you have so much regard to his memory as to encourage any design that may have a tendency to the preservation of it from insults or calumnies; and therefore, with some degree of assurance, intreat you to inform the publick, that his life will speedily be published by a person who was favoured with his confidence, and received from himself an account of most of the transactions which he proposes to mention, to the time of his retirement to Swansea in Wales.

"From that period, to his death in the prison of Bristol, the account will be continued from materials still less liable to objection; his own letters, and those of his friends, some of which will be inserted in the work, and abstracts of others subjoined in the margin.

"It may be reasonably imagined, that others may have the same design; but as it is not credible that they can obtain the same materials, it must be expected they will supply from invention the want of intelligence; and that under the title of 'The Life of Savage,' they will publish only a novel, filled with romantick adventures, and imaginary amours. You may therefore, perhaps, gratify the lovers of truth and wit, by giving me leave to inform them in your Magazine, that my account will be published in 8vo. by Mr. Roberts, in Warwick-lane."

[*No signature.*]

In February, 1744, it accordingly came forth from the shop of Roberts, between whom and Johnson I have not traced any connection, except the casual one of this publication. In Johnson's "Life of Savage," although it must be allowed that its moral is the reverse of—*"Respicere exemplar vitæ morumque jubebo,"* a very useful lesson is inculcated, to guard men of warm passions from a too free indulgence of them; and the various incidents are related in so clear and animated a manner, and illuminated throughout with so much philosophy, that it is one of the most interesting narratives in the English language. Sir Joshua Reynolds told me, that upon his return from Italy he met with it in Devonshire, knowing nothing of its authour, and began to read it while he was standing with his arm leaning against a chimney-piece. It seized his attention so strongly, that, not being able to lay down the book till he had finished it, when he attempted to move, he found his arm totally benumbed. The rapidity with which this work was composed, is a wonderful circumstance. Johnson has been heard to say, "I wrote forty-eight of the printed octavo pages of the Life of Savage at a sitting; but then I sat up all night."

It is remarkable, that in this biographical disquisition there appears a very strong symptom of Johnson's prejudice against players; a prejudice that may be attributed to the following causes: first, the imperfection of his organs, which were so defective that he was not susceptible of the fine impressions which theatrical excellence produces upon the generality of mankind; secondly, the cold rejection of his tragedy; and, lastly, the brilliant success of Garrick, who had been his pupil, who had come to London at the same time with him, not in a much more prosperous state than himself, and whose talents he undoubtedly rated low, compared with his own. His being outstripped by his pupil in the race of immediate fame, as well as of fortune, probably made him feel some indignation, as thinking that whatever might be Garrick's merits in his art, the reward was too great when compared with what the most successful efforts of literary labour could attain. At all periods of his life Johnson used to talk contemptuously of players; but in this work he speaks of them with peculiar acrimony; for which, perhaps, there was formerly too much reason from the licentious and dissolute manners of those engaged in that profession. It is but justice to add, that in our own time such a change has taken place, that there is no longer room for such an unfavourable distinction.

In 1745 he published a pamphlet entitled, "Miscellaneous Observations on the Tragedy of Macbeth, with Remarks on Sir T. H.'s (Sir Thomas Hanmer's) Edition of Shakspeare." * To which he affixed, proposals for a new edition of that poet.

As we do not trace any thing else published by him during the course of this year, we may conjecture that he was occupied entirely with that work. But the little encouragement which was given by the publick to his anonymous proposals for the execution of a task which Warburton was known to have undertaken, probably damped his ardour. His pamphlet, however, was highly esteemed, and was fortunate enough to obtain the approbation even of the supercilious Warburton himself, who, in the Preface to his Shakspeare published two years afterwards, thus mentioned it: "As to all those things which have been published under the titles of *Essays, Remarks, Observations,* &c. on Shakspeare, if you except some Critical Notes on Macbeth, given as a specimen of a projected edition, and written, as appears, by a man of parts and genius, the rest are absolutely below a serious notice."

Of this flattering distinction shewn to him by Warburton, a very grateful remembrance was ever entertained by Johnson, who said, "He praised me at a time when praise was of value to me."

In 1746 it is probable that he was still employed upon his Shakspeare, which perhaps he laid aside for a time, upon account of the high expectations which were formed of Warburton's edition of that great poet. It is somewhat curious, that his career appears to have been almost totally suspended in the years 1745 and 1746, those years which were marked by a civil war in Great-Britain, when a rash attempt was made to restore the House of Stuart to the throne. That he had a tenderness for that unfortunate House, is well known; and some may fancifully imagine, that a sympathetick anxiety impeded the exertion of his intellectual powers: but I am inclined to think, that he was, during this time, sketching the outlines of his great philological work.

This year his old pupil and friend, David Garrick, having become joint patentee and manager of Drury-lane theatre, Johnson honoured his opening of it with a Prologue,* which for just and manly dramatick criticism on the whole range of the English stage, as well as for poetical excellence, is unrivalled. Like the celebrated Epilogue to the "Distressed Mother," it was, during the season, often called for by the audience.

But the year 1747 is distinguished as the epoch, when Johnson's arduous and important work, his DICTIONARY OF THE ENGLISH LANGUAGE, was announced to the world, by the publication of its Plan or PROSPECTUS.

How long this immense undertaking had been the object of his contemplation, I do not know. I once asked him by what means he had attained to that astonishing knowledge of our language, by which he was enabled to realise a design of such extent and accumulated difficulty. He told me, that "it was not the effect of particular study; but that it had grown up in his mind insensibly." I have been informed by Mr. James Dodsley, that several years before this period, when Johnson was one day sitting in his brother Robert's shop, he heard his brother suggest to him, that a Dictionary of the English Language would be a work that would be well received by the publick; that Johnson seemed at first to catch at the proposition, but, after a pause, said, in his abrupt decisive manner, "I believe I shall not undertake it." That he, however, had bestowed much thought upon the subject, before he published his "Plan," is evident from the enlarged, clear, and accurate views which it exhibits; and we find him mentioning in that tract, that many of the writers whose testimonies were to be produced as authorities, were selected by Pope; which proves that he had been furnished, probably by Mr. Robert Dodsley, with whatever hints that eminent poet had contributed towards a great literary project, that had been the subject of important consideration in a former reign.

The booksellers who contracted with Johnson, single and unaided, for the execution of a work, which in other countries has not been effected but by the co-operating exertions of many, were Mr. Robert Dodsley, Mr. Charles Hitch, Mr. Andrew Millar, the two Messieurs Longman, and the two Messieurs Knapton. The price stipulated was fifteen hundred and seventy-five pounds.

The "Plan" was addressed to Philip Dormer, Earl of Chesterfield, then one of his Majesty's Principal Secretaries of State; a nobleman who was very ambitious of literary distinction, and who, upon being informed of the design, had expressed himself in terms very favourable to its success. There is, perhaps, in every thing of any consequence, a secret history which it would be amusing to know, could we have it authentically communicated. Johnson told me, "Sir, the way in which the plan of my Dictionary came to be inscribed to Lord Chesterfield, was this: I had neglected to write it by the time appointed. Dodsley suggested a desire to have it addressed to Lord Chesterfield. I laid hold of this as a pretext for delay, that it might be better done, and let Dodsley have his desire. I said to my friend, Dr.

Bathurst, 'Now if any good comes of my addressing to Lord Chesterfield, it will be ascribed to deep policy,' when, in fact, it was only a casual excuse for laziness."

It is worthy of observation, that the "Plan" has not only the substantial merit of comprehension, perspicuity, and precision, but that the language of it is unexceptionably excellent; it being altogether free from that inflation of style, and those uncommon but apt and energetick words, which in some of his writings have been censured, with more petulance than justice; and never was there a more dignified strain of compliment than that in which he courts the attention of one, who, he had been persuaded to believe, would be a respectable patron.

"With regard to questions of purity or propriety, (says he) I was once in doubt whether I should not attribute to myself too much in attempting to decide them, and whether my province was to extend beyond the proposition of the question, and the display of the suffrages on each side; but I have been since determined by your Lordship's opinion, to interpose my own judgement, and shall therefore endeavour to support what appears to me most consonant to grammar and reason. Ausonius thought that modesty forbade him to plead inability for a task to which Cæsar had judged him equal:

Cur me posse negem, posse quod ille putat?

And I may hope, my Lord, that since you, whose authority in our language is so generally acknowledged, have commissioned me to declare my own opinion, I shall be considered as exercising a kind of vicarious jurisdiction; and that the power which might have been denied to my own claim, will be readily allowed me as the delegate of your Lordship."

This passage proves, that Johnson's addressing his "Plan" to Lord Chesterfield was not merely in consequence of the result of a report by means of Dodsley, that the Earl favoured the design; but that there had been a particular communication with his Lordship concerning it. Dr. Taylor told me, that Johnson sent his "Plan" to him in manuscript, for his perusal; and that when it was lying upon his table,

Mr. William Whitehead happened to pay him a visit, and being shewn it, was highly pleased with such parts of it as he had time to read, and begged to take it home with him, which he was allowed to do; that from him it got into the hands of a noble Lord, who carried it to Lord Chesterfield. When Taylor observed this might be an advantage, Johnson replied, "No, Sir, it would have come out with more bloom, if it had not been seen before by any body."

The opinion conceived of it by another noble authour, appears from the following extract of a letter from the Earl of Orrery to Dr. Birch:

"Caledon, Dec. 30, 1747.

"I have just now seen the specimen of Mr. Johnson's Dictionary, addressed to Lord Chesterfield. I am much pleased with the plan, and I think the specimen is one of the best that I have ever read. Most specimens disgust, rather than prejudice us in favour of the work to follow; but the language of Mr. Johnson's is good, and the arguments are properly and modestly expressed. However, some expressions may be cavilled at, but they are trifles. I'll mention one: the *barren* laurel. The laurel is not barren, in any sense whatever; it bears fruits and flowers. *Sed hœ sunt nugœ*, and I have great expectations from the performance."

That he was fully aware of the arduous nature of the undertaking, he acknowledges; and shews himself perfectly sensible of it in the conclusion of his "Plan;" but he had a noble consciousness of his own abilities, which enabled him to go on with undaunted spirit.

Dr. Adams found him one day busy at his Dictionary, when the following dialogue ensued.—"ADAMS. This is a great work, Sir. How are you to get all the etymologies? JOHNSON. Why, Sir, here is a shelf with Junius, and Skinner, and others; and there is a Welch gentleman who has published a collection of Welch proverbs, who will help me with the Welch. ADAMS. But, Sir, how can you do this in three years? JOHNSON. Sir, I have no doubt that I can do it in three years. ADAMS. But the French Academy, which consists of forty members, took forty years to compile their Dictionary. JOHNSON. Sir, thus it is. This is the proportion. Let me see; forty times forty is sixteen hundred. As three to sixteen hundred, so is the proportion of an Englishman to a Frenchman." With so much ease and pleasantry could he talk of that prodigious labour which he had undertaken to execute.

While the Dictionary was going forward, Johnson lived part of the time in Holborn, part in Gough-square, Fleet-street; and he had an upper room fitted up like a counting-house for the purpose, in which he gave to the copyists their several tasks: The words, partly taken from other dictionaries, and partly supplied by himself, having been first written down with spaces left between them, he delivered in writing their etymologies, definitions, and various significations. The authorities were copied from the books themselves, in which he had marked the passages with a black-lead pencil, the traces of which could easily be effaced. I have seen several of them, in which that trouble had not been taken; so that they were just as when used by the copyists. It is remarkable, that he was so attentive in the choice of the passages in which words were authorised, that one may read page after page of his Dictionary with improvement and pleasure; and it should not pass unobserved, that he has quoted no author whose writings had a tendency to hurt sound religion and morality.

The necessary expence of preparing a work of such magnitude for the press, must have been a considerable deduction from the price stipulated to be paid for the copyright. I understand that nothing was allowed by the booksellers on that account; and I remember his telling me, that a large portion of it having, by mistake, been written upon both sides of the paper, so as to be inconvenient for the compositor, it cost him twenty pounds to have it transcribed upon one side only.

He is now to be considered as "tugging at his oar," as engaged in a steady continued course of occupation, sufficient to employ all his time for some years; and which was the best preventive of that constitutional melancholy which was ever lurking about him, ready to trouble his quiet. But his enlarged and lively mind could not be satisfied without

more diversity of employment, and the pleasure of animated relaxation. He therefore not only exerted his talents
in occasional composition, very different from Lexicogra-
phy, but formed a club in Ivy lane, Paternoster Row, with
a view to enjoy literary discussion, and amuse his evening
hours. The members associated with him in this little society were, his beloved friend Dr. Richard Bathurst, Mr.
Hawkesworth, afterwards well worth his writings, Mr. John
Hawkins, an attorney, and a few others of different professions.

In January, 1749, he published "THE VANITY OF HUMAN
WISHES, being the Tenth Satire of Juvenal imitated." * He,
I believe, composed it the preceding year. Mrs. Johnson,
for the sake of country air, had lodgings at Hampstead, to
which he resorted occasionally, and there the greatest part,
if not the whole, of this Imitation was written. The fervid
rapidity with which it was produced, is scarcely credible. I
have heard him say, that he composed seventy lines of it in
one day, without putting one of them upon paper till they
were finished. I remember when I once regretted to him that
he had not given us more of Juvenal's Satires, he said, he
probably should give more, for he had them all in his head;
by which I understood, that he had the originals and corre-
spondent allusions floating in his mind, which he could,
when he pleased, embody and render permanent without
much labour. Some of them, however, he observed were too
gross for imitation.

The profits of a single poem, however excellent, appear
to have been very small in the last reign, compared with
what a publication of the same size has since been known to
yield. I have mentioned upon Johnson's own authority, that
for his LONDON he had only ten guineas; and now, after
his fame was established, he got for his "Vanity of Human
Wishes" but five guineas more, as is proved by an authentick document in my possession.

His "Vanity of Human Wishes" has less of common life,
but more of a philosophick dignity than his "London." More
readers, therefore, will be delighted with the pointed spirit
of "London," than with the profound reflection of "The
Vanity of Human Wishes." Garrick, for instance, observed

in his sprightly manner, with more vivacity than regard to just discrimination, as is usual with wits, "When Johnson lived much with the Herveys, and saw a good deal of what was passing in life, he wrote his 'London,' which is lively and easy: when he became more retired, he gave us his 'Vanity of Human Wishes,' which is as hard as Greek. Had he gone on to imitate another satire, it would have been as hard as Hebrew." But "The Vanity of Human Wishes" is, in the opinion of the best judges, as high an effort of ethick poetry as any language can shew.

Garrick being now vested with theatrical power by being manager of Drury-lane theatre, he kindly and generously made use of it to bring out Johnson's tragedy, which had been long kept back for want of encouragement. But in this benevolent purpose he met with no small difficulty from the temper of Johnson, which could not brook that a drama which he had formed with much study, and had been obliged to keep more than the nine years of Horace, should be revised and altered at the pleasure of an actor. Yet Garrick knew well, that without some alterations it would not be fit for the stage. A violent dispute having ensued between them, Garrick applied to the Reverend Dr. Taylor to interpose. Johnson was at first very obstinate. "Sir, (said he) the fellow wants me to make Mahomet run mad, that he may have an opportunity of tossing his hands and kicking his heels." He was, however, at last, with difficulty, prevailed on to comply with Garrick's wishes, so as to allow of some changes; but still there were not enough.

Dr. Adams was present the first night of the representation of IRENE, and gave me the following account: "Before the curtain drew up, there were catcalls and whistling, which alarmed Johnson's friends. The Prologue, which was written by himself in a manly strain, soothed the audience, and the play went off tolerably, till it came to the conclusion, when Mrs. Pritchard, the Heroine of the piece, was to be strangled upon the stage, and was to speak two lines with the bow-string round her neck. The audience cried out *'Murder! Murder!'* She several times attempted to speak; but in vain. At last she was obliged to go off the stage alive." This passage was afterwards struck out, and she was carried off to be put to death behind the scenes, as the play now has it. The Epilogue, as Johnson informed me, was written by Sir William Yonge. I know not how his play came to be thus graced by the pen of a person then so eminent in the political world.

Notwithstanding all the support of such performers as Garrick, Barry, Mrs. Cibber, Mrs. Pritchard, and every advantage of dress and decorations, the tragedy of Irene did not please the publick. Mr. Garrick's zeal carried it through for nine nights, so that the authour had his three nights' profits; and from a receipt signed by him, now in the hands of Mr. James Dodsley, it appears that his friend, Mr. Robert Dodsley, gave him one hundred pounds for the copy.

IRENE, considered as a poem, is entitled to the praise of superiour excellence. Analysed into parts, it will furnish a rich store of noble sentiments, fine imagery, and beautiful language; but it is deficient in pathos, in that delicate power of touching the human feelings, which is the principal end of the drama. Indeed Garrick has complained to me, that Johnson not only had not the faculty of producing the impressions of tragedy, but that he had not the sensibility to perceive them. Johnson was wise enough to be convinced that he had not the talents necessary to write successfully for the stage, and never made another attempt in that species of composition.

When asked how he felt upon the ill success of his tragedy, he replied, "Like the Monument!" meaning that he continued firm and unmoved as that column. And let it be remembered, as an admonition to the *genus irritabile* of dramatick writers, that this great man, instead of peevishly complaining of the bad taste of the town, submitted to its decision without a murmur. He had, indeed, upon all occasions a great deference for the general opinion: "A man (said he) who writes a book, thinks himself wiser or wittier than the rest of mankind; he supposes that he can instruct or amuse them, and the publick to whom he appeals, must, after all, be the judges of his pretensions."

On occasion of this play being brought upon the stage, Johnson had a fancy that as a dramatick authour his dress should be more gay than what he ordinarily wore; he therefore appeared behind the scenes, and even in one of the side boxes, in a scarlet waistcoat, with rich gold lace, and a gold-laced hat. He humourously observed to Mr. Langton, "that when in that dress he could not treat people with the same ease as when in his usual plain clothes." Dress indeed, we must allow, has more effect even upon strong minds than one should suppose, without having had the experience of it. His necessary attendance while his play was in rehearsal, and during its performance, brought him acquainted with many of the performers of both sexes, which produced a more favourable opinion of their profession than he had harshly expressed in his Life of Savage. With some of them he kept up an acquaintance as long as he and they lived, and was ever ready to shew them acts of kindness. He for a considerable time used to frequent the *Green-Room,* and seemed to take delight in dissipating his gloom, by mixing in the sprightly chit-chat of the motley circle then to be found there. Mr. David Hume related to me from Mr. Garrick, that Johnson at last denied himself this amusement, from considerations of rigid virtue; saying, "I'll come no more behind your scenes, David; for the silk stockings and white bosoms of your actresses excite my amorous propensities."

In 1750 he came forth in the character for which he was eminently qualified, a majestick teacher of moral and religious wisdom. The vehicle which he chose was that of a periodical paper, which he knew had been, upon former occasions, employed with great success. The Tatler, Spectator, and Guardian, were the last of the kind published in England, which had stood the test of a long trial; and such an interval had now elapsed since their publication, as made him justly think that, to many of his readers, this form of instruction would, in some degree, have the advantage of novelty. A few days before the first of his Essays came out, there started another competitor for fame in the same form, under the title of "The Tatler Revived," which I believe was "born but to die." Johnson was, I think, not very happy in the choice of his title,—"The Rambler;" which certainly is not suited to a series of grave and moral discourses; which the Italians have literally, but ludicrously,

translated by *Il Vagabondo;* and which has been lately assumed as the denomination of a vehicle of licentious tales,
"The Rambler's Magazine." He gave Sir Joshua Reynolds
the following account of its getting this name: "What *must*
be done, Sir, *will* be done. When I was to begin publishing that paper, I was at a loss how to name it. I sat down
at night upon my bedside, and resolved that I would not go
to sleep till I had fixed its title. The Rambler seemed the
best that occurred, and I took it."

With what devout and conscientious sentiments this
paper was undertaken, is evidenced by the following prayer,
which he composed and offered up on the occasion: "Almighty God, the giver of all good things, without whose
help all labour is ineffectual, and without whose grace all
wisdom is folly: grant, I beseech Thee, that in this undertaking thy Holy Spirit may not be with-held from me, but
that I may promote thy glory, and the salvation of myself
and others: grant this, O Lord, for the sake of thy son,
JESUS CHRIST. Amen."

The first paper of the Rambler was published on Tuesday
the 20th of March, 1749-50; and its authour was enabled
to continue it, without interruption, every Tuesday and Saturday, till Saturday the 14th day of March, 1752, on which
day it closed. This is a strong confirmation of the truth of
a remark of his, which I have had occasion to quote elsewhere, that "a man may write at any time, if he will set
himself doggedly to it;" for, notwithstanding his constitutional indolence, his depression of spirits, and his labour in
carrying on his Dictionary, he answered the stated calls of
the press twice a week from the stores of his mind, during
all that time; having received no assistance, except four
billets in No. 10, by Miss Mulso, now Mrs. Chapone; No.
30, by Mrs. Catharine Talbot; No. 97, by Mr. Samuel
Richardson, whom he describes in an introductory note as
"An authour who has enlarged the knowledge of human
nature, and taught the passions to move at the command
of virtue;" and Numbers 44 and 100, by Mrs. Elizabeth
Carter.

Posterity will be astonished when they are told, upon
the authority of Johnson himself, that many of these dis-

63

courses, which we should suppose had been laboured with all the slow attention of literary leisure, were written in haste as the moment pressed, without even being read over by him before they were printed. It can be accounted for only in this way; that by reading and meditation, and a very close inspection of life, he had accumulated a great fund of miscellaneous knowledge, which, by a peculiar promptitude of mind, was ever ready at his call, and which he had constantly accustomed himself to clothe in the most apt and energetick expression. Sir Joshua Reynolds once asked him by what means he had attained his extraordinary accuracy and flow of language. He told him, that he had early laid it down as a fixed rule to do his best on every occasion, and in every company: to impart whatever he knew in the most forcible language he could put it in; and that by constant practice, and never suffering any careless expressions to escape him, or attempting to deliver his thoughts without arranging them in the clearest manner, it became habitual to him.

As the Rambler was entirely the work of one man, there was, of course, such a uniformity in its texture, as very much to exclude the charm of variety; and the grave and often solemn cast of thinking, which distinguished it from other periodical papers, made it, for some time, not generally liked. So slowly did this excellent work, of which twelve editions have now issued from the press, gain upon the world at large, that even in the closing number the authour says, "I have never been much a favourite of the publick." Yet, very soon after its commencement, there were those who felt and acknowledged its uncommon excellence.

Johnson told me, with an amiable fondness, a little pleasing circumstance relative to this work. Mrs. Johnson, in whose judgement and taste he had great confidence, said to him, after a few numbers of the Rambler had come out, "I thought very well of you before; but I did not imagine you could have written any thing equal to this." Distant praise, from whatever quarter, is not so delightful as that of a wife whom a man loves and esteems. Her approbation may be said to "come home to his *bosom;*" and being so near, its effect is most sensible and permanent.

The Rambler has increased in fame as in age. Soon after its first folio edition was concluded, it was published in six duodecimo volumes; and its authour lived to see ten numerous editions of it in London, beside those of Ireland and Scotland. I will venture to say, that in no writings whatever can be found more *bark and steel for the mind,* if I may use the expression; more that can brace and invigorate every manly and noble sentiment.

Though the Rambler was not concluded till the year 1752, I shall, under this year, say all that I have to observe upon it. Some of the translations of the mottos by himself, are admirably done. He acknowledges to have received "elegant translations" of many of them from Mr. James Elphinston; and some are very happily translated by a Mr. *F. Lewis,* of whom I never heard more, except that Johnson thus described him to Mr. Malone: "Sir, he lived in London, and hung loose upon society."

Though Johnson's circumstances were at this time far from being easy, his humane and charitable disposition was constantly exerting itself. Mrs. Anna Williams, daughter of a very ingenious Welsh physician, and a woman of more than ordinary talents and literature, having come to London in hopes of being cured of a cataract in both her eyes, which afterwards ended in total blindness, was kindly received as a constant visitor at his house while Mrs. Johnson lived; and, after her death, having come under his roof in order to have an operation upon her eyes performed with more comfort to her than in lodgings, she had an apartment from him during the rest of her life, at all times when he had a house.

In 1752 he was almost entirely occupied with his Dictionary. The last paper of his Rambler was published March 14, this year; after which, there was a cessation for some time of any exertion of his talents as an essayist.

That there should be a suspension of his literary labours during a part of the year 1752, will not seem strange, when it is considered that soon after closing his Rambler, he suffered the loss which there can be no doubt, affected him with the deepest distress. For on the 17th of March, O. S., his wife died. Why Sir John Hawkins should unwarrantably take upon him even to *suppose* that Johnson's fondness for her was *dissembled* (meaning simulated or assumed,) and to assert, that if it was not the case, "it was a lesson he had learned by rote," I cannot conceive; unless it proceeded from a want of similar feelings in his own breast. To argue from her being much older than Johnson, or any other circumstances, that he could not really love her, is absurd; for love is not a subject of reasoning, but of feeling, and therefore there are no common principles upon which one can persuade another concerning it. Every man feels for himself, and knows how he is affected by particular qualities in the person he admires, the impressions of which are too minute and delicate to be substantiated in language.

The following very solemn and affecting prayer was found after Dr. Johnson's decease, by his servant, Mr. Francis Barber.

"April 26, 1752, being after 12 at Night of the 25th.

"O Lord! Governor of heaven and earth, in whose hands are embodied and departed Spirits, if thou hast ordained the Souls of the Dead to minister to the Living, and appointed my departed Wife to have care of me, grant that I may enjoy the good effects of her attention and ministration, whether exercised by appearance, impulses, dreams, or in any other manner agreeable to thy Government. Forgive my presumption, enlighten my ignorance, and however meaner agents are employed, grant me the blessed influences of thy holy Spirit, through Jesus Christ our Lord. Amen."

What actually followed upon this most interesting piece of devotion by Johnson, we are not informed; but I, whom it has pleased GOD to afflict in a similar manner to that which occasioned it, have certain experience of benignant communication by dreams.

I have been told by Mrs. Desmoulins, who, before her marriage, lived for some time with Mrs. Johnson at Hampstead, that she indulged herself in country air and nice living, at an unsuitable expence, while her husband was drudging in the smoke of London, and that she by no means

3-4
The birthplace of Dr. Johnson, Lichfield, Staffordshire, and (above) Edial Hall near Lichfield where Johnson lived and taught school as a young man.

treated him with that complacency which is the most engaging quality in a wife. But all this is perfectly compatible
with his fondness for her, especially when it is remembered
that he had a high opinion of her understanding, and that
the impressions which her beauty, real or imaginary, had
originally made upon his fancy, being continued by habit,
had not been effaced, though she herself was doubtless
much altered for the worse.

That his sufferings upon the death of his wife were severe,
beyond what are commonly endured, I have no doubt, from
the information of many who were then about him, to none
of whom I give more credit than to Mr. Francis Barber,
his faithful negro servant,[1] who came into his family about
a fortnight after the dismal event.

The circle of his friends at this time was extensive and
various, far beyond what has been generally imagined. To
trace his acquaintance with each particular person, if it
could be done, would be a task, of which the labour would
not be repaid by the advantage. But exceptions are to be
made; one of which must be a friend so eminent as Sir
Joshua Reynolds, who was truly his *dulce decus*, and with
whom he maintained an uninterrupted intimacy to the last
hour of his life. When Johnson lived in Castle-street, Cav-
endish-square, he used frequently to visit two ladies who
lived opposite to him, Miss Cotterells, daughters of Admiral Cotterell. Reynolds used also to visit there, and thus
they met. Mr. Reynolds, as I have observed above, had,
from the first reading of his Life of Savage, conceived a
very high admiration of Johnson's powers of writing. His
conversation no less delighted him; and he cultivated his
acquaintance with the laudable zeal of one who was am-

---

[1] Francis Barber was born in Jamaica, and was brought to England in
1750 by Colonel Bathurst, father of Johnson's very intimate friend, Dr.
Bathurst. He was sent, for some time, to the Reverend Mr. Jackson's
school, at Barton, in Yorkshire. The Colonel by his will left him his freedom, and Dr. Bathurst was willing that he should enter into Johnson's
service, in which he continued from 1752 till Johnson's death, with the
exception of two intervals; in one of which, upon some difference with
his master, he went and served an apothecary in Cheapside, but still
visited Dr. Johnson occasionally; in another, he took a fancy to go to sea.
Part of the time, indeed, he was, by the kindness of his master, at a
school in Northamptonshire, that he might have the advantage of some
learning. So early, and so lasting a connection was there between Dr.
Johnson and this humble friend.

bitious of general improvement. Sir Joshua, indeed, was lucky enough at their very first meeting to make a remark, which was so much above the commonplace style of conversation, that Johnson at once perceived that Reynolds had the habit of thinking for himself. The ladies were regretting the death of a friend, to whom they owed great obligations; upon which Reynolds observed, "You have however, the comfort of being relieved from a burthen of gratitude." They were shocked a little at this alleviating suggestion, as too selfish; but Johnson defended it in his clear and forcible manner, and was much pleased with the *mind*, the fair view of human nature, which it exhibited, like some of the reflections of Rochefoucauld. The consequence was, that he went home with Reynolds, and supped with him.

Sir Joshua told me a pleasant characteristical anecdote of Johnson about the time of their first acquaintance. When they were one evening together at the Miss Cotterells', the then Duchess of Argyle and another lady of high rank came in. Johnson thinking that the Miss Cotterells were too much engrossed by them, and that he and his friend were neglected, as low company of whom they were somewhat ashamed, grew angry; and resolving to shock their supposed pride, by making their great visitors imagine that his friend and he were low indeed, he addressed himself in a low tone to Mr. Reynolds, saying, "How much do you think you and I could get in a week, if we were to *work as hard* as we could?"—as if they had been common mechanicks.

His acquaintance with Bennet Langton, Esq. of Langton, in Lincolnshire, another much valued friend, commenced soon after the conclusion of his Rambler; which that gentleman, then a youth, had read with so much admiration, that he came to London chiefly with a view of endeavouring to be introduced to its authour. By a fortunate chance he happened to take lodgings in a house where Mr. Levet frequently visited; and having mentioned his wish to his landlady, she introduced him to Mr. Levet, who readily obtained Johnson's permission to bring Mr. Langton to him; as, indeed, Johnson, during the whole course of his life, had no shyness, real or affected, but was easy of access to all who were properly recommended, and even wished to see numbers at his *levee,* as his morning circle of company might, with strict propriety, be called. Mr. Langton was exceedingly surprised when the sage first appeared. He had not received the smallest intimation of his figure, dress, or manner. From perusing his writings, he fancied he should see a decent, well-drest, in short, a remarkably decorous philosopher. Instead of which, down from his bed-chamber, about noon, came, as newly risen, a huge, uncouth figure, with a little dark wig which scarcely covered his head, and his clothes hanging loose about him. But his conversation was so rich, so animated, and so forcible, and his religious and political notions so congenial with those in which Langton had been educated, that he conceived for him that veneration and attachment which he ever preserved. Johnson was not the less ready to love Mr. Langton, for his being of a very ancient family; for I have heard him say, with pleasure, "Langton, Sir, has a grant of free warren from Henry the Second; and Cardinal Stephen Langton, in King John's reign, was of this family."

Mr. Langton afterwards went to pursue his studies at Trinity College, Oxford, where he formed an acquaintance with his fellow-student, Mr. Topham Beauclerk; who, though their opinions and modes of life were so different, that it seemed utterly improbable that they should at all agree, had so ardent a love of literature, so acute an understanding, such elegance of manners, and so well discerned the excellent qualities of Mr. Langton, a gentleman eminent not only for worth and learning, but for an inexhaustible fund of entertaining conversation, that they became intimate friends.

Johnson, soon after this acquaintance began, passed a considerable time at Oxford. He at first thought it strange that Langton should associate so much with one who had the character of being loose, both in his principles and practice: but, by degrees, he himself was fascinated. Mr. Beauclerk's being of the St. Alban's family, and, having, in some particulars, a resemblance to Charles the Second, contributed, in Johnson's imagination, to throw a lustre upon his other qualities; and in a short time, the moral, pious

69

Johnson, and the gay dissipated Beauclerk, were companions. "What a coalition! (said Garrick, when he heard of
this:) I shall have my old friend to bail out of the Round-
house." But I can bear testimony that it was a very agreeable association. Beauclerk was too polite, and valued learning and wit too much, to offend Johnson by sallies of infidelity or licentiousness; and Johnson delighted in the good
qualities of Beauclerk, and hoped to correct the evil. Innumerable were the scenes in which Johnson was amused
by these young men. Beauclerk could take more liberty with
him, than any body with whom I ever saw him; but, on the
other hand, Beauclerk was not spared by his respectable
companions, when reproof was proper. Beauclerk had such
a propensity to satire, that at one time Johnson said to him,
"You never open your mouth but with intention to give
pain; and you have often given me pain, not from the
power of what you said, but from seeing your intention." At
another time applying to him, with a slight alteration, a line
of Pope, he said,

" 'Thy love of folly, and thy scorn of fools—'

Every thing thou dost shews the one, and every thing thou
say'st the other." At another time he said to him, "Thy
body is all vice, and thy mind all virtue." Beauclerk not
seeming to relish the compliment, Johnson said, "Nay, Sir,
Alexander the Great, marching in triumph into Babylon,
could not have desired to have had more said to him."

Johnson was some time with Beauclerk at his house at
Windsor, where he was entertained with experiments in
natural philosophy. One Sunday, when the weather was very
fine, Beauclerk enticed him, insensibly, to saunter about
all the morning. They went into a church-yard, in the time
of divine service, and Johnson laid himself down at his
ease upon one of the tomb-stones. "Now, Sir, (said Beauclerk) you are like Hogarth's Idle Apprentice." When Johnson got his pension, Beauclerk said to him, in the humourous phrase of Falstaff, "I hope you'll now purge and live
cleanly, like a gentleman."

One night, when Beauclerk and Langton had supped at a tavern in London, and sat till about three in the morning, it came into their heads to go and knock up Johnson, and see if they could prevail on him to join them in a ramble. They rapped violently at the door of his chambers in the Temple, till at last he appeared in his shirt, with his little black wig on the top of his head, instead of a night-cap, and a poker in his hand, imagining, probably, that some ruffians were coming to attack him. When he discovered who they were, and was told their errand, he smiled, and with great good humour agreed to their proposal: "What, is it you, you dogs! I'll have a frisk with you." He was soon drest, and they sallied forth together into Covent-Garden, where the greengrocers and fruiterers were beginning to arrange their hampers, just come in from the country. Johnson made some attempts to help them; but the honest gardeners stared so at his figure and manner, and odd interference, that he soon saw his services were not relished. They then repaired to one of the neighbouring taverns, and made a bowl of that liquor called *Bishop,* which Johnson had always liked; while in joyous contempt of sleep, from which he had been roused, he repeated the festive lines,

> "Short, Oh short then be thy reign,
> And give us to the world again!"

They did not stay long, but walked down to the Thames, took a boat, and rowed to Billingsgate. Beauclerk and Johnson were so well pleased with their amusement, that they resolved to persevere in dissipation for the rest of the day: but Langton deserted them, being engaged to breakfast with some young Ladies. Johnson scolded him for "leaving his social friends to go and sit with a set of wretched *un-idea'd* girls." Garrick being told of this ramble, said to him smartly, "I heard of your frolick t'other night. You'll be in the Chronicle." Upon which Johnson afterwards observed, "*He* durst not do such a thing. His *wife* would not *let* him!"

The Dictionary, we may believe, afforded Johnson full occupation. As it approached to its conclusion, he probably worked with redoubled vigour, as seamen increase their exertion and alacrity when they have a near prospect of their haven.

Lord Chesterfield, to whom Johnson had paid the high compliment of addressing to his Lordship the Plan of his Dictionary, had behaved to him in such a manner as to excite his contempt and indignation. The world has been for many years amused with a story confidently told, and as confidently repeated with additional circumstances, that a sudden disgust was taken by Johnson upon occasion of his having been one day kept long in waiting in his Lordship's antechamber, for which the reason assigned was, that he had company with him; and that at last, when the door opened, out walked Colley Cibber; and that Johnson was so violently provoked when he found for whom he had been so long excluded, that he went away in a passion, and never would return. I remember having mentioned this story to George Lord Lyttelton, who told me, he was very intimate with Lord Chesterfield; and holding it as a well-known truth, defended Lord Chesterfield by saying, that "Cibber, who had been introduced familiarly by the backstairs, had probably not been there above ten minutes." It may seem strange even to entertain a doubt concerning a story so long and so wildly current, and thus implicitly adopted, if not sanctioned, by the authority which I have mentioned; but Johnson himself assured me, that there was not the least foundation for it. He told me, that there never was any particular incident which produced a quarrel between Lord Chesterfield and him; but that his Lordship's continued neglect was the reason why he resolved to have no connexion with him. When the Dictionary was upon the eve of publication, Lord Chesterfield, who, it is said, had flattered himself with expectations that Johnson would dedicate the work to him, attempted, in a courtly manner, to soothe and insinuate himself with the Sage, conscious, as it should seem, of the cold indifference with which he had treated its learned authour; and further attempted to conciliate him, by writing two papers in "The World," in recommendation of the work; and it must be confessed, that they contain some studied compliments, so finely turned, that if there had been no previous offence, it is probable that Johnson would have been highly delighted. Praise, in general, was pleasing to him; but by praise from a man of rank and elegant accomplishments, he was peculiarly gratified.

His Lordship says, "I think the publick in general, and the republick of letters in particular, are greatly obliged to Mr. Johnson, for having undertaken, and executed so great and desirable a work. Perfection is not to be expected from man: but if we are to judge by the various works of Johnson already published, we have good reason to believe, that he will bring this as near to perfection as any man could do. The plan of it, which he published some years ago, seems to me to be a proof of it. Nothing can be more rationally imagined, or more accurately and elegantly expressed. I therefore recommend the previous perusal of it to all those who intend to buy the Dictionary, and who, I suppose, are all those who can afford it."

*   *   *   *

"It must be owned, that our language is, at present, in a state of anarchy, and hitherto, perhaps, it may not have been the worse for it. During our free and open trade, many words and expressions have been imported, adopted, and naturalized from other languages, which have greatly enriched our own. Let it still preserve what real strength and beauty it may have borrowed from others; but let it not, like the Tarpeian maid, be overwhelmed and crushed by unnecessary ornaments. The time for discrimination seems to be now come. Toleration, adoption, and naturalization have run their lengths. Good order and authority are now necessary. But where shall we find them, and at the same time, the obedience due to them? We must have recourse to the old Roman expedient in times of confusion, and chuse a dictator. Upon this principle, I give my vote for Mr. Johnson, to fill that great and arduous post, and I hereby declare, that I make a total surrender of all my rights and privileges in the English language, as a freeborn British subject, to the said Mr. Johnson, during the term of his dictatorship. Nay more, I will not only obey him like an old Roman, as my dictator, but, like a modern Roman, I will implicitly believe in him as my Pope, and

73

hold him to be infallible while in the chair, but no longer. More than this he cannot well require; for, I presume, that obedience can never be expected, where there is neither terrour to enforce, nor interest to invite it."

*　　*　　*　　*

"But a Grammar, a Dictionary, and a History of our Language, through its several stages, were still wanting at home, and importunately called for from abroad. Mr. Johnson's labours will now, I dare say, very fully supply that want, and greatly contribute to the farther spreading of our language in other countries. Learners were discouraged, by finding no standard to resort to; and, consequently, thought it incapable of any. They will now be undeceived and encouraged."

This courtly device failed of its effect. Johnson, who thought that "all was false and hollow," despised the honeyed words, and was even indignant that Lord Chesterfield should, for a moment, imagine, that he could be the dupe of such an artifice. His expression to me concerning Lord Chesterfield, upon this occasion, was, "Sir, after making great professions, he had, for many years, taken no notice of me; but when my Dictionary was coming out, he fell a scribbling in 'The World' about it. Upon which, I wrote him a letter expressed in civil terms, but such as might shew him that I did not mind what he said or wrote, and that I had done with him."

This is that celebrated letter of which so much has been said, and about which curiosity had been so long excited, without being gratified. I for many years solicited Johnson to favour me with a copy of it, that so excellent a composition might not be lost to posterity. He delayed from time to time to give it me; [1] till at last in 1781, when we were on a visit at Mr. Dilly's, at Southill in Bedfordshire, he

---

[1] Dr. Johnson appeared to have had a remarkable delicacy with respect to the circulation of this letter; for Dr. Douglas, Bishop of Salisbury, informs me, that having many years ago pressed him to be allowed to read it to the second Lord Hardwicke, who was very desirous to hear it, (promising at the same time, that no copy of it should be taken,) Johnson seemed much pleased that it had attracted the attention of a nobleman of such a respectable character; but after pausing some time, declined to comply with the request, saying, with a smile, "No, Sir; I have hurt the dog too much already;" or words to that purpose.

was pleased to dictate it to me from memory. He afterwards found among his papers a copy of it, which he had
dictated to Mr. Baretti, with its title and corrections, in
his own hand-writing. This he gave to Mr. Langton; adding
that if it were to come into print, he wished it to be from
that copy. By Mr. Langton's kindness, I am enabled to enrich my work with a perfect transcript of what the world
has so eagerly desired to see.

"TO THE RIGHT HONOURABLE THE EARL OF CHESTERFIELD.
"MY LORD,   February 7, 1755.
  "I have been lately informed, by the proprietor of the
World, that two papers, in which my Dictionary is recom-
mended to the publick, were written by your Lordship.
To be so distinguished, is an honour, which, being very lit-
tle accustomed to favours from the great, I know not well
how to receive, or in what terms to acknowledge.

  "When, upon some slight encouragement, I first visited
your Lordship, I was overpowered, like the rest of mankind, by the enchantment of your address, and could not
forbear to wish that I might boast myself *Le vainqueur du
vainqueur de la terre;*—that I might obtain that regard for
which I saw the world contending; but I found my attendance so little encouraged, that neither pride nor modesty
would suffer me to continue it. When I had once addressed
your Lordship in publick, I had exhausted all the art of
pleasing which a retired and uncourtly scholar can possess.
I had done all that I could; and no man is well pleased to
have his all neglected, be it ever so little.

  "Seven years, my Lord, have now past, since I waited in
your outward rooms, or was repulsed from your door; during which time I have been pushing on my work through
difficulties, of which it is useless to complain, and have
brought it, at last, to the verge of publication, without one
act of assistance,[1] one word of encouragement, or one smile

---

[1] The following note is subjoined by Mr. Langton. "Dr. Johnson, when
he gave me this copy of his letter, desired that I would annex to it his
information to me, that whereas it is said in the letter that 'no assistance
has been received,' he did once receive from Lord Chesterfield the sum
of ten pounds; but as that was so inconsiderable a sum, he thought the
mention of it could not properly find a place in a letter of the kind that
this was."

of favour. Such treatment I did not expect, for I never had a Patron before.

"The shepherd in Virgil grew at last acquainted with Love, and found him a native of the rocks.

"Is not a Patron, my Lord, one who looks with unconcern on a man struggling for life in the water, and, when he has reached ground, encumbers him with help? The notice which you have been pleased to take of my labours, had it been early, had been kind; but it has been delayed till I am indifferent, and cannot enjoy it; till I am solitary, and cannot impart it; till I am known, and do not want it. I hope it is no very cynical asperity, not to confess obligations where no benefit has been received, or to be unwilling that the publick should consider me as owing that to a Patron, which Providence has enabled me to do for myself.

"Having carried on my work thus far with so little obligation to any favourer of learning, I shall not be disappointed though I should conclude it, if less be possible, with less; for I have been long wakened from that dream of hope, in which I once boasted myself with so much exultation,

"My Lord,
"Your Lordship's most humble
"Most obedient servant,
"SAM. JOHNSON."

"While this was the talk of the town, (says Dr. Adams, in a letter to me) I happened to visit Dr. Warburton, who finding that I was acquainted with Johnson, desired me earnestly to carry his compliments to him, and to tell him, that he honoured him for his manly behaviour in rejecting these condescensions of Lord Chesterfield, and for resenting the treatment he had received from him with a proper spirit. Johnson was visibly pleased with this compliment, for he had always a high opinion of Warburton. Indeed, the force of mind which appeared in this letter, was congenial with that which Warburton himself amply possessed.

There is a curious minute circumstance which struck me, in comparing the various editions of Johnson's Imitations of Juvenal. In the tenth Satire one of the couplets upon the vanity of wishes even for literary distinction stood thus:

> "Yet think what ills the scholar's life assail,
> Toil, envy, want, the *garret*, and the jail."

But after experiencing the uneasiness which Lord Chesterfield's fallacious patronage made him feel, he dismissed the word *garret* from the sad group, and in all the subsequent editions the line stands,

> "Toil, envy, want, the *Patron*, and the jail."

That Lord Chesterfield must have been mortified by the lofty contempt, and polite, yet keen, satire with which Johnson exhibited him to himself in this letter, it is impossible to doubt. He, however, with that glossy duplicity which was his constant study, affected to be quite unconcerned. Dr. Adams mentioned to Mr. Robert Dodsley that he was sorry Johnson had written his letter to Lord Chesterfield. Dodsley, with the true feelings of trade, said "he was very sorry too; for that he had a property in the Dictionary, to which his Lordship's patronage might have been of consequence." He then told Dr. Adams, that Lord Chesterfield had shewn him the letter. "I should have imagined (replied Dr. Adams) that Lord Chesterfield would have concealed it." "Poh! (said Dodsley) do you think a letter from Johnson could hurt Lord Chesterfield? Not at all, Sir. It lay upon his table, where any body might see it. He read it to me; said, 'this man has great powers,' pointed out the severest passages, and observed how well they were expressed." This air of indifference, which imposed upon the worthy Dodsley, was certainly nothing but a specimen of that dissimulation which Lord Chesterfield inculcated as one of the most essential lessons for the conduct of life. His Lordship endeavoured to justify himself to Dodsley from the charges brought against him by Johnson; but we may judge of the flimsiness of his defence, from his having excused his neglect of Johnson, by saying, that "he had heard he had changed his lodgings, and did not know where he lived;"

as if there could have been the smallest difficulty to inform himself of that circumstance, by enquiring in the literary circle with which his Lordship was well acquainted, and was, indeed, himself, one of its ornaments.

Dr. Adams expostulated with Johnson, and suggested, that his not being admitted when he called on him, was probably not to be imputed to Lord Chesterfield; for his Lordship had declared to Dodsley, that "he would have turned off the best servant he ever had, if he had known that he denied him to a man who would have been always more than welcome;" and in confirmation of this, he insisted on Lord Chesterfield's general affability and easiness of access, especially to literary men. "Sir, (said Johnson) that is not Lord Chesterfield; he is the proudest man this day existing." "No, (said Dr. Adams) there is one person, at least, as proud; I think, by your own account you are the prouder man of the two." "But mine (replied Johnson instantly) was *defensive* pride." This, as Dr. Adams well observed, was one of those happy turns for which he was so remarkably ready.

Johnson having now explicitly avowed his opinion of Lord Chesterfield, did not refrain from expressing himself concerning that nobleman with pointed freedom: "This man (said he) I thought had been a Lord among wits; but, I find, he is only a wit among Lords!" And when his Letters to his natural son were published, he observed, that "they teach the morals of a whore, and the manners of a dancing-master."

The character of a "respectable Hottentot," in Lord Chesterfield's letters, has been generally understood to be meant for Johnson, and I have no doubt that it was.

The degree of Master of Arts, which, it has been observed, could not be obtained for him at an early period of his life, was now considered as an honour of considerable importance, in order to grace the title-page of his Dictionary; and his character in the literary world being by this time deservedly high, his friends thought that, if proper exertions were made, the University of Oxford would pay him the compliment. In 1755 we behold him to great advantage; his degree of Master of Arts conferred upon him, his Dictionary published, his correspondence animated, his benevolence exercised.

Mr. Andrew Millar, bookseller in the Strand, took the principal charge of conducting the publication of Johnson's Dictionary; and as the patience of the proprietors was repeatedly tried and almost exhausted, by their expecting that the work would be compleated, within the time which Johnson had sanguinely supposed, the learned author was often goaded to dispatch, more especially as he had received all the copy money, by different drafts, a considerable time before he had finished his task. When the messenger who carried the last sheet to Millar returned, Johnson asked him, "Well, what did he say?"—"Sir, (answered the messenger) he said, thank GOD I have done with him." "I am glad (replied Johnson, with a smile,) that he thanks GOD for any thing." It is remarkable, that those with whom Johnson chiefly contracted for his literary labours were Scotchmen, Mr. Millar and Mr. Strahan. Millar, though himself no great judge of literature, had good sense enough to have for his friends very able men, to give him their opinion and advice in the purchase of copyright; the consequence of which was his acquiring a very large fortune, with liberality. Johnson said of him, "I respect Millar, Sir; he has raised the price of literature."

The Dictionary, with a Grammar and History of the English Language, being now at length published, in two volumes folio, the world contemplated with wonder so stupendous a work achieved by one man, while other countries had thought such undertakings fit only for whole academies. Vast as his powers were, I cannot but think that his imagination deceived him, when he supposed that by constant application he might have performed the task in three years. Let the Preface be attentively perused, in which is given, in a clear, strong, and glowing style, a comprehensive, yet particular view of what he had done; and it will be evident, that the time he employed upon it was comparatively short. I am unwilling to swell my book with long quotations from what is in every body's hands, and I believe there are few prose compositions in the English language that are read with more delight, or are more impressed upon the memory, than that preliminary discourse.

The extensive reading which was absolutely necessary for the accumulation of authorities, and which alone may account for Johnson's retentive mind being enriched with a very large and various store of knowledge and imagery, must have occupied several years. The Preface furnishes an eminent instance of a double talent, of which Johnson was fully conscious. Sir Joshua Reynolds heard him say, "There are two things which I am confident I can do very well: one is an introduction to any literary work, stating what it is to contain, and how it should be executed in the most perfect manner: the other is a conclusion, shewing from various causes why the execution has not been equal to what the authour promised to himself and to the publick."

How should puny scribblers be abashed and disappointed, when they find him displaying a perfect theory of lexicographical excellence, yet at the same time candidly and modestly allowing that he "had not satisfied his own expectations." Here was a fair occasion for the exercise of Johnson's modesty, when he was called upon to compare his own arduous performance, not with those of other individuals, (in which case his inflexible regard to truth would have been violated had he affected diffidence,) but with speculative perfection; as he, who can outstrip all his competitors in the race, may yet be sensible of his deficiency when he runs against time. Well might he say, that "the English Dictionary was written with little assistance of the learned;" for he told me, that the only aid which he received was a paper containing twenty etymologies, sent to him by a person then unknown, who he was afterwards informed was Dr. Pearce, Bishop of Rochester. The etymologies, though they exhibit learning and judgement, are not, I think, entitled to the first praise amongst the various parts of this immense work. The definitions have always appeared to me such astonishing proofs of acuteness of intellect and precision of language, as indicate a genius of the highest rank. This it is which marks the superior excellence of Johnson's Dictionary over others equally or even more voluminous, and must have made it a work of much greater mental labour than mere Lexicons, or *Word-Books,* as the Dutch call them. They, who will make the experiment of trying how they can define a few words of whatever nature, will soon be satisfied of the unquestionable justice of this observation, which I can assure my readers is founded upon much study, and upon communication with more minds than my own.

A few of his definitions must be admitted to be erroneous. Thus *Windward* and *Leeward,* though directly of opposite meaning, are defined identically the same way; as to which inconsiderable specks it is enough to observe, that his Preface announces that he was aware there might be many such in so immense a work; nor was he at all disconcerted when an instance was pointed out to him. A lady once asked him how he came to define *Pastern* the *knee* of a horse: instead of making an elaborate defence, as she expected, he at once answered, "Ignorance, Madam, pure ignorance." His definition of *Network* has been often quoted with sportive malignity, as obscuring a thing in itself very plain. But to these frivolous censures no other answer is necessary than that with which we are furnished by his own Preface. "To explain, requires the use of terms less abstruse than that which is to be explained, and such terms cannot always be found. For as nothing can be proved but by supposing something intuitively known, and evident without proof, so nothing can be defined but by the use of words too plain to admit of definition. Sometimes easier words are changed into harder; as, *burial,* into *sepulture* or *interment; dry,* into *desiccative; dryness,* into *siccity* or *aridity; fit* into *paroxism;* for the *easiest* word, whatever it be, can never be translated into one more easy."

His introducing his own opinions, and even prejudices, under general definitions of words, while at the same time the original meaning of the words is not explained, as his *Tory, Whig, Pension, Oats, Excise,*[1] and a few more, can-

---

[1] He thus defines Excise: "A hateful tax levied upon commodities, and adjudged not by the common judges of property, but wretches hired by those to whom Excise is paid." The Commissioners of Excise being offended by this severe reflection, consulted Mr. Murray, then Attorney-General, to know whether redress could be legally obtained. I wished to

not be fully defended, and must be placed to the account of capricious and humorous indulgence. Talking to me upon this subject when we were at Ashbourne in 1777, he mentioned a still stronger instance of the predominance of his private feelings in the composition of this work, than any now to be found in it. "You know, Sir, Lord Gower forsook the old Jacobite interest. When I came to the *Renegado,* after telling that it meant 'one who deserts to the enemy, a revolter,' I added, *Sometimes we say a* GOWER. Thus it went to the press: but the printer had more wit than I, and struck it out."

Let it, however, be remembered, that this indulgence does not display itself only in sarcasm towards others, but sometimes in playful allusion to the notions commonly entertained of his own laborious task. Thus: *"Grub-street,* the name of a street in London, much inhabited by writers of small histories, *dictionaries,* and temporary poems; whence, any mean production is called *Grub-street."—"Lexicographer,* a writer of dictionaries, a *harmless drudge."*

At the time when he was concluding his very eloquent Preface, Johnson's mind appears to have been in such a state of depression, that we cannot contemplate without wonder the vigourous and splendid thoughts which so highly distinguish that performance. "I (says he) may surely be contented without the praise of perfection, which if I could obtain in this gloom of solitude, what would it avail me? I have protracted my work till most of those whom I wished to please have sunk into the grave; and success and miscarriage are empty sounds. I therefore dismiss it with frigid tranquillity, having little to fear or hope from censure or from praise." That this indifference was rather a temporary than an habitual feeling, appears, I think, from his letters to Mr. Warton; and however he may have been affected for the moment, certain it is that the honours which his great

---

have procured for my readers a copy of the opinion which he gave, and which may now be justly considered as history: but the mysterious secrecy of office it seems would not permit it. I am, however, informed by very good authority, that its import was, that the passage might be considered as actionable; but that it would be more prudent in the board not to prosecute. Johnson never made the smallest alteration in this passage.

work procured him, both at home and abroad, were very grateful to him. His friend the Earl of Corke and Orrery, being at Florence, presented it to the *Accademia della Crusca.* That Academy sent Johnson their *Vocabolario,* and the French Academy sent him their *Dictionnaire,* which Mr. Langton had the pleasure to convey to him.

It must undoubtedly seem strange, that the conclusion of his Preface should be expressed in terms so desponding, when it is considered that the authour was then only in his forty-sixth year. But we must ascribe its gloom to that miserable dejection of spirits to which he was constitutionally subject, and which was aggravated by the death of his wife two years before. I have heard it ingeniously observed by a lady of rank and elegance, that "his melancholy was then at its meridian." It pleased GOD to grant him almost thirty years of life after this time; and once when he was in a placid frame of mind, he was obliged to own to me that he had enjoyed happier days, and had many more friends, since that gloomy hour, than before.

It is a sad saying, that "most of those whom he wished to please had sunk into the grave;" and his case at forty-five was singularly unhappy, unless the circle of his friends was very narrow. I have often thought, that as longevity is generally desired, and I believe, generally expected, it would be wise to be continually adding to the number of our friends, that the loss of some may be supplied by others. Friendship, "the wine of life," should, like a well-stocked cellar, be thus continually renewed; and it is consolatory to think, that although we can seldom add what will equal the generous *first growths* of our youth, yet friendship becomes insensibly old in much less time than is commonly imagined, and not many years are required to make it very mellow and pleasant. *Warmth* will, no doubt, make a considerable difference. Men of affectionate temper and bright fancy will coalesce a great deal sooner than those who are cold and dull.

The proposition which I have now endeavoured to illustrate was, at a subsequent period of his life, the opinion of Johnson himself. He said to Sir Joshua Reynolds, "If a man does not make new acquaintance as he advances through life, he will soon find himself left alone. A man, Sir, should keep his friendship *in constant repair."*

The celebrated Mr. Wilkes, whose notions and habits of life were very opposite to his, but who was ever eminent for literature and vivacity, sallied forth with a little *Jeu d'Esprit* upon the following passage in his Grammar of the English Tongue, prefixed to the Dictionary; *"H* seldom, perhaps never, begins any but the first syllable." In an essay printed in "the Public Advertiser," this lively writer enumerated many instances in opposition to this remark; for example, "The authour of this observation must be a man of a quick *appre-hension,* and of a most *compre-hensive* genius." The position is undoubtedly expressed with too much latitude.

This light sally, we may suppose, made no great impression on our Lexicographer; for we find that he did not alter the passage till many years afterwards.[1]

In 1756 Johnson found that the great fame of his Dictionary had not set him above the necessity of "making provision for the day that was passing over him." No royal or noble patron extended a munificent hand to give independence to the man who had conferred stability on the language of his country. We may feel indignant that there should have been such unworthy neglect; but we must, at the same time, congratulate ourselves, when we consider, that to this very neglect, operating to rouse the natural indolence of his constitution, we owe many valuable productions, which otherwise, perhaps, might never have appeared.

He had spent, during the progress of the work, the money for which he had contracted to write his Dictionary. We have seen that the reward of his labour was only fifteen hundred and seventy-five pounds; and when the expence of amanuenses and paper, and other articles, are deducted, his clear profit was very inconsiderable. I once said to him, "I am sorry, Sir, you did not get more for your Dictionary."

---

[1] In the third edition, published in 1773, he left out the words *perhaps never,* and added the following paragraph:
"It sometimes begins middle or final syllables in words compounded, as *block-head,* or derived from the Latin, as *comprehended."*

84

His answer was, "I am sorry too. But it was very well. The booksellers are generous liberal-minded men." He, upon all occasions, did ample justice to their character in this respect. He considered them as the patrons of literature; and, indeed, although they have eventually been considerable gainers by his Dictionary, it is to them that we owe its having been undertaken and carried through at the risk of great expence, for they were not absolutely sure of being indemnified.

His defence of tea against Mr. Jonas Hanway's violent attack upon that elegant and popular beverage, shews how very well a man of genius can write upon the slightest subject, when he writes, as the Italians say, *con amore:* I suppose no person ever enjoyed with more relish the infusion of that fragrant leaf than Johnson. The quantities which he drank of it at all hours were so great, that his nerves must have been uncommonly strong, not to have been extremely relaxed by such an intemperate use of it. He assured me, that he never felt the least inconvenience from it; which is a proof that the fault of his constitution was rather a too great tension of fibres, than the contrary. Mr. Hanway wrote an angry answer to Johnson's review of his Essay on Tea, and Johnson, after a full and deliberate pause, made a reply to it; the only instance, I believe, in the whole course of his life when he condescended to oppose any thing that was written against him.

He this year [1757] resumed his scheme of giving an edition of Shakspeare with notes. He issued proposals of considerable length, in which he shewed that he perfectly well knew what variety of research such an undertaking required; but his indolence prevented him from pursuing it with that diligence which alone can collect those scattered facts, that genius, however acute, penetrating, and luminous, cannot discover by its own force. It is remarkable, that at this time his fancied activity was for the moment so vigourous, that he promised his work should be published before Christmas, 1757. Yet nine years elapsed before it saw the light. His throes in bringing it forth had been severe and remittent; and at last we may almost conclude that the Cæsarian operation was performed by the knife of Churchill, whose upbraiding satire, I dare say, made Johnson's friends urge him to dispatch.

> "He for subscribers baits his hook,
> And takes your cash; but where's the book?
> No matter where; wise fear, you know,
> Forbids the robbing of a foe;
> But what,' to serve our private ends,
> Forbids the cheating of our friends?"

On the fifteenth of April he began a new periodical paper, entitled "THE IDLER." * These essays were continued till April 5, 1760.

The IDLER is evidently the work of the same mind which produced the RAMBLER, but has less body and more spirit. It has more variety of real life, and greater facility of language. He describes the miseries of idleness, with the lively sensations of one who has felt them; and in his private memorandums while engaged in it, we find "This year I hope to learn diligence." Many of these excellent essays were written as hastily as an ordinary letter. Mr. Langton remembers Johnson, when on a visit at Oxford, asking him one evening how long it was till the post went out; and on being told about half an hour, he exclaimed, "then we shall do very well." He upon this instantly sat down and finished an Idler, which it was necessary should be in London the next day. Mr. Langton having signified a wish to read it, "Sir, (said he,) you shall not do more than I have done myself." He then folded it up, and sent it off.

Yet there are in the Idler several papers which shew as much profundity of thought, and labour of language, as any of this great man's writings.

In 1759, in the month of January, his mother died at the great age of ninety, an event which deeply affected him; not that "his mind had acquired no firmness by the contemplation of morality;" but that his reverential affection for her was not abated by years, as indeed he retained all his tender feelings even to the latest period of his life. I have been told, that he regretted much his not having gone to visit his mother for several years previous to her death.

But he was constantly engaged in literary labours which confined him to London; and though he had not the comfort of seeing his aged parent, he contributed to her support.

"To Mrs. Johnson, in Lichfield.
"HONOURED MADAM,

"The account which Miss [Porter] gives me of your health, pierces my heart. God comfort, and preserve you, and save you, for the sake of Jesus Christ.

"I would have Miss read to you from time to time the Passion of our Saviour, and sometimes the sentences in the Communion Service, beginning—*Come unto me all ye that travail and are heavy laden, and I will give you rest.*

"I have just now read a physical book, which inclines me to think that a strong infusion of the bark would do you good. Do, dear mother, try it.

"Pray, send me your blessing, and forgive all that I have done amiss to you. And whatever you would have done, and what debts you would have paid first, or any thing else that you would direct, let Miss put it down; I shall endeavour to obey you.

"I have got twelve guineas to send you, but unhappily am at a loss how to send it to-night. If I cannot send it to-night, it will come by the next post.

"Pray, do not omit any thing mentioned in this letter. God bless you for ever and ever.

"I am
"Your dutiful Son,
"Sam. Johnson."
"Jan. 13, 1758."

"To Miss Porter, at Mrs. Johnson's, in Lichfield.
"MY DEAR MISS,

"I think myself obliged to you beyond all expression of gratitude for your care of my dear mother. God grant it may not be without success. Tell Kitty, that I shall never forget her tenderness for her mistress. Whatever you can do, continue to do. My heart is very full.

"I hope you received twelve guineas on Monday. I found

a way of sending them by means of the Postmaster, after I had written my letter, and hope they came safe. I will send you more in a few days. GOD bless you all.

"I am, my dear,
"Your most obliged
"and most humble Servant,
"SAM. JOHNSON."

"Jan. 16, 1759."

"Over the leaf is a letter to my mother."

"DEAR HONOURED MOTHER,

"Your weakness afflicts me beyond what I am willing to communicate to you. I do not think you unfit to face death, but I know not how to bear the thought of losing you. Endeavour to do all you [can] for yourself. Eat as much as you can.

"I pray often for you; do you pray for me.—I have nothing to add to my last letter.

"I am, dear, dear Mother
"Your dutiful Son,
"SAM. JOHNSON."

"Jan. 16, 1759."

"To MRS. JOHNSON, IN LICHFIELD.

"DEAR HONOURED MOTHER,

"I fear you are too ill for long letters; therefore I will only tell you, you have from me all the regard that can possibly subsist in the heart. I pray GOD to bless you for evermore, for Jesus Christ's sake. Amen.

"Let Miss write to me every post, however short.

"I am, dear Mother,
"Your dutiful Son,
"SAM. JOHNSON."

"Jan. 18, 1759."

"To MISS PORTER, AT MRS. JOHNSON'S, IN LICHFIELD.

"DEAR MISS,

"I will, if it be possible, come down to you. GOD grant I may yet [find] my dear mother breathing and sensible. Do

5

A portrait of "Tetty," Dr. Johnson's wife. Although she was twice his age, Johnson is supposed to have said to a friend, "Sir, it was a love marriage on both sides."

not tell her, lest I disappoint her. If I miss to write next post, I am on the road.

> "I am, my dearest Miss,
> "Your most humble servant,
> "SAM. JOHNSON."

"Jan. 20, 1759

> *"On the other side."*

"DEAR HONOURED MOTHER,

"Neither your condition nor your character make it fit for me to say much. You have been the best mother, and I believe the best woman in the world. I thank you for your indulgence to me, and beg forgiveness of all that I have done ill, and all that I have omitted to do well. GOD grant you his Holy Spirit, and receive you to everlasting happiness, for Jesus Christ's sake. Amen. Lord Jesus receive your spirit. Amen.

> "I am, dear, dear Mother,
> "Your dutiful Son,
> "SAM. JOHNSON."

"Jan. 20, 1759."

Soon after this event, he wrote his "RASSELAS, PRINCE OF ABYSSINIA:" * concerning the publication of which Sir John Hawkins guesses vaguely and idly, instead of having taken the trouble to inform himself with authentick precision. Not to trouble my readers with a repetition of the Knight's reveries, I have to mention, that the late Mr. Strahan the printer told me, that Johnson wrote it, that with the profits he might defray the expence of his mother's funeral, and pay some little debts which she had left. He told Sir Joshua Reynolds, that he composed it in the evenings of one week, sent it to the press in portions as it was written, and had never since read it over. Mr. Strahan, Mr. Johnson, and Mr. Dodsley, purchased it for a hundred pounds, but afterwards paid him twenty-five pounds more, when it came to a second edition.

Considering the large sums which have been received for compilations, and works requiring not much more genius than compilations, we cannot but wonder at the very low price which he was content to receive for this admirable performance; which, though he had written nothing else, would have rendered his name immortal in the world of literature. None of his writings has been so extensively diffused over Europe; for it has been translated into most, if not all, of the modern languages. This Tale, with all the charms of oriental imagery, and all the force and beauty of which the English language is capable, leads us through the most important scenes of human life, and shews us that this stage of our being is full of "vanity and vexation of spirit." To those who look no further than the present life, or who maintain that human nature has not fallen from the state in which it was created, the instruction of this sublime story will be of no avail. But they who think justly, and feel with strong sensibility, will listen with eagerness and admiration to its truth and wisdom. Voltaire's CANDIDE, written to refute the system of Optimism, which it has accomplished with brilliant success, is wonderfully similar in its plan and conduct to Johnson's RASSELAS; insomuch, that I have heard Johnson say, that if they had not been published so closely one after the other that there was not time for imitation, it would have been in vain to deny that the scheme of that which came latest was taken from the other. Though the proposition illustrated by both these works was the same, namely, that in our present state there is more evil than good, the intention of the writers was very different. Voltaire, I am afraid, meant only by wanton profaneness to obtain a sportive victory over religion, and to discredit the belief of a superintending Providence: Johnson meant, by shewing the unsatisfactory nature of things temporal, to direct the hopes of man to things eternal. Rasselas, as was observed to me by a very accomplished lady, may be considered as a more enlarged and more deeply philosophical discourse in prose, upon the interesting truth, which in his "Vanity of Human Wishes" he had so successfully enforced in verse.

His negro servant, Francis Barber, having left him, and been some time at sea, not pressed as has been supposed, but with his own consent, it appears from a letter to John Wilkes, Esq., from Dr. Smollett, that his master kindly interested himself in procuring his release from a state of life of which Johnson always expressed the utmost abhorrence. He said, "No man will be a sailor who has contrivance enough to get himself into a jail; for being in a ship is being in a jail, with the chance of being drowned." And at another time, "A man in a jail has more room, better food, and commonly better company." The letter was as follows:

"Chelsea, March 16, 1759.

"DEAR SIR,

"I am again your petitioner, in behalf of that great CHAM of literature, Samuel Johnson. His black servant, whose name is Francis Barber has been pressed on board the Stag Frigate, Captain Angel, and our lexicographer is in great distress. He says, the boy is a sickly lad, of a delicate frame, and particularly subject to a malady in his throat, which renders him very unfit for his Majesty's service. You know what matter of animosity the said Johnson has against you: and I dare say you desire no other opportunity of resenting it, than that of laying him under an obligation. He was humble enough to desire my assistance on this occasion, though he and I were never cater-cousins; and I gave him to understand that I would make application to my friend Mr. Wilkes, who, perhaps, by his interest with Dr. Hay and Mr. Elliot, might be able to procure the discharge of his lacquey. It would be superfluous to say more on the subject, which I leave to your own consideration; but I cannot let slip this opportunity of declaring that I am, with the most inviolable esteem and attachment, dear Sir,

"Your affectionate obliged humble servant,

"T. SMOLLETT."

Mr. Wilkes, who upon all occasions has acted as a private gentleman, with most polite liberality, applied to his friend Sir George Hay, then one of the Lords Commissioners of the Admiralty; and Francis Barber was discharged, as he has told me, without any wish of his own. He found his old master in Chambers in the Inner Temple, and returned to his service.

The accession of George the Third to the throne of these

kingdoms, opened a new and brighter prospect to men of literary merit, who had been honoured with no mark of royal favour in the preceding reign. His present Majesty's education in this country, as well as his taste and beneficence, prompted him to be the patron of science and the arts; and early this year Johnson having been represented to him as a very learned and good man, without any certain provision, his Majesty was pleased to grant him a pension of three hundred pounds a year. The Earl of Bute, who was then Prime Minister, had the honour to announce this instance of his Sovereign's bounty, concerning which, many and various stories, all equally erroneous, have been propagated; maliciously representing it as a political bribe to Johnson, to desert his avowed principles, and become the tool of a government which he held to be founded in usurpation. I have taken care to have it in my power to refute them from the most authentick information. Lord Bute told me, that Mr. Wedderburne, now Lord Loughborough, was the person who first mentioned this subject to him. Lord Loughborough told me, that the pension was granted to Johnson solely as the reward of his literary merit, without any stipulation whatever, or even tacit understanding that he should write for administration. His Lordship added, that he was confident the political tracts which Johnson afterwards did write, as they were entirely consonant with his own opinions, would have been written by him, though no pension had been granted to him.

Mr. Thomas Sheridan and Mr. Murphy, who then lived a good deal both with him and Mr. Wedderburne, told me, that they previously talked with Johnson upon this matter, and that it was perfectly understood by all parties that the pension was merely honorary. Sir Joshua Reynolds told me, that Johnson called on him after his Majesty's intention had been notified to him, and said he wished to consult his friends as to the propriety of his accepting this mark of the royal favour, after the definitions which he had given in his Dictionary of *pension* and *pensioners*. He said he should not have Sir Joshua's answer till next day, when he would call again, and desired he might think of it. Sir Joshua answered that he was clear to give his opinion then, that there could be no objection to his receiving from the King a reward for literary merit; and that certainly the definitions in his Dictionary were not applicable to him. Johnson, it should seem, was satisfied, for he did not call again till he had accepted the pension, and had waited on Lord Bute to thank him. He then told Sir Joshua that Lord Bute said to him expressly, "It is not given you for any thing you are to do, but for what you have done."

Mr. Murphy and the late Mr. Sheridan severally contended for the distinction of having been the first who mentioned to Mr. Wedderburne that Johnson ought to have a pension. When I spoke of this to Lord Loughborough, wishing to know if he recollected the prime mover in the business, he said "All his friends assisted:" and when I told him that Mr. Sheridan strenuously asserted his claim to it, his Lordship said, "He rang the bell." And it is but just to add that Mr. Sheridan told me, that when he communicated to Dr. Johnson that a pension was to be granted him, he replied in a fervour of gratitude, "The English language does not afford me terms adequate to my feelings on this occasion. I must have recourse to the French. I am *pénétré* with his Majesty's goodness." When I repeated this to Dr. Johnson, he did not contradict it.

"To the Right Honourable the Earl of Bute.
"my lord,

"When the bills were yesterday delivered to me by Mr. Wedderburne, I was informed by him of the future favours which his Majesty has, by your Lordship's recommendation, been induced to intend for me.

"Bounty always receives part of its value from the manner in which it is bestowed; your Lordship's kindness includes every circumstance that can gratify delicacy, or enforce obligation. You have conferred your favours on a man who has neither alliance nor interest, who has not merited them by services, nor courted them by officiousness; you have spared him the shame of solicitation, and the anxiety of suspense.

"What has been thus elegantly given, will, I hope, not be reproachfully enjoyed; I shall endeavour to give your

Lordship the only recompense which generosity desires,—
the gratification of finding that your benefits are not improperly bestowed. I am, my Lord,
> "Your Lordship's most obliged,
> "Most obedient, and most humble servant,
> > "SAM. JOHNSON."

"July 20, 1762."

This year his friend, Sir Joshua Reynolds, paid a visit of
some weeks to his native country, Devonshire, in which
he was accompanied by Johnson, who was much pleased
with this jaunt, and declared he had derived from it a great
accession of new ideas. He was entertained at the seats
of several noblemen and gentlemen in the west of England; [1]
but the greatest part of this time was passed at Plymouth,
where the magnificence of the navy, the ship-building and
all its circumstances, afforded him a grand subject of contemplation. The Commissioner of the Dock-yard paid him
the compliment of ordering the yacht to convey him and
his friend to the Eddystone, to which they accordingly
sailed. But the weather was so tempestuous that they could
not land.

This is to me a memorable year [1763]; for in it I had the
happiness to obtain the acquaintance of that extraordinary
man whose memoirs I am now writing; an acquaintance
which I shall ever esteem as one of the most fortunate circumstances in my life. Though then but two-and-twenty,
I had for several years read his works with delight and instruction, and had the highest reverence for their authour,
which had grown up in my fancy into a kind of mysterious
veneration, by figuring to myself a state of solemn elevated
abstraction, in which I supposed him to live in the immense metropolis of London. Mr. Gentleman, a native of
Ireland, who passed some years in Scotland as a player,

---

[1] At one of these seats Dr. Amyat, Physician in London, told me he
happened to meet him. In order to amuse him till dinner should be
ready, he was taken out to walk in the garden. The master of the house,
thinking it proper to introduce something scientifick into the conversation, addressed him thus: "Are you a botanist, Dr. Johnson?" "No, Sir,
(answered Johnson,) I am not a botanist; and, (alluding, no doubt, to
his near sightedness) should I wish to become a botanist, I must first turn
myself into a reptile."

and as an instructor in the English language, a man whose
talents and worth were depressed by misfortunes, had given
me a representation of the figure and manner of DICTION-
ARY JOHNSON! as he was then generally called; [1] and during
my first visit to London, which was for three months in
1760, Mr. Derrick the poet, who was Gentleman's friend
and countryman, flattered me with hopes that he would introduce me to Johnson, an honour of which I was very ambitious. But he never found an opportunity; which made me
doubt that he had promised to do what was not in his
power; till Johnson some years afterwards told me, "Derrick, Sir, might very well have introduced you. I had a
kindness for Derrick, and am sorry he is dead."

In the summer of 1761 Mr. Thomas Sheridan was at
Edinburgh, and delivered lectures upon the English Language and Publick Speaking to large and respectable audi-
ences. I was often in his company, and heard him frequently
expatiate upon Johnson's extraordinary knowledge, talents,
and virtues, repeat his pointed sayings, describe his particularities, and boast of his being his guest sometimes till two
or three in the morning. At his house I hoped to have many
opportunities of seeing the sage, as Mr. Sheridan obligingly
assured me I should not be disappointed. .

When I returned to London in the end of 1762, to my
surprise and regret I found an irreconcileable difference had
taken place between Johnson and Sheridan. A pension of
two hundred pounds a year had been given to Sheridan.
Johnson, who, as has been already mentioned, thought
slightingly of Sheridan's art, upon hearing that he was also
pensioned, exclaimed, "What! have they given *him* a pension? Then it is time for me to give up mine." Whether this
proceeded from a momentary indignation, as if it were an
affront to his exalted merit that a player should be rewarded
in the same manner with him, or was the sudden effect of a
fit of peevishness, it was unluckily said, and, indeed, can-

---

[1] As great men of antiquity such as Scipio *Africanus* had an epithet
added to their names, in consequence of some celebrated action, so my
illustrious friend was often called DICTIONARY JOHNSON, from that wonderful achievement of genius and labour, his "Dictionary of the English
Language;" the merit of which I contemplate with more and more admiration.

not be justified. Mr. Sheridan's pension was granted to him not as a player, but as a sufferer in the cause of government, when he was manager of the Theatre Royal in Ireland, when parties ran high in 1753. And it must also be allowed that he was a man of literature, and had considerably improved the arts of reading and speaking with distinctness and propriety.

Johnson complained that a man who disliked him repeated his sarcasm to Mr. Sheridan, without telling him what followed, which was, that after a pause he added, "However, I am glad that Mr. Sheridan has a pension, for he is a very good man." Sheridan could never forgive this hasty contemptuous expression. It rankled in his mind; and though I informed him of all that Johnson said, and that he would be very glad to meet him amicably, he positively declined repeated offers which I made, and once went off abruptly from a house where he and I were engaged to dine, because he was told that Dr. Johnson was to be there.

Mr. Thomas Davies the actor, who then kept a bookseller's shop in Russel-street, Covent-garden, told me that Johnson was very much his friend, and came frequently to his house, where he more than once invited me to meet him: but by some unlucky accident or other he was prevented from coming to us.

At last, on Monday the 16th of May, when I was sitting in Mr. Davies's back-parlour, after having drunk tea with him and Mrs. Davies, Johnson unexpectedly came into the shop; and Mr. Davies having perceived him through the glass-door in the room in which we were sitting, advancing towards us,—he announced his awful approach to me, somewhat in the manner of an actor in the part of Horatio, when he addresses Hamlet on the appearance of his father's ghost, "Look, my Lord, it comes." I found that I had a very perfect idea of Johnson's figure, from the portrait of him painted by Sir Joshua Reynolds soon after he had published his Dictionary, in the attitude of sitting in his easy chair in deep meditation; which was the first picture his friend did for him, which Sir Joshua very kindly presented to me, and from which an engraving has been made for this work. Mr. Davies mentioned my name, and respect-

fully introduced me to him. I was much agitated; and recollecting his prejudice against the Scotch, of which I had
heard much, I said to Davies, "Don't tell where I come
from."—"From Scotland," cried Davies, roguishly. "Mr.
Johnson, (said I) I do indeed come from Scotland, but I
cannot help it." I am willing to flatter myself that I meant
this as light pleasantry to soothe and conciliate him, and
not as an humiliating abasement at the expence of my country. But however that might be, this speech was somewhat
unlucky; for with that quickness of wit for which he was
so remarkable, he seized the expression "come from Scotland," which I used in the sense of being of that country;
and, as if I had said that I had come away from it, or left
it, retorted, "That, Sir, I find, is what a very great many
of your countrymen cannot help." This stroke stunned me a
good deal; and when we had sat down, I felt myself not a
little embarrassed, and apprehensive of what might come
next. He then addressed himself to Davies: "What do you
think of Garrick? He has refused me an order for the play
for Miss Williams, because he knows the house will be full,
and that an order would be worth three shillings." Eager
to take any opening to get into conversation with him, I
ventured to say, "O, Sir, I cannot think Mr. Garrick would
grudge such a trifle to you." "Sir, (said he, with a stern
look,) I have known David Garrick longer than you have
done: and I know no right you have to talk to me on the
subject." Perhaps I deserved this check; for it was rather
presumptuous in me, an entire stranger, to express any
doubt of the justice of his animadversion upon his old acquaintance and pupil.[1] I now felt myself much mortified,
and began to think, that the hope which I had long indulged
of obtaining his acquaintance was blasted. And, in truth,
had not my ardour been uncommonly strong, and my resolution uncommonly persevering, so rough a reception might
have deterred me for ever from making any further at-

---

[1] That this was a momentary sally against Garrick there can be no
doubt; for at Johnson's desire he had, some years before, given a benefit-
night at his theatre to this very person, by which she had got two hundred pounds. Johnson, indeed, upon all other occasions, when I was in
his company, praised the very liberal charity of Garrick. I once mentioned
to him, "It is observed, Sir, that you attack Garrick yourself, but will
suffer nobody else to do it." JOHNSON, (smiling) "Why, Sir, that is true."

tempts. Fortunately, however, I remained upon the field not wholly discomfited; and was soon rewarded by hearing some of his conversation, of which I preserved the following short minute, without marking the questions and observations by which it was produced.

"People (he remarked) may be taken in once, who imagine that an authour is greater in private life than other men. Uncommon parts require uncommon opportunities for their exertion.

"In barbarous society, superiority of parts is of real consequence. Great strength or great wisdom is of much value to an individual. But in more polished times there are people to do every thing for money; and then there are a number of other superiorities, such as those of birth and fortune, and rank, that dissipate men's attention, and leave no extraordinary share of respect for personal and intellectual superiority. This is wisely ordered by Providence, to preserve some equality among mankind."

Speaking of one who with more than ordinary boldness attacked publick measures and the royal family, he said, "I think he is safe from the law, but he is an abusive scoundrel; and instead of applying to my Lord Chief Justice to punish him, I would send half a dozen footmen and have him well ducked."

I was highly pleased with the extraordinary vigour of his conversation, and regretted that I was drawn away from it by an engagement at another place. I had, for a part of the evening, been left alone with him, and had ventured to make an observation now and then, which he received very civilly; so that I was satisfied that though there was a roughness in his manner, there was no ill-nature in his disposition. Davies followed me to the door, and when I complained to him a little of the hard blows which the great man had given me, he kindly took upon him to console me by saying, "Don't be uneasy. I can see he likes you very well."

A few days afterwards I called on Davies, and asked him if he thought I might take the liberty of waiting on Mr. Johnson at his chambers in the Temple. He said I certainly might, and that Mr. Johnson would take it as a compliment.

So on Tuesday the 24th of May, after having been enlivened by the witty sallies of Messieurs Thornton, Wilkes,
Churchill, and Lloyd, with whom I had passed the morning, I boldly repaired to Johnson. His chambers were on
the first floor of No. 1, Inner-Temple-lane, and I entered
them with an impression given me by the Reverend Dr.
Blair, of Edinburgh, who had been introduced to him not
long before, and described his having "found the Giant in
his den"; an expression which, when I came to be pretty
well acquainted with Johnson, I repeated to him, and he
was diverted at this picturesque account of himself. Dr.
Blair had been presented to him by Dr. James Fordyce. At
this time the controversy concerning the pieces published by
Mr. James Macpherson, as translations of Ossian, was at its
height. Johnson had all along denied their authenticity; and,
what was still more provoking to their admirers, maintained
that they had no merit. The subject having been introduced
by Dr. Fordyce, Dr. Blair, relying on the internal evidence
of their antiquity, asked Dr. Johnson whether he thought
any man of a modern age could have written such poems?
Johnson replied, "Yes, Sir, many men, many women, and
many children." Johnson at this time, did not know that
Dr. Blair had just published a Dissertation, not only de-
fending their authenticity, but seriously ranking them with
the poems of Homer and Virgil; and when he was afterwards informed of this circumstance, he expressed some
displeasure at Dr. Fordyce's having suggested the topick,
and said, "I am not sorry that they got thus much for their
pains. Sir, it was like leading one to talk of a book, when
the authour is concealed behind the door."

He received me very courteously: but, it must be confessed, that his apartment, and furniture, and morning
dress, were sufficiently uncouth. His brown suit of cloaths
looked very rusty: he had on a little old shrivelled un-
powdered wig, which was too small for his head; his shirt-
neck and knees of his breeches were loose; his black worsted
stockings ill drawn up; and he had a pair of unbuckled
shoes by way of slippers. But all these slovenly particularities were forgotten the moment that he began to talk. Some

gentlemen, whom I do not recollect, were sitting with him; and when they went away, I also rose; but he said to me, "Nay, don't go."—"Sir, (said I), I am afraid that I intrude upon you. It is benevolent to allow me to sit and hear you." He seemed pleased with this compliment, which I sincerely paid him, and answered, "Sir, I am obliged to any man who visits me."—I have preserved the following short minute of what passed this day.

"Madness frequently discovers itself merely by unnecessary deviation from the usual modes of the world. My poor friend Smart showed the disturbance of his mind, by falling upon his knees, and saying his prayers in the street, or in any other unusual place. Now although, rationally speaking, it is greater madness not to pray at all, than to pray as Smart did, I am afraid there are so many who do not pray, that their understanding is not called in question."

Concerning this unfortunate poet, Christopher Smart, who was confined in a mad-house, he had, at another time, the following conversation with Dr. Burney.—BURNEY. "How does poor Smart do, Sir; is he likely to recover?" JOHNSON. "It seems as if his mind had ceased to struggle with the disease; for he grows fat upon it." BURNEY. "Perhaps, Sir, that may be from want of exercise." JOHNSON. "No, Sir; he has partly as much exercise as he used to have, for he digs in the garden. Indeed, before his confinement, he used for exercise to walk to the alehouse; but he was *carried* back again. I did not think he ought to be shut up. His infirmities were not noxious to society. He insisted on people praying with him; and I'd as lief pray with Kit Smart as any one else. Another charge was, that he did not love clean linen; and I have no passion for it."

Johnson continued. "Mankind have a great aversion to intellectual labour; but even supposing knowledge to be easily attainable, more people would be content to be ignorant than would take even a little trouble to acquire it.

"The morality of an action depends on the motive from which we act. If I fling half a crown to a beggar with intention to break his head, and he picks it up and buys victuals with it, the physical effect is good; but, with respect to me, the action is very wrong. So, religious exercises, if not per-

100

formed with an intention to please GOD, avail us nothing. As our Saviour says of those who perform them from other motives, 'Verily they have their reward.' "

"The Christian religion has very strong evidences. It, indeed, appears in some degree strange to reason; but in History we have undoubted facts, against which, in reasoning *à priori,* we have more arguments than we have for them; but then, testimony has great weight, and casts the balance."

Talking of Garrick, he said, "He is the first man in the world for sprightly conversation."

When I rose a second time, he again pressed me to stay, which I did.

He told me, that he generally went abroad at four in the afternoon, and seldom came home till two in the morning. I took the liberty to ask if he did not think it wrong to live thus, and not make more use of his great talents. He owned it was a bad habit. On reviewing, at the distance of many years, my journal of this period, I wonder how, at my first visit, I ventured to talk to him so freely, and that he bore it with so much indulgence.

Before we parted, he was so good as to promise to favour me with his company one evening at my lodgings: and, as I took my leave, shook me cordially by the hand. It is almost needless to add, that I felt no little elation at having now so happily established an acquaintance of which I had been so long ambitious.

I did not visit him again till Monday, June 13, at which time I recollect no part of his conversation, except that when I told him I had been to see Johnson ride upon three horses, he said, "Such a man, Sir, should be encouraged; for his performances shew the extent of the human power in one instance, and thus tend to raise our opinion of the faculties of man. He shews what may be attained by persevering application; so that every man may hope that by giving as much application, although perhaps he may never ride three horses at a time, or dance upon a wire, yet he may be equally expert in whatever profession he has chosen to pursue."

He again shook me by the hand at parting, and asked me why I did not come oftener to him. Trusting that I was now in his good graces, I answered, that he had not given me much encouragement, and reminded him of the check I had received from him at our first interview. "Poh, poh! (said he, with a complacent smile), never mind these things. Come to me as often as you can. I shall be glad to see you."

I had learnt that his place of frequent resort was the Mitre tavern in Fleet-street, where he loved to sit up late, and I begged I might be allowed to pass an evening with him there soon, which he promised I should. A few days afterwards I met him near Templebar, about one o'clock in the morning, and asked him if he would then go to the Mitre. "Sir, (said he) it is too late; they won't let us in. But I'll go with you another night with all my heart."

A revolution of some importance in my plan of life had just taken place; for instead of procuring a commission in the foot-guards, which was my own inclination, I had, in compliance with my father's wishes, agreed to study the law, and was soon to set out for Utrecht, to hear the lectures of an excellent Civilian in that University, and then to proceed on my travels. Though very desirous of obtaining Dr. Johnson's advice and instructions on the mode of pursuing my studies, I was at this time so occupied, shall I call it? or so dissipated, by the amusements of London, that our next meeting was not till Saturday, June 25, when happening to dine at Clifton's eating-house, in Butcher-row, I was surprised to perceive Johnson come in and take his seat at another table.

He agreed to meet me in the evening at the Mitre. I called on him, and we went thither at nine. We had a good supper, and port wine, of which he then sometimes drank a bottle. The orthodox high-church sound of the MITRE,— the figure and manner of the celebrated SAMUEL JOHNSON, —the extraordinary power and precision of his conversation, and the pride arising from finding myself admitted as his companion, produced a variety of sensations, and a pleasing elevation of mind beyond what I had ever before experienced.

Finding him in a placid humour, and wishing to avail myself of the opportunity which I fortunately had of consulting a sage, to hear whose wisdom, I conceived, in the ardour of youthful imagination, that men filled with a noble enthusiasm for intellectual improvement would gladly have resorted from distant lands;—I opened my mind to him ingenuously, and gave him a little sketch of my life, to which he was pleased to listen with great attention.

I acknowledged, that though educated very strictly in the principles of religion, I had for some time been misled into a certain degree of infidelity; but that I was come now to a better way of thinking, and was fully satisfied of the truth of the Christian revelation, though I was not clear as to every point considered to be orthodox. Being at all times a curious examiner of the human mind, and pleased with an undisguised display of what had passed in it, he called to me with warmth, "Give me your hand; I have taken a liking to you." He then began to descant upon the force of testimony, and the little we could know of final causes; so that the objections of, why was it so? or why was it not so? ought not to disturb us; adding, that he himself had at one period been guilty of a temporary neglect of religion, but that it was not the result of argument, but mere absence of thought.

After having given credit to reports of his bigotry, I was agreeably surprised when he expressed the following very liberal sentiment, which has the additional value of obviating an objection to our holy religion, founded upon the discordant tenets of Christians themselves: "For my part, Sir, I think all Christians, whether Papists or Protestants, agree in the essential articles, and that their differences are trivial, and rather political than religious."

Our conversation proceeded. "Sir, (said he,) I am a friend to subordination, as most conducive to the happiness of society. There is a reciprocal pleasure in governing and being governed."

"Dr. Goldsmith is one of the first men we now have as an authour, and he is a very worthy man too. He has been loose in his principles, but he is coming right."

I mentioned Mallet's tragedy of "ELVIRA," which had been acted the preceding winter at Drury-lane, and that the Honourable Andrew Erskine, Mr. Dempster, and myself, had joined in writing a pamphlet, entitled "Critical Strictures" against it. That the mildness of Dempster's disposition had, however, relented; and he had candidly said, "We have hardly a right to abuse this tragedy; for bad as it is, how vain should either of us be to write one not near so good." JOHNSON. "Why no, Sir; this is not reasoning. You *may* abuse a tragedy, though you cannot write one. You may scold a carpenter who has made you a bad table, though you cannot make a table. It is not your trade to make tables."

He proceeded: "Your going abroad, Sir, and breaking off idle habits, may be of great importance to you. I would go where there are courts and learned men. There is a good deal of Spain that has not been perambulated. I would have you go thither. A man of inferiour talents to yours may furnish us with useful observations upon that country." His supposing me, at that period of life, capable of writing an account of my travels that would deserve to be read, elated me not a little.

I appeal to every impartial reader whether this faithful detail of his frankness, complacency, and kindness to a young man, a stranger and a Scotchman, does not refute the unjust opinion of the harshness of his general demeanour. His occasional reproofs of folly, impudence, or impiety, and even the sudden sallies of his constitutional irritability of temper, which have been preserved for the poignancy of their wit, have produced that opinion among those who had not considered that such instances, though collected by Mrs. Piozzi into a small volume, and read over in a few hours, were, in fact, scattered through a long series of years: years, in which his time was chiefly spent in instructing and delighting mankind by his writings and conversation, in acts of piety to GOD, and good-will to men.

I complained to him that I had not yet acquired much knowledge, and asked his advice as to my studies. He said, "Don't talk of study now. I will give you a plan; but it will require some time to consider of it." "It is very good in you (I replied,) to allow me to be with you thus. Had it been foretold to me some years ago that I should pass an evening with the authour of the RAMBLER, how should I have exulted!" What I then expressed was sincerely from the heart. He was satisfied that it was, and cordially answered, "Sir, I am glad we have met. I hope we shall pass many evenings and mornings too, together." We finished a couple of bottles of port, and sat till between one and two in the morning.

As Dr. Oliver Goldsmith will frequently appear in this narrative I shall endeavour to make my readers in some degree acquainted with his singular character. He was a native of Ireland, and a contemporary with Mr. Burke, at Trinity College, Dublin, but did not then give much promise of future celebrity. He, however, observed to Mr. Malone, that "though he made no great figure in mathematicks, which was a study in much repute there, he could turn an Ode of Horace into English better than any of them." He afterwards studied physick at Edinburgh, and upon the Continent: and I have been informed, was enabled to pursue his travels on foot, partly by demanding at Universities to enter the lists as a disputant, by which, according to the custom of many of them, he was entitled to the premium of a crown, when luckily for him his challenge was not accepted; so that, as I once observed to Dr. Johnson, he *disputed* his passage through Europe. He then came to England, and was employed successively in the capacities of an usher to an academy, a corrector of the press, a reviewer, and a writer for a news-paper. He had sagacity enough to cultivate assiduously the acquaintance of Johnson, and his faculties were gradually enlarged by the contemplation of such a model. To me and many others it appeared that he studiously copied the manner of Johnson, though, indeed, upon a smaller scale.

At this time I think he had published nothing with his name, though it was pretty generally known that *one Dr. Goldsmith* was the authour of "An Enquiry into the present State of polite Learning in Europe," and of "The Citizen of the World," a series of letters supposed to be written from London by a Chinese. No man had the art of displaying with more advantage as a writer, whatever literary acquisitions he made. His mind resembled a fertile, but thin soil. There was a quick, but not a strong vegetation, of whatever chanced to be thrown upon it. No deep root could be struck. The oak of the forest did not grow there: but the elegant shrubbery and the fragrant parterre appeared in gay succession. It has been generally circulated and believed that he was a mere fool in conversation;[1] but, in truth, this has been greatly exaggerated. He had, no doubt, a more than common share of that hurry of ideas which we often find in his countrymen, and which sometimes produces a laughable confusion in expressing them. He was very much what the French call *un étourdi*, and from vanity and an eager desire of being conspicuous wherever he was, he frequently talked carelessly without knowledge of the subject, or even without thought. His person was short, his countenance coarse and vulgar, his deportment that of a scholar awkwardly affecting the easy gentleman. Those who were in any way distinguished, excited envy in him to so ridiculous an excess, that the instances of it are hardly credible. When accompanying two beautiful young ladies with their mother on a tour in France, he was seriously angry that more attention was paid to them than to him; and once at the exhibition of the *Fantoccini* in London, when those who sat next him observed with what dexterity a puppet was made to toss a pike, he could not bear that it should have such praise, and exclaimed with some warmth, "Pshaw! I can do it better myself."[2]

He, I am afraid, had no settled system of any sort, so that his conduct must not be strictly scrutinized; but his affections were social and generous, and when he had money he gave it away very liberally. His desire of imaginary con-

---

[1] In allusion to this, Mr. Horace Walpole, who admired his writings, said he was "an inspired idiot"; and Garrick described him as one
"——for shortness called Noll,
Who wrote like an angel, and talk'd like poor Poll."
Sir Joshua Reynolds mentioned to me that he frequently heard Goldsmith talk warmly of the pleasure of being liked, and observe how hard it would be if literary excellence should preclude a man from that satisfaction, which he perceived it often did, from the envy which attended it; and therefore Sir Joshua was convinced that he was intentionally more absurd, in order to lessen himself in social intercourse, trusting that his character would be sufficiently supported by his work. If it indeed was his intention to appear absurd in company, he was often very successful. But with due deference to Sir Joshua's ingenuity, I think the conjecture too refined.

[2] He went home with Mr. Burke to supper; and broke his shin by attempting to exhibit to the company how much better he could jump over a stick than the puppets.

sequence predominated over his attention to truth. When he began to rise into notice, he said he had a brother who was Dean of Durham, a fiction so easily detected, that it is wonderful how he should have been so inconsiderate as to hazard it. He boasted to me at this time of the power of his pen in commanding money, which I believe was true in a certain degree, though in the instance he gave he was by no means correct. He told me that he had sold a novel for four hundred pounds. This was his "Vicar of Wakefield." But Johnson informed me, that he had made the bargain for Goldsmith, and the price was sixty pounds. "And, Sir, (said he,) a sufficient price too, when it was sold; for then the fame of Goldsmith had not been elevated, as it afterwards was, by his 'Traveller;' and the bookseller had such faint hopes of profit by his bargain, that he kept the manuscript by him a long time, and did not publish it till after the 'Traveller' had appeared. Then, to be sure, it was accidentally worth more money."

Mrs. Piozzi and Sir John Hawkins have strangely misstated the history of Goldsmith's situation and Johnson's friendly interference, when this novel was sold. I shall give it authentically from Johnson's own exact narration:

"I received one morning a message from poor Goldsmith that he was in great distress, and as it was not in his power to come to me, begging that I would come to him as soon as possible. I sent him a guinea, and promised to come to him directly. I accordingly went as soon as I was drest, and found that his landlady had arrested him for his rent, at which he was in a violent passion. I perceived that he had already changed my guinea, and had got a bottle of Madeira and a glass before him. I put the cork into the bottle, desired he would be calm, and began to talk to him of the means by which he might be extricated. He then told me that he had a novel ready for the press, which he produced to me. I looked into it, and saw its merit; told the landlady I should soon return, and having gone to a bookseller sold it for sixty pounds. I brought Goldsmith the money, and he discharged his rent, not without rating his landlady in a high tone for having used him so ill."

My next meeting with Johnson was on Friday the 1st of July, when he and I and Dr. Goldsmith supped at the Mitre. I was before this time pretty well acquainted with Goldsmith, who was one of the brighest ornaments of the Johnsonian school. Goldsmith's respectful attachment to Johnson was then at its height; for his own literary reputation had not yet distinguished him so much as to excite a vain desire of competition with his great Master. He had increased my admiration of the goodness of Johnson's heart, by incidental remarks in the course of conversation, such as, when I mentioned Mr. Levet, whom he entertained under his roof, "He is poor and honest, which is recommendation enough to Johnson;" and when I wondered that he was very kind to a man of whom I had heard a very bad character, "He is now become miserable, and that insures the protection of Johnson."

Goldsmith attempting this evening to maintain, I suppose from an affectation of paradox, "that knowledge was not desirable on its own account, for it often was a source of unhappiness." JOHNSON. "Why, Sir, that knowledge may in some cases produce unhappiness, I allow. But, upon the whole, knowledge, *per se*, is certainly an object which every man would wish to attain, although, perhaps, he may not take the trouble necessary for attaining it."

Dr. John Campbell, the celebrated political and biographical writer, being mentioned, Johnson said, "Campbell is a man of much knowledge, and has a good share of imagination. His 'Hermippus Redivivus' is very entertaining, as an account of the Hermetick philosophy, and as furnishing a curious history of the extravagances of the human mind. If it were merely imaginary, it would be nothing at all. Campbell is not always rigidly careful of truth in his conversation; but I do not believe there is any thing of this carelessness in his books. Campbell is a good man, a pious man. I am afraid he has not been in the inside of a church for many years; but he never passes a church without pulling off his hat. This shews that he has good principles. I used to go pretty often to Campbell's on a Sunday evening till I began to consider that the shoals of Scotchmen who flocked about him might probably say, when any thing of mine was well done, 'Ay, ay, he has learnt this of CAW-MELL!' "

On Tuesday the 5th of July, I again visited Johnson. He told me he had looked into the poems of a pretty voluminous writer, Mr. (now Dr.) John Ogilvie, one of the Presbyterian ministers of Scotland, which had lately come out, but could find no thinking in them. BOSWELL. "Is there not imagination in them, Sir?" JOHNSON. "Why, Sir, there is in them what *was* imagination, but it is no more imagination in *him,* than sound is sound in the echo. And his diction too is not his own. We have long ago seen *white-robed innocence,* and *flower-bespangled meads."*

Talking of London, he observed, "Sir, if you wish to have a just notion of the magnitude of this city, you must not be satisfied with seeing its great streets and squares, but must survey the innumerable little lanes and courts. It is not in the showy evolutions of buildings, but in the multiplicity of human habitations which are crowded together, that the wonderful immensity of London consists."—I have often amused myself with thinking how different a place London is to different people. They, whose narrow minds are contracted to the consideration of some one particular pursuit, view it only through that medium. A politician thinks of it merely as the seat of government in its different departments; a grazier, as a vast market for cattle; a mercantile man, as a place where a prodigious deal of business is done upon 'Change; a dramatick enthusiast, as the grand scene of theatrical entertainments; a man of pleasure, as an assemblage of taverns, and the great emporium for ladies of easy virtue. But the intellectual man is struck with it, as comprehending the whole of human life in all its variety, the contemplation of which is inexhaustible.

On Wednesday, July 6, he was engaged to sup with me at my lodgings in Downing-street, Westminster. But on the preceding night my landlord having behaved very rudely to me and some company who were with me, I had resolved not to remain another night in his house. I was exceedingly uneasy at the awkward appearance I supposed I should make to Johnson and the other gentleman whom I had invited, not being able to receive them at home, and being obliged to order supper at the Mitre. I went to Johnson in the morning, and talked of it as of a serious distress. He laughed, and said, "Consider, Sir, how insignificant this will appear a twelvemonth hence."—Were this considera- tion to be applied to most of the little vexatious incidents of life, by which our quiet is too often disturbed, it would prevent many painful sensations. I have tried it frequently with good effect. "There is nothing (continued he) in this mighty misfortune; nay, we shall be better at the Mitre." I told him that I had been at Sir John Fielding's office, com- plaining of my landlord, and had been informed, that though I had taken my lodgings for a year, I might, upon proof of his bad behaviour, quit them when I pleased, with- out being under an obligation to pay rent for any longer time than while I possessed them. The fertility of Johnson's mind could shew itself even upon so small a matter as this. "Why, Sir, (said he,) I suppose this must be the law, since you have been told so in Bow-street. But, if your landlord could hold you to your bargain, and the lodgings should be yours for a year, you may certainly use them as you think fit. So, Sir, you may quarter two life-guardmen upon him; or you may send the greatest scoundrel you can find into your apartments; or you may say that you want to make some experiments in natural philosophy, and may burn a large quantity of assafœtida in his house."

I had as my guests this evening at the Mitre tavern, Dr. Johnson, Dr. Goldsmith, Mr. Thomas Davies, Mr. Eccles, an Irish gentleman, for whose agreeable company I was obliged to Mr. Davies, and the Reverend Mr. John Ogilvie, who was desirous of being in company with my illustrious friend, while I in my turn, was proud to have the honour of shewing one of my countrymen upon what easy terms Johnson permitted me to live with him.

Goldsmith, as usual, endeavoured, with too much eager- ness, to *shine,* and disputed very warmly with Johnson against the well known maxim of the British constitution, "the King can do no wrong;" affirming, that, "what was morally false could not be politically true; and as the King might, in the exercise of his regal power, command and cause the doing of what was wrong, it certainly might be

6

Bennet Langton, one of Johnson's closest friends. The two first
met in London in 1752. Johnson said of him, " I know not who
will go to Heaven if Langton does not."

said, in sense and in reason, that he could do wrong." JOHNSON. "Sir, you are to consider, that in our constitution, according to its true principles, the King is the head, he is supreme: he is above every thing, and there is no power by which he can be tried. Therefore, it is, Sir, that we hold the King can do no wrong; that whatever may happen to be wrong in government may not be above our reach, by being ascribed to Majesty. Redress is always to be had against oppression, by punishing the immediate agents. The King, though he should command, cannot force a Judge to condemn a man unjustly; therefore it is the Judge whom we prosecute and punish. Political institutions are formed upon the consideration of what will most frequently tend to the good of the whole, although now and then exceptions may occur. Thus it is better in general that a nation should have a supreme legislative power, although it may at times be abused. And then, Sir, there is this consideration, that *if the abuse be enormous, Nature will rise up, and claiming her original rights, overturn a corrupt political system.*" I mark this animated sentence with peculiar pleasure, as a noble instance of that truly dignified spirit of freedom which ever glowed in his heart, though he was charged with slavish tenets by superficial observers; because he was at all times indignant against that false patriotism, that pretended love of freedom, that unruly restlessness which is inconsistent with the stable authority of any good government.

Mr. Ogilvie was unlucky enough to choose for the topick of his conversation the praises of his native country. He began by saying, that there was very rich land around Edinburgh. Goldsmith, who had studied physick there, contradicted this, very untruly, with a sneering laugh. Disconcerted a little by this, Mr. Ogilvie then took a new ground, where, I suppose, he thought himself perfectly safe; for he observed, that Scotland had a great many noble wild prospects. JOHNSON. "I believe, Sir, you have a great many. Norway, too, has noble wild prospects; and Lapland is remarkable for prodigious noble wild prospects. But, Sir, let me tell you, the noblest prospect which a Scotchman ever sees, is the high road that leads him to England!" This unexpected and pointed sally produced a roar of applause.

111

On the 14th we had another evening by ourselves at the Mitre. Feeling myself now quite at ease as his companion, though I had all possible reverence for him, I expressed a regret that I could not be so easy with my father, though he was not much older than Johnson, and certainly however respectable had not more learning and greater abilities to depress me. I asked him the reason of this. JOHNSON. "Why, Sir, I am a man of the world. I live in the world, and I take in some degree, the colour of the world as it moves along. Your father is a Judge in a remote part of the island, and all his notions are taken from the old world. Besides, Sir, there must always be a struggle between a father and son, while one aims at power and the other at independence." I said, I was afraid my father would force me to be a lawyer. JOHNSON. "Sir, you need not be afraid of his forcing you to be a laborious practising lawyer; that is not in his power. For as the proverb says, 'One man may lead a horse to the water, but twenty cannot make him drink.' He may be displeased that you are not what he wishes you to be; but that displeasure will not go far. If he insists only on your having as much law as is necessary for a man of property, and then endeavours to get you into Parliament, he is quite in the right."

He enlarged very convincingly upon the excellence of rhyme over blank verse in English poetry. I mentioned to him that Dr. Adam Smith, in his lectures upon composition, when I studied under him in the College of Glasgow, had maintained the same opinion strenuously, and I repeated some of his arguments. JOHNSON. "Sir, I was once in company with Smith, and we did not take to each other; but had I known that he loved rhyme as much as you tell me he does, I should have HUGGED him."

"Idleness is a disease which must be combated; but I would not advise a rigid adherence to a particular plan of study. I myself have never persisted in any plan for two days together. A man ought to read just as inclination leads him; for what he reads as a task will do him little good. A young man should read five hours in a day, and so may acquire a great deal of knowledge."

I described to him an impudent fellow from Scotland,

who affected to be a savage, and railed at all established systems. JOHNSON. "There is nothing surprizing in this, Sir. He wants to make himself conspicuous. He would tumble in a hogstye, as long as you looked at him and called to him to come out. But let him alone, never mind him, and he'll soon give it over."

I added that the same person maintained that there was no distinction between virtue and vice. JOHNSON. "Why, Sir, if the fellow does not think as he speaks, he is lying; and I see not what honour he can propose to himself from having the character of a lyar. But if he does really think that there is no distinction between virtue and vice, why, Sir, when he leaves our houses let us count our spoons."

He recommended to me to keep a journal of my life, full and unreserved. He said it would be a very good exercise, and would yield me great satisfaction when the particulars were faded from my remembrance. I was uncommonly fortunate in having had a previous coincidence of opinion with him upon this subject, for I had kept such a journal for some time; and it was no small pleasure to me to have this to tell him, and to receive his approbation. He counselled me to keep it private, and said I might surely have a friend who would burn it in case of my death. From this habit I have been enabled to give the world so many anecdotes, which would otherwise have been lost to posterity. I mentioned that I was afraid I put into my journal too many little incidents. JOHNSON. "There is nothing, Sir, too little for so little a creature as man. It is by studying little things that we attain the great art of having as little misery and as much happiness as possible."

Next morning Mr. Dempster happened to call on me, and was so much struck even with the imperfect account which I gave him of Dr. Johnson's conversation, that to his honour be it recorded, when I complained that drinking port and sitting up late with him, affected my nerves for some time after, he said, "One had better be palsied at eighteen than not keep company with such a man."

On Tuesday, July 18, I found tall Sir Thomas Robinson sitting with Johnson. Sir Thomas said, that the King of Prussia valued himself upon three things;—upon being a hero, a musician, and an authour. JOHNSON. "Pretty well, Sir, for one man. As to his being an authour, I have not looked at his poetry; but his prose is poor stuff. He writes just as you may suppose Voltaire's foot-boy to do, who has been his amanuensis. He has such parts as the valet might have, and about as much of the colouring of the style as might be got by transcribing his works." When I was at Ferney, I repeated this to Voltaire, in order to reconcile him somewhat to Johnson, whom he, in affecting the English mode of expression, had previously characterised as "a superstitious dog;" but after hearing such a criticism on Frederick the Great, with whom he was then on bad terms, he exclaimed, "An honest fellow!"

On Wednesday, July 20, Dr. Johnson, Mr. Dempster, and my uncle Dr. Boswell, who happened to be now in London, supped with me. JOHNSON. "Pity is not natural to man. Children are always cruel. Savages are always cruel. Pity is acquired and improved by the cultivation of reason. We may have uneasy sensations for seeing a creature in distress, without pity; for we have not pity unless we wish to relieve them. When I am on my way to dine with a friend, and finding it late, have bid the coachman make haste, if I happen to attend when he whips his horses, I may feel unpleasantly that the animals are put to pain, but I do not wish him to desist. No, Sir, I wish him to drive on."

Mr. Dempster having endeavoured to maintain that intrinsick merit *ought* to make the only distinction amongst mankind. JOHNSON. "Why, Sir, mankind have found that this cannot be. How shall we determine the proportion of intrinsick merit? Were that to be the only distinction amongst mankind, we should soon quarrel about the degrees of it. Were all distinctions abolished, the strongest would not long acquiesce, but would endeavour to obtain a superiority by their bodily strength. But, Sir, as subordination is very necessary for society, and contentions for superiority very dangerous, mankind, that is to say, all civilised nations, have settled it upon a plain invariable principle. A man is born to hereditary rank; or his being appointed to certain offices, gives him a certain rank. Subordination tends greatly to human happiness. Were we all upon an equality, we should have no other enjoyment than mere animal pleasure."

Next morning I found him alone, and have preserved the following fragments of his conversation. Of a gentleman who was mentioned, he said, "I have not met with any man for a long time who has given me such general displeasure. He is totally unfixed in his principles, and wants to puzzle other people." I said his principles had been poisoned by a noted infidel writer, but that he was, nevertheless, a benevolent good man. JOHNSON. "We can have no dependence upon that instinctive, that constitutional goodness which is not founded upon principle. I grant you that such a man may be a very amiable member of society. I can conceive him placed in such a situation that he is not much tempted to deviate from what is right; and as every man prefers virtue, when there is not some strong incitement to transgress its precepts, I can conceive him doing nothing wrong. But if such a man stood in need of money, I should not like to trust him; and I should certainly not trust him with young ladies, for *there* there is always temptation. Hume, and other sceptical innovators, are vain men, and will gratify themselves at any expence. Truth will not afford sufficient food to their vanity; so they have betaken themselves to errour. Truth, Sir, is a cow which will yield such people no more milk, and so they are gone to milk the bull. If I could have allowed myself to gratify my vanity at the expence of truth, what fame might I have acquired. Every thing which Hume has advanced against Christianity had passed through my mind long before he wrote. Always remember this, that after a system is well settled upon positive evidence, a few partial objections ought not to shake it. The human mind is so limited, that it cannot take in all the parts of a subject, so that there may be objections raised against any thing. There are objections against a *plenum,* and objections against a *vacuum;* yet one of them must certainly be true."

I mentioned Hume's argument against the belief of miracles, that it is more probable that the witnesses to the truth of them are mistaken, or speak falsely, than that the miracles should be true. JOHNSON. "Why, Sir, the great difficulty of proving miracles should make us very cautious in believing them. But let us consider; although GOD has made Nature to operate by certain fixed laws, yet it is not unreasonable to think that he may suspend those laws, in order to establish a system highly advantageous to mankind. Now the Christian Religion is a most beneficial system, as it gives us light and certainty where we were before in darkness and doubt. The miracles which prove it are attested by men who had no interest in deceiving us; but who, on the contrary, were told that they should suffer persecution, and did actually lay down their lives in confirmation of the truth of the facts which they asserted. Indeed, for some centuries the heathens did not pretend to deny the miracles; but said they were performed by the aid of evil spirits. This is a circumstance of great weight. Then, Sir, when we take the proofs derived from prophecies which have been so exactly fulfilled, we have most satisfactory evidence. Supposing a miracle possible, as to which, in my opinion, there can be no doubt, we have as strong evidence for the miracles in support of Christianity, as the nature of the thing admits."

At night, Mr. Johnson and I supped in a private room at the Turk's Head coffee-house, in the Strand. "I encourage this house (said he,) for the mistress of it is a good civil woman, and has not much business."

"Sir, I love the acquaintance of young people; because, in the first place, I don't like to think myself growing old. In the next place, young acquaintances must last longest, if they do last; and then, Sir, young men have more virtue than old men; they have more generous sentiments in every respect. I love the young dogs of this age, they have more wit and humour and knowledge of life than we had; but then the dogs are not so good scholars. Sir, in my early years I read very hard. It is a sad reflection but a true one, that I knew almost as much at eighteen as I do now. My judgement, to be sure, was not so good; but, I had all the facts. I remember very well, when I was at Oxford, an old gentleman said to me, 'Young man, ply your book diligently now, and acquire a stock of knowledge; for when years come upon you, you will find that poring upon books will be but an irksome task.' "

116

He again insisted on the duty of maintaining subordination of rank. "Sir, I would no more deprive a nobleman of his respect, than of his money. I consider myself as acting a part in the great system of society, and I do to others as I would have them to do to me. I would behave to a nobleman as I should expect he would behave to me, were I a nobleman and he Sam. Johnson. Sir, there is one Mrs. Macaulay in this town, a great republican. One day when I was at her house, I put on a very grave countenance, and said to her, 'Madam, I am now become a convert to your way of thinking. I am convinced that all mankind are upon an equal footing; and to give you an unquestionable proof, Madam, that I am in earnest, here is a very sensible, civil, well-behaved fellow-citizen, your footman; I desire that he may be allowed to sit down and dine with us.' I thus, Sir, shewed her the absurdity of the levelling doctrine. She has never liked me since. Sir, your levellers wish to level *down* as far as themselves; but they cannot bear levelling *up* to themselves. They would all have some people under them; why not then have some people above them?" I mentioned a certain authour who disgusted me by his forwardness, and by shewing no deference to noblemen into whose company he was admitted. JOHNSON. "Suppose a shoemaker should claim an equality with him, as he does with a Lord: how he would stare. 'Why, Sir, do you stare? (says the shoemaker,) I do great service to society. 'Tis true, I am paid for doing it; but so are you, Sir: and I am sorry to say it, better paid than I am, for doing something not so necessary. For mankind could do better without your books, than without my shoes.' Thus, Sir, there would be a perpetual struggle for precedence, were there no fixed invariable rules for the distinction of rank, which creates no jealousy, as it is allowed to be accidental."

A writer of deserved eminence being mentioned, Johnson said, "Why, Sir, he is a man of good parts, but being originally poor, he has got a love of mean company and low jocularity; a very bad thing, Sir. To laugh is good, and to talk is good. But you ought no more to think it enough if you laugh, than you are to think it enough if you talk. You may laugh in as many ways as you talk; and surely *every* way of talking that is practised cannot be esteemed."

I spoke of Sir James Macdonald as a young man of most distinguished merit, who united the highest reputation at Eton and Oxford, with the patriarchal spirit of a great Highland Chieftain. I mentioned that Sir James had said to me, that he had never seen Mr. Johnson, but he had a great respect for him, though at the same time it was mixed with some degree of terrour. JOHNSON. "Sir, if he were to be acquainted with me, it might lessen both."

He maintained that a boy at school was the happiest of human beings. I supported a different opinion, from which I have never yet varied, that a man is happier: and I enlarged upon the anxiety and sufferings which are endured at school. JOHNSON. "Ah! Sir, a boy's being flogged is not so severe as a man's having the hiss of the world against him. Men have a solicitude about fame; and the greater share they have of it, the more afraid they are of losing it."

We talked of the education of children; and I asked him what he thought was best to teach them first. JOHNSON. "Sir, it is no matter what you teach them first, any more than what leg you shall put into your breeches first. Sir, you may stand disputing which is best to put in first, but in the mean time your breech is bare. Sir, while you are considering which of two things you should teach your child first, another boy has learnt them both."

On Thursday, July 28, we again supped in private at the Turk's Head coffee-house. JOHNSON. "Swift has a higher reputation than he deserves. His excellence is strong sense; for his humour, though very well, is not remarkably good. I doubt whether the 'Tale of a Tub' be his; for he never owned it, and it is much above his usual manner."

The conversation then took a philosophical turn. JOHNSON. "Human experience, which is constantly contradicting theory, is the great test of truth. A system, built upon the discoveries of a great many minds, is always of more strength, than what is produced by the mere workings of any one mind, which, of itself, can do little. There is not so poor a book in the world that would not be a prodigious effort were it wrought out entirely by a single mind, without

118

the aid of prior investigators. The French writers are superficial, because they are not scholars, and so proceed upon the mere power of their own minds; and we see how very little power they have."

"As to the Christian Religion, Sir, besides the strong evidence which we have for it, there is a balance in its favour from the number of great men who have been convinced of its truth, after a serious consideration of the question. Grotius was an acute man, a lawyer, a man accustomed to examine evidence, and he was convinced. Grotius was not a recluse, but a man of the world, who certainly had no bias to the side of religion. Sir Isaac Newton set out an infidel, and came to be a very firm believer."

As we walked along the Strand to-night, arm in arm, a woman of the town accosted us, in the usual enticing manner. "No, no, my girl, (said Johnson) it won't do." He, however, did not treat her with harshness; and we talked of the wretched life of such women, and agreed, that much more misery than happiness, upon the whole, is produced by illicit commerce between the sexes.

On Saturday, July 30, Dr. Johnson and I took a sculler at the Temple-stairs, and set out for Greenwich. I asked him if he really thought a knowledge of the Greek and Latin languages an essential requisite to a good education. JOHNSON. "Most certainly, Sir; for those who know them have a very great advantage over those who do not. Nay, Sir, it is wonderful what a difference learning makes upon people even in the common intercourse of life, which does not appear to be much connected with it." "And yet, (said I) people go through the world very well, and carry on the business of life to good advantage, without learning." JOHNSON. "Why, Sir, that may be true in cases where learning cannot possibly be of any use; for instance, this boy rows us as well without learning, as if he could sing the song of Orpheus to the Argonauts, who were the first sailors." He then called to the boy, "What would you give, my lad, to know about the Argonauts?" "Sir, (said the boy) I would give what I have." Johnson was much pleased with his answer, and we gave him a double fare. Dr. Johnson then turning to me, "Sir, (said he) a desire of knowledge is the natural feeling of mankind; and every human being, whose mind is not debauched, will be willing to give all that he has, to get knowledge."

We landed at the Old Swan, and walked to Billingsgate, where we took oars and moved smoothly along the silver Thames. It was a very fine day. We were entertained with the immense number and variety of ships that were lying at anchor, and with the beautiful country on each side of the river.

I talked of preaching, and of the great success which those called methodists have. JOHNSON. "Sir, it is owing to their expressing themselves in a plain and familiar manner, which is the only way to do good to the common people, and which clergymen of genius and learning ought to do from a principle of duty, when it is suited to their congregations; a practice, for which they will be praised by men of sense. To insist against drunkenness as a crime, because it debases reason, the noblest faculty of man, would be of no service to the common people; but to tell them that they may die in a fit of drunkenness, and shew them how dreadful that would be, cannot fail to make a deep impression. Sir, when your Scotch clergy give up their homely manner, religion will soon decay in that country." Let this observation, as Johnson meant it, be ever remembered.

We walked in the evening in Greenwich Park. He asked me, I suppose, by way of trying my disposition, "Is not this very fine?" Having no exquisite relish of the beauties of Nature, and being more delighted with "the busy hum of men," I answered, "Yes, Sir; but not equal to Fleet-street." JOHNSON. "You are right, Sir."

I am aware that many of my readers may censure my want of taste. Let me, however, shelter myself under the authority of a very fashionable Baronet in the brilliant world, who, on his attention being called to the fragrance of a May evening in the country, observed, "This may be very well; but for my part, I prefer the smell of a flambeau at the play-house."

We staid so long at Greenwich, that our sail up the river, in our return to London, was by no means so pleasant as in the morning; for the night air was so cold that it made me shiver. I was the more sensible of it from having sat up all the night before recollecting and writing in my Journal what I thought worthy of preservation; an exertion, which, during the first part of my acquaintance with Johnson, I frequently made. I remember having sat up four nights in one week, without being much incommoded in the day time.

Johnson, whose robust frame was not in the least affected by the cold, scolded me, as if my shivering had been a paltry effeminacy, saying, "Why do you shiver?"

After we had talked of my setting out for Holland, he said, "I must see thee out of England; I will accompany you to Harwich." I could not find words to express what I felt upon this unexpected and very great mark of his affectionate regard.

Next day, Sunday, July 31, I told him I had been that morning at a meeting of the people called Quakers, where I had heard a woman preach. JOHNSON. "Sir, a woman's preaching is like a dog's walking on his hind legs. It is not done well; but you are surprised to find it done at all."

On Tuesday, August 2, (the day of my departure from London having been fixed for the 5th,) Dr. Johnson did me the honour to pass a part of the morning with me at my Chambers. He said, that "he always felt an inclination to do nothing." I observed, that it was strange to think that the most indolent man in Britain had written the most laborious work, THE ENGLISH DICTIONARY.

I complained to him that my love of London and of his company was such, that I shrunk almost from the thought of going away even to travel, which is generally so much desired by young men. He roused me by manly and spirited conversation. He advised me, when settled in any place abroad, to study with an eagerness after knowledge, and to apply to Greek an hour every day; and when I was moving about, to read diligently the great book of mankind.

On Friday, August 5, we set out early in the morning in the Harwich stage-coach. A fat elderly gentlewoman, and a young Dutchman, seemed the most inclined among us to conversation. At the inn where we dined, the gentlewoman said that she had done her best to educate her children;

and, particularly, that she had never suffered them to be a moment idle. JOHNSON. "I wish, Madam, you would educate me too; for I have been an idle fellow all my life." "I am sure, Sir, (said she) you have not been idle." JOHNSON. "Nay, Madam, it is very true; and that gentleman there, (pointing to me,) has been idle. He was idle at Edinburgh. His father sent him to Glasgow, where he continued to be idle. He then came to London, where he has been very idle; and now he is going to Utrecht, where he will be as idle as ever." I asked him privately how he could expose me so. JOHNSON. "Poh, poh! (said he) they knew nothing about you, and will think of it no more." Though by no means niggardly, his attention to what was generally right was so minute, that having observed at one of the stages that I ostentatiously gave a shilling to the coachman, when the custom was for each passenger to give only six-pence, he took me aside and scolded me, saying that what I had done would make the coachman dissatisfied with all the rest of the passengers who gave him no more than his due. This was a just reprimand; for in whatever way a man may indulge his generosity or his vanity in spending his money, for the sake of others he ought not to raise the price of any article for which there is a constant demand.

At supper this night he talked of good eating with uncommon satisfaction. "Some people (said he,) have a foolish way of not minding, or pretending not to mind, what they eat. For my part, I mind my belly very studiously, and very carefully; for I look upon it, that he who does not mind his belly, will hardly mind any thing else." He now appeared to me *Jean Bull philosophe,* and he was for the moment, not only serious, but vehement. Yet I have heard him, upon other occasions, talk with great contempt of people who were anxious to gratify their palates; and the 206th number of his Rambler is a masterly essay against gulosity. His practice, indeed, I must acknowledge, may be considered as casting the balance of his different opinions upon this subject; for I never knew any man who relished good eating more than he did. When at table, he was totally absorbed in the business of the moment; his looks seemed rivetted to his plate; nor would he, unless when in very high company, say one word, or even pay the least attention to what was said by others, till he had satisfied his appetite: which was so fierce, and indulged with such intenseness, that while in the act of eating, the veins of his forehead swelled, and generally a strong perspiration was visible. To those whose sensations were delicate, this could not but be disgusting; and it was doubtless not very suitable to the character of a philosopher, who should be distinguished by self-command. But it must be owned, that Johnson, though he could be rigidly *abstemious,* was not a *temperate* man either in eating or drinking. He could refrain, but he could not use moderately. He told me, that he had fasted two days without inconvenience, and that he had never been hungry but once. They who beheld with wonder how much he could eat upon all occasions, when his dinner was to his taste, could not easily conceive what he must have meant by hunger; and not only was he remarkable for the extraordinary quantity which he eat, but he was, or affected to be, a man of very nice discernment in the science of cookery. He used to descant critically on the dishes which had been at table where he had dined or supped, and to recollect very minutely what he had liked. I remember when he was in Scotland, his praising *"Gordon's palates,"* (a dish of palates at the Honourable Alexander Gordon's) with a warmth of expression which might have done honour to more important subjects. "As for Maclaurin's imitation of a *made dish,* it was a wretched attempt." He about the same time was so much displeased with the performances of a nobleman's French cook, that he exclaimed with vehemence, "I'd throw such a rascal into the river;" and he then proceeded to alarm a lady at whose house he was to sup, by the following manifesto of his skill: "I, Madam, who live at a variety of good tables, am a much better judge of cookery, than any person who has a very tolerable cook, but lives much at home; for his palate is gradually adapted to the taste of his cook: whereas, Madam, in trying by a wider range, I can more exquisitely judge." When invited to dine, even with an intimate friend, he was not pleased if something better than a plain dinner was not prepared for him. I have heard him say on such an occasion, "This was a good dinner enough, to be sure: but it was not a dinner to *ask* a man to." On the other hand, he was wont to express, with great glee, his satisfaction when he had been entertained quite to his mind. One day when he had dined with his neighbour and landlord, in Boltcourt, Mr. Allen, the printer, whose old housekeeper had studied his taste in every thing, he pronounced this eulogy: "Sir, we could not have had a better dinner, had there been a *Synod of Cooks.*"

Dr. Johnson talked of that studied behaviour which many have recommended and practised. He disapproved of it; and said, "I never considered whether I should be a grave man, or a merry man, but just let inclination, for the time, have its course."

Next day we got to Harwich, to dinner; and my passage in the packet-boat to Helvoetsluys being secured, and my baggage put on board, we dined at our inn by ourselves. I happened to say, it would be terrible if he should not find a speedy opportunity of returning to London, and be confined in so dull a place. JOHNSON. "Don't, Sir, accustom yourself to use big words for little matters. It would *not* be *terrible,* though I *were* to be detained some time here." The practice of using words of disproportionate magnitude, is, no doubt, too frequent every where; but, I think, most remarkable among the French, of which, all who have travelled in France must have been struck with innumerable instances.

We went and looked at the church, and having gone into it, and walked up to the altar, Johnson, whose piety was constant and fervent, sent me to my knees, saying, "Now that you are going to leave your native country, recommend yourself to the protection of your CREATOR and REDEEMER."

After we came out of the church, we stood talking for some time together of Bishop Berkeley's ingenious sophistry to prove the non-existence of matter, and that every thing in the universe is merely ideal. I observed, that though we are satisfied his doctrine is not true, it is impossible to refute it. I never shall forget the alacrity with which Johnson answered, striking his foot with mighty force against a large stone, till he rebounded from it,—"I refute it *thus*."

My reverend friend walked down with me to the beach, where we embraced and parted with tenderness, and engaged to correspond by letters. I said, "I hope, Sir, you will not forget me in my absence." JOHNSON. "Nay, Sir, it is more likely you should forget me, than that I should forget you." As the vessel put out to sea, I kept my eyes upon him for a considerable time, while he remained rolling his majestic frame in his usual manner; and at last I perceived him walk back into the town, and he disappeared.

Utrecht seeming at first very dull to me, after the animated scenes of London, my spirits were grievously affected; and I wrote to Johnson a plaintive and desponding letter, to which he paid no regard. Afterwards, when I had acquired a firmer tone of mind, I wrote him a second letter, expressing much anxiety to hear from him. At length I received the following epistle, which was of important service to me, and, I trust, will be so to many others.

"*A Mr.* BOSWELL, *à la Cour de l'Empereur*, UTRECHT.
"DEAR SIR,

"You are not to think yourself forgotten, or criminally neglected, that you have had yet no letter from me. I love to see my friends, to hear from them, to talk to them, and to talk of them; but it is not without a considerable effort of resolution that I prevail upon myself to write. I would not, however, gratify my own indolence by the omission of any important duty, or any office of real kindness.

"To tell you that I am or am not well, that I have or have not been in the country, that I drank your health in the room in which we last sat together, and that your acquaintance continue to speak of you with their former kindness, topicks with which those letters are commonly filled which are written only for the sake of writing, I seldom shall think worth communicating; but if I can have it in my power to calm any harassing disquiet, to excite any virtuous desire, to rectify any important opinion, or fortify any generous resolution, you need not doubt but I shall at least wish to prefer the pleasure of gratifying a friend much less esteemed than yourself, before the gloomy calm of idle

vacancy. Whether I shall easily arrive at an exact punctu-
ality of correspondence, I cannot tell. I shall, at present, expect that you will receive this in return for two which I
have had from you. The first, indeed, gave me an account
so hopeless of the state of your mind, that it hardly admitted or deserved an answer; by the second I was much
better pleased; and the pleasure will still be increased by
such a narrative of the progress of your studies, as may
evince the continuance of an equal and rational application
of your mind to some useful enquiry.

"You will, perhaps, wish to ask, what study I would
recommend. I shall not speak of theology, because it ought
not to be considered as a question whether you shall endeavour to know the will of GOD.

"I shall, therefore, consider only such studies as we are
at liberty to pursue or to neglect; and of these I know not
how you will make a better choice, than by studying the
civil law as your father advises, and the ancient languages,
as you had determined for yourself; at least resolve, while
you remain in any settled residence, to spend a certain
number of hours every day amongst your books. The dissipation of thought of which you complain, is nothing more
than the vacillation of a mind suspended between different
motives, and changing its direction as any motive gains or
loses strength. If you can but kindle in your mind any
strong desire; if you can but keep predominant any wish for
some particular excellence or attainment, the gusts of imagination will break away, without any effect upon your conduct, and commonly without any traces left upon the
memory.

"There lurks, perhaps, in every human heart a desire of
distinction, which inclines every man first to hope, and then
to believe, that nature has given him something peculiar to
himself. This vanity makes one mind nurse aversion, and
another actuate desires, till they rise by art much above
their original state of power; and as affectation in time improves to habit, they at last tyrannise over him who at first
encouraged them only for show. Every desire is a viper in
the bosom, who, while he was chill, was harmless; but when
warmth gave him strength, exerted it in poison. You know

126

a gentleman, who, when first he set his foot in the gay world, as he prepared himself to whirl in the vortex of pleasure, imagined a total indifference and universal negligence to be the most agreeable concomitants of youth, and the strongest indication of an airy temper and a quick apprehension. Vacant to every object, and sensible of every impulse, he thought that all appearance of diligence would deduct something from the reputation of genius; and hoped that he should appear to attain, amidst all the ease of carelessness, and all the tumult of diversion, that knowledge and those accomplishments which mortals of the common fabrick obtain only by mute abstraction and solitary drudgery. He tried this scheme of life awhile, was made weary of it by his sense and his virtue; he then wished to return to his studies; and finding long habits of idleness and pleasure harder to be cured than he expected, still willing to retain his claim to some extraordinary prerogatives, resolved the common consequences of irregularity into an unalterable decree of destiny, and concluded that Nature had originally formed him incapable of rational employment.

"Let all such fancies, illusive and destructive, be banished henceforward from your thoughts for ever. Resolve, and keep your resolution; choose, and pursue your choice. If you spend this day in study, you will find yourself still more able to study to-morrow; not that you are to expect that you shall at once obtain a complete victory. Depravity is not very easily overcome. Resolution will sometimes relax, and diligence will sometimes be interrupted; but let no accidental surprise or deviation, whether short or long, dispose you to despondency. Consider these failings as incident to all mankind. Begin again where you left off, and endeavour to avoid the seducements that prevailed over you before.

"This, my dear Boswell, is advice which, perhaps, has been often given you, and given you without effect. But this advice, if you will not take from others, you must take from your own reflections, if you purpose to do the duties of the station to which the bounty of Providence has called you.

"Let me have a long letter from you as soon as you can. I hope you continue your Journal, and enrich it with many observations upon the country in which you reside. It will be a favour if you can get me any books in the Frisick language, and can enquire how the poor are maintained in the Seven Provinces. I am, dear Sir,

"Your most affectionate servant,

"SAM. JOHNSON."

"London, Dec. 8, 1763."

Early in 1764 Johnson paid a visit to the Langton family, at their seat of Langton in Lincolnshire, where he passed some time, much to his satisfaction. Soon after his return to London, which was in February, was founded that CLUB which existed long without a name, but at Mr. Garrick's funeral became distinguished by the title of THE LITERARY CLUB. Sir Joshua Reynolds had the merit of being the first proposer of it, to which Johnson acceded; and the original members were, Sir Joshua Reynolds, Dr. Johnson, Mr. Edmund Burke, Dr. Nugent, Mr. Beauclerk, Mr. Langton, Dr. Goldsmith, Mr. Chamier, and Sir John Hawkins. They met at the Turk's Head, in Gerrard-street, Soho, one evening in every week, at seven, and generally continued their conversation till a pretty late hour. This club has been gradually increased to its present number, thirty-five. After about ten years, instead of supping weekly, it was resolved to dine together once a fortnight during the meeting of Parliament. Their original tavern having been converted into a private house, they moved first to Prince's in Sackville-street, then to Le Telier's in Dover-street, and now meet at Parsloe's, St. James's-street. Between the time of its formation, and the time at which this work is passing through the press, (June 1792,) the following persons, now dead, were members of it: Mr. Dunning, (afterwards Lord Ashburton,) Mr. Samuel Dyer, Mr. Garrick, Dr. Shipley Bishop of St. Asaph, Mr. Vesey, Mr. Thomas Warton, and Dr. Adam Smith. The present members are, Mr. Burke, Mr. Langton, Lord Charlemont, Sir Robert Chambers, Dr. Percy Bishop of Dromore, Dr. Barnard Bishop of Killaloe, Dr. Marlay Bishop of Clonfert, Mr. Fox, Dr. George Fordyce, Sir William Scott, Sir Joseph Banks, Sir Charles Bunbury, Mr. Windham of Norfolk, Mr. Sheridan, Mr. Gibbon, Sir William Jones, Mr. Colman, Mr. Steevens, Dr. Burney, Dr. Joseph Warton, Mr. Malone, Lord Ossory, Lord Spencer, Lord Lucan, Lord Palmerston, Lord Eliot, Lord Macartney, Mr. Richard Burke, junior, Sir William Hamilton, Dr. Warren, Mr. Courtenay, Dr. Hinchliffe Bishop of Peterborough, the Duke of Leeds, Dr. Douglas Bishop of Salisbury, and the writer of this account.

Sir John Hawkins represents himself as a *"seceder"* from this society, and assigns as the reason for his *"withdrawing"* himself from it, that its late hours were inconsistent with his domestick arrangements. In this he is not accurate; for the fact was, that he one evening attacked Mr. Burke, in so rude a manner, that all the company testified their displeasure; and at their next meeting his reception was such, that he never came again.[1]

Not very long after the institution of our club, Sir Joshua Reynolds was speaking of it to Garrick. "I like it much, (said he,) I think I shall be of you." When Sir Joshua mentioned this to Dr. Johnson, he was much displeased with the actor's conceit. *"He'll be of us,* (said Johnson) how does he know we will *permit* him? the first Duke in England has no right to hold such language." However, when Garrick was regularly proposed some time afterwards, Johnson, though he had taken a momentary offence at his arrogance, warmly and kindly supported him, and he was accordingly elected, was a most agreeable member, and continued to attend our meetings to the time of his death.

The ease and the independence to which he had at last attained by royal munificence, increased his natural indolence. In his "Meditations," he thus accuses himself: "GOOD FRIDAY, April 20, 1764. I have made no reformation; I have lived totally useless, more sensual in thought, and more addicted to wine and meat."

---

[1] From Sir Joshua Reynolds.
[The knight having refused to pay his portion of the reckoning for supper, because he usually eat no supper at home, Johnson observed, "Sir John, Sir, is a very *unclubable* man."—BURNEY.]

About this time he was afflicted with a very severe return of the hypochondriack disorder, which was ever lurking about him. He was so ill, as, notwithstanding his remarkable love of company, to be entirely averse to society, the most fatal symptom of that malady. Dr. Adams told me, that, as an old friend he was admitted to visit him, and that he found him in a deplorable state, sighing, groaning, talking to himself, and restlessly walking from room to room. He then used this emphatical expression of the misery which he felt: "I would consent to have a limb amputated to recover my spirits."

Talking to himself was, indeed, one of his singularities ever since I knew him. I was certain that he was frequently uttering pious ejaculations; for fragments of the Lord's Prayer have been distinctly overheard. His friend Mr. Thomas Davies, of whom Churchill says,

"That Davies hath a very pretty wife,—"

when Dr. Johnson muttered—"lead us not into temptation," used with waggish and gallant humour to whisper Mrs. Davies, "You, my dear, are the cause of this."

He had another particularity, of which none of his friends even ventured to ask an explanation. It appeared to me some superstitious habit, which he had contracted early, and from which he had never called upon his reason to disentangle him. This was his anxious care to go out or in at a door or passage, by a certain number of steps from a certain point, or at least so as that either his right or his left foot, (I am not certain which,) should constantly make the first actual movement when he came close to the door or passage. Thus I conjecture: for I have, upon innumerable occasions, observed him suddenly stop, and then seem to count his steps with a deep earnestness; and when he had neglected or gone wrong in this sort of magical movement, I have seen him go back again, put himself in a proper posture to begin the ceremony, and, having gone through it, break from his abstraction, walk briskly on, and join his companion. A strange instance of something of this nature, even when on horseback, happened when he was in the Isle of Sky. Sir Joshua Reynolds has observed him to go a good way about, rather than cross a particular alley in Leicester-fields; but this Sir Joshua imputed to his having had some disagreeable recollection associated with it.

That the most minute singularities which belonged to him, and made very observable parts of his appearance and manner, may not be omitted, it is requisite to mention, that while talking or even musing as he sat in his chair, he commonly held his head to one side towards his right shoulder, and shook it in a tremulous manner, moving his body backwards and forwards, and rubbing his left knee in the same direction, with the palm of his hand. In the intervals of articulating he made various sounds with his mouth; sometimes as if ruminating, or what is called chewing the cud, sometimes giving a half whistle, sometimes making his tongue play backwards from the roof of his mouth, as if clucking like a hen, and sometimes protruding it against his upper gums in front, as if pronouncing quickly under his breath, *too, too, too:* all this accompanied sometimes with a thoughtful look, but more frequently with a smile. Generally when he had concluded a period, in the course of a dispute, by which time he was a good deal exhausted by violence and vociferation, he used to blow out his breath like a whale. This I suppose was a relief to his lungs; and seemed in him to be a contemptuous mode of expression, as if he had made the arguments of his opponent fly like chaff before the wind.

Trinity College, Dublin, at this time surprised Johnson with a spontaneous compliment of the highest academical honours, by creating him Doctor of Laws. This unsolicited mark of distinction, conferred on so great a literary character, did much honour to the judgement and liberal spirit of that learned body.

This year was distinguished by his being introduced into the family of Mr. Thrale, one of the most eminent brewers in England, and member of Parliament for the borough of Southwark. Foreigners are not a little amazed, when they hear of brewers, distillers, and men in similar departments of trade, held forth as persons of considerable consequence. In this great commercial country it is natural that a situation which produces much wealth should be considered as very respectable; and, no doubt, honest industry is entitled to esteem. But, perhaps, the too rapid advances of men of low extraction tends to lessen the value of that distinction by birth and gentility, which has ever been found beneficial to the grand scheme of subordination. Johnson used to give this account of the rise of Mr. Thrale's father: "He worked at six shillings a week for twenty years in the great brewery, which afterwards was his own. The proprietor of it had an only daughter, who was married to a nobleman. It was not fit that a peer should continue the business. On the old man's death, therefore, the brewery was to be sold. To find a purchaser for so large a property was a difficult matter; and, after some time, it was suggested, that it would be adviseable to treat with Thrale, a sensible, active, honest man, who had been employed in the house, and to transfer the whole to him for thirty thousand pounds, security being taken upon the property. This was accordingly settled. In eleven years Thrale paid the purchase-money. He acquired a large fortune, and lived to be a member of Parliament for Southwark. But what was most remarkable was the liberality with which he used his riches. He gave his son and daughters the best education. The esteem which his good conduct procured him from the nobleman who had married his master's daughter, made him to be treated with much attention; and his son, both at school and at the University of Oxford, associated with young men of the first rank. His allowance from his father, after he left college, was splendid; not less than a thousand a year. This, in a man who had risen as old Thrale did, was a very extraordinary instance of generosity. He used to say, 'If this young dog does not find so much after I am gone as he expects, let him remember that he has had a great deal in my own time.' "

The son, though in affluent circumstances, had good sense enough to carry on his father's trade, which was of such extent, that I remember he once told me, he would not quit it for an annuity of ten thousand a year; "Not (said he,) that I get ten thousand a year by it, but it is an estate to a family." Having left daughters only, the property was sold for the immense sum of one hundred and thirty-five thou-

7
The cover of the first edition of Dr. Johnson's famous *Dictionary of the English Language*, published in 1755.

sand pounds; a magnificent proof of what may be done by fair trade in a long period of time.

Mr. Thrale had married Miss Hester Lynch Salusbury, of good Welch extraction, a lady of lively talents, improved by education. That Johnson's introduction into Mr. Thrale's family, which contributed so much to the happiness of his life, was owing to her desire for his conversation, is a very probable and the general supposition: but it is not the truth. Mr. Murphy, who was intimate with Mr. Thrale, having spoken very highly of Dr. Johnson, he was requested to make them acquainted. This being mentioned to Johnson, he accepted of an invitation to dinner at Thrale's, and was so much pleased with his reception, both by Mr. and Mrs. Thrale, and they so much pleased with him, that his invitations to their house were more and more frequent, till at last he became one of the family, and an apartment was appropriated to him, both in their house at Southwark and in their villa at Streatham.

Johnson had a very sincere esteem for Mr. Thrale, as a man of excellent principles, a good scholar, well skilled in trade, of a sound understanding, and of manners such as presented the character of a plain independent English 'Squire. As this family will frequently be mentioned in the course of the following pages, and as a false notion has prevailed that Mr. Thrale was inferiour, and in some degree insignificant, compared with Mrs. Thrale, it may be proper to give a true state of the case from the authority of Johnson himself in his own words.

"I know no man, (said he,) who is more master of his wife and family than Thrale. If he but holds up a finger, he is obeyed. It is a great mistake to suppose that she is above him in literary attainments. She is more flippant; but he has ten times her learning: he is a regular scholar; but her learning is that of a school-boy in one of the lower forms." My readers may naturally wish for some representation of the figures of this couple. Mr. Thrale was tall, well proportioned, and stately. As for *Madam*, or *my Mistress*, by which epithets Johnson used to mention Mrs. Thrale, she was short, plump, and brisk. She has herself given us a lively view of the idea which Johnson had of her person, on her appearing before him in a dark-coloured gown: "You little creatures should never wear those sort of clothes, however; they are unsuitable in every way. What! have not all insects gay colours!" Mr. Thrale gave his wife a liberal indulgence, both in the choice of their company, and in the mode of entertaining them. He understood and valued Johnson, without remission, from their first acquaintance to the day of his death. Mrs. Thrale was enchanted with Johnson's conversation for its own sake, and had also a very allowable vanity in appearing to be honoured with the attention of so celebrated a man.

Nothing could be more fortunate for Johnson than this connection. He had at Mr. Thrale's all the comforts and even luxuries of life: his melancholy was diverted, and his irregular habits lessened by association with an agreeable and well ordered family. He was treated with the utmost respect, and even affection. The vivacity of Mrs. Thrale's literary talk roused him to cheerfulness and exertion, even when they were alone. But this was not often the case; for he found here a constant succession of what gave him the highest enjoyment, the society of the learned, the witty, and the eminent in every way; who were assembled in numerous companies; called forth his wonderful powers, and gratified him with admiration, to which no man could be insensible.

In the October of this year he at length gave to the world his edition of Shakspeare, which, if it had no other merit but that of producing his Preface, in which the excellencies and defects of that immortal bard are displayed with a masterly hand, the nation would have had no reason to complain. A blind indiscriminate admiration of Shakspeare had exposed the British nation to the ridicule of foreigners. Johnson, by candidly admitting the faults of his poet, had the more credit in bestowing on him deserved and indisputable praise; and doubtless none of all his panegyrists have done him half so much honour. Their praise was like that of a counsel, upon his own side of the cause; Johnson's was like the grave, well considered, and impartial opinion of the judge, which falls from his lips with weight, and is received with reverence. What he did as a commentator has no small share of merit, though his researches were not so ample, and his investigations so acute as they might have been; which we now certainly know from the labours of other able and ingenious cricks who have followed him.

His Shakspeare was virulently attacked by Mr. William Kenrick, who obtained the degree of LL.D. from a Scotch University, and wrote for the booksellers in a great variety of branches. Though he certainly was not without considerable merit, he wrote with so little regard to decency, and principles, and decorum, and in so hasty a manner, that his reputation was neither extensive nor lasting. I remember one evening, when some of his works were mentioned, Dr. Goldsmith said, he had never heard of them; upon which Dr. Johnson observed, "Sir, he is one of the many who have made themselves *publick*, without making themselves *known*."

In his Preface to Shakspeare, Johnson treated Voltaire very contemptuously, observing, upon some of his remarks, "These are the petty cavils of petty minds." Voltaire, in revenge, made an attack upon Johnson, in one of his numerous literary sallies which I remember to have read; but there being no general index to his voluminous works, have searched in vain, and therefore cannot quote it.

Voltaire was an antagonist with whom I thought Johnson should not disdain to contend. I pressed him to answer. He said, he perhaps might; but he never did.

I returned to London in February, and found Dr. Johnson in a good house in Johnson's court, Fleet-street, in which he had accommodated Mrs. Williams with an apartment on the ground floor, while Mr. Levett occupied his post in the garret: his faithful Francis was still attending upon him. He received me with much kindness. The fragments of our first conversation, which I have preserved, are these: I told him that Voltaire, in a conversation with me, had distinguished Pope and Dryden thus:—"Pope drives a handsome chariot, with a couple of neat trim nags; Dryden a coach, and six stately horses." JOHNSON. "Why, Sir, the truth is they both drive coaches and six; but Dryden's horses are either galloping or stumbling: Pope's go at

135

a steady even trot." He said of Goldsmith's "Traveller," which had been published in my absence, "There has not been so fine a poem since Pope's time."

At night I supped with him at the Mitre Tavern, that we might renew our social intimacy at the original place of meeting. But there was now a considerable difference in his way of living. Having had an illness, in which he was advised to leave off wine, he had, from that period, continued to abstain from it, and drank only water, or lemonade.

I told him that a foreign friend of his, whom I had met with abroad, was so wretchedly perverted to infidelity, that he treated the hopes of immortality with brutal levity; and said, "As man dies like a dog, let him lie like a dog." JOHNSON. "If he dies like a dog, *let* him lie like a dog." I added, that this man said to me, "I hate mankind, for I think myself one of the best of them, and I know how bad I am." JOHNSON. "Sir, he must be very singular in his opinion, if he thinks himself one of the best of men; for none of his friends think him so."—He said, "No honest man could be a Deist; for no man could be so after a fair examination of the proofs of Christianity." I named Hume. JOHNSON. "No, Sir; Hume owned to a clergyman in the bishoprick of Durham, that he had never read the New Testament with attention."—I mentioned Hume's notion, that all who are happy are equally happy; a little Miss with a new gown at a dancing-school ball, a General at the head of a victorious army, and an orator, after having made an eloquent speech in a great assembly. JOHNSON. "Sir, that all who are happy, are equally happy, is not true. A peasant and a philosopher may be equally *satisfied*, but not equally *happy*. Happiness consists in the multiplicity of agreeable consciousness. A peasant has not capacity for having equal happiness with a philosopher." I remember this very question very happily illustrated in opposition to Hume, by the Reverend Mr. Robert Brown, at Utrecht. "A small drinking-glass and a large one, (said he,) may be equally full; but the large one holds more than the small."

Dr. Johnson was very kind this evening, and said to me, "You have now lived five-and-twenty years, and you have employed them well." "Alas, Sir, (said I,) I fear not. Do I

know history? Do I know mathematicks? Do I know law?"
JOHNSON. "Why, Sir, though you may know no science so
well as to be able to teach it, and no profession so well as
to be able to follow it, your general mass of knowledge of
books and men renders you very capable to make yourself
master of any science, or fit yourself for any profession."
I mentioned that a gay friend had advised me against being
a lawyer, because I should be excelled by plodding block-
heads. JOHNSON. "Why, Sir, in the formulary and statutory
part of law, a plodding blockhead may excel; but in the ingenious and rational part of it a plodding blockhead can
never excel."

I talked of the mode adopted by some to rise in the
world, by courting great men, and asked him whether he
had ever submitted to it. JOHNSON. "Why, Sir, I never was
near enough to great men, to court them. You may be
prudently attached to great men, and yet independent. You
are not to do what you think wrong; and, Sir, you are to
calculate, and not pay too dear for what you get. You must
not give a shilling's worth of court for sixpence worth of
good. But if you can get a shilling's worth of good for six-
pence worth of court, you are a fool if you do not pay
court."

Our next meeting at the Mitre was on Saturday the 15th
of February, when I presented to him my old and most intimate friend, the Reverend Mr. Temple, then of Cambridge. I having mentioned that I had passed some time
with Rousseau in his wild retreat, and having quoted some
remark made by Mr. Wilkes, with whom I had spent many
pleasant hours in Italy, Johnson said, (sarcastically,) "It
seems, Sir, you have kept very good company abroad,
Rousseau and Wilkes!" Thinking it enough to defend one
at a time, I said nothing as to my gay friend, but answered
with a smile, "My dear Sir, you don't call Rousseau bad
company. Do you really think *him* a bad man?" JOHNSON.
"Sir, if you are talking jestingly of this, I don't talk with
you. If you mean to be serious, I think him one of the
worst of men; a rascal, who ought to be hunted out of society, as he has been. Three or four nations have expelled
him: and it is a shame that he is protected in this country."

BOSWELL. "I don't deny, Sir, but that his novel may, per-haps, do harm; but I cannot think his intention was bad." JOHNSON. "Sir, that will not do. We cannot prove any man's intention to be bad. You may shoot a man through the head, and say you intended to miss him; but the Judge will order you to be hanged. An alleged want of intention, when evil is committed, will not be allowed in a court of justice. Rousseau, Sir, is a very bad man. I would sooner sign a sentence for his transportation, than that of any felon who has gone from the Old Bailey these many years. Yes, I should like to have him work in the plantations." BOS-WELL. "Sir, do you think him as bad a man as Voltaire?" JOHNSON. "Why, Sir, it is difficult to settle the proportion of iniquity between them."

On his favourite subject of subordination, Johnson said, "So far is it from being true that men are naturally equal, that no two people can be half an hour together, but one shall acquire an evident superiority over the other."

I mentioned the advice given us by philosophers, to con-sole ourselves, when distressed or embarrassed, by thinking of those who are in a worse situation than ourselves. This, I observed, could not apply to all, for there must be some who have nobody worse than they are. JOHNSON. "Why, to be sure, Sir, there are; but they don't know it. There is no being so poor and so contemptible, who does not think there is somebody still poorer, and still more contempt-ible."

One evening, when a young gentleman teased him with an account of the infidelity of his servant, who, he said, would not believe the scriptures, because he could not read them in the original tongues, and be sure that they were not invented; "Why, foolish fellow, (said Johnson,) has he any better authority for almost every thing that he believes?" BOSWELL. "Then the vulgar, Sir, never can know they are right, but must submit themselves to the learned." JOHN-SON. "To be sure, Sir. The vulgar are the children of the State, and must be taught like children." BOSWELL. "Then, Sir, a poor Turk must be a Mahometan, just as a poor Eng-lishman must be a Christian?" JOHNSON. "Why, yes, Sir; and what then? This now is such stuff as I used to talk to my mother, when I first began to think myself a clever fellow; and she ought to have whipt me for it."

Another evening Dr. Goldsmith and I called on him, with the hope of prevailing on him to sup with us at the Mitre. We found him indisposed, and resolved not to go abroad. "Come then, (said Goldsmith,) we will not go to the Mitre to-night, since we cannot have the big man with us." Johnson then called for a bottle of port, of which Goldsmith and I partook, while our friend, now a water-drinker, sat by us. GOLDSMITH. "I think, Mr. Johnson, you don't go near the theatres now. You give yourself no more concern about a new play, than if you had never had any thing to do with the stage." JOHNSON. "Why, Sir, our tastes greatly alter. The lad does not care for the child's rattle, and the old man does not care for the young man's whore." GOLDSMITH. "Nay, Sir; but your Muse was not a whore." JOHNSON. "Sir, I do not think she was. But as we advance in the journey of life we drop some of the things which have pleased us; whether it be that we are fatigued and don't choose to carry so many things any farther, or that we find other things which we like better." BOSWELL. "But, Sir, why don't you give us something in some other way?" GOLDSMITH. "Ay, Sir, we have a claim upon you." JOHNSON. "No, Sir, I am not obliged to do any more. No man is obliged to do as much as he can do. A man is to have part of his life to himself. If a soldier has fought a good many campaigns, he is not to be blamed, if he retires to ease and tranquillity. A physician, who has practised long in a great city, may be excused, if he retires to a small town, and takes less practice. Now, Sir, the good I can do by my conversation bears the same proportion to the good I can do by my writings, that the practice of a physician, retired to a small town, does to his practice in a great city." BOSWELL. "But I wonder, Sir, you have not more pleasure in writing than in not writing." JOHNSON. "Sir, you *may* wonder."

He talked of making verses, and observed, "The great difficulty is, to know when you have made good ones. When composing, I have generally had them in my mind, perhaps fifty at a time, walking up and down in my room; and then

I have written them down, and often, from laziness, have written only half lines. I have written a hundred lines in a day. I remember, I wrote a hundred lines of 'The Vanity of Human Wishes' in a day. Doctor, (turning to Goldsmith,) I am not quite idle; I made one line t'other day; but I made no more." GOLDSMITH. "Let us hear it; we'll put a bad one to it." JOHNSON. "No, Sir; I have forgot it."

In February, 1767, there happened one of the most remarkable incidents of Johnson's life, which gratified his monarchical enthusiasm, and which he loved to relate with all its circumstances, when requested by his friends. This was his being honoured by a private conversation with his Majesty, in the library at the Queen's house. He had frequently visited those splendid rooms, and noble collection of books, which he used to say was more numerous and curious than he supposed any person could have made in the time which the King had employed. Mr. Barnard, the librarian, took care that he should have every accommodation that should contribute to his ease and convenience, while indulging his literary taste in that place: so that he had here a very agreeable resource at leisure hours.

His Majesty having been informed of his occasional visits, was pleased to signify a desire that he should be told when Dr. Johnson came next to the library. Accordingly, the next time that Johnson did come, as soon as he was fairly engaged with a book, on which, while he sat by the fire, he seemed quite intent, Mr. Barnard stole round to the apartment where the King was, and, in obedience to his Majesty's commands, mentioned that Dr. Johnson was then in the library. His Majesty said he was at leisure, and would go to him: upon which Mr. Barnard took one of the candles that stood on the King's table, and lighted his Majesty through a suite of rooms, till they came to a private door into the library, of which his Majesty had the key. Being entered, Mr. Barnard stepped forward hastily to Dr. Johnson, who was still in a profound study, and whispered him, "Sir, here is the King." Johnson started up, and stood still. His Majesty approached him, and at once was courteously easy.

His Majesty began by observing, that he understood he

came sometimes to the library; and then mentioned his having heard that the Doctor had been lately at Oxford, asked
him if he was not fond of going thither. To which Johnson
answered, that he was indeed fond of going to Oxford
sometimes, but was likewise glad to come back again. The
King then asked him what they were doing at Oxford.
Johnson answered, he could not much commend their diligence, but that in some respects they were mended, for they
had put their press under better regulations, and were at
that time printing Polybius. He was then asked whether
there were better libraries at Oxford or Cambridge. He answered, he believed the Bodleian was larger than any they
had at Cambridge; at the same time adding, "I hope,
whether we have more books or not than they have at Cambridge, we shall make as good use of them as they do."
Being asked whether All-Souls or Christ-Church library
was the largest, he answered, "All-Souls library is the largest we have, except the Bodleian." "Ay, (said the King,)
that is the publick library."

His Majesty enquired if he was then writing any thing.
He answered, he was not, for he had pretty well told the
world what he knew, and must now read to acquire more
knowledge. The King, as it should seem with a view to urge
him to rely on his own stores as an original writer, and to
continue his labours, then said, "I do not think you borrow
much from any body." Johnson said, he thought he had already done his part as a writer. "I should have thought so
too, (said the King,) if you had not written so well."—
Johnson observed to me, upon this, that "No man could
have paid a handsomer compliment; and it was fit for a
King to pay. It was decisive." When asked by another
friend, at Sir Joshua Reynold's, whether he made any reply to this high compliment, he answered, "No, Sir. When
the King had said it, it was to be so. It was not for me to
bandy civilities with my Sovereign."

His Majesty having observed to him that he supposed he
must have read a great deal; Johnson answered, that he
thought more than he read; that he had read a great deal in
the early part of his life, but having fallen into ill health,
he had not been able to read much, compared with others.

His Majesty then asked him what he thought of Lord Lyttelton's history, which was then just published. Johnson said, he thought his style pretty good, but that he had blamed Henry the Second rather too much. "Why, (said the King,) they seldom do these things by halves." "No, Sir, (answered Johnson,) not to Kings." But fearing to be misunderstood, he proceeded to explain himself; and immediately subjoined, "That for those who spoke worse of Kings than they deserved, he could find no excuse; but that he could more easily conceive how some might speak better of them than they deserved, without any ill intention; for, as Kings had much in their power to give, those who were favoured by them would frequently, from gratitude, exaggerate their praises: and as this proceeded from a good motive, it was certainly excusable, as far as errour could be excusable."

The King then asked him what he thought of Dr. Hill. Johnson answered, that he was an ingenious man, but had no veracity; and immediately mentioned, as an instance of it, an assertion of that writer, that he had seen objects magnified to a much greater degree by using three or four microscopes at a time than by using one. "Now, (added Johnson,) every one acquainted with microscopes knows, that the more of them he looks through, the less the object will appear." "Why, (replied the King,) this is not only telling an untruth, but telling it clumsily; for, if that be the case, every one who can look through a microscope will be able to detect him."

"I now, (said Johnson to his friends, when relating what had passed,) began to consider that I was deprecating this man in the estimation of his Sovereign, and thought it was time for me to say something that might be more favourable." He added, therefore, that Dr. Hill was, notwithstanding, a very curious observer; and if he would have been contented to tell the world no more than he knew, he might have been a very considerable man, and needed not to have recourse to such mean expedients to raise his reputation.

His Majesty expressed a desire to have the literary biography of this country ably executed, and proposed to Dr.

Johnson to undertake it. Johnson signified his readiness to comply with his Majesty's wishes.

During the whole of this interview, Johnson talked to his Majesty with profound respect, but still in his firm manly manner, with a sonorous voice, and never in that subdued tone which is commonly used at the levee and in the drawing room. After the King withdrew, Johnson shewed himself highly pleased with his Majesty's conversation, and gracious behaviour. He said to Mr. Barnard, "Sir, they may talk of the King as they will; but he is the finest gentleman I have ever seen." And he afterwards observed to Mr. Langton, "Sir, his manners are those of as fine a gentleman as we may suppose Lewis the Fourteenth or Charles the Second."

At Sir Joshua Reynolds's, where a circle of Johnson's friends was collected round him to hear his account of this memorable conversation, Dr. Joseph Warton, in his frank and lively manner, was very active in pressing him to mention the particulars. "Come now, Sir, this is an interesting matter; do favour us with it." Johnson, with great good humour, complied.

He told them, "I found his Majesty wished I should talk and I made it my business to talk. I find it does a man good to be talked to by his sovereign. In the first place, a man cannot be in a passion—." Here some question interrupted him, which is to be regretted, as he certainly would have pointed out and illustrated many circumstances of advantage, from being in a situation, where the powers of the mind are at once excited to vigorous exertion, and tempered by reverential awe.

During all the time in which Dr. Johnson was employed in relating to the circle at Sir Joshua Reynolds's the particulars of what passed between the King and him, Dr. Goldsmith remained unmoved upon a sopha at some distance, affecting not to join in the least in the eager curiosity of the company. He assigned as a reason for his gloom and seeming inattention, that he apprehended Johnson had relinquished his purpose of furnishing him with a Prologue to his play, with the hopes of which he had been flattered; but it was strongly suspected that he was fretting with chagrin and envy at the singular honour Dr. Johnson had lately enjoyed. At length, the frankness, and simplicity of his natural character prevailed. He sprung from the sopha, advanced to Johnson, and in a kind of flutter, from imagining himself in the situation which he had just been hearing described, exclaimed, "Well, you acquitted yourself in this conversation better than I should have done; for I should have bowed and stammered through the whole of it."

An essay, written by Mr. Deane, a Divine of the Church of England, maintaining the future life of brutes, by an explication of certain parts of the scriptures, was mentioned, and the doctrine insisted on by a gentleman who seemed fond of curious speculation. Johnson, who did not like to hear of any thing concerning a future state which was not authorized by the regular canons of orthodoxy, discouraged this talk; and being offended at its continuation, he watched an opportunity to give the gentleman a blow of reprehension. So, when the poor speculatist, with a serious metaphysical pensive face, addressed him, "But really, Sir, when we see a very sensible dog, we don't know what to think of him," Johnson, rolling with joy at the thought which beamed in his eye, turned quickly round, and replied, "True, Sir: and when we see a very foolish *fellow,* we don't know what to think of *him.*" He then rose up, strided to the fire, and stood for some time laughing and exulting.

I told him that I had several times when in Italy, seen the experiment of placing a scorpion within a circle of burning coals; that it ran round and round in extreme pain; and finding no way to escape, retired to the centre, and like a true Stoick philosopher, darted its sting into its head, and thus at once, freed itself from its woes. *"This must end 'em."* I said, this was a curious fact, as it shewed deliberate suicide in a reptile. Johnson would not admit the fact. He said, Maupertuis was of opinion that it does not kill itself, but dies of the heat, that it gets to the centre of the circle, as the coolest place; that its turning its tail in upon its head is merely a convulsion, and that it does not sting itself. He said he would be satisfied if the great anatomist Morgagni, after dissecting a scorpion on which the experiment had been tried, should certify that its sting had penetrated into its head.

He talked of the heinousness of the crime of adultery, by which the peace of families was destroyed. He said, "Confusion of progeny constitutes the essence of the crime; and therefore a woman who breaks her marriage vows is much more criminal than a man who does it. A man, to be sure, is criminal in the sight of GOD; but he does not do his wife a very material injury, if he does not insult her; if, for instance, from mere wantonness of appetite, he steals privately to her chambermaid. Sir, a wife ought not greatly to resent this. I would not receive home a daughter who had run away from her husband on that account. A wife should study to reclaim her husband by more attention to please him. Sir, a man will not, once in a hundred instances, leave his wife and go to a harlot, if his wife has not been negligent of pleasing."

I asked him if it was not hard that one deviation from chastity should so absolutely ruin a young woman. JOHNSON. "Why no, Sir; it is the great principle which she is taught. When she has given up that principle, she has given up every notion of female honour and virtue, which are all included in chastity."

A gentleman talked to him of a lady whom he greatly admired and wished to marry, but was afraid of her superiority of talents. "Sir, (said he,) you need not be afraid; marry her. Before a year goes about, you'll find that reason much weaker, and that wit not so bright." Yet the gentleman may be justified in his apprehension by one of Dr. Johnson's admirable sentences in his life of Waller: "He doubtless praised many whom he would have been afraid to marry; and, perhaps, married one whom he would have been ashamed to praise. Many qualities contribute to domestick happiness, upon which poetry has no colours to bestow: and many airs and sallies may delight imagination, which he who flatters them never can approve."

He praised Signor Baretti. "His account of Italy is a very entertaining book; and, Sir, I know no man who carries his head higher in conversation than Baretti. There are strong powers in his mind. He has not, indeed, many hooks; but with what hooks he has, he grapples very forcibly."

His sincere regard for Francis Barber, his faithful negro servant, made him so desirous of his further improvement, that he now placed him at school at Bishop Stortford, in Hertfordshire. This humane attention does Johnson's heart much honour.

Soon afterwards, he supped at the Crown and Anchor tavern, in the Strand, with a company whom I collected to meet him. They were Dr. Percy, now Bishop of Dromore, Dr. Douglas, now Bishop of Salisbury, Mr. Langton, Dr. Robertson the Historian, Dr. Hugh Blair, and Mr. Thomas Davies, who wished much to be introduced to these eminent Scotch literati; but on the present occasion, he had very little opportunity of hearing them talk, for with an excess of prudence, for which Johnson afterwards found fault with them, they hardly opened their lips, and that only to say something which they were certain would not expose them to the sword of Goliath; such was their anxiety for their fame when in the presence of Johnson. He was this evening in remarkable vigour of mind, and eager to exert himself in conversation, which he did with great readiness and fluency.

He was vehement against old Dr. Mounsey, of Chelsea College, as "a fellow who swore and talked bawdy." "I have often been in his company, (said Dr. Percy,) and never heard him swear or talk bawdy." Mr. Davies who sat next to Dr. Percy, having after this had some conversation aside with him, made a discovery which, in his zeal to pay court to Dr. Johnson, he eagerly proclaimed aloud from the foot of the table: "O, Sir, I have found out a very good reason why Dr. Percy never heard Mounsey swear or talk bawdy, for he tells me he never saw him but at the Duke of Northumberland's table." "And so, Sir, (said Dr. Johnson loudly to Dr. Percy) you would shield this man from the charge of swearing and talking bawdy, because he did not do so at the Duke of Northumberland's table. Sir, you might as well tell us that you had seen him hold up his hand at the Old Bailey, and he neither swore nor talked bawdy; or that you had seen him in the cart at Tyburn, and he neither

swore nor talked bawdy. And is it thus, Sir, that you presume to controvert what I have related?" Dr. Johnson's animadversion was uttered in such a manner, that Dr. Percy
seemed to be displeased, and soon afterwards left the company, of which Johnson did not at that time take any
notice.

Swift having been mentioned, Johnson, as usual, treated
him with little respect as an authour. Some of us endeavoured to support the Dean of St. Patrick's, by various arguments. One in particular praised his "Conduct of the Allies."
JOHNSON. "Sir, his 'Conduct of the Allies' is a performance
of very little ability." "Surely, Sir, (said Dr. Douglas,) you
must allow it has strong facts." JOHNSON. "Why yes, Sir;
but what is that to the merit of the composition? In the
Sessions-paper of the Old Bailey there are strong facts.
House-breaking is a strong fact; robbery is a strong fact;
and murder is a *mighty* strong fact: but is great praise due
to the historian of those strong facts? No, Sir, Swift has told
what he had to tell distinctly enough, but that is all. He had
to count ten, and he has counted it right."

When I called upon Dr. Johnson next morning, I found
him highly satisfied with his colloquial prowess the preceding evening. "Well, (said he,) we had good talk." Bos-
WELL. "Yes, Sir, you tossed and gored several persons."

The late Alexander Earl of Eglintoune, who loved wit
more than wine, and men of genius more than sycophants,
had a great admiration of Johnson; but from the remarkable elegance of his own manners, was, perhaps, too deli-
cately sensible of the roughness which sometimes appeared
in Johnson's behaviour. One evening about this time, when
his Lordship did me the honour to sup at my lodgings with
Dr. Robertson and several other men of literary distinction,
he regretted that Johnson had not been educated with more
refinement, and lived more in polished society. "No, no,
my Lord, (said Signor Baretti,) do with him what you
would, he would always have been a bear." "True, (answered the Earl, with a smile,) but he would have been a
dancing bear."

To obviate all the reflections which have gone round
the world to Johnson's prejudice, by applying to him the

epithet of a *bear*, let me impress upon my readers a just and happy saying of my friend Goldsmith, who knew him well: "Johnson, to be sure, has a roughness in his manner: but no man alive has a more tender heart. *He has nothing of the bear but his skin.*"

In 1769, so far as I can discover, the publick was favoured with nothing of Johnson's composition, either for himself or any of his friends. His Majesty having the preceding year instituted the Royal Academy of Arts in London, Johnson had now the honour of being appointed Professor in Ancient Literature.

I came to London in the autumn, and having informed him that I was going to be married in a few months, I wished to have as much of his conversation as I could before engaging in a state of life which would probably keep me more in Scotland, and prevent me seeing him so often as when I was a single man; but I found he was at Brighthelmstone with Mr. and Mrs. Thrale.

From Brighthelmstone Dr. Johnson wrote me the following letter, which they who may think that I ought to have suppressed, must have less ardent feelings than I have always avowed.

"To James Boswell, Esq.

"dear sir,

*   *   *   *

"I am glad that you are going to be married; and as I wish you well in things of less importance, wish you well with proportionate ardour in this crisis of your life. What I can contribute to your happiness, I should be very unwilling to withhold; for I have always loved and valued you, and shall love you and value you still more, as you become more regular and useful: effects which a happy marriage will hardly fail to produce.

*   *   *   *

"I am, dear Sir,
"Your most affectionate humble Servant,
"Sam. Johnson."

"Brighthelmstone,
Sept. 9, 1769."

After his return to town, we met frequently, and I continued the practice of making notes of his conversation, though not with so much assiduity as I wish I had done. At this time, indeed, I had a sufficient excuse for not being able to appropriate so much time to my journal; for General Paoli, after Corsica had been overpowered by the monarchy of France, was now no longer at the head of his brave countrymen, but having with difficulty escaped from his native island, had sought an asylum in Great-Britain; and it was my duty, as well as my pleasure, to attend much upon him. Such particulars of Johnson's conversation at this period as I have committed to writing, I shall here introduce, without any strict attention to methodical arrangement. Sometimes short notes of different days shall be blended together, and sometimes a day may seem important enough to be separately distinguished.

On the 30th of September we dined together at the Mitre. I attempted to argue for the superiour happiness of the savage life, upon the usual fanciful topicks. JOHNSON. "Sir, there can be nothing more false. The savages have no bodily advantages beyond those of civilised men. They have not better health; and as to care or mental uneasiness, they are not above it, but below it, like bears. No, Sir; you are not to talk such paradox: let me have no more on't. It cannot entertain, far less can it instruct. Lord Monboddo, one of your Scotch Judges, talked a great deal of such nonsense. I suffered *him;* but I will not suffer *you.*" BOSWELL. "But, Sir, does not Rousseau talk such nonsense?" JOHNSON. "True, Sir, but Rousseau *knows* he is talking nonsense, and laughs at the world for staring at him." BOSWELL. "How so, Sir?" JOHNSON. "Why, Sir, a man who talks nonsense so well, must know that he is talking nonsense. But I am *afraid,* (chuckling and laughing,) Monboddo does *not* know that he is talking nonsense."

Talking of a London life, he said, "The happiness of London is not to be conceived but by those who have been in it. I will venture to say, there is more learning and science within the circumference of ten miles from where we now sit, than in all the rest of the kingdom." BOSWELL. "The only disadvantage is the great distance at which people live from one another." JOHNSON. "Yes, Sir; but that is occasioned by the largeness of it, which is the cause of all the other advantages." BOSWELL. "Sometimes I have been in the humour of wishing to retire to a desart." JOHNSON. "Sir, you have desart enough in Scotland."

Although I had promised myself a great deal of instructive conversation with him on the conduct of the married state, of which I had then a near prospect, he did not say much upon that topick. Mr. Seward heard him once say, that "a man has a very bad chance for happiness in that state, unless he marries a woman of very strong and fixed principles of religion." He maintained to me contrary to the common notion, that a woman would not be the worse wife for being learned; in which, from all that I have observed of *Artemisias*, I humbly differed from him.

When I censured a gentleman of my acquaintance for marrying a second time, as it shewed a disregard of his first wife, he said "Not at all, Sir. On the contrary, were he not to marry again, it might be concluded that his first wife had given him a disgust to marriage; but by taking a second wife he pays the highest compliment to the first, by shewing that she made him so happy as a married man, that he wishes to be so a second time." So ingenious a turn did he give to this delicate question. And yet, on another occasion, he owned that he once had almost asked a promise of Mrs. Johnson that she would not marry again, but had checked himself. Indeed I cannot help thinking, that in his case the request would have been unreasonable; for if Mrs. Johnson forgot, or thought it no injury to the memory of her first love,—the husband of her youth and the father of her children,—to make a second marriage, why should she be precluded from a third, should she be so inclined? In Johnson's persevering fond appropriation of his *Tetty*, even after her decease, he seems totally to have overlooked the prior claim of the honest Birmingham trader. I presume that her having been married before had, at times, given him some uneasiness; for I remember his observing upon the marriage of one of our common friends, "He has done a very foolish thing, Sir; he has married a widow, when he might have had a maid."

On Thursday, October 19, I passed the evening with him at his house. I complained that he had not mentioned Garrick in his Preface to Shakspeare; and asked him if he did not admire him. JOHNSON. "Yes, as 'a poor player, who frets and struts his hour upon the stage;'—as a shadow." BOSWELL. "But has he not brought Shakspeare into notice?" JOHNSON. "Sir, to allow that, would be to lampoon the age. Many of Shakspeare's plays are the worse for being acted: Macbeth, for instance." BOSWELL. "What, Sir, is nothing gained by decoration and action? Indeed, I do wish that you had mentioned Garrick." JOHNSON. "My dear Sir, had I mentioned him, I must have mentioned many more; Mrs. Pritchard, Mrs. Cibber,—nay, and Mr. Cibber too; he too altered Shakspeare." BOSWELL. "You have read his apology, Sir?" JOHNSON. "Yes, it is very entertaining. But as for Cibber himself, taking from his conversation all that he ought not to have said, he was a poor creature. I remember when he brought me one of his Odes to have my opinion of it, I could not bear such nonsense, and would not let him read it to the end; so little respect had I for *that great man!* (laughing.) Yet I remember Richardson wondering that I could treat him with familiarity."

I mentioned to him that I had seen the execution of several convicts at Tyburn, two days before, and that none of them seemed to be under any concern. JOHNSON. "Most of them, Sir, have never thought at all." BOSWELL. "But is not the fear of death natural to man?" JOHNSON. "So much so, Sir, that the whole of life is but keeping away the thoughts of it." He then, in a low and earnest tone, talked of his meditating upon the awful hour of his own dissolution, and in what manner he should conduct himself upon that occasion: "I know not (said he,) whether I should wish to have a friend by me, or have it all between GOD and myself."

Talking of our feeling for the distresses of others;— JOHNSON. "Why, Sir, there is much noise made about it, but it is greatly exaggerated. No, Sir, we have a certain degree of feeling to prompt us to do good; more than that, Providence does not intend. It would be misery to no purpose." BOSWELL. "But suppose now, Sir, that one of your intimate friends were apprehended for an offence for which he might be hanged." JOHNSON. "I should do what I could to bail him, and give him any other assistance; but if he were once fairly hanged, I should not suffer." BOSWELL. "Would you eat your dinner that day, Sir?" JOHNSON. "Yes, Sir; and eat it as if he were eating it with me. Why, there's Baretti, who is to be tried for his life to-morrow, friends have risen up for him on every side; yet if he should be hanged, none of them will eat a slice of plum-pudding the less. Sir, that sympathetick feeling goes a very little way in depressing the mind."

Next day, October 20, he appeared, for the only time I suppose in his life, as a witness in a Court of Justice, being called to give evidence to the character of Mr. Baretti, who having stabbed a man in the street, was arraigned at the Old Bailey for murder. Never did such a constellation of genius enlighten the aweful Sessions House, emphatically called JUSTICE HALL; Mr. Burke, Mr. Garrick, Mr. Beauclerk, and Dr. Johnson: and undoubtedly their favourable testimony had due weight with the Court and Jury. Johnson gave his evidence in a slow, deliberate, and distinct manner, which was uncommonly impressive. It is well known that Mr. Baretti was acquitted.

Russia being mentioned as likely to become a great empire, by the rapid increase of population:—JOHNSON. "Why, Sir, I see no prospect of their propagating more. They can have no more children than they can get. I know of no way to make them breed more than they do. It is not from reason and prudence that people marry, but from inclination. A man is poor; he thinks, 'I cannot be worse, and so I'll e'en take Peggy.' " BOSWELL. "But have not nations been more populous at one period than another?" JOHNSON. "Yes, Sir; but that has been owing to the people being less thinned at one period than another, whether by emigrations, war, or pestilence, not by their being more or less prolifick. Births at all times bear the same proportion to the same number of people."

He observed, "Providence has wisely ordered that the

more numerous men are, the more difficult it is for them to agree in any thing, and so they are governed. There is no doubt, that if the poor should reason, 'We'll be the poor no longer, we'll make the rich take their turn,' they could easily do it, were it not that they can't agree. So the common soldiers, though so much more numerous than their officers, are governed by them for the same reason."

He said, "Mankind have a strong attachment to the habitations to which they have been accustomed. You see the inhabitants of Norway do not with one consent quit it, and go to some part of America, where there is a mild climate, and where they may have the same produce from land, with the tenth part of the labour. No, Sir; their affection for their old dwellings, and the terrour of a general change, keep them at home. Thus, we see many of the finest spots in the world thinly inhabited, and many rugged spots well inhabited."

I had hired a Bohemian as my servant while I remained in London, and being much pleased with him, I asked Dr. Johnson whether his being a Roman Catholick should prevent my taking him with me to Scotland. JOHNSON. "Why no, Sir. If *he* has no objections, you can have none." BOSWELL. "So, Sir, you are no great enemy to the Roman Catholick religion." JOHNSON. "No more, Sir, than to the Presbyterian religion." BOSWELL. "You are joking." JOHNSON. "No, Sir, I really think so. Nay, Sir, of the two, I prefer the Popish." BOSWELL. "How so, Sir?" JOHNSON. "Why, Sir, the Presbyterians have no church, no apostolical ordination." BOSWELL. "And do you think that absolutely essential, Sir?" JOHNSON. "Why, Sir, as it was an apostolical institution, I think it is dangerous to be without it. And, Sir, the Presbyterians have no publick worship: they have no form of prayer in which they know they are to join. They go to hear a man pray, and are to judge whether they will join with him." BOSWELL. "But, Sir, their doctrine is the same with that of the Church of England. Their confession of faith, and the thirty-nine articles contain the same points, even the doctrine of predestination." JOHNSON. "Why, yes, Sir; predestination was a part of the clamour of the times, so it is mentioned in our articles, but with as little positiveness as could be." BOSWELL. "Is it necessary, Sir, to believe all the thirty-nine articles?" JOHNson. "Why, Sir, that is a question which has been much agitated. Some have thought it necessary that they should all be believed; others have considered them to be only articles of peace, that is to say, you are not to preach against them."

I proceeded: "What do you think, Sir, of Purgatory, as believed by the Roman Catholicks?" JOHNSON. "Why, Sir, it is a very harmless doctrine. They are of opinion that the generality of mankind are neither so obstinately wicked as to deserve everlasting punishment, nor so good as to merit being admitted into the society of blessed spirits; and therefore that GOD is graciously pleased to allow of a middle state, where they may be purified by certain degrees of suffering. You see, Sir, there is nothing unreasonable in this." BOSWELL. "But then, Sir, their masses for the dead?" JOHNson. "Why, Sir, if it be once established that there are souls in purgatory, it is as proper to pray for *them,* as for our brethren of mankind who are yet in this life." BOSWELL. "The idolatry of the Mass?" JOHNSON. "Sir, there is no idolatry in the Mass. They believe GOD to be there, and they adore him." BOSWELL. "The worship of Saints?" JOHNSON. "Sir, they do not worship saints; they invoke them; they only ask their prayers. I am talking all this time of the *doctrines* of the Church of Rome. I grant you that in *practice,* Purgatory is made a lucrative imposition, and that the people do become idolatrous as they recommend themselves to the tutelary protection of particular saints. I think their giving the sacrament only in one kind is criminal, because it is contrary to the express institution of CHRIST, and I wonder how the Council of Trent admitted it." BOSWELL. "Confession?" JOHNSON. "Why, I don't know but that is a good thing. The scripture says, 'Confess your faults one to another,' and the priests confess as well as the laity. Then it must be considered that their absolution is only upon repentance, and often upon penance also. You think your sins may be forgiven without penance, upon repentance alone."

154

DICTIONARY

OF THE

ENGLISH LANGUAGE:

IN WHICH

The WORDS are deduced from their ORIGINALS,

AND

ILLUSTRATED in their DIFFERENT SIGNIFICATIONS

BY

EXAMPLES from the beſt WRITERS.

TO WHICH ARE PREFIXED,

A HISTORY of the LANGUAGE,

AND

An ENGLISH GRAMMAR.

By SAMUEL JOHNSON, A.M.

In TWO VOLUMES.

VOL. I.

Cum tabulis animum cenſoris ſumet honeſti :
Audebit quæcunque parum ſplendoris habebunt,
Et ſine pondere erunt, et honore indigna ferentur.
Verba movere loco ; quamvis invita recedant,
Et verſentur adhuc intra penetralia Veſtæ :
Obſcurata diu populo bonus eruet, atque
Proferet in lucem ſpecioſa vocabula rerum,
Quæ priſcis memorata Catonibus atque Cethegis,
Nunc ſitus informis premit et deſerta vetuſtas.　　　　Hor.

LONDON

Printed by W. Strahan,

For J. and P. Knapton ; T. and T. Longman ; C. Hitch and L. Hawes ;
A. Millar ; and R. and J. Dodsley.

MDCCLV.

8
The title page of the first edition of Dr. Johnson's *Dictionary*. Its
publication brought him his first fame and a degree from Oxford.

When we were alone, I introduced the subject of death, and endeavoured to maintain that the fear of it might be got over. I told him that David Hume said to me, he was no more uneasy to think he should *not be* after his life, than that he *had not been* before he began to exist. JOHNSON. "Sir, if he really thinks so, his perceptions are disturbed; he is mad; if he does not think so, he lies. He may tell you, he holds his finger in the flame of a candle, without feeling pain; would you believe him? When he dies, he at least gives up all he has." BOSWELL. "Foote, Sir, told me, that when he was very ill he was not afraid to die." JOHNSON. "It is not true, Sir. Hold a pistol to Foote's breast, or to Hume's breast, and threaten to kill them, and you'll see how they behave." BOSWELL. "But may we not fortify our minds for the approach of death?"—Here I am sensible I was in the wrong, to bring before his view what he ever looked upon with horrour; for although when in a celestial frame of mind in his "Vanity of Human Wishes," he has supposed death to be "kind Nature's signal for retreat," from this state of being to "a happier seat," his thoughts upon this awful change were in general full of dismal apprehensions. His mind resembled the vast amphitheatre, the Colisæum at Rome. In the centre stood his judgement, which like a mighty gladiator, combated those apprehensions that, like the wild beasts of the *Arena*, were all around in cells, ready to be let out upon him. After a conflict, he drives them back into their dens; but not killing them, they were still assailing him. To my question, whether we might not fortify our minds for the approach of death, he answered, in a passion, "No, Sir, let it alone. It matters not how a man dies, but how he lives. The act of dying is not of importance, it lasts so short a time." He added, (with an earnest look,) "A man knows it must be so, and submits. It will do him no good to whine."

I attempted to continue the conversation. He was so provoked, that he said: "Give us no more of this;" and was thrown into such a state of agitation, that he expressed himself in a way that alarmed and distressed me; shewed an impatience that I should leave him, and when I was going away, called to me sternly, "Don't let us meet to-mor-row."

I went home exceedingly uneasy. All the harsh observations which I had ever heard made upon his character, crowded into my mind; and I seemed to myself like the man who had put his head into the lion's mouth a great many times with perfect safety, but at last had it bit off.

Next morning I sent him a note, stating that I might have been in the wrong, but it was not intentionally; he was therefore, I could not help thinking, too severe upon me. That notwithstanding our agreement not to meet that day, I would call on him in my way to the city, and stay five minutes by my watch. "You are, (said I) in my mind, since last night, surrounded with cloud and storm. Let me have a glimpse of sunshine, and go about my affairs in serenity and cheerfulness."

Upon entering his study, I was glad that he was not alone, which would have made our meeting more awkward. There were with him Mr. Stevens and Mr. Tyers, both of whom I now saw for the first time. My note had, on his own reflection, softened him, for he received me very complacently; so that I unexpectedly found myself at ease; and joined in the conversation.

I whispered him, "Well, Sir, you are now in good humour." JOHNSON. "Yes, Sir." I was going to leave him, and had got as far as the staircase. He stopped me, and smiling, said, "Get you gone *in;*" a curious mode of inviting me to stay, which I accordingly did for some time longer.

This little incidental quarrel and reconciliation, which, perhaps, I may be thought to have detailed too minutely, must be esteemed as one of many proofs which his friends had, that though he might be charged with *bad humour* at times, he was always a *good-natured man;* and I have heard Sir Joshua Reynolds, a nice and delicate observer of manners, particularly remark, that when upon any occasion Johnson had been rough to any person in company, he took the first opportunity of reconciliation, by drinking to him, or addressing his discourse to him; but if he found his dignified indirect overtures sullenly neglected, he was

156

quite indifferent, and considered himself as having done all that he ought to do, and the other as now in the wrong.

"To Mr. Francis Barber, at Mrs. Clapp's, Bishop-
Stortford, Hertfordshire

"dear francis,

"I am at last sat down to write to you, and should very much blame myself for having neglected you so long, if I did not impute that and many other failings to want of health. I hope not to be so long silent again. I am very well satisfied with your progress, if you can really perform the exercises which you are set; and I hope Mr. Ellis does not suffer you to impose on him, or on yourself.

"Make my compliments to Mr. Ellis, and to Mrs. Clapp, and Mr. Smith.

"Let me know what English books you read for your entertainment. You can never be wise unless you love reading.

"Do not imagine that I shall forget or forsake you; for if, when I examine you, I find that you have not lost your time, you shall want no encouragement from

"Yours affectionately,
"Sam. Johnson."

"London, Sept. 25, 1770."

I shall present my readers with some *Collectanea*, obligingly furnished to me by the Rev. Dr. Maxwell, of Falkland, in Ireland, some time assistant preacher at the Temple, and for many years the social friend of Johnson.

"He frequently gave all the silver in his pocket to the poor, who watched him, between his house and the tavern where he dined. He walked the streets at all hours, and said he was never robbed, for the rogues knew he had little money, nor had the appearance of having much.

"Though the most accessible and communicative man alive, yet when he suspected he was invited to be exhibited, he constantly spurned the invitation.

"Two young women from Staffordshire visited him when I was present, to consult him on the subject of methodism, to which they were inclined. 'Come, (said he,) you pretty fools, dine with Maxwell and me at the Mitre, and we will talk over that subject;' which they did, and after dinner he took one of them upon his knee, and fondled her for half an hour together.

"Burton's 'Anatomy of Melancholy,' he said, was the only book that ever took him out of bed two hours sooner than he wished to rise.

"On my observing to him that a certain gentleman had remained silent the whole evening, in the midst of a very brilliant and learned society, 'Sir, (said he,) the conversation overflowed, and drowned him.'

"Speaking of the *inward light,* to which some methodists pretended, he said, it was a principle utterly incompatible with social or civil security. 'If a man (said he,) pretends to a principle of action of which I can know nothing, nay, not so much as that he has it, but only that he pretends to it; how can I tell what that person may be prompted to do? When a person professes to be governed by a written as-certained law, I can then know where to find him.'

"Being asked by a young nobleman, what was become of the gallantry and military spirit of the old English no-bility, he replied, 'Why, my Lord, I'll tell you what is be-come of it: it is gone into the city to look for a fortune.'

"Speaking of a dull tiresome fellow, whom he chanced to meet, he said, 'That fellow seems to me to possess but one idea, and that is a wrong one.'

"A gentleman who had been very unhappy in marriage, married immediately after his wife died: Johnson said, it was the triumph of hope over experience.

"He observed that a man of sense and education should meet a suitable companion in a wife. It was a miserable thing when the conversation could only be such as, whether the mutton should be boiled or roasted, and probably a dis-pute about that.

"He said, foppery was never cured; it was the bad stam-ina of the mind, which, like those of the body, were never rectified: once a coxcomb always a coxcomb.

"To find a substitution for violated morality, he said, was the leading feature in all perversions of religion.

"He observed, 'it was a most mortifying reflection for any man to consider, *what he had done,* compared with what *he might have done.'*

"He said few people had intellectual resources sufficient to forego the pleasures of wine. They could not otherwise contrive how to fill the interval between dinner and supper.

"One evening at Mrs. Montagu's, where a splendid company was assembled, consisting of the most eminent literary characters, I thought he seemed highly pleased with the respect and attention that were shewn him, and asked him, on our return home, if he was not highly gratified by his visit: 'No, Sir, (said he) not highly *gratified;* yet I do not recollect to have passed many evenings *with fewer objections.'*"

On Tuesday, March 31, he and I dined at General Paoli's. A question was started whether the state of marriage was natural to man. JOHNSON. "Sir, it is so far from being natural for a man and woman to live in a state of marriage, that we find all the motives which they have for remaining in that connection, and the restraints which civilised society imposes to prevent separation, are hardly sufficient to keep them together." The General said, that in a state of nature a man and woman uniting together, would form a strong and constant affection, by the mutual pleasure each would receive; and that the same causes of dissention would not arise between them, as occur between husband and wife in a civilised state. JOHNSON. "Sir, they would have dissentions enough though of another kind. One would choose to go a hunting in this wood, the other in that; one would choose to go a fishing in this lake, the other in that; or, perhaps, one would choose to go a hunting, when the other would choose to go a fishing; and so they would part. Besides, Sir, a savage man and a savage woman meet by chance; and when the man sees another woman that pleases him better, he will leave the first."

We then fell into a disquisition whether there is any beauty independent of utility. The General maintained there was not. Dr. Johnson maintained that there was; and he in-

159

stanced a coffee cup which he held in his hand, the painting of which was of no real use, as the cup could hold the coffee equally well if plain; yet, the painting was beautiful.

We talked of the strange custom of swearing in conversation. The General said, that all barbarous nations swore from a certain violence of temper, that could not be confined to earth, but was always reaching at the powers above. He said, too, that there was greater variety of swearing, in proportion as there was a greater variety of religious ceremonies.

Dr. Johnson went home with me to my lodgings in Conduit-street and drank tea, previous to our going to the Pantheon, which neither of us had seen before.

We then walked to the Pantheon. The first view of it did not strike us so much as Ranelagh, of which he said, the *"coup d'œil* was the finest thing he had ever seen." The truth is, Ranelagh is of a more beautiful form; more of it, or rather indeed the whole *rotunda,* appears at once, and it is better lighted. However, as Johnson observed, we saw the Pantheon in time of mourning, when there was a dull uniformity; whereas we had seen Ranelagh, when the view was enlivened with a gay profusion of colours. Mrs. Bosville, of Gunthwait, in Yorkshire, joined us, and entered into conversation with us. Johnson said to me afterwards, "Sir, this is a mighty intelligent lady."

I said there was not half a guinea's worth of pleasure in seeing this place. JOHNSON. "But, Sir, there is half a guinea's worth of inferiority to other people in not having seen it." BOSWELL. "I doubt, Sir, whether there are many happy people here." JOHNSON. "Yes, Sir, there are many happy people here. There are many people here who are watching hundreds, and who think hundreds are watching them."

Happening to meet Sir Adam Ferguson, I presented him to Dr. Johnson. Sir Adam expressed some apprehension that the Pantheon would encourage luxury. "Sir, (said Johnson,) I am a great friend to publick amusements; for they keep people from vice. You now (addressing himself to me,) would have been with a wench, had you not been here.—O! I forgot you were married."

I mentioned a cause in which I had appeared as counsel at the bar of the General Assembly of the Church of Scotland, where a *Probationer,* (as one licensed to preach, but not yet ordained, is called,) was opposed in his application to be inducted, because it was alledged that he had been guilty of fornication five years before. JOHNSON. "Why, Sir, if he has repented, it is not a sufficient objection. A man who is good enough to go to heaven, is good enough to be a clergyman." I told him, that by the rules of the Church of Scotland, in their "Book of Discipline," if a *scandal* as it is called, is not prosecuted for five years, it cannot afterwards be proceeded upon, "unless it be *of a heinous nature,* or again become flagrant;" and that hence a question arose, whether fornication was a sin of a heinous nature; and that I had maintained, that it did not deserve that epithet, in as much as it was not one of those sins which argue very great depravity of heart: in short, was not, in the general acceptation of mankind a heinous sin. JOHNSON. "No, Sir, it is not a heinous sin. A heinous sin is that for which a man is punished with death or banishment." BOSWELL. "But, Sir, after I had argued that it was not a heinous sin, an old clergyman rose up, and repeating the text of scripture denouncing judgement against whoremongers, asked, whether, considering this, there could be any doubt of fornication being a heinous sin." JOHNSON. "Why, Sir, observe the word *whoremonger.* Every sin, if persisted in, will become heinous. Whoremonger is a dealer in whores as ironmonger is a dealer in iron. But as you don't call a man an ironmonger for buying and selling a penknife; so you don't call a man a whoremonger for getting one wench with child."

On Monday, April 6, I dined with him at Sir Alexander Macdonald's, where was a young officer in the regimentals of the Scots Royal, who talked with a vivacity, fluency, and precision so uncommon, that he attracted particular attention. He proved to be the Honourable Thomas Erskine, youngest brother to the Earl of Buchan, who has since risen into such brilliant reputation at the bar in Westminster-hall.

Fielding being mentioned, Johnson exclaimed, "he was a blockhead;" and upon my expressing my astonishment at so strange an assertion, he said, "What I mean by his being a blockhead is, that he was a barren rascal." BOSWELL. "Will you not allow, Sir, that he draws very natural pictures of human life?" JOHNSON. "Why, Sir, it is of very low life. Richardson used to say, that had he not known who Fielding was, he should have believed he was an ostler. Sir, there is more knowledge of the heart in one letter of Richardson's, than in all 'Tom Jones.' I, indeed, never read 'Joseph Andrews.'" ERSKINE. "Surely, Sir, Richardson is very tedious." JOHNSON. "Why, Sir, if you were to read Richardson for the story, your impatience would be so much fretted that you would hang yourself. But you must read him for the sentiment, and consider the story as only giving occasion to the sentiment."—I have already given my opinion of Fielding; but I cannot refrain from repeating here my wonder at Johnson's excessive and unaccountable depreciation of one of the best writers that England has produced. "Tom Jones" has stood the test of publick opinion with such success, as to have established its great merit, both for the story, the sentiments, and the manners, and also the varieties of diction, so as to leave no doubt of its having an animated truth of execution throughout.

We talked of gaming, and animadverted on it with severity. JOHNSON. "Nay, gentlemen, let us not aggravate the matter. It is not roguery to play with a man who is ignorant of the game, while you are master of it, and so win his money; for he thinks he can play better than you, as you think you can play better than he; and the superior skill carries it." ERSKINE. "He is a fool, but you are not a rogue." JOHNSON. "That's much about the truth, Sir. It must be considered, that a man who only does what every one of the society to which he belongs would do, is not a dishonest man. In the republick of Sparta, it was agreed, that stealing was not dishonourable, if not discovered. I do not commend a society where there is an agreement that would not otherwise be fair, shall be fair; but I maintain, that an individual of any society, who practises what is allowed, is not a dishonest man." BOSWELL. "So then, Sir, you do not think ill of a man who wins perhaps forty thousand pounds in a winter?" JOHNSON. "Sir, I do not call a gamester a dishonest man; but I call him an unsocial man, an unprofitable man. Gaming is a mode of transferring property without producing any intermediate good. Trade gives employment to numbers, and so produces intermediate good."

Mr. Erskine told us, that when he was in the island of Minorca, he not only read prayers, but preached two sermons to the regiment. He seemed to object to the passage in scripture, where we are told that the angel of the Lord smote in one night forty thousand Assyrians. "Sir, (said Johnson,) you should recollect that there was a supernatural interposition; they were destroyed by pestilence. You are not to suppose that the angel of the LORD went about and stabbed each of them with a dagger, or knocked them on the head, man by man."

I talked of the recent expulsion of six students from the University of Oxford, who were methodists, and would not desist from publickly praying and exhorting. JOHNSON. "Sir, that expulsion was extremely just and proper. What have they to do at an University, who are not willing to be taught, but will presume to teach? Where is religion to be learnt, but at an University? Sir, they were examined, and found to be mighty ignorant fellows." BOSWELL. "But, was it not hard, Sir, to expel them, for I am told they were good beings?" JOHNSON. "I believe they might be good beings; but they were not fit to be in the University of Oxford. A cow is a very good animal in the field; but we turn her out of a garden."

Desirous of calling Johnson forth to talk, and exercise his wit, though I should myself be the object of it, I resolutely ventured to undertake the defence of convivial indulgence in wine, though he was not to-night in the most genial humour. After urging the common plausible topicks, I at last had recourse to the maxim, *in vino veritas*, a man who is well warmed with wine will speak truth. JOHNSON. "Why, Sir, that may be an argument for drinking, if you suppose men in general to be liars. But, Sir, I would not keep company with a fellow, who lyes as long as he is sober, and whom you must make drunk before you can get a word of truth out of him."

Mr. Langton told us, he was about to establish a school upon his estate, but it had been suggested to him, that it might have a tendency to make the people less industrious. JOHNSON. "No, Sir. While learning to read and write is a distinction, the few who have that distinction may be the less inclined to work; but when every body learns to read and write, it is no longer a distinction. A man who has a laced waistcoat is too fine a man to work; but if every body had laced waistcoats, we should have people working in laced waistcoats. There are no people whatever more industrious, none who work more, than our manufacturers; yet they have all learned to read and write. Sir, you must not neglect doing a thing immediately good, from fear of remote evil;—from fear of its being abused. A man who has candles may sit up too late, which he would not do if he had not candles; but nobody will deny that the art of making candles, by which light is continued to us beyond the time that the sun gives us light, is a valuable art, and ought to be preserved." BOSWELL. "But, Sir, would it not be better to follow Nature; and go to bed and rise just as nature gives us light or withholds it?" JOHNSON. "No, Sir; for then we should have no kind of equality in the partition of our time between sleeping and waking. It would be very different in different seasons and in different places. In some of the northern parts of Scotland how little light is there in the depth of winter!"

I regretted the reflection in his Preface to Shakspeare against Garrick, to whom we cannot but apply the following passage: "I collated such copies as I could procure, and wished for more, but have not found the collectors of these rarities very communicative." I told him, that Garrick had complained to me of it, and had vindicated himself by assuring me, that Johnson was made welcome to the full use of his collection, and that he left the key of it with a servant, with orders to have a fire and every convenience for him. I found Johnson's notion was, that Garrick wanted to be courted for them, and that, on the contrary, Garrick should have courted him, and sent him the plays of his own accord. But, indeed, considering the slovenly and careless manner in which books were treated by Johnson, it could not be expected that scarce and valuable editions should have been lent to him.

A gentleman having to some of the usual arguments for drinking added this: "You know, Sir, drinking drives away care, and makes us forget whatever is disagreeable. Would not you allow a man to drink for that reason?" JOHNSON. "Yes, Sir, if he sat next *you*."

A learned gentleman, who in the course of conversation wished to inform us of this simple fact, that the Counsel upon the circuit at Shrewsbury were much bitten by fleas, took, I suppose, seven or eight minutes in relating it circumstantially. He in a plenitude of phrase told us, that large bales of woollen cloth were lodged in the town-hall;— that by reason of this, fleas nestled there in prodigious numbers; that the lodgings of the counsel were near the town-hall:—and that those little animals moved from place to place with wonderful agility. Johnson sat in great impatience till the gentleman had finished his tedious narrative, and then burst out (playfully however,) "It is a pity, Sir, that you have not seen a lion; for a flea has taken you such a time, that a lion must have served you a twelvemonth."

He would not allow Scotland to derive any credit from Lord Mansfield; for he was educated in England. "Much (said he,) may be made of a Scotchman, if he be *caught* young."

I mentioned a friend of mine who had resided long in Spain, and was unwilling to return to Britain. JOHNSON. "Sir, he is attached to some woman." BOSWELL. "I rather believe, Sir, it is the fine climate which keeps him there." JOHNSON. "Nay, Sir, how can you talk so? What is *climate* to happiness? Place me in the heart of Asia should I not be exiled? What proportion does climate bear to the complex system of human life? You may advise me to live at Bologna to eat sausages. The sausages there are the best in the world; they lose much by being carried."

At Mr. Thrale's, in the evening, he repeated his usual

paradoxical declamation against action in publick speaking. "Action can have no effect upon reasonable minds. It may augment poise, but it never can enforce argument. If you speak to a dog, you use action; you hold up your hand thus, because he is a brute; and in proportion as men are removed from brutes, action will have the less influence upon them." MRS. THRALE. "What then, Sir, becomes of Demosthenes's saying? 'Action, action, action!' " JOHNSON. "Demosthenes, Madam, spoke to an assembly of brutes; to a barbarous people."

Lord Chesterfield being mentioned, Johnson remarked, that almost all of that celebrated nobleman's witty sayings were puns. He, however, allowed the merit of good wit to his Lordship's saying of Lord Tyrawley and himself, when both very old and infirm: "Tyrawley and I have been dead these two years; but we don't choose to have it known."

I told him that Goldsmith had said to me a few days before, "As I take my shoes from the shoemaker, and my coat from the taylor, so I take my religion from the priest." I regretted this loose way of talking. JOHNSON. "Sir, he knows nothing; he has made up his mind about nothing."

He owned that he thought Hawkesworth was one of his imitators, but he did not think Goldsmith was. Goldsmith, he said, had great merit. BOSWELL. "But, Sir, he is much indebted to you for his getting so high in the publick estimation." JOHNSON. "Why, Sir, he has perhaps got *sooner* to it by his intimacy with me."

Goldsmith, though his vanity often excited him to occasional competition, had a very high regard for Johnson, which he had at this time expressed in the strongest manner in the Dedication of his Comedy, entitled, "She Stoops to Conquer." [1]

He told me that he had twelve or fourteen times attempted to keep a journal of his life but never could persevere. He advised me to do it. "The great thing to be recorded, (said he,) is the state of your own mind; and you

[1] "By inscribing this slight performance to you, I do not mean so much to compliment you as myself. It may do me some honour to inform the publick, that I have lived many years in intimacy with you. It may serve the interests of mankind also to inform them, that the greatest wit may be found in a character, without impairing the most unaffected piety."

should write down every thing that you remember, but you cannot judge at first what is good or bad; and write immediately while the impression is fresh, for it will not be the same a week afterwards."

I again solicited him to communicate to me the particulars of his early life. He said, "You shall have them all for two-pence. I hope you shall know a great deal more of me before you write my Life." He mentioned to me this day many circumstances, which I wrote down when I went home, and have interwoven in the former part of this narrative.

On Tuesday, April 13, he and Dr. Goldsmith and I dined at General Oglethorpe's. Goldsmith expatiated on the common topick, that the race of our people was degenerated, and that this was owing to luxury. JOHNSON. "Sir, in the first place, I doubt the fact. I believe there are as many tall men in England now, as ever there were. But, secondly, supposing the stature of our people to be diminished, that is not owing to luxury; for, Sir, consider to how very small a proportion of our people luxury can reach. Our soldiery, surely, are not luxurious, who live on six-pence a day; and the same remark will apply to almost all the other classes. Luxury, so far as it reaches the poor, will do good to the race of people; it will strengthen and multiply them. Sir, no nation was ever hurt by luxury; for, as I said before, it can reach but to a very few. I admit that the great increase of commerce and manufactures hurts the military spirit of a people; because it produces a competition for something else than martial honours,—a competition for riches. It also hurts the bodies of the people; for you will observe, there is no man who works at any particular trade, but you may know him from his appearance to do so. One part or the other of his body being more used than the rest, he is in some degree deformed: but, Sir, that is not luxury. A tailor sits cross-legged; but that is not luxury." GOLDSMITH. "Come, you're just going to the same place by another road." JOHNSON. "Nay, Sir, I say that is not *luxury*. Let us take a walk from Charing-cross to Whitechapel, through, I suppose, the greatest series of shops in the world, what is there in any of these shops, (if you except gin-shops,) that can do any human being any harm?" GOLDSMITH. "Well, Sir, I'll accept your challenge. The very next shop to Northumberland-house is a pickle-shop." JOHNSON. "Well, Sir: do we not know that a maid can in one afternoon make pickles sufficient to serve a whole family for a year? nay, that five pickle-shops can serve all the kingdom? Besides, Sir, there is no harm done to any body by the making of pickles, or the eating of pickles."

We drank tea with the ladies; and Goldsmith sung Tony Lumpkin's song in his comedy, "She Stoops to Conquer," and a very pretty one, to an Irish tune, which he had designed foɪ Miss Hardcastle: but as Mrs. Bulkeley, who played the part, could not sing, it was left out. He afterwards wrote it down for me, by which means it was preserved, and now appears amongst his poems. Dr. Johnson, in his way home, stopped at my lodgings in Piccadilly, and sat with me, drinking tea a second time, till a late hour.

On Wednesday, April 21, I dined with him at Mr. Thrale's. The modes of living in different countries, and the various views with which men travel in quest of new scenes, having been talked of, a learned gentleman who holds a considerable office in the law expatiated on the happiness of a savage life, and mentioned an instance of an officer who had actually lived for some time in the wilds of America, of whom, when in that state, he quoted this reflection with an air of admiration, as if it had been deeply philosophical: "Here am I, free and unrestrained, amidst the rude magnificence of Nature, with this Indian woman by my side, and this gun, with which I can procure food when I want it: what more can be desired for human happiness?" It did not require much sagacity to foresee that such a sentiment would not be permitted to pass without due animadversion. JOHNSON. "Do not allow yourself, Sir, to be imposed upon by such gross absurdity. It is sad stuff; it is brutish. If a bull could speak, he might as well exclaim,—Here am I with this cow and this grass; what being can enjoy better felicity?"

We talked of the melancholy end of a gentleman who had destroyed himself. JOHNSON. "It was owing to imaginary difficulties in his affairs, which, had he talked with any friend, would soon have vanished." BOSWELL. "Do you think, Sir, that all who commit suicide are mad?" JOHNSON. "Sir, they are often not universally disordered in their intellects, but one passion presses so upon them, that they yield to it, and commit suicide, as a passionate man will stab another." He added, "I have often thought, that after a man has taken the resolution to kill himself, it is not courage in him to do any thing, however desperate, because he has nothing to fear." GOLDSMITH. "I don't see that." JOHNSON. "Nay, but my dear Sir, why should not you see what every one else sees?" GOLDSMITH. "It is for fear of something that he has resolved to kill himself: and will not that timid disposition restrain him?" JOHNSON. "It does not signify that the fear of something made him resolve; it is upon the state of his mind, after the resolution is taken, that I argue. Suppose a man, either from fear, or pride, or conscience, or whatever motive, has resolved to kill himself; when once the resolution is taken, he has nothing to fear. He may then go and take the King of Prussia by the nose, at the head of his army. He cannot fear the rack, who is resolved to kill himself. When Eustace Budgel was walking down to the Thames, determined to drown himself, he might, if he pleased, without any apprehension of danger, have turned aside, and first set fire to St. James's palace."

On Tuesday, April 27, Mr. Beauclerk and I called on him in the morning. He said, "Goldsmith should not be for ever attempting to shine in conversation: he has not temper for it, he is so much mortified when he fails. Sir, a game of jokes is composed partly of skill, partly of chance, a man may be beat at times by one who has not the tenth part of his wit. Now Goldsmith's putting himself against another, is like a man laying a hundred to one who cannot spare the hundred. It is not worth a man's while. A man should not lay a hundred to one, unless he can easily spare it, though he has a hundred chances for him: he can get but a guinea, and he may lose a hundred. Goldsmith is in this state. When he contends, if he gets the better, it is a very little addition to a man of his literary reputation: if he does not get the better, he is miserably vexed."

Johnson's own superlative powers of wit set him above

any risk of such uneasiness. Garrick had remarked to me of him, a few days before, "Rabelais and all other wits are nothing compared with him. You may be diverted by them; but Johnson gives you a forcible hug, and shakes laughter out of you, whether you will or no."

Goldsmith, however, was often very fortunate in his witty contests, even when he entered the lists with Johnson himself. Sir Joshua Reynolds was in company with them one day, when Goldsmith said, that he thought he could write a good fable, mentioned the simplicity which that kind of composition requires, and observed, that in most fables the animals introduced seldom talk in character. "For instance, (said he,) the fable of the little fishes, who saw birds fly over their heads, and envying them, petitioned Jupiter to be changed into birds. The skill (continued he,) consists in making them talk like little fishes." While he indulged himself in this fanciful reverie, he observed Johnson shaking his sides, and laughing. Upon which he smartly proceeded, "Why, Dr. Johnson, this is not so easy as you seem to think; for if you were to make little fishes talk, they would talk like WHALES."

On Thursday, April 29, I dined with him at General Oglethorpe's, where were Sir Joshua Reynolds, Mr. Langton, Dr. Goldsmith, and Mr. Thrale. I was very desirous to get Dr. Johnson absolutely fixed in his resolution to go with me to the Hebrides this year; and I told him that I had received a letter from Dr. Robertson the historian, upon the subject, with which he was much pleased, and now talked in such a manner of his long intended tour, that I was satisfied he meant to fulfil his engagement.

The custom of eating dogs at Otaheite being mentioned, Goldsmith observed, that this was also a custom in China: that a dog-butcher is as common there as any other butcher; and that when he walks abroad all the dogs fall on him. JOHNSON. "That is not owing to his killing dogs, Sir. I remember a butcher at Lichfield, whom a dog that was in the house where I lived, always attacked. It is the smell of carnage which provokes this, let the animals he has killed be what they may." GOLDSMITH. "Yes, there is a general abhorrence in animals at the signs of massacre. If you put a tub full of blood into a stable, the horses are like to go mad." JOHNSON. "I doubt that." GOLDSMITH. "Nay, Sir, it is a fact well authenticated." THRALE. "You had better prove it before you put it into your book on natural history. You may do it in my stable if you will." JOHNSON. "Nay, Sir, I would not have him prove it. If he is content to take his information from others, he may get through his book with little trouble, and without much endangering his reputation. But if he makes experiments for so comprehensive a book as his, there would be no end to them; his erroneous assertions would then fall upon himself; and he might be blamed for not having made experiments as to every particular."

The character of Mallet having been introduced, and spoken of slightingly by Goldsmith; JOHNSON. "Why, Sir, Mallet had talents enough to keep his literary reputation alive as long as he himself lived; and that, let me tell you, is a good deal." GOLDSMITH. "But I cannot agree that it was so. His literary reputation was dead long before his natural death. I consider an authour's literary reputation to be alive only while his name will insure a good price for his copy from the booksellers. I will get you (to Johnson,) a hundred guineas for any thing whatever that you shall write, if you put your name to it."

Dr. Goldsmith's new play, "She Stoops to Conquer," being mentioned; JOHNSON. "I know of no comedy for many years that has so much exhilarated an audience, that has answered so much the great end of comedy—making an audience merry."

On Friday, April 30, I dined with him at Mr. Beauclerk's, where were Lord Charlemont, Sir Joshua Reynolds, and some more members of the LITERARY CLUB, whom he had obligingly invited to meet me, as I was this evening to be ballotted for as candidate for admission into that distinguished society. Johnson had done me the honour to propose me, and Beauclerk was very zealous for me.

Goldsmith being mentioned; JOHNSON. "It is amazing how little Goldsmith knows. He seldom comes where he is not more ignorant than any one else." SIR JOSHUA REYNOLDS. "Yet there is no man whose company is more liked."

JOHNSON. "To be sure, Sir. When people find a man of the most distinguished abilities as a writer, their inferiour while he is with them, it must be highly gratifying to them. What Goldsmith comically says of himself is very true,—he always gets the better when he argues alone; meaning, that he is master of a subject in his study, and can write well upon it; but when he comes into company, grows confused, and unable to talk. Take him as a poet, his 'Traveller' is a very fine performance; ay, and so is his 'Deserted Village,' were it not sometimes too much the echo of his 'Traveller.' Whether, indeed, we take him as a poet,—as a comick writer,—or as an historian, he stands in the first class." BOSWELL. "An historian! My dear Sir, you surely will not rank his compilation of the Roman History with the works of other historians of this age?" JOHNSON. "Why, who are before him?" BOSWELL. "Hume,—Robertson,—Lord Lyttelton." JOHNSON. (His antipathy to the Scotch beginning to rise.) "I have not read Hume; but, doubtless, Goldsmith's History is better than the *verbiage* of Robertson, or the foppery of Dalrymple." BOSWELL. "Will you not admit the superiority of Robertson, in whose history we find such penetration—such painting?" JOHNSON. "Sir, you must consider how that penetration and that painting are employed. It is not history, it is imagination. He who describes what he never saw, draws from fancy. Robertson paints minds as Sir Joshua paints faces in a history-piece: he imagines an heroick countenance. You must look upon Robertson's work as romance and try it by that standard. History it is not. Besides, Sir, it is the great excellence of a writer to put into his book as much as his book will hold. Goldsmith has done this in his History. Now Robertson might have put twice as much into his book. Robertson is like a man who has packed gold in wool; the wool takes up more room than the gold. No, Sir; I always thought Robertson would be crushed by his own weight,—would be buried under his own ornaments. Goldsmith tells you shortly all you want to know: Robertson detains you a great deal too long. No man will read Robertson's cumbrous detail a second time; but Goldsmith's plain narrative will please again and again. I would say to Robertson what an old tutor of a

college said to one of his pupils: 'Read over your compositions, and wherever you meet with a passage which you
think is particularly fine, strike it out.' Goldsmith's abridgement is better than that of Lucious Florus or Eutropius;
and I will venture to say, that if you compare him with Vertot, in the same places of the Roman History, you will find
that he excels Vertot. Sir, he has the art of compiling, and
of saying every thing he has to say in a pleasing manner.
He is now writing a Natural History, and will make it as
entertaining as a Persian Tale."

Johnson praised John Bunyan highly. "His 'Pilgrim's
Progress' has great merit, both for invention, imagination,
and the conduct of the story; and it has had the best evidence of its merit, the general and continued approbation
of mankind. Few books, I believe, have had a more extensive sale. It is remarkable, that it begins very much like the
poem of Dante; yet there was no translation of Dante when
Bunyan wrote. There is reason to think that he had read
Spenser."

A proposition which had been agitated, that monuments
to eminent persons should, for the time to come, be erected
in St. Paul's church as well as in Westminster-abbey, was
mentioned; and it was asked, who should be honoured by
having his monument first erected there. Somebody suggested Pope. JOHNSON. "Why, Sir, as Pope was a Roman
Catholick, I would not have his to be first. I think Milton's
rather should have the precedence. I think more highly of
him now than I did at twenty. There is more thinking in
him and in Butler, than in any of our poets."

The gentlemen went away to their club, and I was left
at Beauclerk's till the fate of my election should be announced to me. I sat in a state of anxiety which even the
charming conversation of Lady Di Beauclerk could not entirely dissipate. In a short time I received the agreeable
intelligence that I was chosen. I hastened to the place of
meeting, and was introduced to such a society as can seldom be found. Mr. Edmund Burke, whom I then saw for
the first time, and whose splendid talents had long made
me ardently wish for his acquaintance; Dr. Nugent, Mr.
Garrick, Dr. Goldsmith, Mr. (afterwards Sir William)

Jones, and the company with whom I had dined. Upon my entrance, Johnson placed himself behind a chair, on which he leaned as on a desk or pulpit, and with humorous formality gave me a *Charge*, pointing out the conduct expected from me as a good member of this club.

I dined with him at the house of my friends, Messieurs Edward and Charles Dilly, booksellers in the Poultry: there were present, their elder brother Mr. Dilly of Bedfordshire, Dr. Goldsmith, Mr. Langton, Mr. Claxton, Reverend Dr. Mayo, a dissenting minister, the Reverend Mr. Toplady, and my friend the Reverend Mr. Temple.

I introduced the subject of toleration. JOHNSON. "Every society has a right to preserve publick peace and order, and therefore has a good right to prohibit the propagation of opinions which have a dangerous tendency: To say the *magistrate* has this right, is using an inadequate word: it is the *society* for which the magistrate is agent. He may be morally or theologically wrong in restraining the propagation of opinions which he thinks dangerous, but he is politically right." MAYO. "I am of opinion, Sir, that every man is entitled to liberty of conscience in religion; and that the magistrate cannot restrain that right." JOHNSON. "Sir, I agree with you. Every man has a right to liberty of conscience, and with that the magistrate cannot interfere. People confound liberty of thinking with liberty of talking; nay, with liberty of preaching. Every man has a physical right to think as he pleases; for it cannot be discovered how he thinks. He has not a moral right, for he ought to inform himself, and think justly. But, Sir, no member of a society has a right to *teach* any doctrine contrary to what the society holds to be true. The magistrate, I say, may be wrong in what he thinks; but while he thinks himself right, he may and ought to enforce what he thinks." MAYO. "Then, Sir, we are to remain always in errour, and truth never can prevail; and the magistrate was right in persecuting the first Christians." JOHNSON. "Sir, the only method by which religious truth can be established is by martyrdom. The magistrate has a right to enforce what he thinks; and he who is conscious of the truth has a right to suffer. I am afraid there is no other way of ascertaining the truth, but by persecution on the one hand and enduring it on the other." GOLDSMITH. "But how is a man to act, Sir? Though firmly convinced of the truth of his doctrine, may he not think it wrong to expose himself to persecution? Has he a right to do so? Is it not, as it were, committing voluntary suicide?" JOHNSON. "Sir, as to voluntary suicide, as you call it, there are twenty thousand men in an army who will go without scruple to be shot at, and mount a breach for five-pence a day." GOLDSMITH. "But have they a moral right to do this?" JOHNSON. "Nay, Sir, if you will not take the universal opinion of mankind, I have nothing to say. If mankind cannot defend their own way of thinking, I cannot defend it. Sir, if a man is in doubt whether it would be better for him to expose himself to martyrdom or not, he should not do it. He must be convinced that he has a delegation from heaven." GOLDSMITH. "I would consider whether there is the greater chance of good or evil upon the whole. If I see a man who has fallen into a well, I would wish to help him out; but if there is a greater probability that he shall pull me in, than that I shall pull him out, I would not attempt it. So were I to go to Turkey, I might wish to convert the grand Signor to the Christian faith; but when I considered that I should probably be put to death without effectuating my purpose in any degree, I should keep myself quiet." JOHNSON. "Sir, you must consider that we have perfect and imperfect obligations. Perfect obligations, which are generally not to do something, are clear and positive; as, 'thou shalt not kill.' But charity, for instance, is not definable by limits. It is a duty to give to the poor; but no man can say how much another should give to the poor, or when a man has given too little to save his soul. In the same manner it is a duty to instruct the ignorant, and of consequence to convert infidels to Christianity; but no man in the common course of things is obliged to carry this to such a degree as to incur the danger of martyrdom, as no man is obliged to strip himself to the shirt, in order to give charity. I have said, that a man must be persuaded that he has a particular delegation from heaven." GOLDSMITH. "How is this to be known? Our first reformers, who were burnt for not believing bread and wine to be

175

was repulsed from your Board, during which time I have been pushing on my work through difficulties of which it is useless to complain, and have brought it at last to the verge of Publication without one Act of assistance, one word of encouragement, or one smile of favour. Such treatment I did not expect, for I never had a Patron before. [The Shepherd in Virgil grew at last acquainted with Love, and found him a Native of the Rocks. ~~Is~~ Is not a Patron, My Lord, one who looks with unconcern on a Man struggling for Life in the water and when he has reached ground encumbers him with help? The notice which you have been pleased to take of my Labours, had it been early, had been kind; but it has been delayed till I am indifferent and cannot enjoy it, till I am solitary and cannot impart it, till I am known and do not want it not to confess obligation where no benefit has been received, or to be unwilling that the Public should consider me as owing that to a Patron, which Providence has enabled me to do for myself.

Having carried on my work thus far with so little obligation to any Favourer of Learning I shall not be disappointed though it should conclude it, if less be possible, with less, for I have been long wakened from that dream of hope, in which I once boasted myself with so much exultation,

My Lord,

Your Lordship's Most humble Most Obedient Servant

S. J—

Doctor Johnson, when he gave me this Copy of his Letter desired that I would annex to it his Information to me, that whereas it is said in the Letter, "that no assistance has been received," he did once receive from L.[d] C. the Sum of ten pounds; but as that was so inconsiderable a Sum, he thought the mention of it could not properly find place in a Letter of the kind that this was.

9

A copy, in Dr. Johnson's own handwriting, of his famous letter to the Earl of Chesterfield refusing in no uncertain terms his tardy offer of patronage for the *Dictionary*. The letter is supposed to have given the death blow to the ancient system of patronage for needy authors.

CHRIST"—JOHNSON. (interrupting him,) "Sir, they were not burnt for not believing bread and wine to be CHRIST, but for insulting those who did believe it. And, Sir, when the first reformers began, they did not intend to be martyred: as many of them ran away as could." BOSWELL. "But, Sir, there was your countryman Elwal, who you told me challenged King George with his black-guards and his red-guards." JOHNSON. "My countryman, Elwal, Sir, should have been put in the stocks: a proper pulpit for him; and he'd have had a numerous audience. A man who preaches in the stocks will always have hearers enough." BOSWELL. "But Elwal thought himself in the right." JOHNSON. "We are not providing for mad people; there are places for them in the neighbourhood." (meaning Moorfields.) MAYO. "But, Sir, is it not very hard that I should not be allowed to teach my children what I really believe to be the truth?" JOHNSON. "Why, Sir, you might contrive to teach your children *extrà scandalum;* but, Sir, the magistrate, if he knows it, has a right to restrain you. Suppose you teach your children to be thieves?" MAYO. "This is making a joke of the subject." JOHNSON. "Nay, Sir, take it thus:—that you teach them the community of goods: for which there are as many plausible arguments as for most erroneous doctrines. You teach them that all things at first were in common, and that no man had a right to anything but as he laid his hands upon it; and that this still is, or ought to be, the rule amongst mankind. Here, Sir, you sap a great principle in society,—property. And don't you think the magistrate would have a right to prevent you? Or, suppose you should teach your children the notion of the Adamites, and they should run naked into the streets, would not the magistrate have a right to flog 'em into their doublets?" MAYO. "I think the magistrate has no right to interfere till there is some overt act." BOSWELL. "So, Sir, though he sees an enemy to the state charging a blunderbuss, he is not to interfere till it is fired off!" MAYO. "He must be sure of its direction against the state." JOHNSON. "The magistrate is to judge of that.—He has no right to restrain your thinking, because the evil centers in yourself. If a man were sitting at this table, and chopping off his fingers, the magistrate, as guardian of the community, has no authority to restrain him, however he might do it from kindness as a parent.— Though, indeed, upon more consideration, I think he may; as it is probable, that he who is chopping off his own fingers, may soon proceed to chop off those of other people. If I think it right to steal Mr. Dilly's plate, I am a bad man; but he can say nothing to me. If I make an open declaration that I think so, he will keep me out of his house. If I put forth my hand, I shall be sent to Newgate. This is the gradation of thinking, preaching, and acting: if a man thinks erroneously, he may keep his thoughts to himself, and nobody will trouble him; if he preaches erroneous doctrine, society may expel him; if he acts in consequence of it, the law takes place, and he is hanged." MAYO. "But, Sir, ought not Christians to have liberty of conscience?" JOHNSON. "I have already told you so, Sir. You are coming back to where you were." BOSWELL. "Dr. Mayo is always taking a return postchaise, and going the stage over again. He has it at half-price." JOHNSON. "Dr. Mayo, like other champions for unlimited toleration, has got a set of words.[1] Sir, it is no matter, politically, whether the magistrate be right or wrong. Suppose a club were to be formed, to drink confusion to King George the Third, and a happy restoration to Charles the Third; this would be very bad with respect to the State; but every member of that club must either conform to its rules, or be turned out of it. Old Baxter, I remember, maintains, that the magistrate should 'tolerate all things that are tolerable.' This is no good definition of toleration upon any principle; but it shews that he thought some things were not tolerable." TOPLADY. "Sir, you have untwisted this difficult subject with great dexterity."

During this argument, Goldsmith sat in restless agitation, from a wish to get in and *shine*. Finding himself excluded, he had taken his hat to go away, but remained for some time with it in his hand, like a gamester, who, at the close

---

[1] Dr. Mayo's calm temper and steady perseverance, rendered him an admirable subject for the exercise of Dr. Johnson's powerful abilities. He never flinched: but, after reiterated blows, remained seemingly unmoved as at the first. The scintillations of Johnson's genius flashed every time he was struck, without his receiving any injury. Hence he obtained the epithet of THE LITERARY ANVIL.

of a long night, lingers for a little while, to see if he can have a favourable opening to finish with success. Once when he was beginning to speak, he found himself over-powered by the loud voice of Johnson, who was at the opposite end of the table, and did not perceive Goldsmith's attempt. Thus disappointed of his wish to obtain the attention of the company, Goldsmith in a passion threw down his hat, looking angrily at Johnson, and exclaimed in a bitter tone, *"Take it."* When Toplady was going to speak, Johnson uttered some sound, which led Goldsmith to think that he was beginning again, and taking the words from Toplady. Upon which, he seized this opportunity of venting his own envy and spleen, under the pretext of supporting another person: "Sir, (said he to Johnson,) the gentleman has heard you patiently for an hour: pray allow us now to hear him." JOHNSON. (sternly.) "Sir, I was not interrupting the gentleman. I was only giving him a signal of my attention. Sir, you are impertinent." Goldsmith made no reply, but continued in the company for some time.

He and Mr. Langton and I went together to THE CLUB, where we found Mr. Burke, Mr. Garrick, and some other members, and amongst them our friend Goldsmith, who sat silently brooding over Johnson's reprimand to him after dinner. Johnson perceived this, and said aside to some of us, "I'll make Goldsmith forgive me;" and then called to him in a loud voice, "Dr. Goldsmith,—something passed to-day where you and I dined; I ask your pardon." Goldsmith answered placidly, "It must be much from you, Sir, that I take ill." And so at once the difference was over, and they were on as easy terms as ever, and Goldsmith rattled away as usual.

In our way to the club to-night, when I regretted that Goldsmith would, upon every occasion, endeavour to shine, by which he often exposed himself, Mr. Langton observed, that he was not like Addison, who was content with the fame of his writings, and did not aim also at excellency in conversation, for which he found himself unfit; and that he said to a lady who complained of his having talked little in company, "Madam, I have but nine-pence in ready money, but I can draw for a thousand pounds." I observed that Goldsmith had a great deal of Gold in his cabinet, but, not content with that, was always taking out his purse. JOHNSON. "Yes, Sir, and that so often an empty purse!"

Goldsmith's incessant desire of being conspicuous in company, was the occasion of his sometimes appearing to such disadvantage as one should hardly have supposed possible in a man of his genius. When his literary reputation had risen deservedly high, and his society was much courted, he became very jealous of the extraordinary attention which was every where paid to Johnson. One evening, in a circle of wits, he found fault with me for talking of Johnson as entitled to the honour of unquestionable superiority. "Sir, (said he,) you are for making a monarchy of what should be a republick."

He was still more mortified, when talking in a company with fluent vivacity, and, as he flattered himself, to the admiration of all who were present; a German who sat next him, and perceived Johnson rolling himself, as if about to speak, suddenly stopped him, saying, "Stay, stay,—Toctor Shonson is going to say something." This was, no doubt, very provoking, especially to one so irritable as Goldsmith, who frequently mentioned it with strong expressions of indignation.

It may also be observed, that Goldsmith was sometimes content to be treated with an easy familiarity, but upon occasions, would be consequential and important. An instance of this occurred in a small particular. Johnson had a way of contracting the names of his friends: as Beauclerk, Beau; Boswell, Bozzy; Langton, Lanky; Murphy, Mur; Sheridan, Sherry. I remember one day, when Tom Davies was telling that Dr. Johnson said, "We are all in labour for a name to *Goldy's* play," Goldsmith seemed displeased that such a liberty should be taken with his name, and said, "I have often desired him not to call me *Goldy*." Tom was remarkably attentive to the most minute circumstance about Johnson. I recollect his telling me once, on my arrival in London, "Sir, our great friend has made an improvement on his appellation of old Mr. Sheridan. He calls him now *Sherry derry*."

On Sunday, May 8, I dined with Johnson at Mr. Langton's with Dr. Beattie and some other company. He descanted on the subject of Literary Property. "There seems (said he,) to be in authours a stronger right of property than that by occupancy; a metaphysical right, a right, as it were, of creation, which should from its nature be perpetual; but the consent of nations is against it; and indeed reason and the interest of learning are against it; for were it to be perpetual, no book, however useful, could be universally diffused amongst mankind, should the proprietor take it into his head to restrain its circulation. No book could have the advantage of being edited with notes, however necessary to its elucidation, should the proprietor perversely oppose it. For the general good of the world, therefore, whatever valuable work has once been created by an authour, and issued out by him, should be understood as no longer in his power, but as belonging to the publick; at the same time the authour is entitled to an adequate reward. This he should have by an exclusive right to his work for a considerable number of years."

On Monday, May 9, as I was to set out on my return to Scotland next morning, I was desirous to see as much of Dr. Johnson as I could. But I first called on Goldsmith to take leave of him. The jealousy and envy which, though possessed of many most amiable qualities, he frankly avowed, broke out violently at this interview. Upon another occasion, when Goldsmith confessed himself to be of an envious disposition, I contended with Johnson that we ought not to be angry with him, he was so candid in owning it. "Nay, Sir, (said Johnson,) we must be angry that a man has such a super-abundance of an odious quality, that he cannot keep it within his own breast, but it boils over:" In my opinion, however, Goldsmith had not more of it than other people have, but only talked of it freely.

He now seemed very angry that Johnson was going to be a traveller; said "he would be a dead weight for me to carry, and that I should never be able to lug him along through the Highlands and Hebrides." Nor would he patiently allow me to enlarge upon Johnson's wonderful abilities; but exclaimed, "Is he like Burke, who winds into a subject like a serpent?" "But, (said I,) Johnson is the Hercules who strangled serpents in his cradle."

In a letter from Edinburgh, dated the 29th of May, I pressed him to persevere in his resolution to make this year the projected visit to the Hebrides, of which he and I had talked for many years, and which I was confident would afford us much entertainment.

His stay in Scotland was from the 18th of August, on which day he arrived, till the 22d of November, when he set out on his return to London; and I believe ninety-four days were never passed by any man in a more vigorous exertion.

He came by the way of Berwick upon Tweed to Edinburgh, where he remained a few days, and then went by St. Andrews, Aberdeen, Inverness, and Fort Augustus, to the Hebrides, to visit which was the principal object he had in view. He visited the isles of Sky, Rasay, Col, Mull, Inchkenneth, and Icolmkill. He travelled through Argyleshire by Inverary, and from thence by Lochlomond and Dunbarton to Glasgow, then by Loudon to Auchinleck in Ayrshire, the seat of my family, and then by Hamilton, back to Edinburgh, where he again spent some time. He thus saw the four Universities of Scotland, its three principal cities, and as much of the Highland and insular life as was sufficient for his philosophical contemplation. I had the pleasure of accompanying him during the whole of his journey. He was respectfully entertained by the great, the learned, and the elegant, wherever he went; nor was he less delighted with the hospitality which he experienced in humbler life.

His various adventures, and the force and vivacity of his mind, as exercised during this peregrination, upon innumerable topicks, have been faithfully, and to the best of my abilities, displayed in my "Journal of a Tour to the Hebrides," to which, as the publick has been pleased to honour it by a very extensive circulation, I beg leave to refer, as to a separate and remarkable portion of his life, which may be there seen in detail, and which exhibits as striking a view of his powers in conversation, as his works do of his excellence in writing.

181

During his stay at Edinburgh, after his return from the Hebrides, he was at great pains to obtain information concerning Scotland; and it will appear from his subsequent letters, that he was not less solicitous for intelligence on this subject after his return to London.

"To James Boswell, Esq.

"DEAR SIR,

"I came home last night, without any incommodity, danger, or weariness, and am ready to begin a new journey. I shall go to Oxford on Monday. I know Mrs. Boswell wished me well to go; [1] her wishes have not been disappointed. Mrs. Williams has received Sir A.'s letter.

"Make my compliments to all those to whom my compliments may be welcome.

"Let the box be sent as soon as it can, and let me know when to expect it.

"Enquire, if you can, the order of the Clans: Macdonald is first, Maclean second; further I cannot go. Quicken Dr. Webster.

"I am, Sir,
"Yours affectionately
"Sam. Johnson."

"Nov. 27, 1773."

"Mr. Boswell to Dr. Johnson.
"Edinburgh, Dec. 2, 1773.

*   *   *   *

"You shall have what information I can procure as to the order of the Clans. A gentleman of the name of Grant tells me, that there is no settled order among them; and he

---

[1] In this he shewed a very acute penetration. My wife paid him the most assiduous and respectful attention, while he was our guest; so that I wonder how he discovered her wishing for his departure. The truth is, that his irregular hours and uncouth habits, such as turning the candles with their heads downwards, when they did not burn bright enough, and letting the wax drop upon the carpet, could not but be disagreeable to a lady. Besides, she had not that high admiration of him which was felt by most of those who knew him; and what was very natural to a female mind, she thought he had too much influence over her husband. She once in a little warmth, made, with more point than justice, this remark upon that subject: "I have seen many a bear led by a man; but I never before saw a man led by a bear."

says, that the Macdonalds were not placed upon the right of the army at Culloden; the Stuarts were. I shall, however, examine witnesses of every name that I can find here. Dr. Webster shall be quickened too. I like your little memorandums; they are symptoms of your being in earnest with your book of northern travels.

"Your box shall be sent next week by sea. You will find in it some pieces of the broom bush, which you saw growing on the old castle of Auchinleck. The wood has a curious appearance when sawn across. You may either have a little writing-standish made of it, or get it formed into boards for a treatise on witchcraft, by way of a suitable binding."

* * * *

On the 5th of March I wrote to him, requesting his counsel whether I should this spring come to London. I stated to him on the one hand some pecuniary embarrassments, which, together with my wife's situation at that time, made me hesitate: and, on the other, the pleasure and improvement which my annual visit to the metropolis always afforded me; and particularly mentioned a peculiar satisfaction which I experienced in celebrating the festival of Easter in St. Paul's cathedral: that to my fancy it appeared like going up to Jerusalem at the feast of the Passover; and that the strong devotion which I felt on that occasion diffused its influence on my mind through the rest of the year.

"To JAMES BOSWELL, ESQ.

[*Not dated, but written about the 15th of March.*]

"DEAR SIR,

"I am ashamed to think that since I received your letter I have passed so many days without answering it.

"I think there is no great difficulty in resolving your doubts. The reasons for which you are inclined to visit London, are, I think, not of sufficient strength to answer the objections. That you should delight to come once a year to the fountain of intelligence and pleasure, is very natural; but both information and pleasure must be regulated by propriety. Pleasure, which cannot be obtained but by unseasonable or unsuitable expence, must always end in pain; and pleasure, which must be enjoyed at the expence of another's pain, can never be such as a worthy mind can fully delight in.

"What improvement you might gain by coming to London, you may easily supply or easily compensate, by enjoining yourself some particular study at home, or opening some new avenue to information. Edinburgh is not yet exhausted; and I am sure you will find no pleasure here which can deserve either that you should anticipate any part of your future fortune, or that you should condemn yourself and your lady to penurious frugality for the rest of the year.

"I need not tell you what regard you owe to Mrs. Boswell's entreaties; or how much you ought to study the happiness of her who studies yours with so much diligence, and of whose kindness you enjoy such good effects. Life cannot subsist in society but by reciprocal concessions. She permitted you to ramble last year, you must permit her now to keep you at home.

"Your last reason is so serious, that I am unwilling to oppose it. Yet you must remember, that your image of worshipping once a year in a certain place, in imitation of the Jews, is but a comparison; and *simile non est idem;* if the annual resort to Jerusalem was a duty to the Jews, it was a duty because it was commanded; and you have no such command, therefore no such duty. It may be dangerous to receive too readily, and indulge too fondly, opinions, from which, perhaps, no pious mind is wholly disengaged, of local sanctity and local devotion. You know what strange effects they have produced over a great part of the Christian world. I am now writing, and you, when you read this, are reading under the eye of Omnipresence.

"To what degree fancy is to be admitted into religious offices, it would require much deliberation to determine. I am far from intending totally to exclude it. Fancy is a faculty bestowed by our Creator, and it is reasonable that all his gifts should be used to his glory, that all our faculties should co-operate in his worship; but they are to co-operate according to the will of him that gave them, according to the order which his wisdom has established. As ceremonies prudential or convenient are less obligatory than positive ordinances, as bodily worship is only the token to others or ourselves of mental adoration, so Fancy is always to act in subordination to Reason. We may take Fancy for a companion, but must follow Reason as our guide. We may allow Fancy to suggest certain ideas in certain places; but Reason must always be heard, when she tells us, that those ideas and those places have no natural or necessary relation. When we enter a church we habitually recall to mind the duty of adoration, but we must not omit adoration for want of a temple: because we know, and ought to remember, that the Universal Lord is everywhere present; and that, therefore, to come to Jona, or to Jerusalem, though it may be useful, cannot be necessary.

"Thus I have answered your letter, and have not answered it negligently. I love you too well to be careless when you are serious.

"I think I shall be very diligent next week about our travels, which I have too long neglected. I am, dear Sir,
"Your most, &c.
"SAM. JOHNSON."
"Compliments to Madam and Miss."

"To JAMES BOSWELL, ESQ.
"DEAR SIR,
"I wish you could have looked over my book before the printer, but it could not easily be. I suspect some mistakes; but as I deal, perhaps, more in notions than in facts, the matter is not great, and the second edition will be mended, if any such there be. The press will go on slowly for a time, because I am going into Wales to-morrow.

* * * *

"Of poor dear Dr. Goldsmith [1] there is little to be told, more than the papers have made publick. He died of a fever, made, I am afraid, more violent by uneasiness of mind. His debts began to be heavy, and all his resources

[1] Dr. Goldsmith died April 4, this year.

185

were exhausted. Sir Joshua is of opinion that he owed not less than two thousand pounds. Was ever poet so trusted before?

* * * *

"I am, dear Sir,
"Your most affectionate servant,
"SAM. JOHNSON."

"July 4, 1774."

"My compliments to all the three ladies."

"To BENNET LANGTON, ESQ. AT LANGTON,
NEAR SPILSBY, LINCOLNSHIRE.

"DEAR SIR,

"You have reason to reproach me that I have left your last letter so long unanswered, but I had nothing particular to say. Chambers, you find, is gone far, and poor Goldsmith is gone much further. He died of a fever, exasperated, as I believe, by the fear of distress. He had raised money and squandered it, by every artifice of acquisition and folly of expence. But let not his frailties be remembered; he was a very great man.

"I have just begun to print my Journey to the Hebrides, and am leaving the press to take another journey into Wales, whither Mr. Thrale is going, to take possession of, at least, five hundred a year, fallen to his lady. All at Streatham, that are alive, are well.

"I have never recovered from the last dreadful illness, but flatter myself that I grow gradually better; much, however, yet remains to mend. Κύριε ἐλέησον.

* * * *

"Do not be sullen now, but let me find a letter when I come back. I am, dear Sir,
"Your affectionate, humble servant,
"SAM. JOHNSON."

"July 5, 1774."

His "Journey to the Western Islands of Scotland," * is a most valuable performance. It abounds in extensive philosophical views of society, and in ingenious sentiment and lively description. A considerable part of it, indeed, consists of speculations, which many years before he saw the wild regions which we visited together, probably had employed his attention, though the actual sight of those scenes undoubtedly quickened and augmented them. Mr. Orme, the very able historian, agreed with me in this opinion, which he thus strongly expressed:—"There are in that book thoughts, which, by long revolution in the great mind of Johnson, have been formed and polished like pebbles rolled in the ocean!"

That he was to some degree of excess a *true-born Englishman*, so as to have entertained an undue prejudice against both the country and the people of Scotland, must be allowed. But it was a prejudice of the head and not of the heart. He had no ill will to the Scotch; for, if he had been conscious of that, he never would have thrown himself into the bosom of their country, and trusted to the protection of its remote inhabitants with a fearless confidence. His remark upon the nakedness of the country, from its being denuded of trees, was made after having travelled two hundred miles along the Eastern coast, where certainly trees are not to be found near the road; and he said it was "a map of the road" which he gave.

On Tuesday, March 21, I arrived in London; and on repairing to Dr. Johnson's before dinner, found him in his study, sitting with Mr. Peter Garrick, the elder brother of David, strongly resembling him in countenance and voice, but of more sedate and placid manners.

The doubts which, in my correspondence with him, I had ventured to state as to the justice and wisdom of the conduct of Great-Britain towards the American colonies, while I at the same time requested that he would enable me to inform myself upon that momentous subject, he had altogether disregarded; and had recently published a pamphlet, entitled "Taxation no Tyranny; an answer to the Resolutions and Address of the American Congress." *

He had long before indulged most unfavourable sentiments of our fellow-subjects in America. For, as early as 1769, I was told by Dr. John Campbell, that he had said of them, "Sir, they are a race of convicts, and ought to

187

be thankful for any thing we allow them short of hanging."

Of this performance I avoided to talk with him; for I had now formed a clear and settled opinion, that the people of America were well warranted to resist a claim that their fellow-subjects in the mother-country should have the entire command of their fortunes, by taxing them without their own consent; and the extreme violence which it breathed, appeared to me so unsuitable to the mildness of a Christian philosopher, and so directly opposite to the principles of peace which he had so beautifully recommended in his pamphlet respecting Falkland's Islands, that I was sorry to see him appear in so unfavourable a light. Besides, I could not perceive in it that ability of argument, or that felicity of expression, for which he was, upon other occasions, so eminent. Positive assertion, sarcastical severity, and extravagant ridicule, which he himself reprobated as a test of truth, were united in this rhapsody.

That this pamphlet was written at the desire of those who were then in power, I have no doubt; and, indeed, he owned to me, that it had been revised and curtailed by some of them. He told me, that they had struck out one passage, which was to this effect: "That the Colonists could with no solidity argue from their not having been taxed while in their infancy, that they should not now be taxed. We do not put a calf into the plow; we wait till he is an ox." He said, "They struck it out either critically as too ludicrous, or politically as too exasperating. I care not which. It was their business. If an architect says I will build five stories, and the man who employs him says, I will have only three, the employer is to decide." "Yes, Sir, (said I,) in ordinary cases. But should it be so when the architect gives his skill and labour *gratis?*"

His pamphlets in support of the measures of administration were published on his own account, and he afterwards collected them into a volume, with the title of "Political Tracts, by the Authour of the Rambler."

These pamphlets drew upon him numerous attacks. Against the common weapons of literary warfare he was hardened; but there were two instances of animadversion which I communicated to him, and from what I could judge, both from his silence and his looks, appeared to me to impress him much.

One was, "A Letter to Dr. Samuel Johnson, occasioned by his late political Publications." It appeared previous to his "Taxation no Tyranny," and was written by Dr. Joseph Towers. In that performance, Dr. Johnson was treated with the respect due to so eminent a man, while his conduct as a political writer was boldly and pointedly arraigned, as inconsistent with the character of one, who, if he did employ his pen upon politicks, "it might reasonably be expected should distinguish himself, not by party violence and rancour, but by moderation and by wisdom."

It concluded thus: "I would, however, wish you to remember, should you again address the publick under the character of a political writer, that luxuriance of imagination or energy of language, will ill compensate for the want of candour, of justice, and of truth. And I shall only add, that should I hereafter be disposed to read, as I heretofore have done, the most excellent of all your performances, 'THE RAMBLER,' the pleasure which I have been accustomed to find in it will be much diminished by the reflection that the writer of so moral, so elegant, and so valuable a work, was capable of prostituting his talents in such productions as 'The False Alarm,' the 'Thoughts on the Transactions respecting Falkland's Islands,' and 'The Patriot.' "

The other instance was a paragraph of a letter to me, from my old and most intimate friend the Reverend Mr. Temple, who wrote the character of Gray, which has had the honour to be adopted both by Mr. Mason and Dr. Johnson in their accounts of that poet. The words were, "How can your great, I will not say your *pious*, but your *moral* friend, support the barbarous measures of administration, which they have not the face to ask even their infidel pensioner Hume to defend?"

However confident of the rectitude of his own mind, Johnson may have felt sincere uneasiness that his conduct should be erroneously imputed to unworthy motives, by good men; and that the influence of his valuable writings should on that account be in any degree obstructed or lessened.

189

On Friday, March 24, I met him at the LITERARY CLUB. Johnson was in high spirits this evening and talked with great animation and success. He attacked Swift, as he used to do upon all occasions. "The 'Tale of a Tub' is so much superiour to his other writings, that one can hardly believe he was the authour of it: there is in it such a vigour of mind, such a swarm of thoughts, so much of nature, and art, and life." I wondered to hear him say of "Gulliver's Travels," "When once you have thought of big men and little men, it is very easy to do all the rest." I endeavoured to make a stand for Swift, and tried to rouse those who were much more able to defend him; but in vain. Johnson at last, of his own accord, allowed very great merit to the inventory of articles found in the pocket of "the Man Mountain," particularly the description of his watch, which it was conjectured was his GOD, as he consulted it upon all occasions. He observed, that "Swift put his name to but two things, (after he had a name to put,) 'The Plan for the Improvement of the English language,' and the last, 'Drapier's Letter.' "

Garrick, when he pleased, could imitate Johnson very exactly; for that great actor, with his distinguished powers of expression which were so universally admired, possessed also an admirable talent of mimicry. He was always jealous that Johnson spoke lightly of him. I recollect his exhibiting him to me one day, as if saying, "Davy has some convivial pleasantry about him, but 'tis a futile fellow;" which he uttered perfectly with the tone and air of Johnson.

I cannot too frequently request of my readers, while they peruse my account of Johnson's conversation, to endeavour to keep in mind his deliberate and strong utterance. His mode of speaking was indeed very impressive; and I wish it could be preserved as musick is written.[1]

I won a small bet from Lady Diana Beauclerk, by asking

---

[1] My noble friend Lord Pembroke said once to me at Wilton, with a happy pleasantry and some truth, that "Dr. Johnson's sayings would not appear so extraordinary, were it not for his *bow-wow-way*." The sayings themselves are generally of sterling merit; but, doubtless, his *manner* was an addition to their effect; and therefore should be attended to as much as may be. It is necessary, however, to guard those who were not acquainted with him, against overcharged imitations or caricatures of his manner.

him as to one of his particularities, which her Ladyship laid I durst not do. It seems he had been frequently observed at the Club to put into his pocket the Seville oranges, after he had squeezed the juice of them into the drink which he made for himself. Beauclerk and Garrick talked of it to me, and seemed to think that he had a strange unwillingness to be discovered. We could not divine what he did with them; and this was the bold question to be put. I saw on his table the spoils of the preceding night, some fresh peels nicely scraped and cut into pieces. "O, Sir, (said I,) I now partly see what you do with the squeezed oranges which you put into your pocket at the Club." JOHNSON. "I have a great love for them." BOSWELL. "And pray, Sir, what do you do with them? You scrape them it seems, very neatly, and what next?" JOHNSON. "Let them dry, Sir." BOSWELL. "And what next?" JOHNSON. "Nay, Sir, you shall know their fate no further." BOSWELL. "Then the world must be left in the dark. It must be said (assuming a mock solemnity,) he scraped them and let them dry, but what he did with them next, he never could be prevailed upon to tell." JOHNSON. "Nay, Sir, you should say it more emphatically:—he could not be prevailed upon, even by his dearest friends, to tell."

He had this morning received his Diploma as Doctor of Laws from the University of Oxford. He did not vaunt of his new dignity, but I understood he was highly pleased with it.

I visited him by appointment in the evening, and we drank tea with Mrs. Williams. He told me that he had been in the company of a gentleman whose extraordinary travels had been much the subject of conversation. But I found he had not listened to him with that full confidence, without which there is little satisfaction in the society of travellers. I was curious to hear what opinion so able a judge as Johnson had formed of his abilities, and I asked if he was not a man of sense. JOHNSON. "Why, Sir, he is not a distinct relater; and I should say, he is neither abounding nor deficient in sense. I did not perceive any superiority of understanding." BOSWELL. "But will you not allow him a nobleness of resolution, in penetrating into distant regions?" JOHNSON. "That, Sir, is not to the present purpose: We are talking of sense. A fighting cock has a nobleness of resolution."

His "Taxation no Tyranny" being mentioned, he said, "I think I have not been attacked enough for it. Attack is the re-action; I never think I have hit hard, unless it rebounds."

On Thursday, April 6, I dined with him at Mr. Thomas Davies's, with Mr. Hicky, the painter, and my old acquaintance, Mr. Moody, the player.

Dr. Johnson, as usual, spoke contemptuously of Colley Cibber. "It is wonderful that a man, who for forty years had lived with the great and the witty, should have acquired so ill the talents of conversation: and he had but half to furnish; for one half of what he said was oaths." He, however, allowed considerable merit to some of his comedies, and said there was no reason to believe that the "Careless Husband" was not written by himself. Davies said, he was the first dramatick writer who introduced genteel ladies upon the stage. Johnson refuted his observation by instancing several such characters in comedies before his time. DAVIES. (trying to defend himself for a charge of ignorance,) "I mean genteel moral characters." "I think (said Hicky,) gentility and morality are inseparable." BOSWELL. "By no means, Sir. The genteelest characters are often the most immoral. Does not Lord Chesterfield give precepts for uniting wickedness and the graces? A man, indeed, is not genteel when he gets drunk; but most vices may be committed very genteely: a man may debauch his friend's wife genteely: he may cheat at cards genteely." HICKY. "I do not think *that* is genteel." BOSWELL. "Sir, it may not be like a gentleman, but it may be genteel." JOHNSON. "You are meaning two different things. One means exteriour grace; the other honour. It is certain that a man may be very immoral with exteriour grace. Lovelace, in 'Clarissa,' is a very genteel and a very wicked character. Tom Hervey, who died t'other day, though a vicious man, was one of the genteelest men that ever lived."

I mentioned that Dr. Thomas Campbell had come from Ireland to London, principally to see Dr. Johnson. He seemed angry at this observation. DAVIES. "Why, you know, Sir, there came a man from Spain to see Livy; and Corelli came to England to see Purcell, and, when he heard he was dead, went directly back again to Italy." JOHNSON. "I should not have wished to be dead to disappoint Campbell, had he been so foolish as you represent him; but I should have wished to have been a hundred miles off." This was apparently perverse; and I do believe it was not his real way of thinking: he could not but like a man who came so far to see him. He laughed with some complacency, when I told him Campbell's odd expression to me concerning him: "That having seen such a man, was a thing to talk of a century hence,"—as if he could live so long.

JOHNSON. "When a man writes from his own mind, he writes very rapidly.[1] The greatest part of a writer's time is spent in reading, in order to write; a man will turn over half a library to make one book."

The mention of [a] wolf had led Johnson to think of other wild beasts; and while Sir Joshua Reynolds and Mr. Langton were carrying on a dialogue about something which engaged them earnestly, he, in the midst of it, broke out, "Pennant tells of Bears.—" [what he added, I have forgotten.] They went on, which he being dull of hearing, did not perceive, or, if he did, was not willing to break off his talk; so he continued to vociferate his remarks, and *Bear* ("like a word in a catch" as Beauclerk said,) was repeatedly heard at intervals, which coming from him who, by those who did not know him, had been so often assimilated to that ferocious animal, while we who were sitting around could hardly stifle laughter, produced a very ludicrous effect. Silence having ensued, he proceeded: "We are told, that the black bear is innocent; but I should not like to trust myself with him." Mr. Gibbon muttered in a low tone of voice, "I should not like to trust myself with *you*." This piece of sarcastick pleasantry was a prudent resolution, if applied to a competition of abilities.

[1] Johnson certainly did, who had a mind stored with knowledge, and teeming with imagery: but the observation is not applicable to writers in general.

Patriotism having become one of our topicks, Johnson suddenly uttered, in a strong determined tone, an apophthegm, at which many will start: "Patriotism is the last refuge of a scoundrel." But let it be considered, that he did not mean a real and generous love of our country, but that pretended patriotism which so many, in all ages and countries, have made a cloak for self interest. I maintained, that certainly all patriots were not scoundrels.

Mrs. Pritchard being mentioned, he said, "Her playing was quite mechanical. It is wonderful how little mind she had. Sir, she had never read the tragedy of Macbeth all through. She no more thought of the play out of which her part was taken, than a shoemaker thinks of the skin, out of which the piece of leather, of which he is making a pair of shoes, is cut."

On Saturday, May 8, I dined with him at Mr. Thrale's, where we met the Irish Dr. Campbell. Johnson had supped the night before at Mrs. Abbington's with some fashionable people whom he named; and he seemed much pleased with having made one in so elegant a circle. Nor did he omit to pique his *mistress* a little with jealousy of her housewifery; for he said, (with a smile,) "Mrs. Abbington's jelly, my dear lady, was better than yours."

Mrs. Thrale, who frequently practised a coarse mode of flattery, by repeating his *bon-mots* in his hearing, told us that he had said, a certain celebrated actor was just fit to stand at the door of an auction-room with a long pole, and cry "Pray, gentlemen, walk in;" and that a certain authour, upon hearing this, had said, that another still more celebrated actor was fit for nothing better than that, and would pick your pocket after you came out. JOHNSON. "Nay, my dear lady, there is no wit in what our friend added; there is only abuse. You may as well say of any man that he will pick a pocket. Besides, the man who is stationed at the door does not pick people's pockets; that is done within, by the auctioneer."

On Monday, April 10, I dined with him at General Oglethorpe's, with Mr. Langton and the Irish Dr. Campbell, whom the general had obligingly given me leave to bring with me. This learned gentleman was thus gratified with a very high intellectual feast, by not only being in company with Dr. Johnson, but with General Oglethorpe, who had been so long a celebrated name both at home and abroad.

He this day enlarged upon Pope's melancholy remark,

"Man never *is*, but always *to be* blest."

He asserted, that *the present* was never a happy state to any human being; but that, as every part of life, of which we are conscious, was at some point of time a period yet to come, in which felicity was expected, there was some happiness produced by hope. Being pressed upon this subject, and asked if he really was of opinion that though, in general, happiness was very rare in human life, a man was not sometimes happy in the moment that was present, he answered, "Never, but when he is drunk."

He observed, "All knowledge is of itself of some value. There is nothing so minute or inconsiderable, that I would not rather know it than not. In the same manner, all power, of whatever sort, is of itself desirable. A man would not submit to learn to hem a ruffle, of his wife, or his wife's maid: but if a mere wish could attain it, he would rather wish to be able to hem a ruffle."

I told him that our friend Goldsmith had said to me that he had come too late into the world, for that Pope and other poets had taken up the places in the Temple of Fame; so that as but a few at any period can possess poetical reputation, a man of genius can now hardly acquire it. JOHNSON. "That is one of the most sensible things I ever heard of Goldsmith. It is difficult to get literary fame, and it is every day growing more difficult. Ah, Sir, that should make a man think of securing happiness in another world, which all who try sincerely for it may attain. In comparison of that, how little are all other things! The belief of immortality is impressed upon all men, and all men act under an impression of it, however they may talk, and though, perhaps, they may be scarcely sensible of it." I said, it appeared to me that some people had not the least notion of immortality; and I mentioned a distinguished gentleman of our acquaintance. JOHNSON. "Sir, if it were not for the notion of immortality, he would cut a throat to fill his pockets." When I quoted this to Beauclerk, who knew much more of the gentleman than we did, he said in his acid manner, "He would cut a throat to fill his pockets, if it were not for fear of being hanged."

He took occasion to enlarge on the advantages of reading and combated the idle superficial notion, that knowledge enough may be acquired in conversation. "The foundation (said he) must be laid by reading. General principles must be had from books which, however, must be brought to the test of real life. In conversation you never get a system. What is said upon a subject is to be gathered from a hundred people. The parts of a truth, which a man gets thus, are at such a distance from each other that he never attains to a full view."

On Tuesday, April 11, he and I were engaged to go with Sir Joshua Reynolds to dine with Mr. Cambridge, at his beautiful villa on the banks of the Thames, near Twickenham. Dr. Johnson's tardiness was such, that Sir Joshua, who had an appointment at Richmond, early in the day, was obliged to go by himself on horseback, leaving his coach to Johnson and me. Johnson was in such good spirits, that every thing seemed to please him as we drove along.

Our conversation turned on a variety of subjects. He thought portrait-painting an improper employment for a woman. "Publick practice of any art, (he observed,) and staring in men's faces, is very indelicate in a female." I happened to start a question, whether when a man knows that some of his intimate friends are invited to the house of another friend, with whom they are all equally intimate, he may join them without an invitation. JOHNSON. "No, Sir; he is not to go when he is not invited. They may be invited on purpose to abuse him" (smiling).

As a curious instance how little a man knows, or wishes to know his own character in the world, or, rather as a convincing proof that Johnson's roughness was only external, and did not proceed from his heart, I insert the following dialogue. JOHNSON. "It is wonderful, Sir, how rare a quality good humour is in life. We meet with very few good humoured men." I mentioned four of our friends, none of whom he would allow to be good humoured. One was *acid,* another was *muddy,* and to the others he had objections which have escaped me. Then, shaking his head and stretching himself at ease in the coach, and smiling with much complacency, he turned to me and said, "I look upon *myself* as a good humoured fellow." The epithet *fellow,* applied to the great Lexicographer, the stately Moralist, the Masterly Critick, as if he had been *Sam* Johnson, a mere pleasant companion, was highly diverting; and this light notion of himself struck me with wonder. I answered, also smiling, "No, no, Sir; that will *not* do. You are good natured, but not good humoured: you are irascible. You have not patience with folly and absurdity. I believe you would pardon them, if there were time to deprecate your vengeance; but punishment follows so quick after sentence, that they cannot escape."

He talked of Isaac Walton's Lives, which was one of his most favourite books. Dr. Donne's Life, he said, was the most perfect of them. He observed, that "it was wonderful that Walton, who was in a very low situation in life, should have been familiarly received by so many great men, and that at a time when the ranks of society were kept more separate than they are now." He supposed that Walton had then given up his business as a linen-draper and semp-ster, and was only an authour; [1] and added, "that he was a great panegyrist." BOSWELL. "No quality will get a man more friends than a disposition to admire the qualities of others. I do not mean flattery, but a sincere admiration." JOHNSON. "Nay, Sir, flattery pleases very generally. In the first place, the flatterer may think what he says to be true; but, in the second place, whether he thinks so or not, he certainly thinks those whom he flatters of consequence enough to be flattered."

No sooner had we made our bow to Mr. Cambridge, in

---

[1] [Johnson's conjecture was erroneous. Walton did not retire from busi-ness till 1643. But in 1664, Dr. King, Bishop of Chichester, in a letter prefixed to his LIVES, mentions his having been familiarly acquainted with him for forty years: and in 1631 he was so intimate with Dr. Donne, that he was one of the friends who attended him on his death bed.—J. BOSWELL.]

his library, than Johnson ran eagerly to one side of the room intent on poring over the backs of the books. Sir Joshua observed, (aside,) "He runs to the books as I do to the pictures: but I have the advantage. I can see much more of the pictures than he can of the books." Mr. Cambridge, upon this, politely said, "Dr. Johnson, I am going with your pardon, to accuse myself, for I have the same custom which I perceive you have. But it seems odd that one should have such a desire to look at the backs of books." Johnson, ever ready for contest, instantly started from his reverie, wheeled about and answered, "Sir, the reason is very plain. Knowledge is of two kinds. We know a subject ourselves, or we know where we can find information upon it. When we enquire into any subject, the first thing we have to do is to know what books have treated of it. This leads us to look at catalogues, and the backs of books in libraries." Sir Joshua observed to me the extraordinary promptitude with which Johnson flew upon an argument. "Yes, (said I,) he has no formal preparation, no flourishing with his sword; he is through your body in an instant."

The common remark as to the utility of reading history being made;—JOHNSON. "We must consider how very little history there is; I mean real authentick history. That certain Kings reigned, and certain battles were fought, we can depend upon as true; but all the colouring, all the philosophy of history is conjecture." BOSWELL. "Then, Sir, you would reduce all history to no better than an almanack, a mere chronological series of remarkable events." Mr. Gibbon, who must at that time have been employed upon his history, of which he published the first volume in the following year, was present; but did not step forth in defence of that species of writing. He probably did not like to *trust* himself with JOHNSON!

"The Beggar's Opera," and the common question, whether it was pernicious in its effects, having been introduced;—JOHNSON. "As to this matter, which has been very much contested, I myself am of opinion, that more influence has been ascribed to 'The Beggar's Opera,' than it in reality ever had; for I do not believe that any man was ever

FLOW. *v. n.* [flopan, Saxon.]

To run or spread as water.

> The god am I, whose yellow water *flows*
> Around these fields, and fattens as it goes. *Dryden's Æn.*

> Fields of light and liquid ether *flow*,
> Purg'd from the pond'rous dregs of earth below. *Dryden.*

> Endless tears *flow* down in streams. *Swift.*

To run: opposed to standing waters.

> With osier floats the standing water strow;
> Of massy stones make bridges, if it *flow*. *Dryden.*

To rise; not to ebb.

> This river hath thrice *flow'd*, no ebb between. *Shakesp.*

To melt.

> Oh that thou wouldst rent the heavens, that the mountains
> might *flow* down at thy presence. *Is. lxiv. 1.*

To proceed; to issue.

> I'll use that tongue I have: if wit *flow* from 't,
> I shall do good. *Shakespeare's Winter's Tale.*

> The knowledge drawn from experience is quite of another
> kind from that which *flows* from speculation or discourse. *South.*

To glide smoothly without asperity: as, a *flowing* period.

> This discourse of Cyprian, and the flowers of rhetorick in
> it, shew him to have been of a great wit and *flowing* elo-
> quence. *Hakewill on Providence.*

To write smoothly; to speak volubly.

> Virgil is sweet and *flowing* in his hexameters. *Dryden.*

> Did sweeter sounds adorn my *flowing* tongue
> Than ever man pronounc'd, or angel sung. *Prior.*

To abound; to be crowded.

> The dry streets *flow'd* with men. *Chapman.*

To be copious; to be full.

> Then shall our names,
> Be in their *flowing* cups freshly remember'd. *Shak. Hen. V.*

> There ev'ry eye with slumb'rous chains she bound,

A typical page of definitions and citations from the first edition of
Samuel Johnson's *Dictionary of the English Language.*

made a rogue by being present at its representation. At the same time I do not deny that it may have some influence, by making the character of a rogue familiar, and in some degree pleasing." [1] Then collecting himself, as it were, to give a heavy stroke: "There is in it such a *labefactation* of all principles as may be injurious to morality."

While he pronounced this response, we sat in a comical sort of restraint, smothering a laugh, which we were afraid might burst out. In his life of Gay, he has been still more decisive as to the inefficiency of "The Beggar's Opera" in corrupting society. But I have ever thought somewhat differently; for, indeed, not only are the gaiety and heroism of a highwayman very captivating to a youthful imagination, but the arguments for adventurous depredation are so plausible, the allusions so lively, and the contrasts with the ordinary and more painful modes of acquiring the property are so artfully displayed, that it requires a cool and strong judgement to resist so imposing an aggregate: yet, I own, I should be very sorry to have "The Beggar's Opera" suppressed; for there is in it so much of a London life, so much brilliant wit, and such a variety of airs, which, from early association of ideas, engage, soothe, and enliven the mind, that no performance which the theatre exhibits, delights me more.

The late *"worthy"* Duke of Queensbury, as Thomson, in his "Seasons," justly characterizes him, told me, that when Gay shewed him "The Beggar's Opera," his Grace's observation was, "This is a very odd thing, Gay; I am satisfied that it is either a very good thing, or a very bad thing." It proved the former, beyond the warmest expectations of the authour or his friends. Mr. Cambridge, however, shewed us to-day, that there was good reason enough to doubt con-

---

[1] A very eminent physician, whose discernment is as acute and penetrating in judging of the human character as it is in his own profession, remarked once at a club where I was, that a lively young man, fond of pleasure, and without money, would hardly resist a solicitation from his mistress to go upon the highway, immediately after being present at the representation of "The Beggar's Opera." I have been told of an ingenious observation by Mr. Gibbon, that "The Beggar's Opera" may, perhaps, have sometimes increased the number of highwaymen; but that it has had a beneficial effect in refining that class of men, making them less ferocious, more polite, in short, more like gentlemen. Upon this Mr. Courtenay said, that "Gay was the Orpheus of highwaymen."

cerning its success. He was told by Quin, that during the first night of its appearance it was long in a very dubious state; that there was a disposition to damn it, and that it was saved by the song,

"Oh ponder well! be not severe!"

the audience being much affected by the innocent looks of Polly, when she came to those two lines, which exhibit at once a painful and ridiculous image,

"For on the rope that hangs my Dear,
Depends poor Polly's life."

Quin himself had so bad an opinion of it, that he refused the part of Captain Macheath, and gave it to Walker, who acquired great celebrity by his grave yet animated performance of it.

Johnson arraigned the modern politicks of this country, as entirely devoid of all principle of whatever kind. "Politicks (said he) are now nothing more than means of rising in the world. With this sole view do men engage in politicks, and their whole conduct proceeds upon it. How different in that respect is the state of the nation now from what it was in the time of Charles the First, during the Usurpation, and after the Restoration, in the time of Charles the Second. Hudibras affords a strong proof how much hold political principles had then upon the minds of men. There is in Hudibras a great deal of bullion which will always last. But to be sure the brightest strokes of his wit owed their force to the impression of the characters, which was upon men's minds at the time; to their knowing them, at table and in the street; in short, being familiar with them; and above all, to his satire being directed against those whom a little while before they had hated and feared. The nation in general has ever been loyal, has been at all times attached to the monarch, though a few daring rebels have been wonderfully powerful for a time. The murder of Charles the First was undoubtedly not committed with the approbation or consent of the people. Had that been the case, Parliament would not have ventured to consign the regicides to their deserved punishment. And we know what exuberance of joy there was when Charles the Second was restored. If Charles the Second had bent all his mind to it, had made it his sole object, he might have been as absolute as Louis the Fourteenth." A gentleman observed he would have done no harm if he had. JOHNSON. "Why, Sir, absolute princes seldom do any harm. But they who are governed by them are governed by chance. There is no security for good government." CAMBRIDGE. "There have been many sad victims to absolute government." JOHNSON. "So, Sir, have there been to popular factions." BOSWELL. "The question is, which is worst, one wild beast or many?"

Johnson praised "THE SPECTATOR," particularly the character of Sir Roger de Coverley. He said, "Sir Roger did not die a violent death, as has been generally fancied. He was not killed; he died only because others were to die, and because his death afforded an opportunity to Addison for some very fine writing. We have the example of Cervantes making Don Quixote die.—I never could see why Sir Roger is represented as a little cracked. It appears to me that the story of the widow was intended to have something superinduced upon it; but the superstructure did not come."

Somebody found fault with writing verses in a dead language, maintaining that they were merely arrangements of so many words, and laughed at the Universities of Oxford and Cambridge, for sending forth collections of them not only in Greek and Latin, but even in Syriack, Arabick, and other more unknown tongues. JOHNSON. "I would have as many of these as possible; I would have verses in every language that there are the means of acquiring. Nobody imagines that an University is to have at once two hundred poets; but it should be able to shew two hundred scholars. Pieresc's death was lamented, I think, in forty languages. And I would have had at every coronation, and every death of a king, every *Gaudium*, and every *Luctus*, University-verses, in as many languages as can be acquired. I would have the world to be thus told, 'Here is a school where everything may be learnt.'"

It being asked whether it was reasonable for a man to be

angry at another whom a woman had preferred to him?—
JOHNSON. "I do not see, Sir, that it is reasonable for a man
to be angry at another, whom a woman has preferred to
him: but angry he is, no doubt; and he is loath to be angry
at himself."

Before setting out for Scotland on the 23d, I was frequently in his company at different places, but during this
period have recorded only two remarks; one concerning
Garrick: "He has not Latin enough. He finds out the Latin
by the meaning rather than the meaning by the Latin." And
another concerning writers of travels, who, he observed,
"were more defective than any other writers."

I passed many hours with him on the 17th, of which I
find all my memorial is, "much laughing." It should seem
he had that day been in a humour for jocularity and merriment, and upon such occasions I never knew a man laugh
more heartily. We may suppose, that the high relish of a
state so different from his habitual gloom, produced more
than ordinary exertions of that distinguishing faculty of
man, which has puzzled philosophers so much to explain.
Johnson's laugh was as remarkable as any circumstance in
his manner. It was a kind of good humoured growl. Tom
Davies described it drolly enough: "He laughs like a rhi-
noceros."

"To JAMES BOSWELL, ESQ.

"DEAR SIR,

"I am returned from the annual ramble into the middle
counties. Having seen nothing I had not seen before, I have
nothing to relate. Time has left that part of the island few
antiquities; and commerce has left the people no singularities. I was glad to go abroad, and, perhaps, glad to come
home; which is, in other words, I was, I am afraid, weary
of being at home, and weary of being abroad. Is not this the
state of life? But, if we confess this weariness, let us not lament it; for all the wise and all the good say, that we may
cure it.

"For the black fumes which rise in your mind, I can
prescribe nothing but that you disperse them by honest
business or innocent pleasure, and by reading, sometimes

easy and sometimes serious. Change of place is useful; and I hope that your residence at Auchinleck will have many good effects.

*   *   *   *

"Mrs. Thrale was so entertained with your 'Journal,'[1] that she almost read herself blind. She has a great regard for you.

"Of Mrs. Boswell, though she knows in her heart that she does not love me, I am always glad to hear any good, and hope that she and the little dear ladies will have neither sickness nor any other affliction. But she knows that she does not care what becomes of me, and for that she may be sure that I think her very much to blame.

"Never, my dear Sir, do you take it into your head to think that I do not love you; you may settle yourself in full confidence both of my love and my esteem; I love you as a kind man, I value you as a worthy man, and hope in time to reverence you as a man of exemplary piety. I hold you, as Hamlet has it, 'in my heart of hearts,' and therefore, it is little to say, that I am, Sir,

"Your affectionate humble Servant,
"SAM. JOHNSON."

"London, August 27, 1775."

When I met him in London the following year, the account which he gave me of his French tour, was, "Sir, I have seen all the visibilities of Paris, and around it; but to have formed an acqaintance with the people there, would have required more time than I could stay. I was just beginning to creep into acquaintance by means of Colonel Drumgold, a very high man, Sir, head of *L'Ecole Militaire,* a most complete character, for he had first been a professor of rhetorick, and then became a soldier. And, Sir, I was very kindly treated by the English Benedictines, and have a cell appropriated to me in their convent."

He observed, "The great in France live very magnificently, but the rest very miserably. There is no happy mid-

---

[1] My "Journal of a Tour to the Hebrides," which that lady read in the original manuscript.

dle state as in England. The shops of Paris are mean; the meat in the markets is such as would be sent to a gaol in England; and Mr. Thrale justly observed, that the cookery of the French was forced upon them by necessity; for they could not eat their meat, unless they added some taste to it. The French are an indelicate people; they will spit upon any place. At Madame ———'s, a literary lady of rank, the footman took the sugar in his fingers, and threw it into my coffee. I was going to put it aside; but hearing it was made on purpose for me, I e'en tasted Tom's fingers. The same lady would needs make tea *à l'Angloise*. The spout of the tea-pot did not pour freely; she bade the footman blow into it. France is worse than Scotland in every thing but climate. Nature has done more for the French; but they have done less for themselves than the Scotch have done."

It happened that Foote was at Paris at the same time with Dr. Johnson, and his description of my friend while there, was abundantly ludicrous. He told me, that the French were quite astonished at his figure and manner, and at his dress, which he obstinately continued exactly as in London;—his brown clothes, black stockings, and plain shirt. He mentioned, that an Irish gentleman said to Johnson, "Sir, you have not seen the best French players." JOHNSON. "Players, Sir! I look on them as no better than creatures set upon tables and joint stools to make faces and produce laughter, like dancing dogs."—"But, Sir, you will allow that some players are better than others?" JOHNSON. "Yes, Sir, as some dogs dance better than others."

When Johnson was in France, he was generally very resolute in speaking Latin. It was a maxim with him that a man should not let himself down, by speaking a language which he speaks imperfectly. Indeed, we must have often observed how inferiour, how much like a child a man appears, who speaks a broken tongue. When Sir Joshua Reynolds, at one of the dinners of the Royal Academy, presented him to a Frenchman of great distinction, he would not deign to speak French, but talked Latin, though his Excellency did not understand it, owing, perhaps, to Johnson's English pronunciation: yet upon another occasion he was observed to speak French to a Frenchman of high rank, who spoke English; and being asked the reason, with some expression of surprise,—he answered, "because I think my French is as good as his English." Though Johnson understood French perfectly, he could not speak it readily, as I have observed at his first interview with General Paoli, in 1769; yet he wrote it, I imagine, pretty well.

Here let me not forget a curious anecdote, as related to me by Mr. Beauclerk, which I shall endeavour to exhibit as well as I can in that gentleman's lively manner; and in justice to him it is proper to add, that Dr. Johnson told me I might rely both on the correctness of his memory, and the fidelity of his narrative. "When Madame de Boufflers was first in England, (said Beauclerk,) she was desirous to see Johnson. I accordingly went with her to his chambers in the Temple, where she was entertained with his conversation for some time. When our visit was over, she and I left him, and were got into Inner Temple-lane when all at once I heard a noise like thunder. This was occasioned by Johnson, who it seems, upon a little recollection, had taken it into his head that he ought to have done the honours of his literary residence to a foreign lady of quality, and eager to show himself a man of gallantry, was hurrying down the stair-case in violent agitation. He overtook us before we reached the Temple-gate, and brushing in between me and Madame de Boufflers, seized her hand, and conducted her to her coach. His dress was a rusty brown morning suit, a pair of old shoes by way of slippers, a little shrivelled wig sticking on the top of his head, and the sleeves of his shirt and the knees of his breeches hanging loose. A considerable crowd of people gathered round, and were not a little struck by this singular appearance."

He spoke Latin with wonderful fluency and elegance. When Père Boscovitch was in England, Johnson dined in company with him at Sir Joshua Reynolds's, and at Dr. Douglas's, now Bishop of Salisbury. Upon both occasions that celebrated foreigner expressed his astonishment at Johnson's Latin conversation.

In the course of this year Dr. Burney informs me that,

"he very frequently met Dr. Johnson at Mr. Thrale's, at Streatham, where fire and candles lasted, and much longer than the patience of the servants subsisted."

A few of Johnson's sayings, which that gentleman recollects, shall here be inserted.

"I never take a nap after dinner but when I have had a bad night, and then the nap takes me."

"The writer of an epitaph should not be considered as saying nothing but what is strictly true. Allowance must be made for some degree of exaggerated praise. In lapidary inscriptions a man is not upon oath."

"There is now less flogging in our great schools than formerly, but then less is learned there; so that what the boys get at one end they lose at the other."

"After having talked slightingly of musick, he was observed to listen very attentively while Miss Thrale played on the harpsichord, and with eagerness he called to her, 'Why don't you dash away like Burney?' Dr. Burney upon this said to him, 'I believe, Sir, we shall make a musician of you at last.' Johnson with candid complacency replied, 'Sir, I shall be glad to have a new sense given to me.' "

"He had come down one morning to the breakfast-room, and been a considerable time by himself before any body appeared. When on a subsequent day he was twitted by Mrs. Thrale for being very late, which he generally was, he defended himself by alluding to the extraordinary morning, when he had been too early. 'Madam, I do not like to come down to *vacuity*.' "

"Dr. Burney having remarked that Mr. Garrick was beginning to look old, he said, 'Why, Sir, you are not to wonder at that; no man's face has had more wear and tear.' "

Not having heard from him for a longer time than I supposed he would be silent, I wrote to him December 18, not in good spirits. "Sometimes I have been afraid that the cold which has gone over Europe this year like a sort of pestilence has seized you severely: sometimes my imagination, which is upon occasions prolifick of evil, hath figured that you may have somehow taken offence at some part of my conduct."

206

"To James Boswell, Esq.

"DEAR SIR,

"Never dream of any offence. How should you offend me? I consider your friendship as a possession, which I intend to hold till you take it from me, and to lament if ever by my fault I should lose it. However, when such suspicions find their way into your mind, always give them vent; I shall make haste to disperse them; but hinder their first ingress if you can. Consider such thoughts as morbid. . . ."

Having arrived in London late on Friday, the 15th of March, [1776] I hastened next morning to wait on Dr. Johnson, at his house; but found he was removed from Johnson's-court, No. 7, to Bolt-court, No. 8, still keeping to his favourite Fleet-street. My reflection at the time upon this change as marked in my Journal, is as follows: "I felt a foolish regret that he had left a court which bore his name; but it was not foolish to be affected with some tenderness of regard for a place in which I had seen him a great deal, from whence I had often issued a better and a happier man than when I went in, and which had often appeared to my imagination while I trod its pavement, in the solemn darkness of the night, to be sacred to wisdom and piety." Being informed that he was at Mr. Thrale's in the Borough, I hastened thither, and found Mrs. Thrale and him at breakfast. I was kindly welcomed. In a moment he was in a full glow of conversation, and I felt myself elevated as if brought into another state of being. Mrs. Thrale and I looked to each other while he talked, and our looks expressed our congenial admiration and affection for him. I shall ever recollect this scene with great pleasure. I exclaimed to her, "I am now intellectually, *Hermippus redivivus,* I am quite restored by him, by transfusion of mind." "There are many (she replied) who admire and respect Mr. Johnson; but you and I *love* him."

I mentioned with much regret the extravagance of the representative of a great family in Scotland, by which there was danger of its being ruined; and as Johnson respected it for its antiquity, he joined with me in thinking it would be happy if this person should die. Mrs. Thrale seemed shocked at this, as feudal barbarity; and said, "I do not understand this preference of the estate to its owner; of the land to the man who walks upon that land." JOHNSON. "Nay, Madam, it is not a preference of the land to its owner; it is the preference of a family to an individual. Here is an establishment in a country, which is of importance for ages, not only to the chief but to his people; an establishment which extends upwards and downwards; that this should be destroyed by one idle fellow is a sad thing."

On Tuesday, March 19, we met in the morning at the Somerset coffee-house in the Strand, where we were taken up by the Oxford coach. He was accompanied by Mr. Gwyn, the architect; and a gentleman of Merton College, whom he did not know, had the fourth seat. We soon got into conversation; for it was very remarkable of Johnson, that the presence of a stranger had no restraint upon his talk. I observed that Garrick, who was about to quit the stage, would soon have an easier life. JOHNSON. "I doubt that, Sir." BOSWELL. "Why, Sir, he will be Atlas with the burthen off his back." JOHNSON. "But I know not, Sir, if he will be so steady without his load. However, he should never play any more, but be entirely the gentleman, and not partly the player: he should no longer subject himself to be hissed by a mob, or to be insolently treated by performers, whom he used to rule with a high hand, and who would gladly retaliate." BOSWELL. "I think he should play once a year for the benefit of decayed actors, as it has been said he means to do." JOHNSON. "Alas, Sir! he will soon be a decayed actor himself."

Johnson expressed his disapprobation of ornamental architecture, such as magnificent columns supporting a portico, or expensive pilasters supporting merely their own capitals, "because it consumes labour disproportionate to its utility." For the same reason he satyrised statuary. "Painting (said he,) consumes labour not disproportionate to its effect; but a fellow will hack half a year at a block of marble to make something in stone that hardly resembles a man. The value of statuary is owing to its difficulty. You would not value the finest head cut upon a carrot."

Gwyn was a fine lively rattling fellow. Dr. Johnson kept him in subjection, but with a kindly authority. The spirit of the artist, however, rose against what he thought a Gothick attack, and he made a brisk defence. "What, Sir, you will allow no value to beauty in architecture or in statuary? Why should we allow it then in writing? Why do you take the trouble to give us so many fine allusions, and bright images, and elegant phrases? You might convey all your instruction without these ornaments." Johnson smiled with complacency; but said, "Why, Sir, all these ornaments are useful, because they obtain an easier reception for truth; but a building is not at all more convenient for being decorated with superfluous carved work."

Gwyn at last was lucky enough to make one reply to Dr. Johnson, which he allowed to be excellent. Johnson censured him for taking down a church which might have stood many years, and building a new one at a different place, for no other reason but that there might be a direct road to a new bridge; and his expression was, "You are taking a church out of the way, that the people may go in a straight line to the bridge."—"No, Sir (said Gwyn,) I am putting the church *in* the way, that the people may not *go out of the way*." JOHNSON. (with a hearty loud laugh of approbation,) "Speak no more. Rest your colloquial fame upon this."

Upon our arrival at Oxford, Dr. Johnson and I went directly to University College, but were disappointed on finding that one of the fellows, his friend, Mr. Scott, who accompanied him from Newcastle to Edinburgh, was gone to the country. We put up at the Angel inn, and passed the evening by ourselves in easy and familiar conversation. Talking of constitutional melancholy, he observed, "A man so afflicted, Sir, must divert distressing thoughts, and not combat with them." BOSWELL. "May not he think them down, Sir?" JOHNSON. "No, Sir. To attempt to *think them down* is madness. He should have a lamp constantly burning in his bed chamber during the night, and if wakefully disturbed, take a book, and read, and compose himself to rest. To have the management of the mind is a great art, and it may be attained in a considerable degree by experience and habitual exercise." BOSWELL. "Should not he provide amusements for himself? Would it not, for instance, be right for him to take a course of chymistry?" JOHNSON. "Let him take a course of chymistry, or a course of rope-dancing, or a course of any thing to which he is inclined at the time. Let him contrive to have as many retreats for his mind as he can, as many things to which it can fly from itself. Burton's 'Anatomy of Melancholy' is a valuable work. It is, perhaps, overloaded with quotation. But there is a great spirit and great power in what Burton says, when he writes from his own mind."

Next morning we visited Dr. Wetherell, Master of University College, with whom Dr. Johnson conferred on the most advantageous mode of disposing of the books printed at the Clarendon press. I often had occasion to remark, Johnson loved business, loved to have his wisdom actually operate on real life.

We then went to Pembroke College, and waited on his old friend Dr. Adams, the master of it, whom I found to be a most polite, pleasing, communicative man. Dr. Adams told us, that in some of the Colleges at Oxford, the fellows had excluded the students from social intercourse with them in the common room. JOHNSON. "They are in the right, Sir: there can be no real conversation, no fair exertion of mind amongst them, if the young men are by; for a man who has a character does not choose to stake it in their presence." BOSWELL. "But, Sir, may there not be very good conversation without a contest for superiority?" JOHNSON. "No animated conversation, Sir, for it cannot be but one or other will come off superiour. I do not mean that the victor must have the better of the argument, for he may take the weak side; but his superiority of parts and knowledge will necessarily appear; and he to whom he thus shews himself superiour is lessened in the eyes of the young men."

We walked with Dr. Adams into the master's garden, and into the common room. JOHNSON. (after a reverie of meditation,) "Ay! Here I used to play at draughts with Phil. Jones and Fludyer. Jones loved beer, and did not get very forward in the church. Fludyer turned out a scoundrel, a Whig, and said he was ashamed of having been bred at Oxford. He had a living at Putney, and got under the eye of some retainers to the court at that time, and so became a violent Whig: but he had been a scoundrel all along to be sure." BOSWELL. "Was he a scoundrel, Sir, in any other way than that of being a political scoundrel? Did he cheat at draughts?" JOHNSON. "Sir, we never played for *money.*"

I expressed a desire to be acquainted with a lady who had been much talked of, and universally celebrated for extraordinary address and insinuation. JOHNSON. "Never believe extraordinary characters which you hear of people. Depend upon it, Sir, they are exaggerated. You do not see one man shoot a great deal higher than another." I mentioned Mr. Burke. JOHNSON. "Yes; Burke *is* an extraordinary man. His stream of mind is perpetual." It is very pleasing to me to record, that Johnson's high estimation of the talents of this gentleman was uniform from their early acquaintance. Sir Joshua Reynolds informs me, that when Mr. Burke was first elected a member of Parliament and Sir John Hawkins expressed a wonder at his attaining a seat Johnson said, "Now we who know Mr. Burke, know, that he will be one of the first men in the country." And once, when Johnson was ill, and unable to exert himself as much as usual without fatigue, Mr. Burke having been mentioned, he said, "That fellow calls forth all my powers. Were I to see Burke now it would kill me." So much was he accustomed to consider conversation as a contest, and such was his notion of Burke as an opponent.

Next morning, Thursday, March 21, we set out in a post-chaise to pursue our ramble. We dined at an excellent inn at Chapel-house, where he expatiated on the felicity of England in its taverns and inns, and triumphed over the French for not having, in any perfection, the tavern life. "There is no private house, (said he,) in which people can enjoy themselves so well, as at a capital tavern. Let there be ever so great plenty of good things, ever so much grandeur, ever so much elegance, ever so much desire that every body should be easy; in the nature of things it cannot be: there must always be some degree of care and anxiety. The master of the house is anxious to entertain his guests; the guests are anxious to be agreeable to him; and no man, but a very impudent dog indeed, can as freely command what is in another man's house, as if it were his own. Whereas, at a tavern, there is a general freedom from anxiety. You are sure you are welcome: and the more noise you make, the more trouble you give, the more good things you call for, the welcomer you are. No servants will attend you with the alacrity which waiters do, who are incited by the prospect of an immediate reward in proportion as they please. No, Sir; there is nothing which has yet been contrived by man, by which so much happiness is produced as by a good tavern or inn."

Dr. Johnson said to me in the morning, "You will see, Sir, at Mr. Hector's, his sister, Mrs. Careless, a clergyman's widow. She was the first woman with whom I was in love. It dropt out of my head imperceptibly; but she and I shall always have a kindness for each other." He laughed at the notion that a man can never be really in love but once, and considered it as a mere romantick fancy.

On our return from Mr. Bolton's, Mr. Hector took me to his house, where we found Johnson sitting placidly at tea, with his *first love;* who though now advanced in years, was a genteel woman, very agreeable and well bred.

When he again talked of Mrs. Careless to-night, he seemed to have had his affection revived; for he said, "If I had married her, it might have been as happy for me." BOSWELL. "Pray, Sir, do you not suppose that there are fifty women in the world, with any one of whom a man may be as happy, as with any one woman in particular?" JOHNSON. "Ay, Sir, fifty thousand." BOSWELL. "Then, Sir, you are not of opinion with some who imagine that certain men and certain women are made for each other: and that they cannot be happy if they miss their counterparts." JOHNSON. "To be sure not, Sir. I believe marriages would in general be as happy, and often more so, if they were all made by the Lord Chancellor, upon a due consideration of the characters and circumstances, without the parties having any choice in the matter."

I wished to have staid at Birmingham to-night, to have talked more with Mr. Hector; but my friend was impatient to reach his native city; so we drove on that stage in the dark, and were long pensive and silent. When we came within the focus of the Lichfield lamps, "Now (said he,) we are getting out of a state of death." We put up at the Three Crowns, not one of the great inns, but a good old fashioned one, which was kept by Mr. Wilkins, and was the very next house to that in which Johnson was born and brought up, and which was still his own property. We had a comfortable supper, and got into high spirits. I felt all my Toryism glow in this old capital of Staffordshire. I could have offered incense *genio loci;* and I indulged in libations of that ale, which Boniface, in "The Beaux Stratagem," recommends with such an eloquent jollity.

Next morning he introduced me to Mrs. Lucy Porter, his step-daughter. She was now an old maid, with much simplicity of manner. She had never been in London. Her brother, a Captain in the navy, had left her a fortune of ten thousand pounds; about a third of which she had laid out in building a stately house, and making a handsome garden, in an elevated situation in Lichfield. Johnson, when here by himself, used to live at her house. She reverenced him, and he had a parental tenderness for her.

We then visited Mr. Peter Garrick, who had that morning received a letter from his brother David, announcing our coming to Lichfield. He was engaged to dinner, but asked us to tea, and to sleep at his house. Johnson, however, would not quit his old acquaintance Wilkins of the Three Crowns. The family likeness of the Garricks was very striking; and Johnson thought that David's vivacity was not so peculiar to himself as was supposed. "Sir, (said he,) I don't know but if Peter had cultivated all the arts of gaiety as much as David has done, he might have been as brisk and lively. Depend upon it, Sir, vivacity is much an art, and depends greatly on habit."

We dined at our inn, and had with us a Mr. Jackson, one of Johnson's schoolfellows, whom he treated with much kindness, though he seemed to be a low man, dull and untaught. He had a coarse grey coat, black waistcoat, greasy leather breeches, and a yellow uncurled wig; and his countenance had the ruddiness which betokens one who is in no haste to "leave his can." He drank only ale. He had tried to

213

be a cutler at Birmingham, but had not succeeded; and now he lived poorly at home, and had some scheme of dressing leather in a better manner than common; to his indistinct account of which, Dr. Johnson listened with patient attention, that he might assist him with his advice. Here was an instance of genuine humanity and real kindness in this great man, who has been most unjustly represented as altogether harsh and destitute of tenderness.

I saw here, for the first time, *oat ale;* and oat cakes, not hard as in Scotland, but soft like a Yorkshire cake, were served at breakfast. It was pleasant to me to find, that *"Oats,"* the *"food of horses,"* were so much used as the *food of the people* in Dr. Johnson's own town. He expatiated in praise of Lichfield and its inhabitants, who, he said, were "the most sober, decent people in England, the genteelest in proportion to their wealth, and spoke the purest English." I doubted as to the last article of this eulogy: for they had several provincial sounds; as *there,* pronounced like *fear,* instead of like *fair; once,* pronounced *woonse,* instead of *wunse* or *wonse.* Johnson himself never got entirely free of those provincial accents. Garrick sometimes used to take him off, squeezing a lemon into a punch-bowl, with uncouth gesticulations, looking round the company, and calling out, "Who's for *poonsh?"* [1]

Very little business appeared to be going forward in Lichfield. I found however two strange manufactures for so inland a place, sail-cloths and streamers for ships; and I observed them making some saddle-cloths, and dressing sheepskins: but upon the whole, the busy hand of industry seemed to be quite slackened. "Surely, Sir, (said I,) you are an idle set of people." "Sir, (said Johnson,) we are a city of philosophers, we work with our heads, and make the boobies of Birmingham work for us with their hands."

On Monday, March 25, we breakfasted at Mrs. Lucy Porter's. Johnson had sent an express to Dr. Taylor's, acquainting him of our being at Lichfield, and Taylor had returned an answer that his post-chaise should come for us

---

[1] [Garrick himself, like the Lichfieldians, always said—*shupreme, shuperior.*—BURNEY.]

this day. While we sat at breakfast, Dr. Johnson received a letter by the post, which seemed to agitate him very much. When he had read it, he exclaimed, "One of the most dreadful things that has happened in my time." The phrase *my time*, like the word *age*, is usually understood to refer to events of a publick or general nature. I imagined something like an assassination of the King—like a gunpowder plot carried into execution—or like another fire of London. When asked, "What is it, Sir?" he answered, "Mr. Thrale has lost his only son!" This was, no doubt, a very great affliction to Mr. and Mrs. Thrale, which their friends would consider accordingly; but from the manner in which the intelligence of it was communicated by Johnson, it appeared for the moment to be comparatively small. I, however, soon felt a sincere concern, and was curious to observe, how Dr. Johnson would be affected. He said, "This is a total extinction to their family, as much as if they were sold into captivity." Upon my mentioning that Mr. Thrale had daughters, who might inherit his wealth;—"Daughters, (said Johnson, warmly,) he'll no more value his daughters than—" I was going to speak.—"Sir, (said he,) don't you know how you yourself think? Sir, he wishes to propagate his name!" In short, I saw male succession strong in his mind, even where there was no name, no family of any long standing. I said, it was lucky he was not present when this misfortune happened. JOHNSON. "It is lucky for *me*. People in distress never think that you feel enough." BOSWELL. "And, Sir, they will have the hope of seeing you, which will be a relief in the mean time; and when you get to them, the pain will be so far abated, that they will be capable of being consoled by you, which, in the first violence of it, I believe, would not be the case." JOHNSON. "No, Sir; violent pain of mind, like violent pain of body, *must* be severely felt." BOSWELL. "I own, Sir, I have not so much feeling for the distress of others, as some people have, or pretend to have; but I know this, that I would do all in my power to relieve them." JOHNSON. "Sir, it is affectation to pretend to feel the distress of others, as much as they do themselves. It is equally so, as if one should pretend to feel as much pain while a friend's leg is cutting off, as he does. No, Sir; you have expressed the rational and just nature of sympathy. I would have gone to the extremity of the earth to have preserved this boy."

He was soon quite calm. The letter was from Mr. Thrale's clerk, and concluded, "I need not say how much they wish to see you in London." He said, "We shall hasten back from Taylor's."

After dinner Dr. Johnson wrote a letter to Mrs. Thrale, on the death of her son. I said it would be very distressing to Thrale, but she would soon forget it, as she had so many things to think of. JOHNSON. "No, Sir, Thrale will forget it first. *She* has many things that she *may* think of. *He* has many things that he *must* think of." This was a very just remark upon the different effects of those light pursuits which occupy a vacant and easy mind, and those serious engagements which arrest attention, and keep us from brooding over grief.

In the evening we went to the Town-hall, which was converted into a temporary theatre, and saw "Theodosius," with "The Stratford Jubilee." I was happy to see Dr. Johnson sitting in a conspicuous part of the pit, and receiving affectionate homage from all his acquaintance. We were quite gay and merry. I afterwards mentioned to him that I condemned myself for being so, when poor Mr. and Mrs. Thrale were in such distress. JOHNSON. "You are wrong, Sir; twenty years hence Mr. and Mrs. Thrale will not suffer much pain from the death of their son. Now, Sir, you are to consider, that distance of place, as well as distance of time, operates upon the human feelings. I would not have you be gay in the presence of the distressed, because it would shock them; but you may be gay at a distance. Pain for the loss of a friend, or of a relation whom we love, is occasioned by the want which we feel. In time the vacuity is filled with something else; or sometimes the vacuity closes up of itself."

Here I shall record some fragments of my friend's conversation during this jaunt.

"Marriage, Sir, is much more necessary to a man than to a woman: for he is much less able to supply himself with domestick comforts. You will recollect my saying to some ladies the other day, that I had often wondered why young women should marry, as they have so much more freedom, and so much more attention paid to them while unmarried, than when married. I indeed did not mention the *strong* reason for their marrying—the *mechanical* reason." BOSWELL. "Why that *is* a strong one. But does not imagination make it much more important than it is in reality? Is it not, to a certain degree, a delusion in us as well as in women?" JOHNSON. "Why yes, Sir! but it is a delusion that is always beginning again." BOSWELL. "I don't know but there is upon the whole more misery than happiness produced by that passion." JOHNSON. "I don't think so, Sir."

"Never speak of a man in his own presence. It is always indelicate, and may be offensive."

"Questioning is not the mode of the conversation among gentlemen. It is assuming a superiority, and it is particularly wrong to question a man concerning himself. There may be parts of his former life which he may not wish to be made known to other persons, or even brought to his own recollection."

I enjoyed the luxury of our approach to London, that metropolis which we both loved so much, for the high and varied intellectual pleasure which it furnishes. I experienced immediate happiness while whirled along with such a companion, and said to him, "Sir, you observed one day at General Oglethorpe's, that a man is never happy for the present, but when he is drunk. Will you not add,—or when driving rapidly in a post-chaise?" JOHNSON. "No, Sir, you are driving rapidly *from* something, or *to* something."

Talking of melancholy, he said, "Some men, and very thinking men too, have not those vexing thoughts. Sir Joshua Reynolds is the same all the year round. Beauclerk, except when ill and in pain, is the same. But I believe most men have them in the degree in which they are capable of having them. If I were in the country, and were distressed by that malady, I would force myself to take a book; and every time I did it I should find it the easier. Melancholy, indeed, should be diverted by every means but drinking."

We stopped at Messieurs Dillys, booksellers in the Poultry; from whence he hurried away, in a hackney coach, to

Mr. Thrale's in the Borough. I called at his house in the evening, having promised to acquaint Mrs. Williams of his safe return; when, to my surprize, I found him sitting with her at tea, and, as I thought, not in a very good humour: for, it seems, when he had got to Mr. Thrale's, he found the coach was at the door waiting to carry Mrs. and Miss Thrale, and Signor Baretti, their Italian master, to Bath. This was not showing the attention which might have been expected to the "Guide, Philosopher, and Friend;" the *Imlac* who had hastened from the country to console a distressed mother, who he understood was very anxious for his return. They had, I found, without ceremony, proceeded on their intended journey.

On Wednesday, April 3, in the morning I found him very busy putting his books in order, and as they were generally very old ones, clouds of dust were flying around him. He had on a pair of large gloves such as hedgers use. His present appearance put me in mind of my uncle, Dr. Boswell's description of him, "A robust genius, born to grapple with whole libraries."

I gave him an account of a conversation which had passed between me and Captain Cook, the day before, at dinner at Sir John Pringle's; and he was much pleased with the conscientious accuracy of that celebrated circumnavigator, who set me right as to many of the exaggerated accounts given by Dr. Hawkesworth of his Voyages. I told him that while I was with the Captain, I catched the enthusiasm of curiosity and adventure, and felt a strong inclination to go with him on his next voyage. JOHNSON. "Why, Sir, a man *does* feel so, till he considers how very little he can learn from such voyages." BOSWELL. "But one is carried away with the general grand and indistinct notion of A VOYAGE ROUND THE WORLD." JOHNSON. "Yes, Sir, but a man is to guard himself against taking a thing in general." I said I was certain that a great part of what we are told by the travellers to the South Sea must be conjecture, because they had not enough of the language of those countries to understand so much as they have related. Objects falling under the observation of the senses might be clearly known; but every thing intellectual, every thing abstract—politicks, morals, and religion, must be darkly guessed. Dr. Johnson was of the same opinion.

I mentioned Mr. Maclaurin's uneasiness on account of a degree of ridicule carelessly thrown on his deceased father, in Goldsmith's "History of Animated Nature," in which that celebrated mathematician is represented as being subject to fits of yawning so violent as to render him incapable of proceeding in his lecture; a story altogether unfounded, but for the publication of which the law would give no reparation. This led us to agitate the question, whether legal redress could be obtained, even when a man's deceased relation was calumniated in a publication. Mr. Murray maintained there should be reparation, unless the authour could justify himself by proving the fact. JOHNSON. "Sir, it is of so much more consequence that truth should be told, than that individuals should not be made uneasy, that it is much better that the law does not restrain writing freely concerning the characters of the dead. Damages will be given to a man who is calumniated in his life-time, because he may be hurt in his worldly interest, or at least hurt in his mind: but the law does not regard that uneasiness which a man feels on having his ancestor calumniated. That is too nice. Let him deny what is said, and let the matter have a fair chance by discussion. But if a man could say nothing against a character but what he can prove, history could not be written; for a great deal is known of men of which proof cannot be brought. A minister may be notoriously known to take bribes, and yet you may not be able to prove it." Mr. Murray suggested, that the authour should be obliged to show some sort of evidence, though he would not require a strict legal proof: but Johnson firmly and resolutely opposed any restraint whatever, as adverse to a free investigation of the characters of mankind.

On Thursday, April 4, having called on Dr. Johnson, I said, it was a pity that truth was not so firm as to bid defiance to all attacks, so that it might be shot at as much as people chose to attempt, and yet remain unhurt. JOHNSON. "Then, Sir, it would not be shot at. Nobody attempts to dispute that two and two make four: but with contests concerning moral truth, human passions are generally mixed, and therefore it must ever be liable to assault and misrepresentation."

On Thursday, April 11, I dined with him at General Paoli's, in whose house I now resided, and where I had ever afterwards the honour of being entertained with the kindest attention as his constant guest, while I was in London, till I had a house of my own there. I mentioned my having that morning introduced to Mr. Garrick, Count Neni, a Flemish Nobleman of great rank and fortune, to whom Garrick talked of Abel Drugger as a *small part;* and related, with pleasant vanity, that a Frenchman, who had seen him in one of his low characters, exclaimed, *"Comment! je ne le crois pas. Ce n'est pas Monsieur Garrick, ce Grand Homme!"* Garrick added, with an appearance of grave recollection, "If I were to begin life again, I think I should not play those low characters." Upon which I observed, "Sir, you would be in the wrong; for your great excellence is your variety of playing, your representing so well, characters so very different." JOHNSON. "Garrick, Sir, was not in earnest in what he said; for, to be sure, his peculiar excellence is his variety; and, perhaps, there is not any one character which has not been as well acted by somebody else, as he could do it." BOSWELL. "Why then, Sir, did he talk so?" JOHNSON. "Why, Sir, to make you answer as you did." BOSWELL. "I don't know, Sir; he seemed to dip deep into his mind for the reflection." JOHNSON. "He had not far to dip, Sir; he had said the same thing, probably, twenty times before."

On Friday, April 12, I dined with him at our friend Tom Davies's. I introduced Aristotle's doctrine in his "Art of Poetry," of "the κάθαρσις ὧν παθημάιων, the purging of passions," as the purpose of tragedy. "But how are the passions to be purged by terrour and pity?" (said I, with an assumed air of ignorance, to incite him to talk, for which it was often necessary to employ some address.) JOHNSON. "Why, Sir, you are to consider what is the meaning of purging in the original sense. It is to expel impurities from the human body. The mind is subject to the same imperfection. The passions are the great movers of

Letter XIV.

To Mrs Thrale

Madam

I can readily find no paper that is not
destined for juridical use. You will wonder that I have
so written, and indeed I wonder too, but I have often
idly put by my purpose. If my omission has given
in any measure, I have the mortification of pain
in that mind which I would most wish to please
am not, I thank God, worse than when I went
and you have no hope that I should grow better
here. But I will shew myself to morrow, and only
in it hope that my letter will come before me
and that you will have forgiven the negligence

 . Madam,

Your, &c.
most humble and
most obedient servant
Sam: Johnson

Dec. 2. 1768.

11
A letter from Dr. Johnson to Mrs. Thrale, the possessor of " that
mind that I would most wish to please." She was his close
companion for many years until her remarriage led to a coldness
between them.

human actions; but they are mixed with such impurities, that it is necessary they should be purged or refined by means of terrour and pity. For instance, ambition is a noble passion; but by seeing upon the stage, that a man who is so excessively ambitious as to raise himself by injustice, is punished, we are terrified at the fatal consequences of such a passion. In the same manner a certain degree of resentment is necessary; but if we see that a man carries it too far, we pity the object of it, and are taught to moderate that passion." My record upon this occasion does great injustice to Johnson's expression, which was so forcible and brilliant, that Mr. Cradock whispered to me, "O that his words were written in a book!"

I observed the great defect of the tragedy of "Othello" was, that it had not a moral; for that no man could resist the circumstances of suspicion which were artfully suggested to Othello's mind. JOHNSON. "In the first place, Sir, we learn from 'Othello' this very useful moral, not to make an unequal match; in the second place, we learn not to yield too readily to suspicion. The handkerchief is merely a trick, though a very pretty trick; but there are no other circumstances of reasonable suspicion, except what is related by Iago of Cassio's warm expressions concerning Desdemona in his sleep; and that depended entirely upon the assertion of one man. No, Sir, I think 'Othello' has more moral than almost any play."

Johnson and I supped this evening at the Crown and Anchor tavern, in company with Sir Joshua Reynolds, Mr. Langton, Mr. Nairne, now one of the Scotch Judges, with the title of Lord Dunsinan, and my very worthy friend, Sir William Forbes, of Pitsligo.

We discussed the question, whether drinking improved conversation and benevolence. Sir Joshua maintained it did. JOHNSON. "No, Sir: before dinner men meet with great inequality of understanding; and those who are conscious of their inferiority, have the modesty not to talk. When they have drunk wine, every man feels himself happy, and loses that modesty, and grows impudent and vociferous: but he is not improved: he is only not sensible of his defects." Sir Joshua said the Doctor was talking of the effects of excess in wine; but that a moderate glass enlivened the mind, by giving a proper circulation to the blood. "I am, (said he,) in very good spirits, when I get up in the morning. By dinner-time I am exhausted; wine puts me in the same state as when I got up: and I am sure that moderate drinking makes people talk better." JOHNSON. "No, Sir; wine gives not light, gay, ideal hilarity; but tumultuous, noisy, clamorous merriment. I have heard none of those drunken,—nay, drunken is a coarse word,—none of those *vinous* flights." SIR JOSHUA. "Because you have sat by, quite sober, and felt an envy of the happiness of those who were drinking." JOHNSON. "Perhaps, contempt.—And, Sir, it is not necessary to be drunk one's self, to relish the wit of drunkenness. Do we not judge of the drunken wit of the dialogue between Iago and Cassio, the most excellent in its kind, when we are quite sober? Wit is wit, by whatever means it is produced; and, if good, will appear so at all times. I admit that the spirits are raised by drinking, as by the common participation of any pleasure: cock-fighting, or bear-baiting, will raise the spirits of a company, as drinking does, though surely they will not improve conversation. I also admit, that there are some sluggish men who are improved by drinking; as there are fruits which are not good till they are rotten. There are such men, but they are medlars. I indeed allow that there have been a very few men of talents who were improved by drinking; but I maintain that I am right as to the effects of drinking in general: and let it be considered, that there is no position, however false in its universality, which is not true of some particular man." Sir William Forbes said, "Might not a man warmed with wine be like a bottle of beer, which is made brisker by being set before the fire?"—"Nay, (said Johnson, laughing,) I cannot answer that: that is too much for me."

I observed, that wine did some people harm, by inflaming, confusing, and irritating their minds; but that the experience of mankind had declared in favour of moderate drinking. JOHNSON. "Sir, I do not say it is wrong to produce self-complacency by drinking; I only deny that it improves the mind. When I drank wine, I scorned to drink it when

222

in company. I have drunk many a bottle by myself; in the first place, because I had need of it to raise my spirits: in the second place, because I would have nobody to witness its effects upon me."

He said, that for general improvement, a man should read whatever his immediate inclination prompts him to; though to be sure, if a man has a science to learn, he must regularly and resolutely advance. He added, "what we read with inclination makes a much stronger impression. If we read without inclination, half the mind is employed in fixing the attention; so there is but one half to be employed on what we read." He told us, he read Fielding's "Amelia" through, without stopping. He said, "if a man begins to read in the middle of a book, and feels an inclination to go on, let him not quit it, to go to the beginning. He may perhaps not feel again the inclination."

"Lord Chesterfield's Letters to his son, I think, might be made a very pretty book. Take out the immorality, and it should be put in the hands of every young gentleman. An elegant manner and easiness of behaviour are acquired gradually and imperceptibly. No man can say, 'I'll be genteel.' There are ten genteel women for one genteel man, because they are more restrained. A man without some degree of restraint is insufferable; but we are all less restrained than women. Were a woman sitting in company to put out her legs before her as most men do, we should be tempted to kick them in." No man was a more attentive and nice observer of behaviour in those in whose company he happened to be, than Johnson; or however strange it may seem to many, had a higher estimation of its refinements. Lord Eliot informs me, that one day when Johnson and he were at dinner in a gentleman's house in London, upon Lord Chesterfield's Letters being mentioned, Johnson surprized the company by this sentence: "Every man of any education would rather be called a rascal, than accused of deficiency in *the graces*." Mr. Gibbon, who was present, turned to a lady who knew Johnson well, and lived much with him, and in his quaint manner, tapping his box, addressed her thus: "Don't you think, Madam, (looking towards Johnson,) that among *all* your acquaintance you could find *one* exception?" The lady smiled, and seemed to acquiesce.

A gentleman, whom I found sitting with him one morning, said, that in his opinion the character of an infidel was more detestable than that of a man notoriously guilty of an atrocious crime. I differed from him, because we are surer of the odiousness of the one, than of the errour of the other. JOHNSON. "Sir, I agree with him; for the infidel would be guilty of any crime if he were inclined to it."

When I complained of having dined at a splendid table without hearing one sentence of conversation worthy of being remembered, he said, "Sir, there seldom is any such conversation." BOSWELL. "Why then meet at table?" JOHNSON. "Why to eat and drink together, and to promote kindness; and, Sir, this is better done when there is no solid conversation: for when there is, people differ in opinion, and get into bad humour, or some of the company who are not capable of such conversation, are left out, and feel themselves uneasy. It was for this reason Sir Robert Walpole said, he always talked bawdy at his table, because in that all could join."

Being irritated by hearing a gentleman ask Mr. Levett a variety of questions concerning him, when he was sitting by, he broke out, "Sir, you have but two topicks, yourself and me. I am sick of both." "A man, (said he,) should not talk of himself, nor much of any particular person. He should take care not to be made a proverb; and, therefore, should avoid having any one topick of which people can say, 'We shall hear him upon it.' There was a Dr. Oldfield, who was always talking of the Duke of Marlborough. He came into a coffee house one day, and told that his Grace had spoken in the House of Lords for half an hour. 'Did he indeed speak for half an hour?' (said Belchier, the surgeon.)—'Yes.'—'And what did he say of Dr. Oldfield?'— 'Nothing.'—'Why then, Sir, he was very ungrateful; for Dr. Oldfield could not have spoken for a quarter of an hour, without saying something of him.' "

I am now to record a very curious incident in Dr. Johnson's life, which fell under my own observation; and which

I am persuaded will, with the liberal-minded, be much to his credit.

My desire of being acquainted with celebrated men of every description, had made me, much about the same time, obtain an introduction to Dr. Samuel Johnson and to John Wilkes, Esq. Two men more different could perhaps not be selected out of all mankind. They had even attacked one another with some asperity in their writings; yet I lived in habits of friendship with both. I could fully relish the excellence of each; for I have ever delighted in that intellectual chymistry, which can separate good qualities from evil in the same person.

Sir John Pringle, "mine own friend and my Father's friend," between whom and Dr. Johnson I in vain wished to establish an acquaintance, as I respected and lived in intimacy with both of them, observed to me once, very ingeniously, "It is not in friendship as in mathematicks, where two things, each equal to a third, are equal between themselves. You agree with Johnson as a middle quality, and you agree with me as a middle quality; but Johnson and I should not agree." Sir John was not sufficiently flexible; so I desisted; knowing, indeed, that the repulsion was equally strong on the part of Johnson; who, I know not from what cause, unless his being a Scotchman, had formed a very erroneous opinion of Sir John. But I conceived an irresistible wish, if possible, to bring Dr. Johnson and Mr. Wilkes together. How to manage it, was a nice and difficult matter.

My worthy booksellers and friends, Messieurs Dilly in the Poultry, at whose hospitable and well-covered table I have seen a greater number of literary men, than at any other, except that of Sir Joshua Reynolds, had invited me to meet Mr. Wilkes and some more gentlemen, on Wednesday, May 15. "Pray (said I,) let us have Dr. Johnson."—"What with Mr. Wilkes? not for the world, (said Mr. Edward Dilly;) Dr. Johnson would never forgive me."—"Come, (said I), if you'll let me negociate for you, I will be answerable that all shall go well." DILLY. "Nay, if you will take it upon you, I am sure I shall be very happy to see them both here."

Notwithstanding the high veneration which I entertained

for Dr. Johnson, I was sensible that he was sometimes a little actuated by the spirit of contradiction, and by means of that I hoped I should gain my point. I was persuaded that if I had come upon him with a direct proposal, "Sir, will you dine in company with Jack Wilkes?" he would have flown into a passion, and would probably have answered, "Dine with Jack Wilkes, Sir! I'd as soon dine with Jack Ketch." I therefore, while we were sitting quietly by ourselves at his house in an evening, took occasion to open my plan thus:—"Mr. Dilly, Sir, sends his respectful compliments to you, and would be happy if you would do him the honour to dine with him on Wednesday next along with me, as I must soon go to Scotland." JOHNSON. "Sir, I am obliged to Mr. Dilly. I will wait upon him—" BOSWELL. "Provided, Sir, I suppose, that the company which he is to have, is agreeable to you." JOHNSON. "What do you mean, Sir? What do you take me for? Do you think I am so ignorant of the world, as to imagine that I am to prescribe to a gentleman what company he is to have at his table?" BOSWELL. "I beg your pardon, Sir, for wishing to prevent you from meeting people whom you might not like. Perhaps he may have some of what he calls his patriotick friends with him." JOHNSON. "Well, Sir, and what then? What care *I* for his *patriotick friends?* Poh!" BOSWELL. "I should not be surprized to find Jack Wilkes there." JOHNSON. "And if Jack Wilkes *should* be there, what is that to *me*, Sir? My dear friend, let us have no more of this. I am sorry to be angry with you; but really it is treating me strangely to talk to me as if I could not meet any company whatever, occasionally." BOSWELL. "Pray, forgive me, Sir: I meant well. But you shall meet whoever comes, for me." Thus I secured him, and told Dilly that he would find him very well pleased to be one of his guests on the day appointed.

Upon the much expected Wednesday, I called on him about half an hour before dinner, as I often did when we were to dine out together, to see that he was ready in time, and to accompany him. I found him buffeting his books, as upon a former occasion, covered with dust, and making no preparation for going abroad. "How is this, Sir? (said I). Don't you recollect that you are to dine at Mr. Dilly's?"

JOHNSON. "Sir, I did not think of going to Dilly's: it went out of my head. I have ordered dinner at home with Mrs. Williams." BOSWELL. "But, my dear Sir, you know you were engaged to Mr. Dilly, and I told him so. He will expect you, and will be much disappointed if you don't come." JOHNSON. "You must talk to Mrs. Williams about this."

Here was a sad dilemma. I feared that what I was so confident I had secured, would yet be frustrated. He had accustomed himself to shew Mrs. Williams such a degree of humane attention, as frequently imposed some restraint upon him; and I knew that if she should be obstinate, he would not stir. I hastened down stairs to the blind lady's room, and told her I was in great uneasiness, for Dr. Johnson had engaged to me to dine this day at Mr. Dilly's, but that he had told me he had forgotten his engagement, and had ordered dinner at home. "Yes, Sir (said she, pretty peevishly,) Dr. Johnson is to dine at home."—"Madam, (said I,) his respect for you is such, that I know he will not leave you, unless you absolutely desire it. But as you have so much of his company, I hope you will be good enough to forego it for a day: as Mr. Dilly is a very worthy man, has frequently had agreeable parties at his house for Dr. Johnson, and will be vexed if the Doctor neglects him to-day. And then, Madam, be pleased to consider my situation; I carried the message, and I assured Mr. Dilly that Dr. Johnson was to come; and no doubt he has made a dinner, and invited a company, and boasted of the honour he expected to have. I shall be quite disgraced if the Doctor is not there." She gradually softened to my solicitations, which were certainly as earnest as most entreaties to ladies upon any occasion, and was graciously pleased to empower me to tell Dr. Johnson, "That all things considered, she thought he should certainly go." I flew back to him, still in dust, and careless of what should be the event, "indifferent in his choice to go or stay;" but as soon as I had announced to him Mrs. Williams's consent, he roared, "Frank, a clean shirt," and was very soon drest. When I had him fairly seated in a hackney-coach with me, I exulted as much as a fortune-hunter who has got an heiress into a post-chaise with him to set out for Gretna-Green.

When we entered Mr. Dilly's drawing-room, he found himself in the midst of a company he did not know. I kept myself snug and silent, watching how he would conduct himself. I observed him whispering to Mr. Dilly, "Who is that gentleman, sir?"—"Mr. Arthur Lee."—JOHNSON. "Too, too, too," (under his breath,) which was one of his habitual mutterings. Mr. Arthur Lee could not but be very obnoxious to Johnson, for he was not only a *patriot*, but an *American*. He was afterwards minister from the United States at the court of Madrid. "And who is the gentleman in lace?"— "Mr. Wilkes, Sir." This information confounded him still more; he had some difficulty to restrain himself, and taking up a book, sat down upon a window-seat and read, or at least kept his eye upon it intently for some time, till he composed himself. His feelings, I dare say, were aukward enough. But he no doubt recollected his having rated me for supposing that he could be at all disconcerted by any company, and he, therefore, resolutely set himself to behave quite as an easy man of the world, who could adapt himself at once to the disposition and manners of those whom he might chance to meet.

The cheering sound of "Dinner is upon the table," dissolved his reverie, and we *all* sat down without any symptom of ill humour. There were present, beside Mr. Wilkes, and Mr. Arthur Lee, who was an old companion of mine when he studied physick at Edinburgh, Mr. (now Sir John) Miller, Dr. Lettsom, and Mr. Slater, the druggist. Mr. Wilkes placed himself next to Dr. Johnson, and behaved to him with so much attention and politeness, that he gained upon him insensibly. No man eat more heartily than Johnson, or loved better what was nice and delicate. Mr. Wilkes was very assiduous in helping him to some fine veal. "Pray give me leave, Sir;—It is better here—A little of the brown—Some fat, Sir—A little of the stuffing—Some gravy—Let me have the pleasure of giving you some butter —Allow me to recommend a squeeze of this orange;—or the lemon, perhaps, may have more zest."—"Sir, Sir, I am obliged to you, Sir," cried Johnson, bowing, and turning his head to him with a look for some time of "surly virtue," but, in a short while, of complacency.

Foote being mentioned, Johnson said, "He is not a good mimick." One of the company added, "A merry Andrew, a buffoon." JOHNSON. "But he has wit too, and is not deficient in ideas, or in fertility and variety of imagery, and not empty of reading; he has knowledge enough to fill up his part. One species of wit he has in an eminent degree, that of escape. You drive him into a corner with both hands; but he's gone, Sir, when you think you have got him—like an animal that jumps over your head. Then he has a great range for wit; he never lets truth stand between him and a jest, and he is sometimes mighty coarse. Garrick is under many restraints from which Foote is free." WILKES. "Garrick's wit is more like Lord Chesterfield's." JOHNSON. "The first time I was in company with Foote was at Fitzherbert's. Having no good opinion of the fellow, I was resolved not to be pleased; and it is very difficult to please a man against his will. I went on eating my dinner pretty sullenly, affecting not to mind him. But the dog was so very comical, that I was obliged to lay down my knife and fork, throw myself back upon my chair, and fairly laugh it out. No, Sir, he was irresistible.[1] He upon one occasion experienced, in an extraordinary degree, the efficacy of his powers of entertaining. Amongst the many and various modes which he tried of getting money, he became a partner with a small-beer brewer, and he was to have a share of the profits for procuring customers amongst his numerous acquaintance. Fitzherbert was one who took his small-beer; but it was so bad that the servants resolved not to drink it. They were at some loss how to notify their resolution, being afraid of offending their master, who they knew liked Foote much as a companion. At last they fixed upon a little black boy, who was rather a favourite, to be their deputy, and deliver their remonstrance; and having invested him with the whole authority of the kitchen, he was to inform Mr. Fitzherbert, in all their names, upon a certain day, that they would drink Foote's small-beer no longer. On that day Foote happened to dine at Fitzherbert's, and this boy served at table; he was so delighted with Foote's stories, and merriment,

[1] Foote told me, that Johnson said of him, "For loud obstreperous broad-faced mirth I know not his equal."

and grimace, that when he went down stairs, he told them, "This is the finest man I have ever seen. I will not deliver your message. I will drink his small-beer."

Somebody observed that Garrick could not have done this. WILKES. "Garrick would have made the small-beer still smaller. He is now leaving the stage; but he will play *Scrub* all his life." I knew that Johnson would let nobody attack Garrick but himself, as Garrick said to me, and I had heard him praise his liberality; so to bring out his commendation of his celebrated pupil, I said, loudly, "I have heard Garrick is liberal." JOHNSON. "Yes, Sir, I know that Garrick has given away more money than any man in England that I am acquainted with, and that not from ostentatious views. Garrick was very poor when he began life; so when he came to have money, he probably was very unskilful in giving away, and saved when he should not. But Garrick began to be liberal as soon as he could; and I am of opinion, the reputation of avarice which he has had, has been very lucky for him, and prevented his having many enemies. You despise a man for avarice, but do not hate him. Garrick might have been much better attacked for living with more splendour than is suitable to a player: if they had had the wit to have assaulted him in that quarter, they might have galled him more. But they have kept clamouring about his avarice, which has rescued him from much obloquy and envy."

Talking of the great difficulty of obtaining authentick information for biography, Johnson told us, "When I was a young fellow I wanted to write the 'Life of Dryden,' and in order to get materials, I applied to the only two persons then alive who had seen him; these were old Swinney, and old Cibber. Swinney's information was no more than this, 'That at Will's coffee-house Dryden had a particular chair for himself, which was set by the fire in winter, and was then called his winter-chair; and that it was carried out for him to the balcony in summer, and was then called his summer-chair.' Cibber could tell no more but 'That he remembered him a decent old man, arbiter of critical disputes at Will's.' You are to consider that Cibber was then at a great distance from Dryden, had perhaps one leg only in the room, and durst not draw in the other." BOSWELL. "Yet Cibber was a man of observation?" JOHNSON. "I think not." BOSWELL. "You will allow his 'Apology' to be well done." JOHNSON. "Very well done, to be sure, Sir. That book is a striking proof of the justice of Pope's remark:

> " 'Each might his several province well command,
>   Would all but stoop to what they understand.' "

BOSWELL. "And his plays are good." JOHNSON. "Yes; but that was his trade; *l'esprit du corps;* he had been all his life among players and play-writers. I wondered that he had so little to say in conversation, for he had kept the best company, and learnt all that can be got by the ear. He abused Pindar to me, and then shewed me an ode of his own, with an absurd couplet, making a linnet soar on an eagle's wing. I told him that when the ancients made a simile, they always made it like something real."

Mr. Arthur Lee mentioned some Scotch who had taken possession of a barren part of America, and wondered why they should choose it. JOHNSON. "Why, Sir, all barrenness is comparative. The *Scotch* would not know it to be barren." BOSWELL. "Come, come, he is flattering the English. You have now been in Scotland, Sir, and say if you did not see meat and drink enough there." JOHNSON. "Why yes, Sir; meat and drink enough to give the inhabitants sufficient strength to run away from home." All these quick and lively sallies were said sportively, quite in jest, and with a smile, which showed that he meant only wit. Upon this topick he and Mr. Wilkes could perfectly assimilate; here was a bond of union between them, and I was conscious that as both of them had visited Caledonia, both were fully satisfied of the strange narrow ignorance of those who imagine that it is a land of famine. But they amused themselves with persevering in the old jokes. When I claimed a superiority for Scotland over England in one respect, that no man can be arrested there for a debt merely because another swears it against him; but there must first be the judgement of a court of law ascertaining its justice; and that a seizure of the person, before judgement is obtained, can take place only, if his creditor should swear that he is about to fly from the country, or, as it is technically expressed, is *in meditatione fugæ:* WILKES. "That, I should think, may be safely sworn of all the Scotch nation." JOHNSON. (To Mr. Wilkes) "You must know, Sir, I lately took my friend Boswell, and shewed him genuine civilised life in an English provincial town. I turned him loose at Lichfield, my native city, that he might see for once real civility: for you know he lives among savages in Scotland, and among rakes in London." WILKES. "Except when he is with grave, sober, decent people, like you and me." JOHNSON. (smiling) "And we ashamed of him."

They were quite frank and easy. Johnson told the story of his asking Mrs. Macaulay to allow her footman to sit down with them, to prove the ridiculousness of the arguments for the equality of mankind; and he said to me afterwards, with a nod of satisfaction, "You saw Mr. Wilkes acquiesced." Wilkes talked with all imaginable freedom of the ludicrous title given to the Attorney-General, *Diabolus Regis;* adding, "I have reason to know something about that officer; for I was prosecuted for a libel." Johnson, who many people would have supposed must have been furiously angry at hearing this talked of so lightly, said not a word. He was now, *indeed,* "a good-humoured fellow."

After dinner we had an accession of Mrs. Knowles, the Quaker lady, well known for her various talents, and of Mr. Alderman Lee. Amidst some patriotick groans, somebody (I think the Alderman) said, "Poor old England is lost." JOHNSON. "Sir, it is not so much to be lamented that old England is lost, as that the Scotch have found it." WILKES. "Had Lord Bute governed Scotland only, I should not have taken the trouble to write his eulogy, and dedicate 'MORTIMER' to him."

Mr. Wilkes held a candle to shew a fine print of a beautiful female figure which hung in the room, and pointed out the elegant contour of the bosom with the finger of an arch connoisseur. He afterwards in a conversation with me waggishly insisted, that all the time Johnson shewed visible signs of a fervent admiration of the corresponding charms of the fair Quaker.

This record, though by no means so perfect as I could wish, will serve to give a notion of a very curious interview, which was not only pleasing at the time, but had the agreeable and benignant effect of reconciling any animosity, and sweetening any acidity, which, in the various bustle of political contest, had been produced in the minds of two men, who though widely different, had so many things in common—classical learning, modern literature, wit and humour, and ready repartee—that it would have been much to be regretted if they had been for ever at a distance from each other.

Mr. Burke gave me much credit for this successful *negotiation;* and pleasantly said, "that there was nothing equal to it in the whole history of the *Corps Diplomatique."*

I attended Dr. Johnson home, and had the satisfaction to hear him tell Mrs. Williams how much he had been pleased with Mr. Wilkes's company, and what an agreeable day he had passed.

On the evening of the next day I took leave of him, being to set out for Scotland. I thanked him with great warmth for all his kindness. "Sir, (said he,) you are very welcome. Nobody repays it with more."

How very false is the notion that has gone round the world of the rough, and passionate, and harsh manners of this great and good man. That he had occasional sallies of heat of temper, and that he was sometimes, perhaps, "too easily provoked" by absurdity and folly, and sometimes too desirous of triumph in colloquial contest, must be allowed. The quickness both of his perception and sensibility disposed him to sudden explosions of satire; to which his extraordinary readiness of wit was a strong and almost irresistible incitement. I admit that the beadle within him was often so eager to apply the lash, that the Judge had not time to consider the case with sufficient deliberation.

That he was occasionally remarkable for violence of temper may be granted: but let us ascertain the degree, and not let it be supposed that he was in a perpetual rage, and never without a club in his hand to knock down every one who approached him. On the contrary, the truth is, that by much the greatest part of his time he was civil, obliging,

233

nay, polite in the true sense of the word; so much so, that many gentlemen who were long acquainted with him never received, or even heard a strong expression from him.

On Sunday evening, Sept. 14, [1777] I arrived at Ashbourne, and drove directly up to Dr. Taylor's door. Dr. Johnson and he appeared before I had got out of the post-chaise, and welcomed me cordially.

I told them that I had travelled all the preceding night, and gone to bed at Leek, in Staffordshire; and that when I rose to go to church in the afternoon, I was informed there had been an earthquake, of which, it seems the shock had been felt in some degree at Ashbourne. JOHNSON. "Sir, it will be much exaggerated in publick talk: for, in the first place, the common people do not accurately adapt their thoughts to the objects; nor, secondly, do they accurately adapt their words to their thoughts: they do not mean to lie; but, taking no pains to be exact, they give you very false accounts. A great part of their language is proverbial. If any thing rocks at all, they say *it rocks like a cradle;* and in this way they go on."

The subject of grief for the loss of relations and friends being introduced, I observed that it was strange to consider how soon it in general wears away. Dr. Taylor mentioned a gentleman of the neighbourhood as the only instance he had ever known of a person who had endeavoured to *retain* grief. He told Dr. Taylor that after his Lady's death, which affected him deeply, he *resolved* that the grief, which he cherished with a kind of sacred fondness, should be lasting; but that he found he could not keep it long. JOHNSON. "All grief for what cannot in the course of nature be helped, soon wears away; in some sooner, indeed, in some later; but it never continues very long, unless where there is madness, such as will make a man have pride so fixed in his mind, as to imagine himself a king; or any other passion in an unreasonable way: for all unnecessary grief is unwise, and therefore will not be long retained by a sound mind. If indeed, the cause of our grief is occasioned by our own misconduct, if grief is mingled with remorse of conscience, it should be lasting." BOSWELL. "But, Sir, we do not approve of a man who very soon forgets the loss of a wife or a friend." JOHNSON. "Sir, we disapprove of him, not because he soon forgets his grief; for the sooner it is forgotten the better, but because we suppose, that if he forgets his wife or his friend soon, he has not had much affection for them."

I was somewhat disappointed in finding that the edition of the English Poets, for which he was to write Prefaces and Lives, was not an undertaking directed by him: but that he was to furnish a Preface and Life to any poet the booksellers pleased. I asked him if he would do this to any dunce's works, if they should ask him. JOHNSON. "Yes, Sir, and *say* he was a dunce." My friend seemed now not much to relish talking of this edition.

Tuesday, September 16, Dr. Taylor thus described to me his old school-fellow and friend, Johnson: "He is a man of a very clear head, great power of words, and a very gay imagination; but there is no disputing with him. He will not hear you, and having a louder voice than you, must roar you down."

I mentioned to Dr. Johnson, that David Hume's persisting in his infidelity, when he was dying, shocked me much. JOHNSON. "Why should it shock you, Sir? Hume owned he had never read the New Testament with attention. Here then was a man who had been at no pains to enquire into the truth of religion, and had continually turned his mind the other way. It was not to be expected that the prospect of death would alter his way of thinking, unless GOD should send an angel to set him right." I said, I had reason to believe that the thought of annihilation gave Hume no pain. JOHNSON. "It was not so, Sir. He had a vanity in being thought easy. It is more probable that he should assume an appearance of ease, than so very improbable a thing should be, as a man not afraid of going (as, in spite of his delusive theory, he cannot be sure but he may go), into an unknown state, and not being uneasy at leaving all he knew. And you are to consider, that upon his own principle of annhilation he had no motive to speak the truth." The horrour of death, which I had always observed in Dr. Johnson, appeared strong to-night. I ventured to tell him, that I had been, for

235

moments in my life, not afraid of death; therefore I could suppose another man in that state of mind for a considerable space of time. He said, "he never had a moment in which death was not terrible to him." He added, that it had been observed, that scarce any man dies in publick, but with apparent resolution; from that desire of praise which never quits us.

Dr. Johnson was much pleased with a remark which I told him was made to me by General Paoli:—"That it is impossible not to be afraid of death; and that those who at the time of dying are not afraid, are not thinking of death, but of applause, or something else, which keeps death out of their sight: so that all men are equally afraid of death when they see it; only some have a power of turning their sight away from it better than others."

Talking of biography, I said, in writing a life, a man's peculiarities should be mentioned, because they mark his character. JOHNSON. "Sir, there is no doubt as to peculiarities: the question is, whether a man's vices should be mentioned; for instance, whether it should be mentioned that Addison and Parnell drank too freely; for people will probably more easily indulge in drinking from knowing this; so that more ill may be done by the example, than good by telling the whole truth." Here was an instance of his varying from himself in talk; for when Lord Hailes and he sat one morning calmly conversing in my house at Edinburgh, I well remember that Dr. Johnson maintained, that "If a man is to write *A Panegyrick,* he may keep vices out of sight: but if he professes to write *A Life,* he must represent it really as it was;" and when I objected to the danger of telling that Parnell drank to excess, he said, that "it would produce an instructive caution to avoid drinking, when it was seen, that even the learning and genius of Parnell could be debased by it." And in the Hebrides he maintained, as appears from my "Journal," that a man's intimate friend should mention his faults, if he writes his life.

Friday, September 19, after breakfast, Dr. Johnson and I set out in Dr. Taylor's chaise to go to Derby. In our way, Johnson strongly expressed his love of driving fast in a post-chaise. "If (said he) I had no duties, and no reference to futurity, I would spend my life in driving briskly in a post-chaise with a pretty woman; but she should be one who could understand me, and would add something to the conversation."

We entered seriously upon a question of much importance to me, which Johnson was pleased to consider with friendly attention. I had long complained to him that I felt myself discontented in Scotland, as too narrow a sphere, and that I wished to make my chief residence in London, the great scene of ambition, instruction, and amusement: a scene, which was to me, comparatively speaking, a heaven upon earth. JOHNSON. "Why, Sir, I never knew any one who had such a *gust* for London as you have: and I cannot blame you for your wish to live there: yet, Sir, were I in your father's place, I should not consent to your settling there; for I have the old feudal notions, and I should be afraid that Auchinleck would be deserted, as you would soon find it more desirable to have a country-seat in a better climate."

I suggested a doubt, that if I were to reside in London, the exquisite zest with which I relished it in occasional visits might go off, and I might grow tired of it. JOHNSON. "Why, Sir, you find no man, at all intellectual, who is willing to leave London. No, Sir, when a man is tired of London, he is tired of life; for there is in London all that life can afford."

We talked of employment being absolutely necessary to preserve the mind from wearying and growing fretful, especially in those who have a tendency to melancholy; and I mentioned to him a saying which somebody had related of an American savage, who, when an European was expatiating on all the advantages of money, put this question: "Will it purchase *occupation?*" JOHNSON. "Depend upon it, Sir, this saying is too refined for a savage. And, Sir, money *will* purchase occupation; it will purchase all the conveniences of life; it will purchase variety of company; it will purchase all sorts of entertainment."

Johnson and Taylor were so different from each other,

that I wondered at their preserving an intimacy. Their having been at school and college together, might, in some degree, account for this; but Sir Joshua Reynolds has furnished me with a stronger reason; for Johnson mentioned to him, that he had been told by Taylor he was to be his heir. I shall not take upon me to animadvert upon this; but certain it is that Johnson paid great attention to Taylor. He now, however, said to me, "Sir, I love him; but I do not love him more; my regard for him does not increase. As it is said in the Apocrypha, 'his talk is of bullocks.' [1] I do not suppose he is very fond of my company. His habits are by no means sufficiently clerical: this he knows that I see; and no man likes to live under the eye of perpetual disapprobation."

I mentioned to Johnson a respectable person of a very strong mind, who had little of that tenderness which is common to human nature; as an instance of which, when I suggested to him that he should invite his son, who had been settled ten years in foreign parts, to come home and pay him a visit, his answer was, "No, no, let him mind his business." JOHNSON. "I do not agree with him, Sir, in this. Getting money is not all a man's business: to cultivate kindness is a valuable part of the business of life."

In the evening, Johnson being in very good spirits, entertained us with several characteristical portraits. I shall present my readers with a series of what I gathered this evening from the Johnsonian garden.

"Did we not hear so much said of Jack Wilkes, we should think more highly of his conversation. Jack has a great variety of talk, Jack is a scholar, and Jack has the manners of a gentleman. But after hearing his name sounded from pole to pole, as the phœnix of convivial felicity, we are disappointed in his company. He has always been *at me:* but I would do Jack a kindness, rather than not. The contest is now over."

"Garrick's gaiety of conversation has delicacy and ele-

---

[1] Ecclesiasticus, chap. xxxviii. v. 25. The whole chapter may be read as an admirable illustration of the superiority of cultivated minds over the gross and illiterate.

gance: Foote makes you laugh more; but Foote has the air of a buffoon paid for entertaining the company. He, indeed, well deserves his hire."

"Colley Cibber once consulted me as to one of his birthday Odes, a long time before it was wanted. I objected very freely to several passages. Cibber lost patience, and would not read his Ode to an end. When we had done with criticism, we walked over to Richardson's, the authour of 'Clarissa,' and I wondered to find Richardson displeased that I 'did not treat Cibber with more *respect.*' Now, Sir, to talk of *respect for a player!*" (smiling disdainfully.) Boswell. "There, Sir, you are always heretical: you never will allow merit to a player." Johnson. "Merit, Sir, what merit? Do you respect a rope-dancer, or a ballad-singer?" Boswell. "No, Sir: but we respect a great player, as a man who can conceive lofty sentiments, and can express them gracefully." Johnson. "What, Sir, a fellow who claps a hump on his back, and a lump on his leg, and cries, '*I am Richard the Third*'? Nay, sir, a ballad-singer is a higher man, for he does two things; he repeats and he sings: there is both recitation and musick in his performance: the player only recites." Boswell. "My dear Sir! you may turn any thing into ridicule. I allow, that a player of farce is not entitled to respect; he does a little thing: but he who can represent exalted characters, and touch the noblest passions, has very respectable powers; and mankind have agreed in admiring great talents for the stage. We must consider, too, that a great player does what very few are capable to do: his art is a very rare faculty. *Who* can repeat Hamlet's soliloquy, 'To be, or not to be,' as Garrick does it?" Johnson. "Any body may. Jemmy, there (a boy about eight years old, who was in the room) will do it as well in a week." Boswell. "No, no, Sir: and as a proof of the merit of great acting, and of the value which mankind set upon it, Garrick has got a hundred thousand pounds." Johnson. "Is getting a hundred thousand pounds a proof of excellence? That has been done by a scoundrel commissary."

This was most fallacious reasoning. I was *sure,* for once, that I had the best side of the argument. I boldly maintained the just distinction between a tragedian and a mere theatrical droll; between those who rouse our terrour and pity, and those who only make us laugh.

On Monday, September 22, when at breakfast, I unguardedly said to Dr. Johnson, "I wish I saw you and Mrs. Macaulay together." He grew very angry; and, after a pause, while a cloud gathered on his brow, he burst out, "No, Sir; you would not see us quarrel, to make you sport. Don't you know that it is very uncivil to *pit* two people against one another?" Then, checking himself, and wishing to be more gentle, he added, "I do not say you should be hanged or drowned for this; but it *is* very uncivil." Dr. Taylor thought him in the wrong, and spoke to him privately of it; but I afterwards acknowledged to Johnson that I was to blame, for I candidly owned, that I meant to express a desire to see a contest between Mrs. Macaulay and him; but then I knew how the contest would end; so that I was to see him triumph." JOHNSON. "Sir, you cannot be sure how a contest will end; and no man has a right to engage two people in a dispute by which their passions may be enflamed, and they may part with bitter resentment against each other. I would sooner keep company with a man from whom I must guard my pockets, than with a man who contrives to bring me into a dispute with somebody that he may hear it. This is the great fault of ——, (naming one of our friends) endeavouring to introduce a subject upon which he knows two people in the company differ." BOSWELL. "But he told me, Sir, he does it for instruction." JOHNSON. "Whatever the motive be, Sir, the man who does so, does very wrong. He has no more right to instruct himself at such risk, than he has to make two people fight a duel, that he may learn how to defend himself."

He found great fault with a gentleman of our acquaintance for keeping a bad table. "Sir, (said he,) when a man is invited to dinner, he is disappointed if he does not get something good. I advised Mrs. Thrale, who has no card-parties at her house, to give sweet-meats, and such good things, in an evening, as are not commonly given, and she would find company enough come to her; for every body

loves to have things which please the palate put in their
way, without trouble or preparation." Such was his attention to the *minutiæ* of life and manners.

One morning after breakfast, when the sun shone bright,
we walked out together, and "pored" for some time with
placid indolence upon an artificial water-fall, which Dr.
Taylor had made by building a strong dyke of stone across
the river behind the garden. It was now somewhat obstructed by branches of trees and other rubbish, which had
come down the river, and settled close to it. Johnson, partly
from a desire to see it play more freely, and partly from
that inclination to activity which will animate, at times,
the most inert and sluggish mortal, took a long pole which
was lying on a bank, and pushed down several parcels of
this wreck with painful assiduity, while I stood quietly by,
wondering to behold the sage thus curiously employed, and
smiling with an humourous satisfaction each time when he
carried his point. He worked till he was quite out of breath;
and having found a large dead cat so heavy that he could
not move it after several efforts, "Come," said he (throwing
down the pole,) "*you* shall take it now;" which I accordingly did, and being a fresh man, soon made the cat tumble over the cascade. This may be laughed at as too tri-
fling to record; but it is a small characteristick trait in the
Flemish picture which I give of my friend, and in which,
therefore, I mark the most minute particulars. And let it be
remembered, that "Æsop at play" is one of the instructive
apologues of antiquity.

Talking of Rochester's Poems, he said, he had given them
to Mr. Steevens to castrate for the edition of the poets, to
which he was to write Prefaces. Dr. Taylor (the only time I
ever heard him say any thing witty) [1] observed, that "if
Rochester had been castrated himself, his exceptionable
poems would not have been written." I asked if Burnet
had not given a good Life of Rochester. JOHNSON. "We
have a good *Death:* there is not much *Life.*" I asked whether
Prior's poems were to be printed entire: Johnson said, they

---

[1] I am told, that Horace, Earl of Oxford, has a collection of *Bon-Mots*
by persons who never said but one.

were. I mentioned Lord Hailes's censure of Prior, in his Preface to a collection of "Sacred Poems," by various hands, published by him at Edinburgh a great many years ago, where he mentions, "those impure tales which will be the eternal opprobrium of their ingenious authour." JOHNson. "Sir, Lord Hailes has forgot. There is nothing in Prior that will excite to lewdness. If Lord Hailes thinks there is, he must be more combustible than other people." I instanced the tale of "Paulo Purganti and his Wife." JOHNSON. "Sir, there is nothing there, but that his wife wanted to be kissed, when poor Paulo was out of pocket. No, Sir, Prior is a lady's book. No lady is ashamed to have it standing in her library."

The hypochondriack disorder being mentioned, Dr. Johnson did not think it so common as I supposed. "Dr. Taylor (said he) is the same one day as another. Burke and Reynolds are the same. Beauclerk, except when in pain, is the same. I am not so myself; but this I do not mention commonly."

I complained of a wretched changefulness, so that I could not preserve, for any long continuance, the same views of any thing. It was most comfortable to me to experience in Dr. Johnson's company, a relief from this uneasiness. His steady vigourous mind held firm before me those objects which my own feeble and tremulous imagination frequently presented in such a wavering state, that my reason could not judge well of them.

Dr. Johnson advised me to-day, to have as many books about me as I could; that I might read upon any subject upon which I had a desire for instruction at the time. "What you read *then*, (said he,) you will remember; but if you have not a book immediately ready, and the subject moulds in your mind, it is a chance if you have again a desire to study it." He added, "If a man never has an eager desire for instruction, he should prescribe a task for himself. But it is better when a man reads from immediate inclination."

He repeated a good many lines of Horace's Odes, while we were in the chaise; I remember particularly the Ode *"Eheu fugaces."*

He said, the dispute as to the comparative excellence of

12

Hester Piozzi (Mrs. Thrale) in 1793. Dr. Johnson first met the Thrales in 1765, and their house became a second home to him. "There are many" Mrs. Thrale said to Boswell, "who admire and respect Mr. Johnson; but you and I *love* him."

Homer or Virgil was inaccurate. "We must consider (said he) whether Homer was not the greatest poet, though Virgil may have produced the finest poem. Virgil was indebted to Homer for the whole invention of the structure of an epick poem, and for many of his beauties."

He told me, that Bacon was a favourite authour with him; but he had never read his works till he was compiling the English Dictionary, in which he said, I might see Bacon very often quoted. Mr. Seward recollects his having mentioned, that a Dictionary of the English Language might be compiled from Bacon's writings alone, and that he had once an intention of giving an edition of Bacon, at least of his English works, and writing the Life of that great man.

Wishing to be satisfied what degree of truth there was in a story which a friend of Johnson's and mine had told me to his disadvantage, I mentioned it to him in direct terms; and it was to this effect: that a gentleman who had lived in great intimacy with him, shewn him much kindness, and even relieved him from a spunging-house, having afterwards fallen into bad circumstances, was one day, when Johnson was at dinner with him, seized for debt, and carried to prison; that Johnson sat still undisturbed, and went on eating and drinking; upon which the gentleman's sister, who was present, could not suppress her indignation: "What, sir, (said she,) are you so unfeeling, as not even to offer to go to my brother in his distress; you who have been so much obliged to him?" And that Johnson answered, "Madam, I owe him no obligation; what he did for me he would have done for a dog."

Johnson assured me, that the story was absolutely false: but like a man conscious of being in the right, and desirous of completely vindicating himself from such a charge, he did not arrogantly rest on a mere denial, and on his general character, but proceeded thus:—"Sir, I was very intimate with that gentleman, and was once relieved by him from an arrest; but I never was present when he was arrested, never knew that he was arrested, and I believe he never was in difficulties after the time when he relieved me. I loved him much; yet, in talking of his general character, I may have said, though I do not remember that I ever did

243

say so; that as his generosity proceeded from no principle, but was a part of his profusion, he would do for a dog what he would do for a friend: but I never applied this remark to any particular instance, and certainly not to his kindness to me. If a profuse man, who does not value his money, and gives a large sum to a whore, gives half as much, or an equally large sum to relieve a friend, it cannot be esteemed as virtue. This was all that I could say of that gentleman; and, if said at all, it must have been said after his death. Sir, I would have gone to the world's end to relieve him. The remark about the dog, if made by me, was such a sally as might escape one when painting a man highly."

On Tuesday, September 23, Johnson was remarkably cordial to me. It being necessary for me to return to Scotland soon, I had fixed on the next day for my setting out, and I felt a tender concern at the thought of parting with him. He had, at this time, frankly communicated to me many particulars, which are inserted in this work in their proper places; and once, when I happened to mention that the expence of my jaunt would come to much more than I had computed, he said, "Why, Sir, if the expence were to be an inconvenience, you would have reason to regret it; but, if you have had the money to spend, I know not that you could have purchased as much pleasure with it in any other way."

He found fault with me for using the phrase to *make* money. "Don't you see (said he) the impropriety of it? To *make* money is to *coin* it: you should say *get* money." The phrase, however, is, I think, pretty current. But Johnson was at all times jealous of infractions upon the genuine English language, and prompt to repress colloquial barbarisms; such as *pledging myself*, for *undertaking; line*, for *department*, or *branch*, as, the *civil line*, the *banking line*. He was particularly indignant against the almost universal use of the word *idea* in the sense of *notion*, or *opinion*, when it is clear that *idea* can only signify something of which an image can be formed in the mind. We may have an *idea* or *image* of a mountain, a tree, a building; but we cannot surely have an *idea* or *image* of an *argument* or *proposition*. Yet we hear the sages of the law "delivering their *ideas* upon the question under consideration;" and the first speakers in parliament "entirely coinciding in the *idea* which has been ably stated by an honourable member;"—or "reprobating an *idea* unconstitutional, and fraught with the most dangerous consequences to a great and free country." Johnson called this "modern cant."

In the evening our gentleman-farmer, and two others, entertained themselves and the company with a great number of tunes on the fiddle. This evening, while some of the tunes of ordinary composition were played with no great skill, my frame was agitated, and I was conscious of a generous attachment to Dr. Johnson, as my preceptor and friend, mixed with an affectionate regret that he was an old man, whom I should probably lose in a short time. I thought I could defend him at the point of my sword. My reverence and affection for him were in full glow. I said to him, "My dear Sir, we must meet every year, if you don't quarrel with me." JOHNSON. "Nay, Sir, you are more likely to quarrel with me, than I with you. My regard for you is greater almost than I have words to express; but I do not chuse to be always repeating it; write it down in the first leaf of your pocket-book, and never doubt of it again."

While Johnson and I stood in calm conference by ourselves in Dr. Taylor's garden, at a pretty late hour in a serene autumn night, looking up to the heavens, I directed the discourse to the subject of a future state. My friend was in a placid and most benignant frame of mind. "Sir, (said he,) I do not imagine that all things will be made clear to us immediately after death, but that the ways of Providence will be explained to us very gradually." I ventured to ask him whether, although the words of some texts of Scripture seemed strong in support of the dreadful doctrine of an eternity of punishment, we might not hope that the denunciation was figurative, and would not literally be executed. JOHNSON. "Sir, you are to consider the intention of punishment in a future state. We have no reason to be sure that we shall then be no longer liable to offend against GOD. We do not know that even the angels are quite in a state of security; nay, we know that some of them have fallen. It may therefore, perhaps, be necessary, in order

245

to preserve both men and angels in a state of rectitude, that they should have continually before them the punishment of those who have deviated from it; but we may hope that by some other means a fall from rectitude may be prevented. Some of the texts of Scripture upon this subject, are, as you observe, indeed strong; but they may admit of a mitigated interpretation." He talked to me upon this awful and delicate question in a gentle tone, and as if afraid to be decisive.

In his review of Dr. Warton's "Essay on the Writings and Genius of Pope," Johnson has given the following salutary caution: "Nothing but experience could evince the frequency of false information, or enable any man to conceive that so many groundless reports should be propagated, as every man of eminence may hear of himself. Some men relate what they think, as what they know; some men of confused memories and habitual inaccuracy, ascribe to one man what belongs to another; and some talk on, without thought or care. A few men are sufficient to broach falsehoods, which are afterwards innocently diffused by successive relaters." Had he lived to read what Sir John Hawkins and Mrs. Piozzi have related concerning himself, how much would he have found his observation illustrated. He was indeed so much impressed with the prevalance of falsehood, voluntary or unintentional, that I never knew any person who upon hearing an extraordinary circumstance told, discovered more of the *incredulus odi*. He would say with a significant look and decisive tone, "It is not so. Do not tell this again." He inculcated upon all his friends the importance of perpetual vigilance against the slightest degrees of falsehood; the effect of which, as Sir Joshua Reynolds observed to me, has been, that all who were of his *school* are distinguished for a love of truth and accuracy, which they would not have possessed in the same degree, if they had not been acquainted with Johnson.

He said, "John Wesley's conversation is good, but he is never at leisure. He is always obliged to go at a certain hour. This is very disagreeable to a man who loves to fold his legs and have out his talk, as I do."

On Friday, April 3, I dined with him in London, in a

company where were present several eminent men, whom
I shall not name, but distinguish their parts in the conversation by different letters.

F. "I have been looking at this famous antique marble
dog of Mr. Jennings, valued at a thousand guineas, said
to be Alcibiades's dog." JOHNSON. "His tail then must be
docked. That was the mark of Alcibiades's dog." E. "A
thousand guineas! The representation of no animal whatever is worth so much. At this rate a dead dog would indeed
be better than a living lion." JOHNSON. "Sir, it is not the
worth of the thing, but the skill in forming it which is
so highly estimated. Every thing that enlarges the sphere
of human powers, that shows man he can do what he
thought he could not do, is valuable. The first man who
balanced a straw upon his nose; Johnson who rode upon
three horses at a time; in short, all such men deserved the
applause of mankind, not on acount of the use of what they
did, but of the dexterity which they exhibited." BOSWELL.
"Yet a misapplication of time and assiduity is not to be
encouraged. Addison, in one of his 'Spectators,' commends
the judgement of a King, who as a suitable reward to a man
that by long perseverance had attained to the art of throwing a barley-corn through the eye of a needle, gave him a
bushel of barley." JOHNSON. "He must have been a King
of Scotland, where barley is scarce." F. "One of the most
remarkable antique figures of an animal is the boar at
Florence." JOHNSON. "The first boar that is well made in
marble, should be preserved as a wonder. When men arrive at a facility of making boars well, then the workman-
ship is not of such value, but they should however be preserved as examples, and as a greater security for the restoration of the art, should it be lost."

R. "Mr. E., I don't mean to flatter, but when posterity
reads one of your speeches in Parliament it will be difficult
to believe that you took so much pains, knowing with certainty that it could produce no effect, that not one vote
would be gained by it." E. "Waiving your compliment to
me, I shall say in general, that it is very well worth while
for a man to take pains to speak well in parliament. A man,
who has vanity, speaks to display his talents; and if a man

speaks well, he gradually establishes a certain reputation and consequence in the general opinion, which sooner or later will have its political reward. Besides, though not one vote is gained, a good speech has its effect. Though an act which has been ably opposed passes into a law, yet in its progress it is modelled, it is softened in such a manner, that we see plainly the Minister has been told, that the members attached to him are so sensible of its injustice or absurdity from what they have heard, that it must be altered." JOHNSON. "And, Sir, there is a gratification of pride. Though we cannot out-vote them we will out-argue them. They shall not do wrong without its being shown both to themselves and to the world." E. "The House of Commons is a mixed body. (I except the minority, which I hold to be pure, [smiling] but I take the whole House.) It is a mass by no means pure; but neither is it wholly corrupt, though there is a large proportion of corruption in it. There are many members who generally go with the Minister, who will not go all lengths. There are many honest well-meaning country gentlemen who are in parliament only to keep up the consequence of their families. Upon most of these a good speech will have influence." JOHNSON. "We are all more or less governed by interest. But interest will not make us do every thing. In a case which admits of doubt, we try to think on the side which is for our interest, and generally bring ourselves to act accordingly. But the subject must admit of diversity of colouring; it must receive a colour on that side. In the House of Commons there are members enough who will not vote what is grossly unjust or absurd. No, Sir, there must always be right enough, or appearance of right, to keep wrong in countenance."

JOHNSON. "I have been reading Thicknesse's Travels, which I think are entertaining." BOSWELL. "What, Sir, a good book?" JOHNSON. "Yes, Sir, to read once; I do not say you are to make a study of it, and digest it; and I believe it to be a true book in his intention. All travellers generally mean to tell truth; though Thicknesse observes, upon Smollett's account of his alarming a whole town in France by firing a blunderbuss, and frightening a French nobleman till he made him tie on his portmanteau, that he would be loth to say Smollett had told two lies in one page; but he had found the only town in France where these things could have happened. Travellers must often be mistaken. In everything, except where mensuration can be applied, they may honestly differ. There has been, of late, a strange turn in travellers to be displeased."

E. "From the experience which I have had,—and I have had a great deal,—I have learnt to think *better* of mankind." JOHNSON. "From my experience I have found them worse in commercial dealings, more disposed to cheat, than I had any notion of; but more disposed to do one another good than I had conceived." J. "Less just and more beneficent." JOHNSON. "And really it is wonderful, considering how much attention is necessary for men to take care of themselves, and ward off immediate evils which press upon them, it is wonderful how much they do for others. As it is said of the greatest liar, that he tells more truth than falsehood; so it may be said of the worst man, that he does more good than evil." BOSWELL. "Perhaps from experience men may be found *happier* than we suppose." JOHNSON. "No, Sir; the more we enquire we shall find men the less happy." P. "As to thinking better or worse of mankind from experience, some cunning people will not be satisfied unless they have put men to the test, as they think. There is a very good story told of Sir Godfrey Kneller, in his character of a justice of the peace. A gentleman brought his servant before him, upon an accusation of having stolen some money from him; but it having come out that he had laid it purposely in the servant's way, in order to try his honesty, Sir Godfrey sent the master to prison." JOHNSON. "To resist temptation once, is not a sufficient proof of honesty. If a servant, indeed, were to resist the continued temptation of silver lying in a window, as some people let it lye, when he is sure his master does not know how much there is of it, he would give a strong proof of honesty. But this is a proof to which you have no right to put a man. You know, humanly speaking, there is a certain degree of temptation, which will overcome any virtue. Now, in so far as you approach temptation to a man, you do him an injury; and, if he is overcome, you share his guilt." P.

"And, when once overcome, it is easier for him to be got the better of again." BOSWELL. "Yes, you are his seducer; you have debauched him. I have known a man resolve to put friendship to the test, by asking a man to lend him money, merely with that view, when he did not want it." JOHNSON. "That is very wrong, Sir. Your friend may be a narrow man, and yet have many good qualities: narrowness may be his only fault. Now you are trying his general character as a friend, by one particular singly, in which he happens to be defective, when, in truth, his character is composed of many particulars."

On Saturday, April 4, I drank tea with Johnson at Dr. Taylor's, where he had dined. He entertained us with an account of a tragedy written by a Dr. Kennedy, (not the Lisbon physician.) "The catastrophe of it (said he) was, that a King, who was jealous of his Queen with his prime-minister, castrated himself. This tragedy was actually shewn about in manuscript to several people, and, amongst others, to Mr. Fitzherbert, who repeated to me two lines of the Prologue:

'Our hero's fate we have but gently touch'd;
The fair might blame us, if it were less couch'd.'

It is hardly to be believed what absurd and indecent images men will introduce into their writings, without being sensible of the absurdity and indecency. I remember Lord Orrery told me, that there was a pamphlet written against Sir Robert Walpole, the whole of which was an allegory on the PHALLICK OBSCENITY. The Duchess of Buckingham asked Lord Orrery *who* this person was? He answered he did not know. She said, she would send to Mr. Pulteney, who, she supposed, could inform her. So then, to prevent her from making herself ridiculous, Lord Orrery sent her Grace a note, in which he gave her to understand what was meant."

I mentioned to him that I had become very weary in a company where I heard not a single intellectual sentence, except that "a man who had been settled ten years in Minorca was become a much inferiour man to what he was

250

in London, because a man's mind grows narrow in a narrow place." JOHNSON. "A man's mind grows narrrow in a narrow place, whose mind is enlarged only because he has lived in a large place: but what is got by books and thinking is preserved in a narrow place as well as in a large place. A man cannot know modes of life as well in Minorca as in London; but he may study mathematics as well in Minorca." BOSWELL. "I don't know, Sir: if you had remained ten years in the Isle of Col, you would not have been the man that you now are." JOHNSON. "Yes, Sir, if I had been there from fifteen to twenty-five; but not if from twenty-five to thirty-five." BOSWELL. "I own, Sir, the spirits which I have in London make me do every thing with more readiness and vigour. I can talk twice as much in London as any where else."

Of Goldsmith, he said, "He was not an agreeable companion, for he talked always for fame. A man who does so, never can be pleasing. The man who talks to unburthen his mind, is the man to delight you. An eminent friend of ours is not so agreeable as the variety of his knowledge would otherwise make him, because he talks partly from ostentation."

This season, there was a whimsical fashion in the newspapers of applying Shakspeare's words to describe living persons well known in the world; which was done under the title of "Modern Characters from Shakspeare;" many of which were admirably adapted. The fancy took so much, that they were afterwards collected into a pamphlet. Somebody said to Johnson, across the table, that he had not been in those characters. "Yes (said he) I have. I should have been sorry to be left out." He then repeated what had been applied to him,

"You must borrow me GARGANTUA's mouth."

Miss Reynolds not perceiving at once the meaning of this, he was obliged to explain it to her, which had something of an aukward and ludicrous effect. "Why, Madam, it has a reference to me, as using big words, which require the mouth of a giant to pronounce them. Gargantua is the name of a giant in Rabelais." BOSWELL. "But, Sir, there is another amongst them for you:

> 'He would not flatter Neptune for his trident,
> Or Jove for his power to thunder.' "

JOHNSON. "There is nothing marked in that. No, Sir, Gargantua is the best."

Talking of fame, for which there is so great a desire, I observed, how little there is of it in reality, compared with the other objects of human attention. "Let every man recollect, and he will be sensible how small a part of his time is employed in talking or thinking of Shakspeare, Voltaire, or any of the most celebrated men that have ever lived, or are now supposed to occupy the attention and admiration of the world. Let this be extracted and compressed; into what a narrow space will it go!" I then slily introduced Mr. Garrick's fame, and his assuming the airs of a great man. JOHNSON. "Sir, it is wonderful how *little* Garrick assumes. No, Sir, Garrick *fortunam reverenter habet*. Consider, Sir; celebrated men, such as you have mentioned, have had their applause at a distance; but Garrick had it dashed in his face, sounded in his ears, and went home every night with the plaudits of a thousand in his *cranium*. Then, Sir, Garrick did not *find*, but *made* his way to the tables, the levees, and almost the bed-chambers of the great. Then, Sir, Garrick had under him a numerous body of people; who, from fear of his power, and hopes of his favour, and admiration of his talents, were constantly submissive to him. And here is a man who has advanced the dignity of his profession. Garrick has made a player a higher character." SCOTT. "And he is a very sprightly writer too." JOHNSON. "Yes, Sir; and all this supported by great wealth of his own acquisition. If all this had happened to me, I should have had a couple of fellows with long poles walking before me, to knock down every body that stood in the way. Consider, if all this had happened to Cibber or Quin, they'd have jumped over the moon.—Yet Garrick speaks to *us*." (smiling.) BOSWELL. "And Garrick is a very good man, a chari-

table man." JOHNSON. "Sir, a liberal man. He has given
away more money than any man in England. There may be
a little vanity mixed: but he has shewn, that money is not
his first object." BOSWELL. "Yet Foote used to say of him,
that he walked out with an intention to do a generous action; but turning the corner of a street, he met with the
ghost of a halfpenny, which frightened him." JOHNSON.
"Why, Sir, that is very true, too; for I never knew a man
of whom it could be said with less certainty to-day, what
he will do to-morrow, than Garrick; it depends so much on
his humour at the time." SCOTT. "I am glad to hear of his
liberality. He has been represented as very saving." JOHN-
SON. "With his domestick saving we have nothing to do. I
remember drinking tea with him long ago, when Peg Wof-
fington made it, and he grumbled at her for making it too
strong.[1] He had then begun to feel money in his purse, and
did not know when he should have enough of it."

We talked of war. JOHNSON. "Every man thinks meanly
of himself for not having been a soldier, or not having been
at sea." BOSWELL. "Lord Mansfield does not." JOHNSON.
"Sir, if Lord Mansfield were in a company of General Officers and Admirals who have been in service, he would
shrink; he'd wish to creep under the table." BOSWELL. "No;
he'd think he could *try* them all." JOHNSON. "Yes, if he
could catch them: but they'd try him much sooner. No, Sir:
were Socrates and Charles the Twelfth of Sweden both
present in any company, and Socrates to say, 'Follow me,
and hear a lecture in philosophy;' and Charles, laying his
hand on his sword, to say, 'Follow me, and dethrone the
Czar;' a man would be ashamed to follow Socrates. Sir,
the impression is universal: yet it is strange. As to the sailor,
when you look down from the quarterdeck to the space
below, you see the utmost extremity of human misery:
such crowding, such filth, such stench!" BOSWELL. "Yet
sailors are happy." JOHNSON. "They are happy as brutes are
happy, with a piece of fresh meat,—with the grossest sen-
suality. But, Sir, the profession of soldiers and sailors has

---

[1] When Johnson told this little anecdote to Sir Joshua Reynolds, he
mentioned a circumstance which he omitted to-day:—"Why (said Garrick) it is as red as blood."

the dignity of danger. Mankind reverence those who have got over fear, which is so general a weakness." SCOTT. "But is not courage mechanical, and to be acquired?" JOHNSON. "Why yes, Sir, in a collective sense. Soldiers consider themselves only as part of a great machine." SCOTT. "We find people fond of being sailors." JOHNSON. "I cannot account for that, any more than I can account for other strange perversions of imagination."

He sometimes could not bear being teazed with questions. I was once present when a gentleman asked so many, as, "What did you do, Sir?" "What did you say, Sir?" that he at last grew enraged, and said, "I will not be put to the *question.* Don't you consider, Sir, that these are not the manners of a gentleman? I will not be baited with *what* and *why;* what is this? what is that? why is a cow's tail long? why is a fox's tail bushy?" The gentleman, who was a good deal out of countenance, said, "Why, Sir, you are so good, that I venture to trouble you." JOHNSON. "Sir, my being so *good* is no reason why you should be so *ill.*"

On Monday, April 13, I dined with Johnson at Mr. Langton's, where were Dr. Porteus, then Bishop of Chester, now of London, and Dr. Stinton. He was at first in a very silent mood. Before dinner he said nothing but "Pretty baby," to one of the children. Langton said very well to me afterwards, that he could repeat Johnson's conversation before dinner, as Johnson had said that he could repeat a complete chapter of "The Natural History of Iceland," from the Danish of *Horrebow,* the whole of which was exactly thus:

"CHAP. LXXII. *Concerning Snakes.*
"There are no snakes to be met with throughout the whole island."

Dr. Mayo having asked Johnson's opinion of Soame Jenyns's "View of the Internal Evidence of the Christian Religion;"—JOHNSON. "I think it a pretty book; not very theological indeed; and there seems to be an affectation of ease and carelessness, as if it were not suitable to his character to be very serious about the matter." BOSWELL. "He may have intended this to introduce his book the better among genteel people, who might be unwilling to read too grave a treatise. There is a general levity in the age. We have physicians now with bag-wigs; may we not have airy divines, at least somewhat less solemn in their appearance than they used to be?" JOHNSON. "Jenyns might mean as you say." BOSWELL. "*You* should like this book, Mrs. Knowles, as it maintains, as your *friends* do, that courage is not a Christian virtue." MRS. KNOWLES. "Yes, indeed, I like him there; but I cannot agree with him, that friendship is not a Christian virtue." JOHNSON. "Why, Madam, strictly speaking, he is right. All friendship is preferring the interest of a friend, to the neglect, or, perhaps, against the interests of others; so that an old Greek said, 'He that has *friends* has *no friend.*' Now Christianity recommends universal benevolence,—to consider all men as our brethren; which is contrary to the virtue of friendship, as described by the ancient philosophers. Surely, Madam, your sect must approve of this; for, you call all men *friends.*" MRS. KNOWLES. "We are commanded to do good to all men, 'but especially to them who are of the household of Faith.'" JOHNSON. "Well, Madam. The household of Faith is wide enough." MRS. KNOWLES. "But, Doctor, our Saviour had twelve Apostles, yet there was *one* whom he *loved.* John was called 'the disciple whom JESUS loved.'" JOHNSON. (with eyes sparkling benignantly) "Very well, indeed, Madam. You have said very well." BOSWELL. "A fine application. Pray, Sir, had you ever thought of it?" JOHNSON. "I had not, Sir."

From this pleasing subject, he, I know not how or why, made a sudden transition to one upon which he was a violent aggressor; for he said, "I am willing to love all mankind, *except an American:*" and his inflammable corruption bursting into horrid fire, he "breathed out threatenings and slaughter;" calling them, "Rascals—Robbers—Pirates;" and exclaiming, he'd "burn and destroy them." Miss Seward, looking to him with mild but steady astonishment, said, "Sir, this is an instance that we are always most violent against those whom we have injured."—He was irritated still more by this delicate and keen reproach; and roared

255

out another tremendous volley which one might fancy could be heard across the Atlantịck. During this tempest I sat in great uneasiness, lamenting his heat of temper; till, by degrees, I diverted his attention to other topicks.

DR. MAYO, (to Dr. Johnson.) "Pray, Sir, have you read Edwards, of New England, on Grace?" JOHNSON. "No, Sir." BOSWELL. "It puzzled me so much as to the freedom of the human will, by stating, with wonderful acute ingenuity, our being actuated by a series of motives which we cannot resist, that the only relief I had was to forget it." MAYO. "But he makes the proper distinction between moral and physical necessity." BOSWELL. "Alas, Sir, they come both to the same thing. You may be bound as hard by chains when covered by leather, as when the iron appears. The argument for the moral necessity of human actions is always, I observe, fortified by supposing universal prescience to be one of the attributes of the Deity." JOHNSON. "You are surer that you are free, than you are of prescience; you are surer that you can lift up your finger or not as you please, than you are of any conclusion from a deduction of reasoning. But let us consider a little the objection from prescience. It is certain I am either to go home to-night or not; that does not prevent my freedom." BOSWELL. "That it is certain you are *either* to go home or not, does not prevent your freedom: because the liberty of choice between the two is compatible with that certainty. But if *one* of these events be certain *now*, you have no *future* power of volition. If it be certain you are to go home to-night, you *must* go home." JOHNSON. "If I am well acquainted with a man, I can judge with great probability how he will act in any case, without his being restrained by my judging. GOD may have this probability increased to certainty." BOSWELL. "When it is increased to *certainty,* freedom ceases, because that cannot be certainly foreknown, which is not certain at the time; but if it be certain at the time, it is a contradiction in terms to maintain that there can be afterwards any *contingency* dependent upon the exercise of will or any thing else." JOHNSON. "All theory is against the freedom of the will; all experience for it."—I did not push the subject any farther. I was glad to find him so mild in discussing a question of the most abstract nature, involved with theological tenets, which he generally would not suffer to be in any degree opposed.

Talking of Miss ――――, a literary lady, he said, "I was obliged to speak to Miss Reynolds, to let her know that I desired she would not flatter me so much." Somebody now observed, "She flatters Garrick." JOHNSON. "She is in the right to flatter Garrick. She is in the right for two reasons; first, because she has the world with her, who have been praising Garrick these thirty years; and secondly, because she is rewarded for it by Garrick. Why should she flatter *me?* I can do nothing for her. Let her carry her praise to a better market. (Then turning to Mrs. Knowles.) You, Madam, have been flattering me all the evening; I wish you would give Boswell a little now. If you knew his merit as well as I do, you would say a great deal; he is the best travelling companion in the world."

I expressed some inclination to publish an account of my *Travels* upon the continent of Europe, for which I had a variety of materials collected. JOHNSON. "I do not say, Sir, you may not publish your travels; but I give you my opinion, that you would lessen yourself by it. What can you tell of countries so well known as those upon the continent of Europe, which you have visited?" BOSWELL. "But I can give an entertaining narrative, with many incidents, anecdotes, *jeux d'esprit,* and remarks, so as to make very pleasant reading." JOHNSON. "Why, Sir, most modern travellers in Europe who have published their travels, have been laughed at: I would not have you added to the number.[1] The world is now not contented to be merely entertained by a traveller's narrative; they want to learn something. Now some of my friends asked me, why I did not give some account of my travels in France. The reason is plain; intelligent readers had seen more of France than I had. *You* might have liked my travels in France, and THE CLUB might have liked them; but, upon the whole, there would have been more ridicule than good produced by them." BOSWELL. "I cannot agree with you, Sir. People would like

―――――
[1] I believe, however, I shall follow my own opinion; for the world has shewn a very flattering partiality to my writings, on many occasions.

to read what you say of any thing. Suppose a face has been painted by fifty painters before; still we love to see it done by Sir Joshua." JOHNSON. "True, Sir, but Sir Joshua cannot paint a face when he has not time to look on it." BOSWELL. "Sir, a sketch of any sort by him is valuable. And, Sir, to talk to you in your own style (raising my voice, and shaking my head,) you *should* have given us your travels in France. I am *sure* I am right, and *there's an end on't.*"

I said to him that it was certainly true, as my friend Dempster had observed in his letter to me upon the subject, that a great part of what was in his "Journey to the Western Islands of Scotland," had been in his mind before he left London. JOHNSON. "Why yes, Sir, the topicks were; and books of travels will be good in proportion to what a man has previously in his mind; his knowing what to observe; his power of contrasting one mode of life with another. As the Spanish proverb says, 'He, who would bring home the wealth of the Indies, must carry the wealth of the Indies with him.' So it is in travelling; a man must carry knowledge with him, if he would bring home knowledge." BOSWELL. "The proverb, I suppose, Sir, means, he must carry a large stock with him to trade with." JOHNSON. "Yes, Sir."

And now I am to give a pretty full account of one of the most curious incidents in Johnson's life, of which he himself has made the following minute on this day: "In my return from church, I was accosted by Edwards, an old fellow-collegian, who had not seen me since 1729. He knew me, and asked if I remembered one Edwards; I did not at first recollect the name, but gradually as we walked along, recovered it, and told him a conversation that had passed at an alehouse between us. My purpose is to continue our acquaintance."

It was in Butcher-row that this meeting happened. Mr. Edwards, who was a decent-looking elderly man in grey clothes, and a wig of many curls, accosted Johnson with familiar confidence, knowing who he was, while Johnson returned his salutation with a courteous formality, as to a stranger. But as soon as Edwards had brought to his recollection their having been at Pembroke-College together nine-and-forty years ago, he seemed much pleased, asked where he lived, and said he should be glad to see him in Bolt-court. EDWARDS. "Ah, Sir! we are old men now." JOHNSON, (who never liked to think of being old:) "Don't let us discourage one another." EDWARDS. "Why, Doctor, you look stout and hearty, I am happy to see you so; for the newspapers told us you were very ill." JOHNSON. "Ay, Sir, they are always telling lies of *us old fellows.*"

Wishing to be present at more of so singular a conversation as that between two fellow-collegians, who had lived forty years in London without ever having chanced to meet, I whispered to Mr. Edwards that Dr. Johnson was going home, and that he had better accompany him now. So Edwards walked along with us, I eagerly assisting to keep up the conversation. Mr. Edwards informed Dr. Johnson that he had practised long as a solicitor in Chancery, but that he now lived in the country upon a little farm, about sixty acres, just by Stevenage in Hertfordshire, and that he came to London (to Barnard's Inn, No. 6,) generally twice a week. Johnson appearing to be in a reverie, Mr. Edwards addressed himself to me, and expatiated on the pleasure of living in the country. BOSWELL. "I have no notion of this, Sir. What you have to entertain you, is, I think, exhausted in half an hour." EDWARDS. "What? don't you love to have hope realized? I see my grass, and my corn, and my trees growing. Now, for instance, I am curious to see if this frost has not nipped my fruit-trees." JOHNSON, (who we did not imagine was attending:) "You find, Sir, you have fears as well as hopes."—So well did he see the whole, when another saw but the half of a subject.

When we got to Dr. Johnson's house, and were seated in his library, the dialogue went on admirably. EDWARDS. "Sir, I remember you would not let us say *prodigious* at College. For even then, Sir, (turning to me,) he was delicate in language, and we all feared him." [1] JOHNSON, (to Edwards:) "From your having practised the law long, Sir, I presume you must be rich." EDWARDS. "No, Sir; I got a good deal of money; but I had a number of poor relations to whom I

---

[1] Johnson said to me afterwards, "Sir, they respected me for literature; and yet it was not great but by comparison. Sir, it is amazing how little literature there is in the world."

gave a great part of it." JOHNSON. "Sir, you have been rich in the most valuable sense of the word." EDWARDS. "But I shall not die rich." JOHNSON. "Nay, sure, Sir, it is better to *live* rich, than to *die* rich." EDWARDS. "I wish I had continued at College." JOHNSON. "Why do you wish that, Sir?" EDWARDS. "Because I think I should have had a much easier life than mine has been. I should have been a parson, and had a good living, like Bloxham and several others, and lived comfortably." JOHNSON. "Sir, the life of a parson, of a conscientious clergyman, is not easy. I have always considered a clergyman as the father of a larger family than he is able to maintain. I would rather have Chancery suits upon my hands than the cure of souls. No, Sir, I do not envy a clergyman's life as an easy life, nor do I envy the clergyman who makes it an easy life."

EDWARDS. "You are a philosopher, Dr. Johnson. I have tried too in my time to be a philosopher; but, I don't know how, cheerfulness was always breaking in."—Mr. Burke, Sir Joshua Reynolds, Mr. Courtenay, Mr. Malone, and, indeed, all the eminent men to whom I have mentioned this, have thought it an exquisite trait of character. The truth is, that philosophy, like religion, is too generally supposed to be hard and severe, at least so grave as to exclude all gaiety.

EDWARDS. "I have been twice married, Doctor. You, I suppose, have never known what it was to have a wife." JOHNSON. "Sir, I have known what it was to have a wife, and (in a solemn tender faultering tone) I have known what it was to *lose a wife*.—It had almost broke my heart."

EDWARDS. "How do you live, Sir? For my part, I must have my regular meals, and a glass of good wine. I find I require it." JOHNSON. "I now drink no wine, Sir. Early in life I drank wine: for many years I drank none. I then for some years drank a great deal." EDWARDS. "Some hogsheads, I warrant you." JOHNSON. "I then had a severe illness, and left it off, and I have never begun it again. I never felt any difference upon myself from eating one thing rather than another, nor from one kind of weather rather than another. There are people, I believe, who feel a difference; but I am not one of them. And as to regular meals, I have fasted from the Sunday's dinner to the Tuesday's dinner, without any inconvenience. I believe it is best to eat just as one is hungry: but a man who is in business, or a man who has a family, must have stated meals. I am a straggler. I may leave this town and go to Grand Cairo, without being missed here or observed there." EDWARDS. "Don't you eat supper, Sir?" JOHNSON. "No, Sir." EDWARDS. "For my part, now, I consider supper as a turn-pike through which one must pass, in order to get to bed."

JOHNSON. "You are a lawyer, Mr. Edwards. Lawyers know life practically. A bookish man should always have them to converse with. They have what he wants." EDWARDS. "I am grown old: I am sixty-five." JOHNSON. "I shall be sixty-eight next birthday. Come, Sir, drink water, and put in for a hundred."

Mr. Edwards mentioned a gentleman who had left his whole fortune to Pembroke College. JOHNSON. "Whether to leave one's whole fortune to a College be right, must depend upon circumstances. I would leave the interest of the fortune I bequeathed to a College to my relations or my friends, for their lives. It is the same thing to a College, which is a permanent society, whether it gets the money now or twenty years hence; and I would wish to make my relations or friends feel the benefit of it."

This interview confirmed my opinion of Johnson's most humane and benevolent heart. His cordial and placid behaviour to an old fellow collegian, a man so different from himself; and his telling him that he would go down to his farm and visit him, shewed a kindness of disposition very rare at an advanced age. He observed, "how wonderful it was that they had both been in London forty years, without having ever once met, and both walkers in the street too!" Mr. Edwards, when going away, again recurred to his consciousness of senility, and looking full in Johnson's face, said to him, "You'll find in Dr. Young,

'O my coevals! remnants of yourselves.' "

Johnson did not relish this at all; but shook his head with impatience. Edwards walked off seemingly highly-pleased with the honour of having been thus noticed by Dr. Johnson. When he was gone, I said to Johnson, I thought him but a weak man. JOHNSON. "Why, yes, Sir. Here is a man who has passed through life without experience: yet I would rather have him with me than a more sensible man who will not talk readily. This man is always willing to say what he has to say." Yet Dr. Johnson had himself by no means that willingness which he praised so much, and I think so justly; for who has not felt the painful effect of the dreary void, when there is a total silence in a company, for any length of time; or, which is as bad, or perhaps worse, when the conversation is with difficulty kept up by a perpetual effort?

Johnson once observed to me, "Tom Tyers described me the best: 'Sir, (said he,) you are like a ghost; you never speak till you are spoken to.' "

Mr. Edwards had said to me aside, that Dr. Johnson should have been of a profession. I repeated the remark to Johnson that I might have his own thoughts on the subject. JOHNSON. "Sir, it *would* have been better that I had been of a profession. I ought to have been a lawyer." BOSWELL. "I do not think, Sir, it would have been better, for we should not have had the English Dictionary." JOHNSON. "But you would have had Reports." BOSWELL. "Aye; but there would not have been another, who could have written the Dictionary. There have been very many good Judges. Suppose you had been Lord Chancellor; you would have delivered opinions with more extent of mind, and in a more ornamented manner, than perhaps any Chancellor ever did, or ever will do. But, I believe, causes have been as judiciously decided as you could have done." JOHNSON. "Yes, Sir. Property has been as well settled."

He told Sir Joshua Reynolds, that once when he dined in a numerous company of booksellers, where the room being small, the head of the table, at which he sat, was almost close to the fire, he persevered in suffering a great deal of inconvenience from the heat, rather than quit his place, and let one of them sit above him.

Goldsmith, in his diverting simplicity, complained one day, in a mixed company, of Lord Camden. "I met him (said he) at Lord Clare's house in the country, and he took no more notice of me than if I had been an ordinary man." The company having laughed heartily, Johnson stood forth in defence of his friend. "Nay, Gentlemen, (said he,) Dr. Goldsmith is in the right. A nobleman ought to have made up to such a man as Goldsmith; and I think it is much against Lord Camden that he neglected him."

Nor could he patiently endure to hear, that such respect as he thought due only to higher intellectual qualities, should be bestowed on men of slighter, though perhaps more amusing, talents. I told him, that one morning, when I went to breakfast with Garrick, who was very vain of his intimacy with Lord Camden, he accosted me thus:—"Pray now, did you—did you meet a little lawyer turning the corner, eh?"—"No, Sir, (said I.) Pray what do you mean by the question?"—"Why, (replied Garrick, with an affected indifference, yet as if standing on tip-toe,) Lord Camden has this moment left me. We have had a long walk together." JOHNSON. "Well, Sir, Garrick talked very properly. Lord Camden *was a little lawyer* to be associating so familiarly with a player."

Sir Joshua Reynolds observed, with great truth, that Johnson considered Garrick to be as it were his *property*. He would allow no man either to blame or to praise Garrick in his presence, without contradicting him.

Having fallen into a very serious frame of mind, in which mutual expressions of kindness passed between us, such as would be thought too vain in me to repeat, I talked with regret of the sad inevitable certainty that one of us must survive the other. JOHNSON. "Yes, Sir, that is an affecting consideration. I remember Swift, in one of his letters to Pope, says, 'I intend to come over, that we may meet once more; and when we must part, it is what happens to all human beings.'" BOSWELL. "The hope that we shall see our departed friends again must support the mind." JOHNSON. "Why, yes, Sir." BOSWELL. "There is a strange unwillingness to part with life, independent of serious fears as to futurity. A reverend friend of ours (naming him) tells me, that he feels an uneasiness at the thoughts of leaving his house, his study, his books." JOHNSON. "This is foolish

263

in *****. A man need not be uneasy on these grounds; for, as he will retain his consciousness, he may say with the philosopher, *Omnia mea mecum porto.*" BOSWELL. "True, Sir; we may carry our books in our heads; but still there is something painful in the thought of leaving for ever what has given us pleasure. I remember, many years ago, when my imagination was warm, and I happened to be in a melancholy mood, it distressed me to think of going into a state of being in which Shakspeare's poetry did not exist. A lady whom I then much admired, a very amiable woman, humoured my fancy, and relieved me by saying, 'The first thing you will meet in the other world, will be an elegant copy of Shakspeare's works presented to you.'" Dr. Johnson smiled benignantly at this, and did not appear to disapprove of the notion.

The gentleman who had dined with us at Dr. Percy's came in. Johnson attacked the Americans with intemperate vehemence of abuse. I said something in their favour; and added, that I was always sorry, when he talked on that subject. This, it seems, exasperated him; though he said nothing at the time. The cloud was charged with sulphureous vapour, which was afterwards to burst in thunder.—We talked of a gentleman who was running out his fortune in London; and I said, "We must get him out of it. All his friends must quarrel with him, and that will soon drive him away." JOHNSON. "Nay, Sir, we'll send *you* to him. If your company does not drive a man out of his house, nothing will." This was a horrible shock, for which there was no visible cause. I afterwards asked him why he had said so harsh a thing. JOHNSON. "Because, Sir, you made me angry about the Americans." BOSWELL. "But why did you not take your revenge directly?" JOHNSON (smiling) "Because, Sir, I had nothing ready. A man cannot strike till he has his weapons." This was a candid and pleasant confession.

He shewed me to-night his drawing-room, very genteely fitted up; and said, "Mrs. Thrale sneered, when I talked of my having asked you and your lady to live at my house. I was obliged to tell her, that you would be in as respectable a situation in my house as in hers. Sir, the insolence

13
Dr. Johnson (with Boswell behind him in the distance) on the
famous walking tour of Scotland the two took together in 1773.
Note the Scottish thistle and " sheltie " ponies. The illustration
comes from Boswell's *Journal of a Tour to the Hebrides*, published
in 1785.

of wealth will creep out." BOSWELL. "She has a little both
of the insolence of wealth, and the conceit of parts." JOHN-
SON. "The insolence of wealth is a wretched thing; but the
conceit of parts has some foundation. To be sure, it should
not be. But who is without it?" BOSWELL. "Yourself, Sir."
JOHNSON. "Why, I play no tricks: I lay no traps." BOS-
WELL. "No, Sir. You are six feet high, and you only do not
stoop."

On Sunday, April 19, being Easter day, after the solem-
nities of the festival in St. Paul's Church, I visited him, but
could not stay to dinner. I expressed a wish to have the arguments for Christianity always in readiness, that my religious faith might be as firm and clear as any proposition
whatever, so that I need not be under the least uneasiness,
when it should be attacked. JOHNSON. "Sir, you cannot answer all objections. You have demonstration for a First
Cause: you see he must be good as well as powerful, because there is nothing to make him otherwise, and goodness of itself is preferable. Yet you have against this, what
is very certain, the unhappiness of human life. This, however, gives us reason to hope for a future state of com-
pensation, that there may be a perfect system. But of that
we were not sure, till we had a positive revelation." I told
him, that his "Rasselas" had often made me unhappy; for
it represented the misery of human life so well, and so convincingly to a thinking mind, that if at any time the impression wore off, and I felt myself easy, I began to suspect
some delusion.

On Monday, April 20, I found him at home in the
morning. We talked of a gentleman who we apprehended
was gradually involving his circumstances by bad management. JOHNSON. "Wasting a fortune is evaporation by a
thousand imperceptible means. If it were a stream, they'd
stop it. You must speak to him. It is really miserable. Were
he a gamester, it could be said he had hopes of winning.
Were he a bankrupt in trade, he might have grown rich;
but he has neither spirit to spend, nor resolution to spare.
He does not spend fast enough to have pleasure from it.
He has the crime of prodigality, and the wretchedness of
parsimony. If a man is killed in a duel, he is killed as many

a one has been killed; but it is a sad thing for a man to lie down and die; to bleed to death, because he has not fortitude enough to sear the wound, or even to stitch it up." I cannot but pause a moment to admire the fecundity of fancy and choice of language, which in this instance, and, indeed, on almost all occasions, he displayed. It was well observed by Dr. Percy, now Bishop of Dromore, "The conversation of Johnson is strong and clear, and may be compared to an antique statue, where every vein and muscle is distinct and bold. Ordinary conversation resembles an inferiour cast."

On Saturday, April 25, I dined with him at Sir Joshua Reynolds's, with the learned Dr. Musgrave, Counsellor Leland of Ireland, son to the historian, Mrs. Cholmondeley, and some more ladies. "The Project," a new poem, was read to the company by Dr. Musgrave. JOHNSON. "Sir, it has no power. Were it not for the well-known names with which it is filled, it would be nothing: the names carry the poet, not the poet the names." MUSGRAVE. "A temporary poem always entertains us." JOHNSON. "So does an account of the criminals hanged yesterday entertain us."

He proceeded:—"Demosthenes Taylor, as he was called, (that is, the Editor of Demosthenes) was the most silent man, the merest statue of a man that I have ever seen. I once dined in company with him, and all he said during the whole time was no more than *Richard.* How a man should say only Richard, it is not easy to imagine. But it was thus: Dr. Douglas was talking of Dr. Zachary Grey, and ascribing to him something that was written by Dr. Richard Grey. So, to correct him, Taylor said, (imitating his affected sententious emphasis and nod) *'Richard.'* "

I happened, I know not how, to say that a pamphlet meant a prose piece. JOHNSON. "No, Sir. A few sheets of poetry unbound are a pamphlet, as much as a few sheets of prose." MUSGRAVE. "A pamphlet may be understood to mean a poetical piece in Westminster-Hall, that is, in formal language; but in common language it is understood to mean prose." JOHNSON. (and here was one of the many instances of his knowing clearly and telling exactly how a thing is,) "A pamphlet is understood in common language to mean prose, only from this, that there is so much more prose written than poetry; as when we say a *book*, prose is understood for the same reason, though a book may as well be in poetry as in prose. We understand what is most general, and we name what is less frequent."

We talked of a lady's verses on Ireland. MISS REYNOLDS. "Have you seen them, Sir?" JOHNSON. "No, Madam, I have seen a translation from Horace, by one of her daughters. She shewed it me." MISS REYNOLDS. "And how was it, Sir?" JOHNSON. "Why, very well for a young Miss's verses;— that is to say, compared with excellence, nothing; but, very well, for the person who wrote them. I am vexed at being shewn verses in that manner." MISS REYNOLDS. "But if they should be good, why not give them hearty praise?" JOHNSON. "Why, Madam, because I have not then got the better of my bad humour from having been shewn them. You must consider, Madam; before-hand they may be bad as well as good. Nobody has a right to put another under such a difficulty, that he must either hurt the person by telling the truth, or hurt himself by telling what is not true." BOSWELL. "A man often shews his writings to people of eminence, to obtain from them, either from their good-nature, or from their not being able to tell the truth firmly, a commendation, of which he may afterwards avail himself." JOHNSON. "Very true, Sir. Therefore the man, who is asked by an authour what he thinks of his work, is put to the torture, and is not obliged to speak the truth; so that what he says is not considered as his opinion; yet he has said it, and cannot retract it; and this authour, when mankind are hunting him with a cannister at his tail, can say, 'I would not have published, had not Johnson, or Reynolds, or Musgrave, or some other good judge commended the work.' Yet I consider it as a very difficult question in conscience, whether one should advise a man not to publish a work, if profit be his object; for the man may say, 'Had it not been for you, I should have had the money.' Now you cannot be sure; for you have only your own opinion, and the publick may think very differently." SIR JOSHUA REYNOLDS. "You must upon such an occasion have two judgements; one as to the real value of the work, the other

267

as to what may please the general taste at the time." JOHN-SON. "But you can be *sure* of neither; and therefore I should scruple much to give a suppressive vote. Both Goldsmith's comedies were once refused; his first by Garrick, his second by Colman, who was prevailed on at last by much solicitation, nay, a kind of force, to bring it on. His 'Vicar of Wakefield' I myself did not think would have had much success. It was written and sold to a bookseller, before his 'Traveller;' but published after; so little expectation had the bookseller from it. Had it been sold after the 'Traveller,' he might have had twice as much money for it, though sixty guineas was no mean price. The bookseller had the advantage of Goldsmith's reputation from 'The Traveller' in the sale, though Goldsmith had it not in selling the copy." SIR JOSHUA REYNOLDS. "The Beggar's Opera affords a proof how strangely people will differ in opinion about a literary performance. Burke thinks it has no merit." JOHNSON. "It was refused by one of the houses; but I should have thought it would succeed, not from any great excellence in the writing, but from the novelty, and the general spirit and gaiety of the piece, which keeps the audience always attentive, and dismisses them in good humour."

He observed, "A man cannot with propriety speak of himself, except he relates simple facts; as, 'I was at Richmond:' or what depends on mensuration; as, 'I am six feet high.' He is sure he has been at Richmond; he is sure he is six feet high: but he cannot be sure he is wise, or that he has any other excellence. Then, all censure of a man's self is oblique praise. It is in order to shew how much he can spare. It has all the invidiousness of self-praise, and all the reproach of falsehood." BOSWELL. "Sometimes it may proceed from a man's strong consciousness of his faults being observed. He knows that others would throw him down, and therefore he had better lie down softly of his own accord."

On Tuesday, April 28, he was engaged to dine at General Paoli's, where, as I have already observed, I was still entertained in elegant hospitality, and with all the ease and comfort of a home. I called on him, and accompanied him in a hackney-coach. We stopped first at the bottom of

Hedge-lane, into which he went to leave a letter, "with good news for a poor man in distress," as he told me. I did not question him particularly as to this. He himself often resembled Lady Bolingbroke's lively description of Pope: that "he was *un politique aux choux et aux raves."* He would say, "I dine to-day in Grosvenor-square;" this might be with a Duke; or, perhaps, "I dine to-day at the other end of the town:" or, "A gentleman of great eminence called on me yesterday."—He loved thus to keep things floating in conjecture: *Omne ignotum pro magnifico est.* I believe I ventured to dissipate the cloud, to unveil the mystery, more freely and frequently than any of his friends. We stopped again at Wirgman's, the well-known *toy-shop,* in St. James's-Street, at the corner of St. James's-Place, to which he had been directed, but not clearly, for he searched about some time, and could not find it at first; and said, "To direct one only to a corner shop is *toying* with one." I suppose he meant this as a play upon the word *toy;* it was the first time that I knew him to stoop to such sport. After he had been some time in the shop, he sent for me to come out of the coach, and help him to choose a pair of silver buckles, as those he had were too small. Probably this alteration in dress had been suggested by Mrs. Thrale, by associating with whom, his external appearance was much improved. He got better cloaths; and the dark colour, from which he never deviated, was enlivened by metal buttons. His wigs, too, were much better; and during their travels in France, he was furnished with a Paris-made wig, of handsome construction. This choosing of silver buckles was a negociation: "Sir, (said he,) I will not have the ridiculous large ones now in fashion; and I will give no more than a guinea for a pair." Such were the *principles* of the business; and, after some examination, he was fitted.

BOSWELL. "I drank chocolate, Sir, this morning with Mr. Eld; and, to my no small surprize, found him to be a *Staffordshire Whig,* a being which I did not believe had existed." JOHNSON. "Sir, there are rascals in all countries." BOSWELL. "Eld said, a Tory was a creature generated between a non-juring parson and one's grandmother." JOHNSON. "And I have always said, the first Whig was the Devil."

269

BOSWELL. "He certainly was, Sir. The Devil was impatient of subordination; he was the first who resisted power:

'Better to reign in Hell, than serve in Heaven.' "

At General Paoli's were Sir Joshua Reynolds, Mr. Langton, Marchese Gherardi of Lombardy, and Mr. John Spottiswoode the younger, of Spottiswoode, the solicitor. At this time fears of an invasion were circulated; to obviate which, Mr. Spottiswoode observed, that Mr. Fraser the engineer, who had lately come from Dunkirk, said, that the French had the same fears of us. JOHNSON. "It is thus that mutual cowardice keeps us in peace. Were one-half of mankind brave, and one-half cowards, the brave would be always beating the cowards. Were all brave, they would lead a very uneasy life; all would be continually fighting: but being all cowards, we go on very well."

We talked of drinking wine. JOHNSON. "I require wine, only when I am alone. I have then often wished for it, and often taken it." SPOTTISWOODE. "What, by way of a companion, Sir?" JOHNSON. "To get rid of myself, to send myself away. Wine gives great pleasure; and every pleasure is of itself a good. It is a good, unless counterbalanced by evil. A man may have a strong reason not to drink wine; and that may be greater than the pleasure. Wine makes a man better pleased with himself. I do not say that it makes him more pleasing to others. Sometimes it does. But the danger is, that while a man grows better pleased with himself, he may be growing less pleasing to others. Wine gives a man nothing. It neither gives him knowledge nor wit; it only animates a man, and enables him to bring out what a dread of the company has repressed. It only puts in motion what has been locked up in frost. But this may be good, or it may be bad." SPOTTISWOODE. "So, Sir, wine is a key which opens a box; but this box may be either full or empty?" JOHNSON. "Nay, Sir, conversation is the key: wine is a pick-lock, which forces open the box, and injures it. A man should cultivate his mind so as to have that confidence and readiness without wine, which wine gives." BOSWELL. "The great difficulty of resisting wine is from benevolence. For instance, a good worthy man asks you to taste his wine, which he has had twenty years in his cellar." JOHNSON. "Sir, all this notion about benevolence arises from a man's imagining himself to be of more importance to 'others, than he really is. They don't care a farthing whether he drinks wine or not." SIR JOSHUA REYNOLDS. "Yes, they do for the time." JOHNSON. "For the time!—If they care this minute, they forget it the next. And as for the good worthy man; how do you know he is good and worthy? No good and worthy man will insist upon another man's drinking wine. As to the wine twenty years in the cellar,—of ten men, three say this, merely because they must say something; three are telling a lie, when they say they have had the wine twenty years;—three would rather save the wine;—one, perhaps, cares. I allow it is something to please one's company; and people are always pleased with those who partake pleasure with them. But after a man has brought himself to relinquish the great personal pleasure which arises from drinking wine, any other consideration is a trifle. To please others by drinking wine, is something only, if there be nothing against it. I should, however, be sorry to offend worthy men:

> 'Curst be the verse, how well so e'er it flow,
> That tends to make one worthy man my foe.' "

BOSWELL. "Curst be the *spring,* the water." JOHNSON. "But let us consider what a sad thing it would be, if we were obliged to drink or do any thing else that may happen to be agreeable to the company where we are." LANGTON. "By the same rule you must join with a gang of cut-purses." JOHNSON. "Yes, Sir: but yet we must do justice to wine; we must allow it the power it possesses. To make a man pleased with himself, let me tell you, is doing a very great thing.

I was at this time myself a water-drinker, upon trial, by Johnson's recommendation. JOHNSON. "Boswell is a bolder combatant than Sir Joshua: he argues for wine without the help of wine; but Sir Joshua with it." SIR JOSHUA REYNOLDS. "But to please one's company is a strong motive." JOHNSON, (who, from drinking only water, supposed every body who drank wine to be elevated,) "I won't argue any more with you, Sir. You are too far gone." SIR JOSHUA. "I should have thought so indeed, Sir, had I made such a speech as you have now done." JOHNSON. (drawing himself in, and, I really thought blushing,) "Nay, don't be angry. I did not mean to offend you." SIR JOSHUA. "At first the taste of wine was disagreeable to me; but I brought myself to drink it, that I might be like other people. The pleasure of drinking wine is so connected with pleasing your company, that altogether there is something of social goodness in it." JOHNSON. "Sir, this is only saying the same thing over again." SIR JOSHUA. "No, this is new." JOHNSON. "You put it in new words, but it is an old thought. This is one of the disadvantages of wine, it makes a man mistake words for thoughts." BOSWELL. "I think it is a new thought; at least, it is in a new *attitude*." JOHNSON. "Nay, Sir, it is only in a new coat; or an old coat with a new facing. (Then laughing heartily.) It is the old dog in a new doublet.—An extraordinary instance, however, may occur where a man's patron will do nothing for him, unless he will drink: *there* may be a good reason for drinking."

I mentioned a nobleman, who I believed was really uneasy, if his company would not drink hard. JOHNSON. "That is from having had people about him whom he has been accustomed to command." BOSWELL. "Supposing I should be *tête-à-tête* with him at table." JOHNSON. "Sir, there is no more reason for your drinking with *him,* than his being sober with *you.*" BOSWELL. "Why, that is true, for it would do him less hurt to be sober, than it would do me to get drunk." JOHNSON. "Yes, Sir; and from what I have heard of him, one would not wish to sacrifice himself to such a man. If he must always have somebody to drink with him, he should buy a slave, and then he would be sure to have it. They who submit to drink as another pleases, make themselves his slaves." BOSWELL. "But, Sir, you will surely make allowance for the duty of hospitality. A gentleman who loves drinking, comes to visit me." JOHNSON. "Sir, a man knows whom he visits; he comes to the table of a sober man." BOSWELL. "But, Sir, you and I should not have been so well received in the Highlands and Hebrides, if I had not drunk with our worthy friends. Had I drunk water only as you did, they would not have been so cordial." JOHNSON. "Sir William Temple mentions, that in his travels through the Netherlands he had two or three gentlemen with him; and when a bumper was necessary, he put it on *them*. Were I to travel again through the islands, I would have Sir Joshua with me to take the bumpers." BOSWELL. "But, Sir, let me put a case. Suppose Sir Joshua should take a jaunt into Scotland; he does me the honour to pay me a visit at my house in the country; I am overjoyed at seeing him; we are quite by ourselves; shall I unsociably and churlishly let him sit drinking by himself? No, no, my dear Sir Joshua, you shall not be treated so, I *will* take a bottle with you."

On Wednesday, April 29, I dined with him at Mr. Allan Ramsay's, where were Lord Binning, Dr. Robertson the historian, Sir Joshua Reynolds, and the Honourable Mrs. Boscawen, widow of the Admiral, and mother of the present Viscount Falmouth; of whom, if it be not presumptuous in me to praise her, I would say, that her manners are the most agreeable, and her conversation the best, of any lady with whom I ever had the happiness to be acquainted. Before Johnson came we talked a good deal of him; Ramsay said, he had always found him a very polite man, and that he treated him with great respect, which he did very sincerely. I said, I worshipped him. ROBERTSON. "But some of you spoil him: you should not worship him; you should worship no man." BOSWELL. "I cannot help worshipping him, he is so much superiour to other men." ROBERTSON. "In criticism, and in wit and conversation, he is no doubt very excellent; but in other respects he is not above other men; he will believe any thing, and will strenuously defend the most minute circumstance connected with the Church of England." BOSWELL. "Believe me, Doctor, you are much mistaken as to this; for when you talk with him calmly in private, he is very liberal in his way of thinking." ROBERTSON. "He and I have been always very gracious; the first time I met him was one evening at Strahan's, where he had just had an unlucky altercation with Adam Smith, to whom he had been so rough, that Strahan, after Smith was

273

gone, had remonstrated with him, and told him that I was coming soon, and that he was uneasy to think that he might behave in the same manner to me. 'No, no, Sir, (said Johnson) I warrant you Robertson and I shall do very well.' Accordingly he was gentle and good-humoured and courteous with me the whole evening; and he has been so upon every occasion that we have met since. I have often said, (laughing) that I have been in a great measure indebted to Smith for my good reception." BOSWELL. "His power of reasoning is very strong, and he has a peculiar art of drawing characters, which is as rare as good portrait painting." SIR JOSHUA REYNOLDS. "He is undoubtedly admirable in this; but, in order to mark the characters which he draws, he overcharges them, and gives people more than they really have, whether of good or bad."

No sooner did he, of whom we had been thus talking so easily, arrive, than we were all as quiet as a school upon the entrance of the head-master; and were very soon sat down to a table covered with such variety of good things, as contributed not a little to dispose him to be pleased.

RAMSAY. "I am old enough to have been a contemporary of Pope. His poetry was highly admired in his life-time, more a great deal than after his death." JOHNSON. "Sir, it has not been less admired since his death; no authours ever had so much fame in their own life-time as Pope and Voltaire; and Pope's poetry has been as much admired since his death as during his life; it has only not been as much talked of, but that is owing to its being now more distant, and people having other writings to talk of. Virgil is less talked of than Pope, and Homer is less talked of than Virgil; but they are not less admired. We must read what the world reads at the moment. It has been maintained that this superfetation, this teeming of the press in modern times, is prejudicial to good literature, because it obliges us to read so much of what is of inferiour value, in order to be in the fashion; so that better works are neglected for want of time, because a man will have more gratification of his vanity in conversation, from having read modern books, than from having read the best works of antiquity. But it must be considered that we have now more knowledge generally diffused; all our ladies read now, which is a great extension. Modern writers are the moons of literature; they shine with reflected light, with light borrowed from the ancients. Greece appears to me to be the fountain of knowledge; Rome of elegance." RAMSAY. "I suppose Homer's 'Iliad' to be a collection of pieces which had been written before his time. I should like to see a translation of it in poetical prose, like the book of Ruth or Job." ROBERTSON. "Would you, Dr. Johnson, who are master of the English language, but try your hand upon a part of it." JOHNSON. "Sir, you could not read it without the pleasure of verse."

Dr. Robertson expatiated on the character of a certain nobleman; that he was one of the strongest-minded men that ever lived; that he would sit in company quite sluggish, while there was nothing to call forth his intellectual vigour; but the moment that any important subject was started, for instance, how this country is to be defended against a French invasion, he would rouse himself, and shew his extraordinary talents with the most powerful ability and animation. JOHNSON. "Yet this man cut his own throat. The true strong and sound mind is the mind that can embrace equally great things and small. Now I am told the King of Prussia will say to a servant, 'Bring me a bottle of such a wine, which came in such a year; it lies in such a corner of the cellars.' I would have a man great in great things, and elegant in little things." He said to me afterwards, when we were by ourselves, "Robertson was in a mighty romantick humour, he talked of one he did not know; but I *downed* him with the King of Prussia."—"Yes, Sir, (said I,) you threw a *bottle* at his head."

Next day, Thursday, April 30, I found him at home by himself. JOHNSON. "Well, Sir, Ramsay gave us a splendid dinner. I love Ramsay. You will not find a man in whose conversation there is more instruction, more information, and more elegance, than in Ramsay's." BOSWELL. "What I admire in Ramsay, is his continuing to be so young." JOHNSON. "Why, yes, Sir; it is to be admired. I value myself upon this, that there is nothing of the old man in my conversation. I am now sixty-eight, and I have no more of it

275

than twenty-eight." BOSWELL. "But, Sir, would not you wish to know old age? He who is never an old man, does not know the whole of human life; for old age is one of the divisions of it." JOHNSON. "Nay, Sir, what talk is this?" BOSWELL. "I mean, Sir, the Sphinx's description of it; —morning, noon, and night. I would know night, as well as morning and noon." JOHNSON. "What, Sir, would you know what it is to feel the evils of old age? Would you have the gout? Would you have decrepitude?"—Seeing him heated, I would not argue any farther; but I was confident that I was in the right. I would, in due time, be a Nestor, an elder of the people; and there *should* be some difference between the conversation of twenty-eight and sixty-eight. A grave picture should not be gay. There is a serene, solemn, placid old age. JOHNSON. "Mrs. Thrale's mother said of me what flattered me much. A clergyman was complaining of want of society in the country where he lived; and said, 'They talk of *runts*;' (that is, young cows.) 'Sir, (said Mrs. Salusbury,) Mr. Johnson would learn to talk of runts:' meaning that I was a man who would make the most of my situation, whatever it was." He added. "I think myself a very polite man."

On Saturday, May 2, I dined with him at Sir Joshua Reynolds's, where there was a very large company, and a great deal of conversation; but owing to some circumstances which I cannot now recollect, I have no record of any part of it, except that there were several people there by no means of the Johnsonian school; so that less attention was paid to him than usual, which put him out of humour; and upon some imaginary offence from me, he attacked me with such rudeness, that I was vexed and angry, because it gave those persons an opportunity of enlarging upon his supposed ferocity, and ill-treatment of his best friends. I was so much hurt, and had my pride so much roused, that I kept away from him for a week; and perhaps, might have kept away much longer, nay, gone to Scotland without seeing him again, had not we fortunately met and been reconciled. To such unhappy chances are human friendships liable.

On Friday, May 8, I dined with him at Mr. Langton's. I

was reserved and silent, which I suppose he perceived, and might recollect the cause. After dinner, when Mr. Langton was called out of the room, and we were by ourselves, he drew his chair near to mine, and said in a tone of conciliating courtesy, "Well, how have you done?" BOSWELL. "Sir, you have made me very uneasy by your behaviour to me when we last were at Sir Joshua Reynolds's. You know, my dear Sir, no man has a greater respect and affection for you, or would sooner go to the end of the world to serve you. Now to treat me so——." He insisted that I had interrupted him, which I assured him was not the case; and proceeded—"But why treat me so before people who neither love you nor me?" JOHNSON. "Well, I am sorry for it. I'll make it up to you twenty different ways, as you please." BOSWELL. "I said to-day to Sir Joshua, when he observed that you *tossed* me sometimes—I don't care how often, or how high he tosses me, when only friends are present, for then I fall upon soft ground: but I do not like falling on stones, which is the case when enemies are present.—I think this is a pretty good image, Sir." JOHNSON. "Sir, it is one of the happiest I have ever heard."

The truth is, there was no venom in the wounds which he inflicted at any time, unless they were irritated by some malignant infusion by other hands. We were instantly as cordial again as ever, and joined in hearty laugh at some ludicrous but innocent peculiarities of one of our friends. BOSWELL. "Do you think, Sir, it is always culpable to laugh at a man to his face?" JOHNSON. "Why, Sir, that depends upon the man and the thing. If it is a slight man, and a slight thing, you may; for you take nothing valuable from him."

Mr. Langton having repeated the anecdote of Addison having distinguished between his powers in conversation and in writing, by saying "I have only nine-pence in my pocket; but I can draw for a thousand pounds;"—JOHNSON. "He had not that retort ready, Sir: he had prepared it beforehand." LANGTON: (turning to me.) "A fine surmise. Set a thief to catch a thief."

Our conversation to-day, I know not how, turned, I think, for the only time at any length, during our long acquaintance, upon the sensual intercourse between the sexes, the delight of which he ascribed chiefly to imagination. "Were it not for imagination, Sir, (said he) a man would be as happy in the arms of a Chambermaid as of a Duchess. But such is the adventitious charm of fancy, that we find men who have violated the best principles of society, and ruined their fame and their fortune, that they might possess a woman of rank." It would not be proper to record the particulars of such a conversation in moments of unreserved frankness, when nobody was present on whom it could have any hurtful effect. That subject, when philosophically treated, may surely employ the mind in a curious discussion, and as innocently, as anatomy; provided that those who do treat it, keep clear of inflammatory incentives.

"From grave to gay, from lively to severe,"—we were soon engaged in very different speculation; humbly and reverently considering and wondering at the universal mystery of all things, as our imperfect faculties can now judge of them. "There are (said he) innumerable questions to which the inquisitive mind can in this state receive no answer: Why do you and I exist? Why was this world created? Since it was to be created, why was it not created sooner?"

On Tuesday, May 12, I waited on the Earl of Marchmont, to know if his Lordship would favour Dr. Johnson with information concerning Pope, whose Life he was about to write. Johnson had not flattered himself with the hopes of receiving any civility from this nobleman; for he said to me, when I mentioned Lord Marchmont as one who could tell him a great deal about Pope,—"Sir, he will tell *me* nothing." I had the honour of being known to his Lordship, and applied to him of myself, without being commissioned by Johnson. His Lordship behaved in the most polite and obliging manner, promised to tell all he recollected about Pope and was so very courteous as to say, "Tell Dr. Johnson, I have a great respect for him, and am ready to shew it in any way I can. I am to be in the city to-morrow, and will call at his house as I return." His Lordship however asked, "Will he write the Lives of the Poets impartially? He was the first that brought Whig and Tory into a

Dictionary. And what do you think of his definition of Excise? Do you know the history of his aversion to the word *transpire?*" Then taking down the folio Dictionary, he shewed it with this censure on its secondary sense: "To escape from secrecy to notice; a sense lately innovated from France, without necessity." The truth was, Lord Bolingbroke, who left the Jacobites, first used it; therefore, it was to be condemned. He should have shewn what word would do for it, if it was unnecessary. I afterwards put the question to Johnson: "Why, Sir, (said he,) *get abroad.*" BOSWELL. "That, Sir, is using two words." JOHNSON. "Sir, there is no end of this. You may as well insist to have a word for old age." BOSWELL. "Well, Sir, Senectus." JOHNSON. "Nay, Sir, to insist always that there should be one word to express a thing in English, because there is one in another language, is to change the language."

I availed myself of this opportunity to hear from his Lordship many particulars both of Pope and Lord Bolingbroke, which I have in writing.

I proposed to Lord Marchmont, that he should revise Johnson's Life of Pope: "So (said his Lordship) you would put me in a dangerous situation. You know he knocked down Osborne, the bookseller."

Elated with the success of my spontaneous exertion to procure material and respectable aid to Johnson for his very favourite work, "The Lives of the Poets," I hastened down to Mr. Thrale's at Streatham, where he now was, that I might insure his being at home next day; and after dinner, when I thought he would receive the good news in the best humour, I announced it eagerly: "I have been at work for you to-day, Sir. I have been with Lord Marchmont. He bade me tell you, he has a great respect for you, and will call on you to-morrow, at one o'clock, and communicate all he knows about Pope."—Here I paused, in full expectation that he would be pleased with this intelligence, would praise my active merit, and would be alert to embrace such an offer from a nobleman. But whether I had shewn an over-exultation, which provoked his spleen, or whether he was seized with a suspicion that I had obtruded him on Lord Marchmont, and humbled him too much; or whether there was any thing more than an unlucky fit of ill-humour, I know not; but to my surprise, the result was,—JOHNSON. "I shall not be in town to-morrow. I don't care to know about Pope." MRS. THRALE: (surprised as I was, and a little angry.) "I suppose, Sir, Mr. Boswell thought, that as you are to write Pope's Life, you would wish to know about him." JOHNSON. "Wish! why yes. If it rained knowledge, I'd hold out my hand; but I would not give myself the trouble to go in quest of it." There was no arguing with him at the moment. Some time afterwards he said, "Lord Marchmont will call on me, and then I shall call on Lord Marchmont." Mrs. Thrale was uneasy at his unaccountable caprice; and told me, that if I did not take care to bring about a meeting between Lord Marchmont and him, it would never take place, which would be a great pity. I sent a card to his Lordship, to be left at Johnson's house, acquainting him, that Dr. Johnson could not be in town next day, but would do himself the honour of waiting on him at another time.—I give this account fairly, as a specimen of that unhappy temper with which this great and good man had occasionally to struggle, from something morbid in his constitution. Let the most censorious of my readers suppose himself to have a violent fit of the toothache, or to have received a severe stroke on the shin-bone, and when in such a state to be asked a question; and if he has any candour, he will not be surprised at the answers which Johnson sometimes gave in moments of irritation, which, let me assure them, is exquisitely painful. But it must not be erroneously supposed that he was, in the smallest degree, careless concerning any work which he undertook, or that he was generally thus peevish. It will be seen that in the following year he had a very agreeable interview with Lord Marchmont, at his Lordship's house; and this very afternoon he soon forgot any fretfulness, and fell into conversation as usual.

Talking of divorces, I asked if Othello's doctrine was not plausible:

"He that is robb'd, not wanting what is stolen,
Let him not know't, and he's not robbed at all."

Dr. Johnson and Mrs. Thrale joined against this. JOHNSON. "Ask any man if he'd wish not to know of such an injury." BOSWELL. "Would you tell your friend to make him unhappy?" JOHNSON. "Perhaps, Sir, I should not; but that would be from prudence on my own account. A man would tell his father." BOSWELL. "Yes; because he would not have spurious children to get any share of the family inheritance." MRS. THRALE. "Or he would tell his brother." BOSWELL. "Certainly, his *elder* brother." JOHNSON. "You would tell your friend of a woman's infamy, to prevent his marrying a whore: there is the same reason to tell him of his wife's infidelity when he is married, to prevent the consequences of imposition. It is a breach of confidence not to tell a friend." BOSWELL. "Would you tell Mr. ——?" (naming a gentleman who assuredly was not in the least danger of such a miserable disgrace, though married to a fine woman.) JOHNSON. "No, Sir; because it would do no good; he is so sluggish, he'd never go to parliament and get a divorce."

After Mrs. Thrale was gone to bed, Johnson and I sat up late. We resumed Sir Joshua Reynolds's argument on the preceding Sunday, that a man would be virtuous though he had no other motive than to preserve his character. JOHNSON. "Sir, it is not true; for as to this world, vice does not hurt a man's character." BOSWELL. "Yes, Sir, debauching a friend's wife will." JOHNSON. "No, Sir. Who thinks the worse of —— for it?" BOSWELL. "Lord —— was not his friend." JOHNSON. "That is only a circumstance, Sir; a slight distinction. He could not get into the house but by Lord ——. A man is chosen Knight of the shire, not the less for having debauched ladies." BOSWELL. "What, Sir, if he debauched the ladies of gentlemen in the county, will not there be a general resentment against him?" JOHNSON. "No, Sir. He will lose those particular gentlemen; but the rest will not trouble their heads about it," (warmly). BOSWELL. "Well, Sir, I cannot think so." JOHNSON. "Nay, Sir, there is no talking with a man who will dispute what everybody knows, (angrily.) Don't you know this?" BOSWELL. "No, Sir; and I wish to think better of your country than you represent it. I knew in Scotland a gentleman obliged to leave it for debauching a lady; and in one of our counties an Earl's brother lost his election, because he had debauched the lady of another Earl in that county, and destroyed the peace of a noble family."

Still he would not yield. He proceeded: "Will you not allow, Sir, that vice does not hurt a man's character so as to obstruct his prosperity in life, when you know that —— was loaded with wealth and honours; a man who had acquired his fortune by such crimes, that his consciousness of them impelled him to cut his own throat?" BOSWELL. "You will recollect, Sir, that Dr. Robertson said, he cut his throat because he was weary of still life; little things not being sufficient to move his great mind." JOHNSON, (very angry.) "Nay, Sir, what stuff is this? You had no more this opinion after Robertson said it, than before. I know nothing more offensive than repeating what one knows to be foolish things, by way of continuing a dispute, to see what a man will answer,—to make him your butt!" (angrier still.) BOSWELL. "My dear Sir, I had no such intention as you seem to suspect; I had not indeed. Might not this nobleman have felt every thing 'weary, stale, flat, and unprofitable,' as Hamlet says?" JOHNSON. "Nay, if you are to bring in gabble, I'll talk no more. I will not, upon my honour."

Looking at Messrs. Dilly's splendid edition of Lord Chesterfield's miscellaneous works, he laughed, and said, "Here are now two speeches ascribed to him, both of which were written by me: and the best of it is, they have found out that one of them is like Demosthenes, and the other like Cicero."

I talked of a country life.—JOHNSON. "Were I to live in the country, I would not devote myself to the acquisition of popularity; I would live in a much better way, much more happily; I would have my time at my own command." BOSWELL. "But, Sir, is it not a sad thing to be at a distance from all our literary friends?" JOHNSON. "Sir, you will by and by have enough of this conversation, which now delights you so much."

As he was a zealous friend of subordination, he was at all times watchful to suppress the vulgar cant against the manners of the great; "High people, Sir, (said he,) are the best; take a hundred ladies of quality, you'll find them better wives, better mothers, more willing to sacrifice their own pleasures to their children, than a hundred other women. Tradeswomen (I mean the wives of tradesmen) in the city, who are worth from ten to fifteen thousand pounds, are the worst creatures upon the earth, grossly ignorant, and thinking viciousness fashionable. Farmers, I think, are often worthless fellows. Few lords will cheat; and, if they do, they'll be ashamed of it: farmers cheat and are not ashamed of it: they have all the sensual vices too of the nobility, with cheating into the bargain. There is as much fornication and adultery amongst farmers as amongst noblemen." BOSWELL. "The notion of the world, Sir, however, is, that the morals of women of quality are worse than those in lower stations." JOHNSON. "Yes, Sir, the licentiousness of one woman of quality makes more noise than that of a number of women in lower stations; then, Sir, you are to consider the malignity of women in the city against women of quality, which will make them believe any thing of them, such as that they call their coachmen to bed. No, Sir, so far as I have observed, the higher in rank, the richer ladies are, they are the better instructed, and the more virtuous."

He this day made the observations upon the similarity between "Rasselas" and "Candide:" which I have inserted in its proper place, when considering his admirable philosophical Romance. He said *"Candide"* he thought had more power in it than any thing that Voltaire had written.

On Tuesday, May 19, I was to set out for Scotland in the evening. He was engaged to dine with me at Mr. Dilly's; I waited upon him to remind him of his appointment and attend him thither; he gave me some salutary counsel, and recommended vigourous resolution against any deviation from moral duty. BOSWELL. "But you would not have me to bind myself by a solemn obligation?" JOHNSON. (much agitated) "What! a vow—O, no, Sir, a vow is a horrible thing, it is a snare for sin. The man who cannot go to heaven without a vow—may go—" Here, standing erect, in the middle of his library, and rolling grand, his pause was truly a curious compound of the solemn and the ludicrous; he half-whistled in his usual way, when pleasant, and he paused, as if checked by religious awe.—Methought he would have added—to Hell—but was restrained. I humoured the dilemma. "What! Sir, (said I,) *'In cœlum jusseris ibit?'* alluding to his imitation of it,

'And bid him go to Hell, to Hell he goes.' "

This year, Johnson gave the world a luminous proof that the vigour of his mind in all its faculties, whether memory, judgement, or imagination, was not in the least abated; for this year came out the first four volumes of his "Prefaces, biographical and critical, to the most eminent of the English Poets," * published by the booksellers of London. The remaining volumes came out in the year 1780. The Poets were selected by the several booksellers who had the honorary copy right, which is still preserved among them by mutual compact, notwithstanding the decision of the House of Lords against the perpetuity of Literary Property. We have his own authority, that by his recommendation the poems of Blackmore, Watts, Pomfret, and Yalden, were added to the collection. Of this work I shall speak more particularly hereafter.

On the 22nd of January, I wrote to him on several topicks, and mentioned that as he had been so good as to permit me to have the proof sheets of his "Lives of the Poets," I had written to his servant, Francis, to take care of them for me.

> "MR. BOSWELL TO DR. JOHNSON.
> "Edinburgh, Feb. 2, 1779.

"MY DEAR SIR,

"Garrick's death is a striking event; not that we should be surprised with the death of any man, who has lived sixty-two years; but because there was a *vivacity* in our late celebrated friend, which drove away the thoughts of *death* from any association with *him*. I am sure you will be tenderly affected with his departure; and I would wish to hear from you upon the subject. I was obliged to him in

my days of effervescence in London, when poor Derrick
was my governour; and since that time I received many
civilities from him. Do you remember how pleasing it was,
when I received a letter from him at Invetary, upon our
first return to civilised living after our Hebridean journey?
I shall always remember him with affection as well as admiration.

               *   *   *   *

"Any fresh instance of the uncertainty of life makes one
embrace more closely a valuable friend. My dear and much
respected Sir, may GOD preserve you long in this world
while I am in it.

"I am ever,
"Your much obliged,
"And affectionate humble servant,
"JAMES BOSWELL."

I arrived [in London] on Monday, March 15, and next
morning at a late hour, found Dr. Johnson sitting over his
tea, attended by Mrs. Desmoulins, Mr. Levett, and a clergyman, who had come to submit some poetical pieces to his
revision. It is wonderful what a number and variety of
writers, some of them even unknown to him, prevailed on
his good-nature to look over their works, and suggest corrections and improvements. My arrival interrupted for a
little while the important business of this true representative
of Bayes; upon its being resumed, I found that the subject
under immediate consideration was a translation, yet in
manuscript, of the *Carmen Seculare* of Horace, which had
this year been set to musick, and performed at a publick
entertainment in London, for the joint benefit of Monsieur
Philidor and Signor Baretti. When Johnson had done reading, the authour asked him bluntly, "If upon the whole it
was a good translation?" Johnson, whose regard for truth
was uncommonly strict, seemed to be puzzled for a moment, what answer to make; as he certainly could not honestly commend the performance: with exquisite address
he evaded the question thus, "Sir, I do not say that it may
not be made a very good translation." Here nothing whatever in favour of the performance was affirmed, and yet

the writer was not shocked. A printed "Ode to the Warlike Genius of Britain" came next in review; the bard was a lank bony figure, with short black hair; he was writhing himself in agitation, while Johnson read, and shewing his teeth in a grin of earnestness, exclaimed in broken sentences, and in a keen sharp tone, "Is that poetry, Sir?—Is it Pindar?" JOHNSON. "Why, Sir, there is here a great deal of what is called poetry." Then, turning to me, the poet cried, "My muse has not been long upon the town, and (pointing to the Ode) it trembles under the hand of the great critick." Johnson, in a tone of displeasure, asked him, "Why do you praise Anson?" I did not trouble him by asking his reason for this question. He proceeded, "Here is an errour, Sir; you have made Genius feminine."—"Palpable, Sir; (cried the enthusiast) I know it. But (in a lower tone) it was to pay a compliment to the Duchess of Devonshire, with which her Grace was pleased. She is walking across Coxheath, in the military uniform, and I suppose her to be the Genius of Britain." JOHNSON. "Sir, you are giving a reason for it; but that will not make it right. You may have a reason why two and two should make five; but they will still make but four."

Although I was several times with him in the course of the following days, such it seems were my occupations, or such my negligence, that I have preserved no memorial of his conversation till Friday, March 26, when I visited him. He said he expected to be attacked on account of his "Lives of the Poets," "However (said he) I would rather be attacked than unnoticed. For the worst thing you can do to an authour is to be silent as to his works. An assault upon a town is a bad thing; but starving it is still worse; an assault may be unsuccessful, you may have more men killed than you kill; but if you starve the town, you are sure of victory."

On Friday, April 2, being Good-Friday, I visited him in the morning as usual; and finding that we insensibly fell into a train of ridicule upon the foibles of one of our friends, a very worthy man, I, by way of a check, quoted some good admonition from "The Government of the Tongue," that very pious book. It happened also remarkably enough, that the subject of the sermon preached to us to-day by Dr.

14
Oliver Goldsmith, author of *The Vicar of Wakefield* and a member of Johnson's Literary Club. A portrait from the studio of Sir Joshua Reynolds.

Burrows, the rector of St. Clement Danes, was the certainty that at the last day we must give an account of "the deeds done in the body;" and amongst various acts of culpability he mentioned evil-speaking. As we were moving slowly along in the crowd from church, Johnson jogged my elbow, and said, "Did you attend to the sermon?"—"Yes, Sir, (said I,) it was very applicable to *us*." He, however, stood upon the defensive. "Why, Sir, the sense of ridicule is given us, and may be lawfully used. The authour of 'The Government of the Tongue' would have us treat all men alike."

On Wednesday, April 7, I dined with him at Sir Joshua Reynolds's. I have not marked what company was there. Johnson harangued upon the qualities of different liquors; and spoke with great contempt of claret, as so weak, that "a man would be drowned by it before it make him drunk." He was persuaded to drink one glass of it, that he might judge, not from recollection, which might be dim, but from immediate sensation. He shook his head, and said, "Poor stuff! No, Sir, claret is the liquor for boys; port for men; but he who aspires to be a hero (smiling) must drink brandy. In the first place, the flavour of brandy is most grateful to the palate; and then brandy will do soonest for a man what drinking *can* do for him. There are, indeed, few who are able to drink brandy. That is a power rather to be wished for than attained. And yet, (proceeded he) as in all pleasure hope is a considerable part, I know not but fruition comes too quick by brandy. Florence wine I think the worst; it is wine only to the eye; it is wine neither while you are drinking it, nor after you have drunk it; it neither pleases the taste, nor exhilarates the spirits." I reminded him how heartily he and I used to drink wine together, when we were first acquainted; and how I used to have a head-ache after sitting up with him. He did not like to have this recalled, or, perhaps, thinking that I boasted improperly, resolved to have a witty stroke at me; "Nay, Sir, it was not the *wine* that made your head ache, but the *sense* that I put into it." BOSWELL. "What, Sir! will sense make the head ache?" JOHNSON. "Yes, Sir, (with a smile) when it is not used to it." No man who has a true relish of pleasantry could be offended at this; especially if Johnson in a long intimacy had given him repeated proofs of his regard and good estimation. I used to say, that as he had given me a thousand pounds in praise, he had a good right now and then to take a guinea from me.

On Thursday, April 8, I dined with him at Mr. Allan Ramsay's, with Lord Graham and some other company. We talked of Shakspeare's witches. JOHNSON. "They are beings of his own creation; they are a compound of malignity and meanness, without any abilities: and are quite different from the Italian magician. King James says in his 'Dæmonology' 'Magicians command the devils: witches are their servants.' The Italian magicians are elegant beings." RAMSAY. "Opera witches, not Drury-lane witches."—

On Friday, April 16, I had been present at the trial of the unfortunate Mr. Hackman, who, in a fit of frantick jealous love, had shot Miss Ray, the favourite of a nobleman. Johnson, in whose company I dined to-day with some other friends, was much interested by my account of what passed, and particularly with his prayer for the mercy of heaven. He said, in a solemn fervid tone, "I hope he *shall* find mercy."

This day a violent altercation arose between Johnson and Beauclerk, which having made much noise at the time, I think it proper, in order to prevent any future misrepresentation, to give a minute account of it.

In talking of Hackman, Johnson argued, as Judge Blackstone had done, that his being furnished with two pistols was a proof that he meant to shoot two persons. Mr. Beauclerk said, "No; for that every wise man who intended to shoot himself, took two pistols, that he might be sure of doing it at once. Lord ——'s cook shot himself with one pistol, and lived ten days in great agony. Mr. ——, who loved buttered muffins, but durst not eat them because they disagreed with his stomach, resolved to shoot himself; and then he eat three buttered muffins for breakfast, before shooting himself, knowing that he should not be troubled with indigestion; *he* had two charged pistols; one was found lying charged upon the table by him, after he had shot himself with the other."—"Well, (said Johnson, with an air of triumph,) you see here one pistol was sufficient." Beauclerk replied smartly, "Because it happened to kill him." And either then or a very little afterwards, being piqued at John- son's triumphant remark, added, "This is what you don't know, and I do." There was then a cessation of the dispute; and some minutes intervened, during which, dinner and the glass went on cheerfully; when Johnson suddenly and abruptly exclaimed, "Mr. Beauclerk, how came you to talk so petulantly to me, as 'This is what you don't know, but what I know?' One thing *I* know, which *you* don't seem to know, that you are very uncivil." BEAUCLERK. "Because *you* began by being uncivil, (which you always are.)" The words in parentheses were, I believe, not heard by Dr. John- son. Here again there was a cessation of arms. Johnson told me, that the reason why he waited at first some time without taking any notice of what Mr. Beauclerk said, was because he was thinking whether he should resent it. But when he considered that there were present a young Lord and an eminent traveller, two men of the world with whom he had never dined before, he was apprehensive that they might think they had a right to take such liberties with him as Beauclerk did, and therefore resolved he would not let it pass; adding, "that he would not appear a coward." A little while after this, the conversation turned on the violence of Hackman's temper. Johnson then said, "It was his business to *command* his temper, as my friend Mr. Beauclerk, should have done some time ago." BEAUCLERK. "I should learn of *you*, Sir." JOHNSON. "Sir, you have given *me* opportunities enough of learning, when I have been in *your* company. No man loves to be treated with contempt." BEAUCLERK. (with a polite inclination towards Johnson) "Sir, you have known me twenty years, and however I may have treated others, you may be sure I could never treat you with contempt." JOHNSON. "Sir, you have said more than was necessary." Thus it ended; and Beauclerk's coach not having come for him till very late, Dr. Johnson and another gentleman sat with him a long time after the rest of the company were gone; and he and I dined at Beauclerk's on the Saturday se'night following.

After this tempest had subsided, I recollect the following particulars of his conversation:

"I am always for getting a boy forward in his learning; for that is a sure good. I would let him at first read *any* English book which happens to engage his attention; because you have done a great deal, when you have brought him to have entertainment from a book. He'll get better books afterwards."

"To be contradicted, in order to force you to talk is mighty unpleasing. You *shine,* indeed; but it is by being *ground.*"

Of a gentleman who made some figure among the *Literati* of his time (Mr. Fitzherbert,) he said, "What eminence he had was by a felicity of manner: he had no more learning than what he could not help."

On Saturday, April 24, I dined with him at Mr. Beauclerk's, with Sir Joshua Reynolds, Mr. Jones (afterwards Sir William,) Mr. Langton, Mr. Steevens, Mr. Paradise, and Dr. Higgins. I mentioned that Mr. Wilkes had attacked Garrick to me, as a man who had no friend. JOHNSON. "I believe he is right, sir. Οι φιγοι, ον φγος—He had friends, but no friend. Garrick was so diffused, he had no man to whom he wished to unbosom himself. He found people always ready to applaud him, and that always for the same thing: so he saw life with great uniformity." I took upon me, for once, to fight with Goliath's weapons, and play the sophist.—"Garrick did not need a friend, as he got from every body all he wanted. What is a friend? One who supports you and comforts you, while others do not. Friendship, you know, Sir, is the cordial drop, 'to make the nauseous draught of life go down:' but if the draught be not nauseous, if it be all sweet, there is no occasion for that drop." JOHNSON. "Many men would not be content to live so. I hope I should not. They would wish to have an intimate friend, with whom they might compare minds, and cherish private virtues." One of the company mentioned Lord Chesterfield, as a man who had no friend. JOHNSON. "There were more materials to make friendship in Garrick, had he not been so diffused." BOSWELL. "Garrick was pure gold, but beat out to thin leaf. Lord Chesterfield was tinsel."

JOHNSON. "Garrick was a very good man, the cheerfulest man of his age; a decent liver in a profession which is supposed to give indulgence to licentiousness; and a man who gave away, freely, money acquired by himself. He began the world with a great hunger for money; the son of a half-pay officer, bred in a family whose study was to make four-pence do as much as others made four-pence halfpenny do. But, when he had got money, he was very liberal." I presumed to animadvert on his eulogy on Garrick, in his "Lives of the Poets." "You say, Sir, his death eclipsed the gaiety of nations." JOHNSON. "I could not have said more nor less. It is the truth; *eclipsed, not extinguished;* and his death *did* eclipse; it was like a storm." BOSWELL. "But why nations? Did his gaiety extend further than his own nation?" JOHNSON. "Why, Sir, some exaggeration must be allowed. Besides, nations may be said—if we allow the Scotch to be a nation, and to have gaiety,—which they have not. *You* are an exception, though. Come, gentlemen, let us candidly admit that there is one Scotchman who is cheerful." BEAU-CLERK. "But he is a very unnatural Scotchman."

Johnson being now better disposed to obtain information concerning Pope than he was last year, sent by me to my Lord Marchmont, a present of those volumes of his "Lives of the Poets," which were at this time published, with a request to have permission to wait on him; and his Lordship, who had called on him twice, obligingly appointed Saturday, the first of May, for receiving us.

On that morning Johnson came to me from Streatham, and after drinking chocolate at General Paoli's, in South-Audley-street, we proceeded to Lord Marchmont's in Curzon-street. His Lordship met us at the door of his library, and with great politeness said to Johnson, "I am not going to make an encomium upon *myself,* by telling you the high respect I have for *you,* Sir." Johnson was exceedingly courteous; and the interview, which lasted about two hours, during which the Earl communicated his anecdotes of Pope, was as agreeable as I could have wished. When we came out, I said to Johnson, that considering his Lordship's civility, I should have been vexed if he had again failed to come. "Sir, (said he,) I would rather have given twenty pounds than not have come." I accompanied him to Streatham, where we dined, and returned to town in the evening.

He said, "Dodsley first mentioned to me the scheme of an English Dictionary; but I had long thought of it." Boswell. "You did not know what you were undertaking." Johnson. "Yes, Sir, I knew very well what I was undertaking,—and very well how to do it,—and have done it very well." Boswell. "An excellent climax! and it *has* availed you. In your Preface you say, 'What would it avail me in this gloom of solitude?' You have been agreeably mistaken."

He, I know not why, shewed upon all occasions an aversion to go to Ireland, where I proposed to him that we should make a tour. Johnson. "It is the last place where I should wish to travel." Boswell. "Should you not like to see Dublin, Sir?" Johnson. "No, Sir; Dublin is only a worse capital." Boswell. "Is not the Giant's-causeway worth seeing?" Johnson. "Worth seeing? yes; but not worth going to see."

Yet he had a kindness for the Irish nation, and thus generously expressed himself to a gentleman from that country, on the subject of an UNION which artful Politicians have often had in view—"Do not make an union with us, Sir. We should unite with you, only to rob you. We should have robbed the Scotch, if they had had any thing of which we could have robbed them."

Of an acquaintance of ours, whose manners and every thing about him, though expensive, were coarse, he said, "Sir, you see in him vulgar prosperity."

On his birth-day, Johnson has this note; "I am now beginning the seventy-second year of my life, with more strength of body, and greater vigour of mind, than I think is common at that age." But still he complains of sleepless nights and idle days, and forgetfulness, or neglect of resolutions. He thus pathetically expresses himself: "Surely I shall not spend my whole life with my own total disapprobation."

Being disappointed in my hopes of meeting Johnson this year, so that I could hear none of his admirable sayings, I shall compensate for this want by inserting a collection of them, for which I am indebted to my worthy friend Mr. Langton, whose kind communications have been separately interwoven in many parts of this work.

"John Gilbert Cooper related, that soon after the publication of his Dictionary, Garrick being asked by Johnson what people said of it, told him, that among other animadversions, it was objected that he cited authorities which were beneath the dignity of such a work, and mentioned Richardson. 'Nay, (said Johnson,) I have done worse than that: I have cited *thee,* David.' "

"He related, that he had once in a dream a contest of wit with some other person, and that he was very much mortified by imagining that his opponent had the better of him. 'Now, (said he,) one may mark here the effect of sleep in weakening the power of reflection; for had not my judgement failed me, I should have seen, that the wit of this supposed antagonist, by whose superiority I felt myself depressed, was as much furnished by me, as that which I thought I had been uttering in my own character.' "

"He thus defined the difference between physical and moral truth: 'Physical truth is, when you tell a thing as it actually is. Moral truth is, when you tell a thing sincerely and precisely as it appears to you. I say such a one walked across the street; if he really did so, I told a physical truth. If I thought so, though I should have been mistaken, I told a moral truth.' "

"Mr. Beauclerk one day repeated to Dr. Johnson Pope's lines,

'Let modest Foster, if he will, excel
Ten metropolitans in preaching well:'

Then asked the Doctor, 'Why did Pope say this?' JOHNSON. 'Sir, he hoped it would vex somebody.' "

"His affection for Topham Beauclerk was so great, that when Beauclerk was labouring under that severe illness which at last occasioned his death, Johnson said, (with a voice faultering with emotion,) 'Sir, I would walk to the extent of the diameter of the earth to save Beauclerk.' "

"Talking on the subject of toleration, one day when some friends were with him in his study, he made his usual remark, that the State has a right to regulate the religion of the people, who are the children of the State. A clergyman having readily acquiesced in this, Johnson, who loved discussion, observed, 'But, Sir, you must go round to other States than our own. You do not know what a Bramin has to say for himself. In short, Sir, I have got no further than this: Every man has a right to utter what he thinks truth, and every other man has a right to knock him down for it. Martyrdom is the test.' "

"A man, he observed, should begin to write soon; for, if he waits till his judgement is matured, his inability, through want of practice to express his conceptions, will make the disproportion so great between what he sees, and what he can attain, that he will probably be discouraged from writing at all. As a proof of the justness of this remark, we may instance what is related of the great Lord Granville; that after he had written his letter giving an account of the battle of Dettingen, he said, 'Here is a letter, expressed in terms not good enough for a tallow-chandler to have used.' "

"Talking of a Court-martial that was sitting upon a very momentous publick occasion, he expressed much doubt of an enlightened decision; and said, that perhaps there was not a member of it, who in the whole course of his life, had ever spent an hour by himself in balancing probabilities."

"Goldsmith one day brought to the CLUB a printed Ode, which he, with others, had been hearing read by its authour in a publick room, at the rate of five shillings each for admission. One of the company having read it aloud, Dr. Johnson said, 'Bolder words and more timorous meaning, I think, never were brought together.' "

"He used to quote with great warmth, the saying of Aristotle recorded by Diogenes Laertius; that there was the same difference between one learned and unlearned, as between the living and the dead."

"Though he used to censure carelessness with great vehemence, he owned, that he once, to avoid the trouble of locking up five guineas, hid them, he forgot where, so that he could not find them."

"A gentleman who introduced his brother to Dr. Johnson, was earnest to recommend him to the Doctor's notice, which he did by saying, 'When we have sat together some time, you'll find my brother grow very entertaining.'—'Sir, (said Johnson,) I can wait.' "

"Drinking tea one day at Garrick's with Mr. Langton, he was questioned if he was not somewhat of a heretic as to Shakspeare; said Garrick, 'I doubt he is a little of an infidel.'—'Sir, (said Johnson) I will stand by the lines I have written on Shakspeare in my Prologue at the opening of your Theatre.' Mr. Langton suggested, that in the line

'And panting Time toil'd after him in vain;'

Johnson might have had in his eye the passage in the 'Tempest,' where Prospero says of Miranda,

'——She will outstrip all praise,
And make it halt behind her.'

Johnson said nothing. Garrick then ventured to observe, 'I do not think that the happiest line in the praise of Shakspeare.' Johnson exclaimed (smiling,) 'Prosaical rogues! next time I write, I'll make both time and space pant.' "

"It is well known that there was formerly a rude custom for those who were sailing upon the Thames, to accost each other as they passed, in the most abusive language they could invent, generally, however, with as much satirical humour as they were capable of producing. Addison gives a specimen of this ribaldry, in number 383 of 'The Spectator,' when Sir Roger de Coverly and he are going to Spring-garden. Johnson was once eminently successful in this species of contest; a fellow having attacked him with some coarse raillery, Johnson answered him thus, 'Sir, your wife, *under pretence of keeping a bawdy-house,* is a receiver of stolen goods.' One evening when he and Mr. Burke and Mr. Langton were in company together, and the admirable scolding of Timon of Athens was mentioned, this instance of Johnson's was quoted, and thought to have at least equal excellence."

"As Johnson always allowed the extraordinary talents of Mr. Burke, so Mr. Burke was fully sensible of the wonderful powers of Johnson. Mr. Langton recollects having passed an evening with both of them, when Mr. Burke repeatedly entered upon topicks which it was evident he would have illustrated with extensive knowledge and richness of expression; but Johnson always seized upon the conversation, in which, however, he acquitted himself in a most masterly manner. As Mr. Burke and Mr. Langton were walking home, Mr. Burke observed that Johnson had been very great that night; Mr. Langton joined in this, but added, he could have wished to hear more from another person; (plainly intimating that he meant Mr. Burke.) 'O, no, (said Mr. Burke) it is enough for me to have rung the bell to him.' "

"Beauclerk having observed to him of one of their friends, that he was aukward at counting money, 'Why, Sir,' said Johnson, 'I am likewise aukward at counting money. But then, Sir, the reason is plain; I have had very little money to count.' "

"He had an abhorrence of affectation. Talking of old Mr. Langton, of whom he said, 'Sir, you will seldom see such a gentleman, such are his stores of literature, such his knowledge in divinity, and such his exemplary life;' he added, 'and, Sir, he has no grimace, no gesticulation, no bursts of admiration on trivial occasions; he never embraces you with an overacted cordiality.' "

"Being in company with a gentleman who thought fit to maintain Dr. Berkeley's ingenious philosophy, that nothing exists but as perceived by some mind; when the gentleman was going away, Johnson said to him, 'Pray, Sir, don't leave us; for we may perhaps forget to think of you, and then you will cease to exist.' "

"Of Dr. Goldsmith he said, 'No man was more foolish when he had not a pen in his hand, or more wise when he had.' "

"Depend upon it, said he, that if a man *talks* of his misfortunes, there is something in them that is not disagreeable to him; for where there is nothing but pure misery, there never is any recourse to the mention of it."

"A man must be a poor beast, that should *read* no more in quantity than he could *utter* aloud."

" 'The applause of a single human being is of great consequence:' This he said to me with great earnestness of manner, very near the time of his decease, on occasion of having desired me to read a letter addressed to him from some person in the North of England; which when I had done, and he asked me what the contents were, as I thought being particular upon it might fatigue him, it being of great length, I only told him in general that it was highly in his praise;—and then he expressed himself as above."

In 1781, Johnson at last completed his "Lives of the Poets," of which he gives this account: "Some time in March I finished the 'Lives of the Poets,' which I wrote in my usual way, dilatorily and hastily, unwilling to work, and working with vigour and haste." In a memorandum previous to this, he says of them: "Written, I hope, in such a manner as may tend to the promotion of piety."

This is the work, which of all Dr. Johnson's writings will perhaps be read most generally, and with most pleasure. Philology and biography were his favourite pursuits, and those who lived most in intimacy with him, heard him upon all occasions, when there was a proper opportunity, take delight in expatiating upon the various merits of the English Poets: upon the niceties of their characters, and the events of their progress through the world which they contributed to illuminate. His mind was so full of that kind of information, and it was so well arranged in his memory, that in performing what he had undertaken in this way, he had little more to do than to put his thoughts upon paper; exhibiting first each Poet's life, and then subjoining a critical examination of his genius and works. But when he began to write, the subject swelled in such a manner, that instead of prefaces to each poet, of no more than a few pages, as he had originally intended, he produced an ample, rich, and most entertaining view of them in every respect.

While the world in general was filled with admiration of Johnson's "Lives of the Poets," there were narrow circles in which prejudice and resentment were fostered, and from which attacks of different sorts issued against him. By some violent Whigs he was arraigned of injustice to Milton; by some Cambridge men of depreciating Gray; and his expressing with a dignified freedom what he really thought of George, Lord Lyttelton, gave offence to some of the friends of that nobleman, and particularly produced a declaration of war against him from Mrs. Montagu, the ingenious Essayist on Shakspeare, between whom and his Lordship a commerce of reciprocal compliments had long been carried on. In this war the smallest powers in alliance with him were of course led to engage, at least on the defensive, and thus I for one, was excluded from the enjoyment of "A Feast of Reason," such as Mr. Cumberland has described, with a keen, yet just and delicate pen, in his "OBSERVER." These minute inconveniences gave not the least disturbance to Johnson. He nobly said, when I talked to him of the feeble, though shrill outcry which had been raised, "Sir, I considered myself as entrusted with a certain portion of truth. I have given my opinion sincerely; let them shew where they think me wrong."

I wrote to him in February, complaining of having been troubled by a recurrence of the perplexing question of Liberty and Necessity;—and mentioning that I hoped soon to meet him again in London.

"To JAMES BOSWELL, ESQ.

"DEAR SIR,

"I hoped you had got rid of all this hypocrisy of misery. What have you to do with Liberty and Necessity? Or what more than to hold your tongue about it? Do not doubt but I shall be most heartily glad to see you here again, for I love every part about you but your affectation of distress.

"I have at last finished my Lives, and have laid up for you a load of copy, all out of order, so that it will amuse you a long time to set it right. Come to me, my dear Bozzy, and let us be as happy as we can. We will go again to the Mitre, and talk old times over.

> "I am, dear Sir,
>> "Yours affectionately,
>>> "SAM. JOHNSON."

"March 14, 1781."

On Monday, March 19, I arrived in London, and on Tuesday, the 20th, met him in Fleet-street, walking, or rather indeed moving along; for his peculiar march is thus described in a very just and picturesque manner, in a short Life of him published very soon after his death:—"When he walked the streets, what with the constant roll of his head, and the concomitant motion of his body, he appeared to make his way by that motion, independent of his feet." That he was often much stared at while he advanced in this manner, may easily be believed; but it was not safe to make sport of one so robust as he was. Mr. Langton saw him one day, in a fit of absence, by a sudden start, drive the load off a porter's back, and walk forward briskly, without being conscious of what he had done. The porter was very angry, but stood still, and eyed the huge figure with much earnestness, till he was satisfied that his wisest course was to be quiet, and take up his burthen again.

Our accidental meeting in the street after a long separation, was a pleasing surprize to us both. He stepped aside with me into Falcon-court, and made kind enquiries about my family, and as we were in a hurry going different ways, I promised to call on him next day; he said he was engaged to go out in the morning. "Early, Sir?" said I. JOHNSON. "Why, Sir, a London morning does not go with the sun."

I waited on him next evening, and he gave me a great portion of his original manuscript of his "Lives of the Poets," which he had preserved for me.

I found on visiting his friend, Mr. Thrale, that he was now very ill, and had removed, I suppose by the solicitation of Mrs. Thrale, to a house in Grosvenor-square. I was sorry to see him sadly changed in his appearance.

He told me I might now have the pleasure to see Dr. Johnson drink wine again, for he had lately returned to it.

When I mentioned this to Johnson, he said, "I drink it now sometimes, but not socially." The first evening that I was with him at Thrale's, I observed he poured a large quantity of it into a glass, and swallowed it greedily. Every thing about his character and manners was forcible and violent; there never was any moderation; many a day did he fast, many a year did he refrain from wine; but when he did eat, it was voraciously; when he did drink wine, it was copiously. He could practise abstinence, but not temperance.

He said, "Mrs. Montagu has dropt me. Now, Sir, there are people whom one should like very well to drop, but would not wish to be dropped by." He certainly was vain of the society of ladies, and could make himself very agreeable to them, when he chose it; Sir Joshua Reynolds agreed with me that he could. Mr. Gibbon, with his usual sneer, controverted it, perhaps in resentment of Johnson's having talked with some disgust of his ugliness, which one would think a *philosopher* would not mind. Dean Marlay wittily observed, "A lady may be vain, when she can turn a wolf-dog into a lap-dog."

His notion of the duty of a member of Parliament, sitting upon an election-committee, was very high; and when he was told of a gentleman upon one of those committees, who read the newspapers part of the time, and slept the rest, while the merits of a vote were examined by the counsel; and as an excuse, when challenged by the chairman for such behaviour, bluntly answered, "I had made up my mind upon that case;"—Johnson, with an indignant contempt, said, "If he was such a rogue as to make up his mind upon a case without hearing it, he should not have been such a fool as to tell it."—"I think (said Mr. Dudley Long, now North) the Doctor has pretty plainly made him out to be both rogue and fool."

Johnson justly considered that the clergy, as persons set apart for the sacred office of serving at the altar, and impressing the minds of men with the awful concerns of a future state, should be somewhat more serious than the generality of mankind, and have a suitable composure of manners. A due sense of the dignity of their profession, independent of higher motives, will ever prevent them from losing their distinction in an indiscriminate socialty; and did such as affect this, know how much it lessens them in the eyes of those whom they think to please by it, they would feel themselves much mortified.

Johnson, and his friend, Beauclerk, were once together in company with several clergymen, who thought that they should appear to advantage, by assuming the lax jollity of *men of the world;* which, as it may be observed in similar cases, they carried to noisy excess. Johnson, who they expected would be *entertained,* sat grave and silent for some time; at last, turning to Beauclerk, he said, by no means in a whisper, "This merriment of parsons is mighty offensive."

Mrs. Thrale mentioned a gentleman who had acquired a fortune of four thousand a year in trade, but was absolutely miserable, because he could not talk in company; so miserable, that he was impelled to lament his situation in the street to ******, whom he hates, and who he knows despises him. "I am a most unhappy man (said he). I am invited to conversations. I go to conversations; but, alas! I have no conversation."—JOHNSON. "Man commonly cannot be successful in different ways. This gentleman has spent, in getting four thousand pounds a year, the time in which he might have learnt to talk; and now he cannot talk." Mr. Perkins made a shrewd and droll remark: "If he had got his four thousand a year as a mountebank, he might have learnt to talk at the same time that he was getting his fortune."

Some other gentlemen came in. The conversation concerning the person whose character Dr. Johnson had treated so slightingly, as he did not know his merit, was resumed. Mrs. Thrale said, "You think so of him, Sir, because he is quiet, and does not exert himself with force. You'll be saying the same thing of Mr. ***** there, who sits as quiet—." This was not well bred; and Johnson did not let it pass without correction. "Nay, Madam, what right have you to talk thus? Both Mr. ***** and I have reason to take it ill. *You* may talk so of Mr. *****; but why do you make *me* do it? Have I said anything against Mr. *****?

You have *set* him, that I might shoot him: but I have not shot him."

One of the gentlemen said, he had seen three folio volumes of Dr. Johnson's sayings collected by me. "I must put you right, Sir, (said I;) for I am very exact in authenticity. You could not see folio volumes, for I have none: you might have seen some in quarto and octavo. This is an inattention which one should guard against." JOHNSON. "Sir, it is a want of concern about veracity. He does not know that he saw *any* volumes. If he had seen them he could have remembered their size."

Mr. Thrale appeared very lethargick to-day. I saw him again on Monday evening, at which time he was not thought to be in immediate danger; but early in the morning of Wednesday the 4th, he expired. Johnson was in the house, and thus mentions the event: "I felt almost the last flutter of his pulse, and looked for the last time upon the face that for fifteen years had never been turned upon me but with respect and benignty." Upon that day there was a *Call* of the LITERARY CLUB; but Johnson apologised for his absence by the following note:

"MR. JOHNSON knows that Sir Joshua Reynolds and the other gentlemen will excuse his incompliance with the Call, when they are told that Mr. Thrale died this morning."

"Wednesday."

Mr. Thrale's death was a very essential loss to Johnson, who, although he did not foresee all that afterwards happened, was sufficiently convinced that the comforts which Mr. Thrale's family afforded him, would now in a great measure cease. He, however, continued to shew a kind attention to his widow and children as long as it was acceptable: and he took upon him, with a very earnest concern, the office of one of his executors, the importance of which seemed greater than usual to him, from his circumstances having been always such, that he had scarcely any share in the real business of life. His friends of the CLUB were in hopes that Mr. Thrale might have made a liberal provision for him for his life, which, as Mr. Thrale left no son, and a very large fortune, it would have been highly to his honour to have done; and, considering Dr. Johnson's age, could not have been of long duration; but he bequeathed him only two hundred pounds, which was the legacy given to each of his executors. I could not but be somewhat diverted by hearing Johnson talk in a pompous manner of his new office, and particularly of the concerns of the brewery, which it was at last resolved should be sold. Lord Lucan tells a very good story, which, if not precisely exact, is certainly characteristical: that when the sale of Thrale's brewery was going forward, Johnson appeared bustling about, with an ink-horn and pen in his button-hole, like an excise-man; and on being asked what he really considered to be the value of the property which was to be disposed of, answered, "We are not here to sell a parcel of boilers and vats, but the potentiality of growing rich beyond the dreams of avarice."

On Friday, April 13, being Good-Friday, I went to St. Clement's church with him as usual. There I saw again his old fellow-collegian, Edwards, to whom I said, "I think, Sir, Dr. Johnson and you meet only at Church." "Sir, (said he,) it is the best place we can meet in, except Heaven, and I hope we shall meet there too." Dr. Johnson told me, that there was very little communication between Edwards and him, after their unexpected renewal of acquaintance. "But (said he, smiling) he met me once, and said, 'I am told you have written a very pretty book called *The Rambler.*' I was unwilling that he should leave the world in total darkness, and sent him a set."

Mr. Berenger visited him to-day, and was very pleasing. We talked of an evening society for conversation at a house in town, of which we were all members, but of which Johnson said, "It will never do, Sir. There is nothing served about there, neither tea, nor coffee, nor lemonade, nor any thing whatever; and depend upon it, Sir, a man does not love to go to a place from whence he comes out exactly as he went in." I endeavoured for argument's sake, to maintain that men of learning and talents might have very good intellectual society, without the aid of any little gratifications of the senses. Berenger joined with Johnson, and

303

said, that without these any meeting would be dull and insipid. He would therefore have all the slight refreshments; nay, it would not be amiss to have some cold meat, and a bottle of wine upon a side-board. "Sir, (said Johnson to me, with an air of triumph,) Mr. Berenger knows the world. Every body loves to have good things furnished to them without any trouble. I told Mrs. Thrale once, that as she did not choose to have card-tables, she should have a profusion of the best sweetmeats, and she would be sure to have company enough come to her." I agreed with my illustrious friend upon this subject; for it has pleased GOD to make man a composite animal, and where there is nothing to refresh the body, the mind will languish.

On Friday, April 20, I spent with him one of the happiest days that I remember to have enjoyed in the whole course of my life. Mrs. Garrick, whose grief for the loss of her husband was, I believe, as sincere as wounded affection and admiration could produce, had this day, for the first time since his death, a select party of his friends to dine with her. The company was, Miss Hannah More, who lived with her, and whom she called her Chaplain; Mrs. Boscawen, Mrs. Elizabeth Carter, Sir Joshua Reynolds, Dr. Burney, Dr. Johnson, and myself. We found ourselves very elegantly entertained at her house in the Adelphi, where I have passed many a pleasing hour with him "who gladdened life." She looked well, talked of her husband with complacency, and while she cast her eyes on his portrait, which hung over the chimney-piece, said, that "death was now the most agreeable object to her." The very semblance of David Garrick was cheering. Mr. Beauclerk, with happy propriety, inscribed under that fine portrait of him, which by Lady Diana's kindness is now the property of my friend Mr. Langton, the following passage from his beloved Shakspeare:

> "————————A merrier man,
> Within the limit of becoming mirth,
> I never spent an hour's talk withal.
> His eye begets occasion for his wit;
> For every object that the one doth catch

The other turns to a mirth-moving jest;
Which his fair tongue (Conceit's expositor)
Delivers in such apt and gracious words,
That aged ears play truant at his tales,
And younger hearings are quite ravished;
So sweet and voluble is his discourse."

We were all in fine spirits; and I whispered to Mrs. Boscawen, "I believe this is as much as can be made of life."
In addition to a splendid entertainment, we were regaled
with Lichfield ale, which had a peculiar appropriate value.
Sir Joshua, and Dr. Burney, and I, drank cordially of it to
Dr. Johnson's health; and though he would not join us, he
as cordially answered, "Gentlemen, I wish you all as well
as you do me."

The general effect of this day dwells upon my mind in
fond remembrance, but I do not find much conversation
recorded. What I have preserved shall be faithfully given.

One of the company mentioned Mr. Thomas Hollis, the
strenuous Whig, who used to send over Europe presents of
democratical books, with their boards stamped with daggers
and caps of liberty. Mrs. Carter said, "He was a bad man:
he used to talk uncharitably." JOHNSON. "Poh! poh!
Madam; who is the worse for being talked of uncharitably?
Besides, he was a dull poor creature as ever lived: and I believe he would not have done harm to a man whom he
knew to be of very opposite principles to his own. I remember once at the Society of Arts, when an advertisement was
to be drawn up, he pointed me out as the man who could
do it best. This, you will observe, was kindness to me. I
however slipt away and escaped it."

Mrs. Carter having said of the same person, "I doubt he
was an Atheist." JOHNSON. "I don't know that. He might
perhaps have become one, if he had had time to ripen,
(smiling.) He might have *exuberated* into an Atheist."

Sir Joshua Reynolds praised "Mudge's Sermons." JOHN-
SON. "Mudge's Sermons are good, but not practical. He
grasps more sense than he can hold; he takes more corn
than he can make into meal; he opens a wide prospect, but
it is so distant, it is indistinct. I love 'Blair's Sermons.'

305

Though the dog is a Scotchman, and a Presbyterian, and every thing he should not be, I was the first to praise them. Such was my candour." (smiling.) MRS. BOSCAWEN. "Such his great merit, to get the better of your prejudices." JOHNSON. "Why, Madam, let us compound the matter; let us ascribe it to my candour, and his merit."

In the evening we had a large company in the drawing-room; several ladies, the Bishop of Killaloe, Dr. Percy, Mr. Chamberlayne of the Treasury, &c. &c. Somebody said, the life of a mere literary man could not be very entertaining. JOHNSON. "But it certainly may. This is a remark which has been made, and repeated, without justice; why should the life of a literary man be less entertaining than the life of any other man? Are there not as interesting varieties in such a life? As a *literary life* it may be very entertaining." BOSWELL. "But it must be better surely, when it is diversified with a little active variety—such as his having gone to Jamaica:—or—his having gone to the Hebrides." Johnson was not displeased at this.

Talking of a very respectable authour, he told us a curious circumstance in his life, which was, that he had married a printer's devil. REYNOLDS. "A Printer's devil, Sir! Why, I thought a printer's devil was a creature with a black face and in rags." JOHNSON. "Yes, Sir. But I suppose he had her face washed, and put clean clothes on her. (Then looking very serious, and very earnest.) And she did not disgrace him;—the woman had a bottom of good sense." The word *bottom* thus introduced, was so ludicrous when contrasted with his gravity, that most of us could not forbear tittering and laughing; though I recollect that the Bishop of Killaloe kept his countenance with perfect steadiness, while Miss Hannah More slyly hid her face behind a lady's back who sat on the same settee with her. His pride could not bear that any expression of his should excite ridicule, when he did not intend it; he therefore resolved to assume and exercise despotick power, glanced sternly around, and called out in a strong tone, "Where's the merriment?" Then collecting himself, and looking awful, to make us feel how he could impose restraint, and as it were searching his mind for a still more ludicrous word, he slowly pronounced, "I say the *woman* was *fundamentally* sensible;" as if he had said, hear this now, and laugh if you dare. We all sat composed as at a funeral.

He and I walked away together; we stopped a little while by the rails of the Adelphi, looking on the Thames, and I said to him with some emotion, that I was now thinking of two friends we had lost, who once lived in the buildings behind us, Beauclerk and Garrick. "Ay, Sir, (said he, tenderly,) and two such friends as cannot be supplied."

He gave us an entertaining account of *Bet Flint,* a woman of the town, who, with some eccentrick talents and much effrontery, forced herself upon his acquaintance. "Bet (said he) wrote her own Life in verse, which she brought to me, wishing that I would furnish her with a Preface to it. (Laughing.) I used to say of her, that she was generally slut and drunkard;—occasionally, whore and thief. She had, however, genteel lodgings, a spinnet on which she played, and a boy that walked before her chair. Poor Bet was taken up on a charge of stealing a counterpane, and tried at the Old Bailey. Chief Justice ——, who loved a wench, summed up favourably, and she was acquitted. After which, Bet said, with a gay and satisfied air, 'Now that the counterpane is *my own,* I shall make a petticoat of it.' "

Mr. Wilkes said to me, loud enough for Dr. Johnson to hear, "Dr. Johnson should make me a present of his 'Lives of the Poets,' as I am a poor patriot, who cannot afford to buy them." Johnson seemed to take no notice of this hint; but in a little while, he called to Mr. Dilly, "Pray, Sir, be so good as to send a set of my Lives to Mr. Wilkes, with my compliments." This was accordingly done; and Mr. Wilkes paid Dr. Johnson a visit, was courteously received, and sat with him a long time.

The company gradually dropped away. Mr. Dilly himself was called down stairs upon business; I left the room for some time; when I returned, I was struck with observing Dr. Samuel Johnson and John Wilkes, Esq. literally *tête-à-tête;* for they were reclined upon their chairs, with their heads leaning almost close to each other, and talking earnestly, in a kind of confidential whisper, of the personal quarrel between George the Second and the King of Prussia. Such a scene of perfectly easy sociality between two such opponents in the war of political controversy, as that which I now beheld would have been an excellent subject for a picture. It presented to my mind the happy days which are foretold in Scripture, when the lion shall lie down with the kid.

After this day there was another pretty long interval, during which Dr. Johnson and I did not meet. When I mentioned it to him with regret, he was pleased to say, "Then, Sir, let us live double."

About this time it was much the fashion for several ladies to have evening assemblies, where the fair sex might participate in conversation with literary and ingenious men, animated by a desire to please. These societies were denominated *Blue-stocking Clubs,* the origin of which title being little known, it may be worth while to relate it. One of the most eminent members of those societies, when they first commenced, was Mr. Stillingfleet, whose dress was remarkable grave, and in particular it was observed, that he wore blue stockings. Such was the excellence of his conversation, that his absence was felt as so great a loss, that it used to be said, "We can do nothing without the *blue-stockings;*" and thus by degrees the title was established. Miss Hannah More has admirably described a *Blue-stocking Club,* in her *"Bas Bleu,"* a poem in which many of the persons who were most conspicuous there are mentioned.

Johnson was prevailed with to come sometimes into these circles, and did not think himself too grave even for the lively Miss Monckton (now Countess of Corke) who used to have the finest *bit of blue* at the house of her mother, Lady Galway. Her vivacity enchanted the Sage, and they used to talk together with all imaginable ease. A singular instance happened one evening, when she insisted that some of Sterne's writings were very pathetick. Johnson bluntly denied it. "I am sure (said she) they have affected *me.*"— "Why (said Johnson, smiling, and rolling himself about,) that is, because, dearest, you're a dunce." When she sometimes afterwards mentioned this to him, he said with equal

15
A self-portrait by Sir Joshua Reynolds, co-founder with Johnson of the Literary Club, whose membership embraced many of the most eminent men in England.

truth and politeness; "Madam, if I had thought so, I certainly should not have said it."

Another evening Johnson's kind indulgence towards me had a pretty difficult trial. I had dined at the Duke of Montrose's with a very agreeable party, and his grace, according to his usual custom, had circulated the bottle very freely. Lord Graham and I went together to Miss Monckton's, where I certainly was in extraordinary spirits, and above all fear or awe. In the midst of a great number of persons of the first rank, amongst whom I recollect with confusion, a noble lady of the most stately decorum, I placed myself next to Johnson, and thinking myself now fully his match, talked to him in a loud and boisterous manner, desirous to let the company know how I could contend with *Ajax*. I particularly remember pressing him upon the value of the pleasures of the imagination and as an illustration of my argument, asking him, "What, Sir, supposing I were to fancy that the —— (naming the most charming Duchess in his Majesty's dominions) were in love with me should I not be very happy?" My friend with much address evaded my interrogatories, and kept me as quiet as possible; but it may easily be conceived how he must have felt. However, when a few days afterwards I waited upon him and made an apology, he behaved with the most friendly gentleness.

While I remained in London this year, Johnson and I dined together at several places. I recollect a placid day at Dr. Butler's, who had now removed from Derby to Lower Grosvenor-street, London; but of his conversation on that and other occasions during this period, I neglected to keep any regular record, and shall therefore insert here some miscellaneous articles which I find in my Johnsonian notes.

His disorderly habits, when "making provision for the day that was passing over him," appear from the following anecdote, communicated to me by Mr. John Nichols:—"In the year 1763, a young bookseller, who was an apprentice to Mr. Whiston, waited on him with a subscription to his 'Shakspeare:' and observing that the Doctor made no entry in any book of the subscriber's name, ventured diffidently to ask, whether he would please to have the gentleman's address, that it might be properly inserted in the printed list of subscribers.—'*I shall print no List of Subscribers;'* said Johnson, with great abruptness: but almost immediately recollecting himself, added, very complacently, 'Sir, I have two very cogent reasons for not printing any list of subscribers;—one, that I have lost all the names,—the other, that I have spent all the money.' "

Johnson could not brook appearing to be worsted in argument, even when he had taken the wrong side, to shew the force and dexterity of his talents. When, therefore, he perceived that his opponent gained ground, he had recourse to some sudden mode of robust sophistry. Once when I was pressing upon him with visible advantage, he stopped me thus:—"My dear Boswell, let's have no more of this; you'll make nothing of it. I'd rather have you whistle a Scotch tune."

Care, however, must be taken to distinguish between Johnson when he "talked for victory," and Johnson when he had no desire but to inform and illustrate.—"One of Johnson's principal talents (says an eminent friend of his) was shewn in maintaining the wrong side of an argument, and in a splendid perversion of the truth.—If you could contrive to have his fair opinion on a subject, and without any bias from personal prejudice, or from a wish to be victorious in argument, it was wisdom itself, not only convincing, but overpowering."

He had, however, all his life habituated himself to consider conversation as a trial of intellectual vigour and skill; and to this I think, we may venture to ascribe that unexampled richness and brilliancy which appeared in his own. As a proof at once of his eagerness for colloquial distinction, and his high notion of this eminent friend, he once addressed him thus: "——, we now have been several hours together; and you have said but one thing for which I envied you."

Goldsmith could sometimes take adventurous liberties with him, and escape unpunished. Beauclerk told me, that when Goldsmith talked of a project for having a third Theatre in London solely for the exhibition of new plays, in order to deliver authours from the supposed tyranny of managers, Johnson treated it slightingly, upon which Goldsmith said, "Ay, ay, this may be nothing to you, who can now shelter yourself behind the corner of a pension;" Johnson bore this with good-humour.

Johnson had called twice on the Bishop of Killaloe before his Lordship set out for Ireland, having missed him the first time. He said, "It would have hung heavy on my heart if I had not seen him. No man ever paid more attention to another than he has done to me; and I have neglected him, not wilfully, but from being otherwise occupied. Always, Sir, set a high value on spontaneous kindness. He whose inclination prompts him to cultivate your friendship of his own accord, will love you more than one whom you have been at pains to attach to you."

Johnson told me, that he was once much pleased to find that a carpenter, who lived near him, was very ready to shew him some things in his business which he wished to see: "It was paying (said he) respect to literature."

I asked him, if he was not dissatisfied with having so small a share of wealth, and none of those distinctions in the state which are the objects of ambition. He had only a pension of three hundred a year. Why was he not in such circumstances as to keep his coach? Why had he not some considerable office? JOHNSON. "Sir, I have never complained of the world; nor do I think that I have reason to complain. It is rather to be wondered at that I have so much. My pension is more out of the usual course of things than any instance that I have known. Here, Sir, was a man avowedly no friend to Government at the time, who got a pension without asking for it. I never courted the great; they sent for me; but I think they now give me up. They are satisfied: they have seen enough of me." Upon my observing that I could not believe this; for they must certainly be highly pleased by his conversation; conscious of his own superiority, he answered, "No, Sir; great Lords and great Ladies don't love to have their mouths stopped." This was very expressive of the effect which the force of his understanding and brilliancy of his fancy could not but produce; and, to be sure, they must have found themselves strangely diminished in his company. When I warmly declared how happy I was at all times to hear him;—"Yes,

311

Sir, (said he); but if you were Lord Chancellor, it would not be so: you would then consider your own dignity."

There was much truth and knowledge of human nature in this remark. But certainly one should think, that in whatever elevated state of life a man who *knew* the value of the conversation of Johnson might be placed, though he might prudently avoid a situation in which he might appear lessened by comparison; yet he would frequently gratify himself in private with the participation of the rich intellectual entertainment which Johnson could furnish. Strange, however, is it, to consider how few of the great sought his society; so that if one were disposed to take occasion for satire on that account, very conspicuous objects present themselves. His noble friend, Lord Elibank, well observed, that if a great man procured an interview with Johnson, and did not wish to see him more, it shewed a mere idle curiosity, and a wretched want of relish for extraordinary powers of mind. Mrs. Thrale justly and wittily accounted for such conduct by saying, that Johnson's conversation was by much too strong for a person accustomed to obsequiousness and flattery; it was *mustard in a young child's mouth!*

One day, when I told him that I was a zealous Tory, but not enough "according to knowledge," and should be obliged to him for "a reason," he was so candid, and expressed himself so well, that I begged of him to repeat what he had said, and I wrote down as follows:

OF TORY AND WHIG.

"A wise Tory and a wise Whig, I believe, will agree. Their principles are the same, though their modes of thinking are different. A high Tory makes government unintelligible: it is lost in the clouds. A violent Whig makes it impracticable: he is for allowing so much liberty to every man, that there is not power enough to govern any man. The prejudice of the Tory is for establishment; the prejudice of the Whig is for innovation. A Tory does not wish to give more real power to Government; but that Government should have more reverence. Then they differ as to the church. The Tory is not for giving more legal power to the

312

Clergy, but wishes they should have a considerable influence founded on the opinion of mankind: the Whig is for limiting and watching them with a narrow jealousy."

On Saturday, June 2, I set out for Scotland, and had promised to pay a visit, in my way, as I sometimes did, at Southill, in Bedfordshire, at the hospitable mansion of 'Squire Dilly, the elder brother of my worthy friends, the booksellers, in the Poultry. Dr. Johnson agreed to be of the party this year, with Mr. Charles Dilly and me, and to go and see Lord Bute's seat at Luton-Hoe. He talked little to us in the carriage, being chiefly occupied in reading Dr. Watson's second volume of "Chemical Essays," which he liked very well, and his own "Prince of Abyssinia," on which he seemed to be intently fixed; having told us, that he had not looked at it since it was first published. I happened to take it out of my pocket this day, and he seized upon it with avidity. He pointed out to me the following remarkable passage: "By what means (said the prince) are the Europeans thus powerful; or why, since they can so easily visit Asia and Africa for trade or conquests, cannot the Asiaticks and Africans invade their coasts, plant colonies in their ports, and give laws to their natural princes? The same wind that carried them back would bring us thither." —"They are more powerful, Sir, than we, (answered Imlack,) because they are wiser. Knowledge will always predominate over ignorance, as man governs the other animals. But why their knowledge is more than ours, I know not what reason can be given, but the unsearchable will of the Supreme Being." He said, "This, Sir, no man can explain otherwise."

Upon the road we talked of the uncertainty of profit with which authours and booksellers engage in the publication of literary works. JOHNSON. "My judgement I have found is no certain rule as to the sale of a book." BOSWELL. "Pray, Sir, have you been much plagued with authours sending you their works to revise?" JOHNSON. "No, Sir; I have been thought a sour surly fellow." BOSWELL. "Very lucky for you, Sir,—in that respect." I must however observe, that notwithstanding what he now said, which he no doubt imagined at the time to be the fact, there was, perhaps, no man who more frequently yielded to the solicitations even of very obscure authours, to read their manuscripts, or more liberally assisted them with advice and correction.

He found himself very happy at 'Squire Dilly's, where there is always abundance of excellent fare, and hearty welcome.

On Sunday, June 3, we all went to Southill church, which is very near to Mr. Dilly's house. It being the first Sunday of the month, the holy sacrament was administered, and I staid to partake of it. When I came afterwards into Dr. Johnson's room, he said, "You did right to stay and receive the communion; I had not thought of it." This seemed to imply that he did not choose to approach the altar without a previous preparation, as to which good men entertain different opinions, some holding that it is irreverent to partake of that ordinance without considerable premeditation; others, that whoever is a sincere Christian, and in a proper frame of mind to discharge any other ritual duty of our religion, may, without scruple, discharge this most solemn one. A middle notion I believe to be the just one, which is, that communicants need not think a long train of preparatory forms indispensably necessary; but neither should they rashly and lightly venture upon so awful and mysterious an institution. Christians must judge, each for himself, what degree of retirement and self-examination is necessary upon each occasion.

Being in a frame of mind which, I hope for the felicity of human nature, many experience,—in fine weather,—at the country-house of a friend,—consoled and elevated by pious exercises,—I expressed myself with an unrestrained fervour to my "Guide, Philosopher, and Friend;" "My dear Sir, I would fain be a good man; and I am very good now. I fear GOD, and honour the King; I wish to do no ill, and to be benevolent to all mankind." He looked at me with a benignant indulgence; but took occasion to give me wise and salutary caution. "Do not, Sir, accustom yourself to trust to *impressions*. There is a middle state of mind between conviction and hypocrisy, of which many are unconscious. By trusting to impressions, a man may gradually come to yield

314

to them, and at length be subject to them, so as not to be a free agent, or what is the same thing in effect, to *suppose* that he is not a free agent. A man who is in that state, should not be suffered to live; if he declares he cannot help acting in a particular way, and is irresistibly impelled, there can be no confidence in him, no more than in a tyger. But, Sir, no man believes himself to be impelled irresistibly; we know that he who says he believes it, lies. Favourable impressions at particular moments, as to the state of our souls, may be deceitful and dangerous. In general no man can be sure of his acceptance with GOD; some, indeed, may have had it revealed to them. St. Paul, who wrought miracles, may have had a miracle wrought on himself, and may have obtained supernatural assurance of pardon, and mercy, and beatitude; yet St. Paul, though he expresses strong hope, also expresses fear, lest having preached to others, he himself should be a cast-away."

The opinion of a learned Bishop of our acquaintance, as to there being merit in religious faith, being mentioned;— JOHNSON. "Why, yes, Sir, the most licentious man, were hell open before him, would not take the most beautiful strumpet to his arms. We must, as the Apostle says, live by faith, not by sight."

I talked to him of original sin, in consequence of the fall of man, and of the atonement made by our SAVIOUR. After some conversation, which he desired me to remember, he, at my request, dictated to me as follows:

"With respect to original sin, the enquiry is not necessary; for whatever is the cause of human corruption, men are evidently and confessedly so corrupt, that all the laws of heaven and earth are insufficient to restrain them from crimes.

"Whatever difficulty there may be in the conception of vicarious punishments, it is an opinion which has had possession of mankind in all ages. There is no nation that has not used the practice of sacrifices. Whoever, therefore, denies the propriety of vicarious punishments, holds an opinion which the sentiments and practice of mankind have contradicted, from the beginning of the world. The great sacrifice for the sins of mankind was offered at the death of

315

the MESSIAH, who is called in scripture, 'The Lamb of GOD, that taketh away the sins of the world.' To judge of the reasonableness of the scheme of redemption, it must be considered as necessary to the government of the universe, that GOD should make known his perpetual and irreconcileable detestation of moral evil. He might indeed punish, and punish only the offenders; but as the end of punishment is not revenge of crimes, but propagation of virtue, it was more becoming the Divine clemency to find another manner of proceeding, less destructive to man, and at least equally powerful to promote goodness. The end of punishment is to reclaim and warn. *That* punishment will both reclaim and warn, which shews evidently such abhorrence of sin in GOD, as may deter us from it, or strike us with dread of vengeance when we have committed it. This is effected by vicarious punishment. Nothing could more testify the opposition between the nature of GOD and moral evil, or more amply display his justice, to men and angels, to all orders and successions of beings, than that it was necessary for the highest and purest nature, even for DIVINITY itself, to pacify the demands of vengeance, by a painful death; of which the natural effect will be, that when justice is appeased, there is a proper place for the exercise of mercy; and that such propitiation shall supply, in some degree, the imperfections of our obedience, and the inefficacy of our repentance: for, obedience and repentance, such as we can perform, are still necessary. Our SAVIOUR has told us, that he did not come to destroy the law but to fulfill: to fulfill the typical law, by the performance of what those types had foreshewn; and the moral law, by precepts of greater purity and higher exaltation."

[Here he said, "GOD bless you with it." I acknowledged myself much obliged to him; but I begged that he would go on as to the propitiation being the chief object of our most holy faith. He then dictated this one other paragraph.]

"The peculiar doctrine of Christianity is, that of an universal sacrifice, and perpetual propitiation. Other prophets only proclaimed the will and the threatenings of GOD. CHRIST satisfied his justice."

Dr. Gibbons, the Dissenting minister, being mentioned,

he said, "I took to Dr. Gibbons." And addressing himself to Mr. Charles Dilly, added, "I shall be glad to see him. Tell him, if he'll call on me, and dawdle over a dish of tea in an afternoon, I shall take it kind."

The Reverend Mr. Smith, Vicar of Southill, a very respectable man, with a very agreeable family, sent an invitation to us to drink tea. I remarked Dr. Johnson's very respectful politeness. Though always fond of changing the scene, he said, "We must have Mr. Dilly's leave. We cannot go from your house, Sir, without your permission." We all went, and were well satisfied with our visit. I however remember nothing particular, except a nice distinction which Dr. Johnson made with respect to the power of memory, maintaining that forgetfulness was a man's own fault. "To remember and to recollect (said he) are different things. A man has not the power to recollect what is not in his mind; but when a thing is in his mind he may remember it."

The remark was occasioned by my leaning back on a chair, which a little before I had perceived to be broken, and pleading forgetfulness as an excuse. "Sir, (said he,) its being broken was certainly in your mind."

When I observed that a housebreaker was in general very timorous;—JOHNSON. "No wonder, Sir; he is afraid of being shot getting *into* a house, or hanged when he has got *out* of it."

He told us, that he had in one day written six sheets of a translation from the French; adding, "I should be glad to see it now. I wish that I had copies of all the pamphlets written against me, as it is said Pope had. Had I known that I should make so much noise in the world, I should have been at pains to collect them. I believe there is hardly a day in which there is not something about me in the newspapers."

On Monday, June 4, we all went to Luton-Hoe, to see Lord Bute's magnificent seat, for which I had obtained a ticket. As we entered the park, I talked in a high style of my old friendship with Lord Mountstuart, and said, "I shall probably be much at this place." The Sage, aware of human vicissitudes, gently checked me: "Don't you be too sure of that." He made two or three peculiar observations; as when shewn the botanical garden, "Is not *every* garden a botanical garden?" When told that there was a shrubbery to the extent of several miles: "That is making a very foolish use of the ground; a little of it is very well." When it was proposed that we should walk on the pleasure-ground; "Don't let us fatigue ourselves. Why should we walk there? Here's a fine tree, let's get to the top of it." But upon the whole, he was very much pleased. He said, "This is one of the places I do not regret having come to see. It is a very stately place, indeed; in the house magnificence is not sacrificed to convenience, nor convenience to magnificence. The library is very splendid; the dignity of the rooms is very great; and the quantity of pictures is beyond expectation, beyond hope."

On Tuesday, June 5, Johnson was to return to London. He was very pleasant at breakfast; I mentioned a friend of mine having resolved never to marry a pretty woman. JOHNSON. "Sir, it is a very foolish resolution to resolve not to marry a pretty woman. Beauty is of itself very estimable. No, Sir, I would prefer a pretty woman, unless there are objections to her. A pretty woman may be foolish; a pretty woman may be wicked; a pretty woman may not like me. But there is no such danger in marrying a pretty woman as is apprehended; she will not be persecuted if she does not invite persecution. A pretty woman, if she has a mind to be wicked, can find a readier way than another; and that is all."

In one of his little memorandum-books is the following minute:

"August 9, 3 P.M. ætat. 72, in the summer-house at Streatham.

"After innumerable resolutions formed and neglected, I have retired hither, to plan a life of greater diligence, in hope that I may yet be useful, and be daily better prepared to appear before my Creator and my Judge, from whose infinite mercy I humbly call for assistance and support.

"My purpose is,

"To pass eight hours every day in some serious employment.

"Having prayed, I purpose to employ the next six weeks upon the Italian language, for my settled study."

How venerably pious does he appear in these moments of solitude, and how spirited are his resolutions for the improvement of his mind, even in elegant literature, at a very advanced period of life, and when afflicted with many complaints.

In 1782, his complaints increased, and the history of his life this year, is little more than a mournful recital of the variations of his illness, in the midst of which, however, it will appear from his letters, that the powers of his mind were in no degree impaired.

At a time when he was less able than he had once been to sustain a shock, he was suddenly deprived of Mr. Levett, which event he thus communicated to Dr. Lawrence.

"SIR,

"Our old friend, Mr. Levett, who was last night eminently cheerful, died this morning. The man who lay in the same room, hearing an uncommon noise, got up and tried to make him speak, but without effect. He then called Mr. Holder, the apothecary, who, though when he came he thought him dead, opened a vein, but could draw no blood. So has ended the long life of a very useful and very blameless man.—I am, Sir,

"Your most humble servant,
"SAM. JOHNSON."

"Jan. 17, 1782."

In one of his memorandum-books in my possession, is the following entry: "January 20, Sunday. Robert Levett was buried in the church-yard of Bridewell, between one and two in the afternoon. He died on Thursday 17, about seven in the morning, by an instantaneous death. He was an old and faithful friend; I have known him from about 46. *Commendavi.* May GOD have mercy on him. May he have mercy on me."

On the 30th of August, I informed him that my honoured father had died that morning; a complaint under which he had long laboured, having suddenly come to a crisis, while I was upon a visit at the seat of Sir Charles Preston, from whence I had hastened the day before, upon receiving a letter by express.

"To JAMES BOSWELL, ESQ.

"DEAR SIR,

"I have struggled through this year with so much infirmity of body, and such strong impressions of the fragility of life, that death, whenever it appears, fills me with melancholy; and I cannot hear without emotion, of the removal of any one, whom I have known, into another state.

"Your father's death had every circumstance that could enable you to bear it; it was at a mature age, and it was expected; and as his general life had been pious, his thoughts had doubtless for many years past been turned upon eternity. That you did not find him sensible must doubtless grieve you; his disposition towards you was undoubtedly that of a kind, though not of a fond father. Kindness, at least actual, is in our power, but fondness is not; and if by negligence or imprudence you had extinguished his fondness, he could not at will rekindle it. Nothing then remained between you but mutual forgiveness of each other's faults, and mutual desire of each other's happiness.

"I shall long to know his final disposition of his fortune.

"You, dear Sir, have now a new station, and have therefore new cares, and new employments. Life, as Cowley seems to say, ought to resemble a well-ordered poem; of which one rule generally received is, that the exordium should be simple, and should promise little. Begin your new course of life with the least shew and the least expence possible; you may at pleasure encrease both, but you cannot easily diminish them. Do not think your estate your own, while any man can call upon you for money which you cannot pay; therefore, begin with timorous parsimony. Let it be your first care not to be in any man's debt.

"When the thoughts are extended to a future state, the present life seems hardly worthy of all those principles of conduct, and maxims of prudence, which one generation of

320

men has transmitted to another; but upon a closer view, when it is perceived how much evil is produced, and how much good is impeded by embarrassment and distress, and how little room the expedients of poverty leave for the exercise of virtue, it grows manifest that the boundless importance of the next life enforces some attention to the interest of this.

"Be kind to the old servants, and secure the kindness of the agents and factors; do not disgust them by asperity, or unwelcome gaiety, or apparent suspicion. From them you must learn the real state of your affairs, the characters of your tenants, and the value of your lands.

"Make my compliments to Mrs. Boswell; I think her expectations from air and exercise are the best that she can form. I hope she will live long and happily.

"I forgot whether I told you that Ramsay has been here; we dined cheerfully together. I entertained lately a young gentleman from Corrichatachin.

"I received your letters only this morning. I am, dear Sir,
Yours, &c.
"SAM. JOHNSON.
"London, Sept. 7, 1782."

The death of Mr. Thrale had made a very material alteration with respect to Johnson's reception in that family. The manly authority of the husband no longer curbed the lively exuberance of the lady; and as her vanity had been fully gratified, by having the Colossus of Literature attached to her for many years, she gradually became less assiduous to please him. Whether her attachment to him was already divided by another object, I am unable to ascertain; but it is plain that Johnson's penetration was alive to her neglect or forced attention; for on the 6th of October this year, we find him making a "parting use of the library" at Streatham, and pronouncing a prayer, which he composed on leaving Mr. Thrale's family.

"Almighty GOD, Father of all mercy, help me by thy grace, that I may, with humble and sincere thankfulness, remember the comforts and conveniences which I have enjoyed at this place; and that I may resign them with holy submission, equally trusting in thy protection when Thou givest, and when Thou takest away. Have mercy upon me, O LORD, have mercy upon me.

"To thy fatherly protection, O LORD, I commend this family. Bless, guide, and defend them, that they may so pass through this world, as finally to enjoy in thy presence everlasting happiness, for JESUS CHRIST's sake. Amen."

One cannot read this prayer, without some emotions not very favourable to the lady whose conduct occasioned it.

In 1783, he was more severely afflicted than ever, but still the same ardour for literature, the same constant piety, the same kindness for his friends, and the same vivacity, both in conversation and writing, distinguished him.

Talking of conversation, he said, "There must, in the first place, be knowledge, there must be materials;—in the second place, there must be a command of words;—in the third place, there must be imagination, to place things in such views as they are not commonly seen in;—and in the fourth place, there must be presence of mind, and a resolution that is not to be overcome by failures; this last is an essential requisite; for want of it many people do not excel in conversation. Now *I* want it; I throw up the game upon losing a trick." I wondered to hear him talk thus of himself, and said, "I don't know, Sir, how this may be; but I am sure you beat other people's cards out of their hands." I doubt whether he heard this remark. While he went on talking triumphantly, I was fixed in admiration, and said to Mrs. Thrale, "O, for short-hand to take this down!"— "You'll carry it all in your head, (said she;) a long head is as good as short-hand."

It has been observed and wondered at, that Mr. Charles Fox never talked with any freedom in the presence of Dr. Johnson; though it is well known, and I myself can witness, that his conversation is various, fluent, and exceedingly agreeable. Johnson's own experience, however, of that gentleman's reserve was a sufficient reason for his going on thus: "Fox never talks in private company; not from any determination not to talk, but because he has not the first motion. A man who is used to the applause of the House of Commons, has no wish for that of a private company. A man accustomed to throw for a thousand pounds, if set down to throw for sixpence, would not be at the pains to count his dice. Burke's talk is the ebullition of his mind; he does not talk from a desire of distinction, but because his mind is full."

After musing for some time, he said, "I wonder how I should have any enemies; for I do harm to nobody." Boswell. "In the first place, Sir, you will be pleased to recollect, that you set out with attacking the Scotch; so you got a whole nation for your enemies." Johnson. "Why, I own, that by my definition of *oats* I meant to vex them." Boswell. "Pray, Sir, can you trace the cause of your antipathy to the Scotch?" Johnson. "I cannot, Sir." Boswell. "Old Mr. Sheridan says, it was because they sold Charles the First." Johnson. "Then, Sir, old Mr. Sheridan has found out a very good reason."

On Sunday, March 23, I breakfasted with Dr. Johnson, who seemed much relieved, having taken opium the night before. He however protested against it, as a remedy that should be given with the utmost reluctance, and only in extreme necessity. I mentioned how commonly it was used in Turkey, and that therefore it could not be so pernicious as he apprehended. He grew warm, and said, "Turks take opium, and Christians take opium; but Russell, in his account of Aleppo, tells us, that it is as disgraceful in Turkey to take too much opium, as it is with us to get drunk. Sir, it is amazing how things are exaggerated. A gentleman was lately telling in a company where I was present, that in France as soon as a man of fashion marries, he takes an opera girl into keeping; and this he mentioned as a general custom. 'Pray, Sir, (said I,) how many opera girls may there be?' He answered, 'About fourscore.' 'Well then, Sir, (said I,) you see there can be no more than fourscore men of fashion who can do this.' "

Mrs. Desmoulins made tea; and she and I talked before him upon a topick which he had once borne patiently from me when we were by ourselves,—his not complaining of the world, because he was not called to some great office, nor had attained to great wealth. He flew into a violent passion, I confess with some justice, and commanded us to have done. "Nobody, (said he) has a right to talk in this manner, to bring before a man his own character, and the events of his life, when he does not choose it should be done. I never have sought the world; the world was not to seek me. It is rather wonderful that so much has been done for me. All the complaints which are made of the world are unjust. I never knew a man of merit neglected: it was generally by his own fault that he failed of success. A man may hide his head in a hole: he may go into the country, and publish a book now and then, which nobody reads, and then complain he is neglected. There is no reason why any person should exert himself for a man who has written a good book: he has not written it for any individual. I may as well make a present to the postman who brings me a letter. When patronage was limited, an authour expected to find a Mæcenas, and complained if he did not find one. Why should he complain? This Mæcenas has others as good as he, or others who have got the start of him."

On the subject of the right employment of wealth, Johnson observed, "A man cannot make a bad use of his money, so far as regards Society, if he does not hoard it; for if he either spends it or lends it out, Society has the benefit. It is in general better to spend money than to give it away; for industry is more promoted by spending money than by giving it away. A man who spends his money is sure he is doing good with it: he is not so sure when he gives it away. A man who spends ten thousand a year will do more good than a man who spends two thousand and gives away eight."

Talking of an acquaintance of ours, whose narratives, which abounded in curious and interesting topicks, were unhappily found to be very fabulous; I mentioned Lord Mansfield's having said to me, "Suppose we believe one *half* of what he tells." JOHNSON. "Ay; but we don't know *which* half to believe. By his lying we lose not only our reverence for him, but all comfort in his conversation." BOSWELL. "May we not take it as amusing fiction?" JOHNSON. "Sir, the misfortune is, that you will insensibly believe as much of it as you incline to believe."

It is remarkable, that notwithstanding their congeniality in politicks, he never was acquainted with a late eminent noble judge, whom I have heard speak of him as a writer, with great respect. Johnson, I know not upon what degree of investigation, entertained no exalted opinion of his Lordship's intellectual character. Talking of him to me one day, he said, "It is wonderful, Sir, with how little real superiority of mind men can make an eminent figure in publick life." He expressed himself to the same purpose concerning another law-lord, who, it seems, once took a fancy to associate with the wits of London; but with so little success, that Foote said, "What can he mean by coming among us? He is not only dull himself, but the cause of dullness in others." Trying him by the test of his colloquial powers, Johnson found him very defective. He once said to Sir Joshua Reynolds, "This man now has been ten years about town, and has made nothing of it;" meaning as a companion. He said to me, "I never heard any thing from him in company that was at all striking; and depend upon it, Sir, it is when you come close to a man in conversation, that you discover what his real abilities are: to make a speech in a publick assembly is a knack. Now I honour Thurlow, Sir; Thurlow is a fine fellow; he fairly puts his mind to yours."

After repeating to him some of his pointed, lively sayings, I said, "It is a pity, Sir, you don't always remember your own good things, that you may have a laugh when you will." JOHNSON. "Nay, Sir, it is better that I forget them, that I may be reminded of them, and have a laugh on their being brought to my recollection."

When I recalled to him his having said as we sailed up Lochlomond, "That if he wore any thing fine, it should be *very* fine;" I observed that all his thoughts were upon a great scale. JOHNSON. "Depend upon it, Sir, every man will have as fine a thing as he can get; as large a diamond for his ring." BOSWELL. "Pardon me, Sir: a man of a narrow mind will not think of it, a slight trinket will satisfy him."

I told him I should send him some "Essays," which I had written, which I hoped he would be so good as to read, and pick out the good ones. JOHNSON. "Nay, Sir, send me only the good ones; don't make *me* pick them."

He said, "How few of his friends' houses would a man choose to be at, when he is sick!" He mentioned one or two. I recollect only Thrale's.

Sir Joshua Reynolds communicated to me the following particulars:

Johnson thought the poems published as translations from Ossian, had so little merit, that he said, "Sir, a man might write such stuff for ever, if he would *abandon* his mind to it."

He said, "A man should pass a part of his time with *the laughers*, by which means any thing ridiculous or particular about him might be presented to his view, and corrected." I observed, he must have been a bold laugher who would have ventured to tell Dr. Johnson of any of his particularities.[1]

Having observed the vain ostentatious importance of many people in quoting the authority of Dukes and Lords, as having been in their company, he said, he went to the other extreme, and did not mention his authority when he should have done it, had it not been that of a Duke or a Lord.

Dr. Goldsmith once said to Dr. Johnson, that he wished for some additional members to the LITERARY CLUB, to give it an agreeable variety; for (said he) there can now be nothing new among us: we have travelled over one another's minds. Johnson seemed a little angry, and said, "Sir, you have not travelled over *my* mind, I promise you." Sir Joshua, however, thought Goldsmith right; observing, that "when people have lived a great deal together, they know what each of them will say on every subject. A new understanding, therefore, is desirable; because though it may only furnish the same sense upon a question which would have been furnished by those with whom we are accustomed to live, yet this sense will have a different colour-

---

[1] I am happy, however, to mention a pleasing instance of his enduring with great gentleness to hear one of his most striking particularities pointed out:—Miss Hunter, a niece of his friend Christopher Smart, when a very young girl, struck by his extraordinary motions, said to him, "Pray, Dr. Johnson, why do you make such strange gestures?"— "From bad habit. (he replied.) Do you, my dear, take care to guard against bad habits." This I was told by the young lady's brother at Margate.

ing; and colouring is of much effect in every thing else as well as in painting."

Johnson used to say that he made it a constant rule to talk as well as he could, both as to sentiment and expression; by which means, what had been originally effort became familiar and easy. The consequence of this, Sir Joshua observed, was, that his common conversation in all companies was such as to secure him universal attention, as something above the usual colloquial style was expected.

Sir Joshua once observed to him, that he had talked above the capacity of some people with whom they had been in company together. "No matter, Sir, (said Johnson); they consider it as a compliment to be talked to, as if they were wiser than they are. So true is this, Sir, that Baxter made it a rule in every sermon that he preached, to say something that was above the capacity of his audience." [1]

Johnson's dexterity in retort, when he seemed to be driven to an extremity by his adversary, was very remarkable. Of his power in this respect, our common friend, Mr. Windham, of Norfolk, has been pleased to furnish me with an eminent instance. However unfavourable to Scotland, he uniformly gave liberal praise to George Buchanan, as a writer. In a conversation concerning the literary merits of the two countries, in which Buchanan was introduced, a Scotchman, imagining that on this ground he should have an undoubted triumph over him, exclaimed, "Ah, Dr. Johnson, what would you have said of Buchanan, had he been an Englishman?"—"Why, Sir, (said Johnson, after a little pause,) I should *not* have said of Buchanan, had he been an *Englishman*, what I will now say of him as a *Scotchman*,—that he was the only man of genius his country ever produced."

Though his usual phrase for conversation was *talk*, yet he made a distinction; for when he once told me that he dined the day before at a friend's house, with "a very pretty

---

[1] The justness of this remark is confirmed by the following story, for which I am indebted to Lord Eliot: A country Parson, who was remarkable for quoting scraps of Latin in his sermons, having died, one of his parishioners was asked how he liked his successor: "He is a very good preacher, (was his answer,) but no *latiner*."

company;" and I asked him if there was good conversation, he answered, "No, Sir; we had *talk* enough, but no *conversation;* there was nothing *discussed.*"

Mr. Hoole told him, he was born in Moorfields, and had received part of his early instruction in Grub-street. "Sir, (said Johnson, smiling,) you have been *regularly* educated." Having asked who was his instructor, and Mr. Hoole having answered, "My uncle, Sir, who was a taylor;" Johnson, recollecting himself, said, "Sir, I knew him; we called him the *metaphysical taylor.* He was of a club in Old-street, with me and George Psalmanazar, and some others: but pray, Sir, was he a good taylor?" Mr. Hoole having answered that he believed he was too mathematical, and used to draw squares and triangles on his shop-board, so that he did not excel in the cut of a coat;—"I am sorry for it, (said Johnson,) for I would have every man to be master of his own business."

In pleasant reference to himself and Mr. Hoole, as brother authours, he often said, "Let you and I, Sir, go together, and eat a beef-steak in Grub-street."

He said to Sir William Scott, "The age is running mad after innovation; and all the business of the world is to be done in a new way; men are to be hanged in a new way; Tyburn itself is not safe from the fury of innovation." It having been argued that this was an improvement.—"No, Sir, (said he, eagerly,) it is *not* an improvement; they object, that the old method drew together a number of spectators. Sir, executions are intended to draw spectators. If they do not draw spectators, they don't answer their purpose. The old method was most satisfactory to all parties; the publick was gratified by a procession; the criminal was supported by it. Why is all this to be swept away?" I perfectly agree with Dr. Johnson upon this head, and am persuaded that executions now, the solemn procession being discontinued, have not nearly the effect which they formerly had. Magistrates both in London, and elsewhere, have, I am afraid, in this, had too much regard to their own ease."

Johnson's attention to precision and clearness in expression was very remarkable. He disapproved of a parenthesis; and I believe in all his voluminous writings, not half a dozen of them will be found. He never used the phrases *the former and the latter*, having observed, that they often occasioned obscurity; he therefore contrived to construct his sentences so as not to have occasion for them, and would even rather repeat the same words, in order to avoid them. Nothing is more common than to mistake surnames, when we hear them carelessly uttered for the first time. To prevent this, he used not only to pronounce them slowly and distinctly, but to take the trouble of spelling them; a practice which I have often followed, and which I wish were general.

Such was the heat and irritability of his blood, that not only did he pare his nails to the quick, but scraped the joints of his fingers with a pen-knife, till they seemed quite red and raw.

The heterogeneous composition of human nature was remarkably exemplified in Johnson. His liberality in giving his money to persons in distress was extraordinary. Yet there lurked about him a propensity to paltry saving. One day I owned to him, that "I was occasionally troubled with a fit of *narrowness*." "Why, Sir, (said he,) so am I. *But I do not tell it*." He has now and then borrowed a shilling of me; and when I asked him for it again, seemed to be rather out of humour. A droll little circumstance once occurred: As if he meant to reprimand my minute exactness as a creditor, he thus addressed me;—"Boswell, *lend* me sixpence—*not to be repaid*."

This great man's attention to small things was very remarkable. As an instance of it, he one day said to me, "Sir, when you get silver in change for a guinea, look carefully at it; you may find some curious piece of coin."

Once, when checking my boasting too frequently of myself in company, he said to me, "Boswell, you often vaunt so much as to provoke ridicule. You put me in mind of a man who was standing in the kitchen of an inn with his back to the fire, and thus accosted the person next him, 'Do you know, Sir, who I am?' 'No, Sir, (said the other,) I have not that advantage.' 'Sir, (said he,) I am the *great* TWALMLEY, who invented the New Floodgate Iron.' "

He was pleased to say to me one morning when we were

329

left alone in his study, "Boswell, I think I am easier with you than with almost any body."

He would not allow Mr. David Hume any credit for his political principles, though similar to his own; saying of him, "Sir, he was a Tory by chance."

His acute observation of human life made him remark, "Sir, there is nothing by which a man exasperates most people more, than by displaying a superior ability of brilliancy in conversation. They seem pleased at the time; but their envy makes them curse him at their hearts."

Johnson's love of little children, which he discovered upon all occasions, calling them "pretty dears," and giving them sweetmeats, was an undoubted proof of the real humanity and gentleness of his disposition.

His uncommon kindness to his servants, and serious concern, not only for their comfort in this world, but their happiness in the next, was another unquestionable evidence of what all, who were intimately acquainted with him, knew to be true.

Nor would it be just under this head, to omit the fondness which he shewed for animals which he had taken under his protection. I never shall forget the indulgence with which he treated Hodge, his cat; for whom he himself used to go out and buy oysters, lest the servants, having that trouble, should take a dislike to the poor creature. I am, unluckily, one of those who have an antipathy to a cat, so that I am uneasy when in the room with one; and I own, I frequently suffered a good deal from the presence of this same Hodge. I recollect him one day scrambling up Dr. Johnson's breast, apparently with much satisfaction, while my friend smiling and half-whistling, rubbed down his back, and pulled him by the tail; and when I observed he was a fine cat, saying "why, yes, Sir, but I have had cats whom I liked better than this;" and then as if perceiving Hodge to be out of countenance, adding, "but he is a very fine cat, a very fine cat indeed."

This reminds me of the ludicrous account which he gave Mr. Langton, of the despicable state of a young gentleman of good family. "Sir, when I heard of him last, he was running about town shooting cats." And then in a sort of

16

A concert at the popular Vauxhall Pleasure Gardens in London.
In this watercolour by Rowlandson, Boswell, Dr. Johnson,
Mrs. Thrale, and Oliver Goldsmith are shown seated at the table
under the arch at left.

kindly reverie, he bethought himself of his own favourite cat, and said, "But Hodge shan't be shot: no, no, Hodge shall not be shot."

He thought Mr. Beauclerk made a shrewd and judicious remark to Mr. Langton, who, after having been for the first time in company with a well known wit about town, was warmly admiring and praising him,—"See him again," said Beauclerk.

Talking of the origin of language;—JOHNSON. "It must have come by inspiration. A thousand, nay, a million of children could not invent a language. While the organs are pliable, there is not understanding enough to form a language; by the time that there is understanding enough, the organs are become stiff. We know that after a certain age we cannot learn to pronounce a new language. No foreigner, who comes to England when advanced in life, ever pronounces English tolerably well; at least such instances are very rare. When I maintain that language must have come by inspiration, I do not mean that inspiration is required for rhetorick, and all the beauties of language; for when once man has language, we can conceive that he may gradually form modifications of it. I mean only that inspiration seems to me to be necessary to give man the faculty of speech; to inform him that he may have speech; which I think he could no more find out without inspiration, than cows or hogs would think of such a faculty."

I have no minute of any interview with Johnson till Thursday, May 15th, when I find what follows: BOSWELL. "I wish much to be in Parliament, Sir." JOHNSON. "Why, Sir, unless you come resolved to support any administration, you would be the worse for being in Parliament, because you would be obliged to live more expensively."— BOSWELL. "Perhaps, Sir, I should be the less happy for being in Parliament. I never would sell my vote, and I should be vexed if things went wrong." JOHNSON. "That's cant, Sir. It would not vex you more in the house than in the gallery: publick affairs vex no man." BOSWELL. "Have not they vexed yourself a little, Sir? Have not you been vexed by all the turbulence of this reign, and by that absurd vote of the House of Commons, 'That the influence of the Crown has increased, is increasing, and ought to be diminished?' " JOHNSON. "Sir, I have never slept an hour less, nor eat an ounce less meat. I would have knocked the factious dogs on the head, to be sure; but I was not *vexed*." BOSWELL. "I declare, Sir, upon my honour, I did imagine I was vexed, and took a pride in it; but it *was*, perhaps, cant; for I own I neither eat less, nor slept less." JOHNSON. "My dear friend, clear your mind of cant. You may *talk* as other people do: you may say to a man, 'Sir, I am your most humble servant.' You are *not* his most humble servant. You may say, 'These are bad times; it is a melancholy thing to be reserved at such times.' You don't mind the times. You tell a man, 'I am sorry you had such bad weather the last day of your journey, and were so much wet.' You don't care sixpence whether he is wet or dry. You may *talk* in this manner; it is a mode of talking in Society: but don't *think* foolishly."

I asked, whether a man naturally virtuous, or one who has overcome wicked inclinations, is the best. JOHNSON. "Sir, to *you*, the man who has overcome wicked inclinations, is not the best. He has more merit to *himself:* I would rather trust my money to a man who has no hands, and so a physical impossibility to steal, than to a man of the most honest principles. There is a witty satirical story of Foote. He had a small bust of Garrick placed upon his bureau. 'You may be surprised (said he) that I allow him to be so near my gold;—but you will observe, he has no hands.' "

I stated to him an anxious thought, by which a sincere Christian might be disturbed, even when conscious of having lived a good life, so far as is consistent with human infirmity; he might fear that he should afterwards fall away, and be guilty of such crimes as would render all his former religion vain. Could there be, upon this awful subject, such a thing as balancing of accounts? Suppose a man who has led a good life for seven years, commits an act of wickedness, and instantly dies; will his former good life have any effect in his favour? JOHNSON. "Sir, if a man has led a good life for seven years, and then is hurried by passion to do what is wrong, and is suddenly carried off, depend upon it he will have the reward of his seven years' good life: GOD will not take a catch of him. Upon this principle Richard Baxter believes that a Suicide may be saved. 'If (says he) it should be objected that what I maintain may encourage suicide, I answer, I am not to tell a lie to prevent it.'" BOSWELL. "But does not the text say, 'As the tree falls, so it must lie?'" JOHNSON. "Yes, Sir; as the tree falls: but,—(after a little pause) that is meant as to the general state of the tree, not what is the effect of a sudden blast." In short, he interpreted the expression as referring to condition, not to position. The common notion, therefore, seems to be erroneous; and Shenstone's witty remark on Divines trying to give the tree a jerk upon a death-bed, to make it lie favourably, is not well founded.

He said, "Get as much force of mind as you can. Live within your income. Always have something saved at the end of the year. Let your imports be more than your exports, and you'll never go far wrong."

I assured him, that in the extensive and various range of his acquaintance there never had been any one who had a more sincere respect and affection for him than I had. He said, "I believe it, Sir. Were I in distress, there is no man to whom I should sooner come than to you. I should like to come and have a cottage in your park, toddle about, live mostly on milk, and be taken care of by Mrs. Boswell. She and I are good friends now; are we not?"

He embraced me, and gave me his blessing, as usual when I was leaving him for any length of time. I walked from his door to-day, with a fearful apprehension of what might happen before I returned.

My anxious apprehensions at parting with him this year, proved to be but too well founded; for not long afterwards he had a dreadful stroke of the palsy, of which there are very full and accurate accounts in letters written by himself to shew with what composure of mind, and resignation to the Divine Will, his steady piety enabled him to behave.

"To Mr. Edmund Allen.

"dear sir,

"It has pleased God, this morning, to deprive me of the powers of speech; and as I do not know but that it may be his further good pleasure to deprive me soon of my senses, I request you will on the receipt of this note, come to me, and act for me, as the exigencies of my case may require.

"I am,

"Sincerely yours,

"Sam. Johnson."

"June 17, 1783."

"To the Reverend Dr. John Taylor.

"dear sir,

"It has pleased God, by a paralytick stroke in the night, to deprive me of speech.

"I am very desirous of Dr. Heberden's assistance, as I think my case is not past remedy. Let me see you as soon as it is possible. Bring Dr. Heberden with you, if you can; but come yourself at all events. I am glad you are so well, when I am so dreadfully attacked.

"I think that by a speedy application of stimulants much may be done. I question if a vomit, vigorous and rough, would not rouse the organs of speech to action. As it is too early to send, I will try to recollect what I can, that can be suspected to have brought on this dreadful distress.

"I have been accustomed to bleed frequently for an asthmatick complaint; but have forborne for some time by Dr. Pepys's persuasion, who perceived my legs beginning to swell. I sometimes alleviate a painful, or more properly an oppressive, constriction of my chest, by opiates; and have lately taken opium frequently, but the last, or two last times, in smaller quantities. My largest dose is three grains, and last night I took but two. You will suggest these things (and they are all that I can call to mind) to Dr. Heberden.

"I am, &c.

"Sam. Johnson."

"June 17, 1783."

Two days after he wrote thus to Mrs. Thrale:

"On Monday, the 16th, I sat for my picture, and walked a considerable way with little inconvenience. In the afternoon and evening I felt myself light and easy, and began to plan schemes of life. Thus I went to bed, and in a short time waked and sat up, as has long been my custom, when I felt a confusion and indistinctness in my head, which lasted, I suppose, about half a minute. I was alarmed, and prayed GOD, that however he might afflict my body, he would spare my understanding. This prayer, that I might try the integrity of my faculties, I made in Latin verse. The lines were not very good, but I knew them not to be very good: I made them easily, and concluded myself to be unimpaired in my faculties.

"Soon after I perceived that I had suffered a paralytick stroke, and that my speech was taken from me. I had no pain, and so little dejection in this dreadful state, that I wondered at my own apathy, and considered that perhaps death itself, when it should come, would excite less horrour than seems now to attend it.

"In order to rouse the vocal organs, I took two drams. Wine has been celebrated for the production of eloquence. I put myself into violent motion, and I think repeated it; but all was in vain. I then went to bed, and strange as it may seem, I think slept. When I saw light, it was time to contrive what I should do. Though GOD stopped my speech, he left me my hand; I enjoyed a mercy which was not granted to my dear friend Lawrence, who now perhaps overlooks me as I am writing, and rejoices that I have what he wanted. My first note was necessarily to my servant, who came in talking, and could not immediately comprehend why he should read what I put into his hands.

"I then wrote a card to Mr. Allen, that I might have a discreet friend at hand, to act as occasion should require. In penning this note, I had some difficulty; my hand, I knew not how nor why, made wrong letters. I then wrote to Dr. Taylor to come to me, and bring Dr. Heberden: and I sent to Dr. Brocklesby, who is my neighbour. My physicians are very friendly, and give me great hopes; but you may imagine my situation. I have so far recovered my vocal powers, as to repeat the Lord's Prayer with no very imperfect articulation. My memory, I hope, yet remains as it was! but such an attack produces solicitude for the safety of every faculty."

Such was the general vigour of his constitution, that he recovered from this alarming and severe attack with wonderful quickness; so that in July he was able to make a visit to Mr. Langton at Rochester, where he passed about a fortnight, and made little excursions as easily as at any time of his life. In August he went as far as the neighbourhood of Salisbury, to Heale, the seat of William Bowles, Esq., a gentleman whom I have heard him praise for exemplary religious order in his family. In his diary I find a short but honourable mention of this visit:—"August 28, I came to Heale without fatigue. 30. I am entertained quite to my mind."

While he was here, he had a letter from Dr. Brocklesby, acquainting him of the death of Mrs. Williams, which affected him a good deal. Though for several years her temper had not been complacent, she had valuable qualities, and her departure left a blank in his house.

He this autumn received a visit from the celebrated Mrs. Siddons. He gives this account of it in one of his letters to Mrs. Thrale [October 27]:—"Mrs. Siddons, in her visit to me, behaved with great modesty and propriety, and left nothing behind her to be censured or despised. Neither praise nor money, the two powerful corrupters of mankind, seemed to have depraved her. I shall be glad to see her again. Her brother Kemble calls on me, and pleases me very well. Mrs. Siddons and I talked of plays; and she told me her intention of exhibiting this winter the characters of Constance, Catharine, and Isabella, in Shakspeare."

Mr. Kemble has favoured me with the following minute of what passed at this visit.

"When Mrs. Siddons came into the room, there happened to be no chair ready for her, which he observing, said with a smile, 'Madam, you who so often occasion a want of seats to other people, will the more easily excuse the want of one yourself.'

"Having placed himself by her, he with great good humour entered upon a consideration of the English drama; and, among other enquiries, particularly asked her which of Shakspeare's characters she was most pleased with. Upon her answering that she thought the character of Queen Catharine, in Henry the Eighth, the most natural:— 'I think so too, Madam, (said he;) and whenever you perform it, I will once more hobble out to the theatre myself.' Mrs. Siddons promised she would do herself the honour of acting his favourite part for him; but many circumstances happened to prevent the representation of King Henry the Eighth during the Doctor's life.

"In the course of the evening he thus gave his opinion upon the merits of some of the principal performers whom he remembered to have seen upon the stage. 'Mrs. Porter, in the vehemence of rage, and Mrs. Clive, in the sprightliness of humour, I have never seen equalled. What Clive did best, she did better than Garrick; but could not do half so many things well; she was a better romp than any I ever saw in nature.—Pritchard, in common life, was a vulgar ideot; she would talk of her *gownd;* but, when she appeared upon the stage, seemed to be inspired by gentility and understanding.—I once talked with Colley Cibber, and thought him ignorant of the principles of his art.— Garrick, Madam, was no declaimer; there was not one of his own scene-shifters who could not have spoken *To be, or not to be,* better than he did; yet he was the only actor I ever saw, whom I could call a master both in tragedy and comedy; though I liked him best in comedy. A true conception of character, and natural expression of it, were his distinguished excellencies.' Having expatiated, with his usual force and eloquence, on Mr. Garrick's extraordinary eminence as an actor, he concluded with this compliment to his social talents; 'And after all, Madam, I thought him less to be envied on the stage than at the head of a table.' "

Johnson, indeed, had thought more upon the subject of

acting than might be generally supposed. Talking of it one day to Mr. Kemble, he said, "Are you, Sir, one of those enthusiasts who believe yourself transformed into the very character you represent?" Upon Mr. Kemble's answering—that he had never felt so strong a persuasion himself; "To be sure not, Sir, (said Johnson;) the thing is impossible. And if Garrick really believed himself to be that monster, Richard the Third, he deserved to be hanged every time he performed it."

In the end of this year he was seized with a spasmodick asthma of such violence, that he was confined to the house in great pain, being sometimes obliged to sit all night in his chair, a recumbent posture being so hurtful to his respiration, that he could not endure lying in bed; and there came upon him at the same time that oppressive and fatal disease, a dropsy. It was a very severe winter, which probably aggravated his complaints; and the solitude in which Mr. Levett and Mrs. Williams had left him, rendered his life very gloomy. Mrs. Desmoulins, who still lived, was herself so very ill, that she could contribute very little to his relief. He, however, had none of that unsocial shyness which we commonly see in people afflicted with sickness. He did not hide his head from the world, in solitary abstraction; he did not deny himself to the visits of his friends and acquaintances; but at all times, when he was not overcome by sleep, was ready for conversation as in his best days.

And now I am arrived at the last year of the life of SAMUEL JOHNSON, a year in which, although passed in severe indisposition, he nevertheless gave many evidences of the continuance of those wondrous powers of mind, which raised him so high in the intellectual world. His conversation and his letters of this year were in no respect inferiour to those of former years.

On Saturday, May 15, I dined with him at Dr. Brocklesby's. One of the company provoked him greatly by doing what he could least of all bear, which was quoting something of his own writing, against what he then maintained. "What, Sir, (cried the gentleman,) do you say to

'The busy day, the peaceful night,
Unfelt, uncounted, glided by?' "

Johnson finding himself thus presented as giving an instance of a man who had lived without uneasiness, was much offended, for he looked upon such a quotation as unfair, his anger burst out in an unjustifiable retort, insinuating that the gentleman's remark was a sally of ebriety; "Sir, there is one passion I would advise you to command: when you have drunk out that glass, don't drink another." Here was exemplified what Goldsmith said of him, with the aid of a very witty image from one of Cibber's Comedies: "There is no arguing with Johnson: for if his pistol misses fire, he knocks you down with the butt end of it."

Johnson, talking of the fear of death, said, "Some people are not afraid, because they look upon salvation as the effect of an absolute decree, and think they feel in themselves the marks of sanctification. Others, and those the most rational in my opinion, look upon salvation as conditional; and as they never can be sure that they have complied with the conditions, they are afraid."

In one of his little manuscript diaries, about this time, I find a short notice, which marks his amiable disposition more certainly than a thousand studied declarations.—"Afternoon spent cheerfully and elegantly, I hope without offence to GOD or man; though in no holy duty, yet in the general exercise and cultivation of benevolence."

On Wednesday, May 19, I sat a part of the evening with him, by ourselves. I observed, that the death of our friends might be a consolation against the fear of our own dissolution, because we might have more friends in the other world than in this. He perhaps felt this a reflection upon his apprehension as to death; and said, with heat, "How can a man know *where* his departed friends are, or whether they will be his friends in the other world? How many friendships have you known formed upon principles of virtue? Most friendships are formed by caprice or by chance, mere confederacies in vice or leagues in folly."

We talked of our worthy friend Mr. Langton. He said, "I know not who will go to Heaven if Langton does not.

Sir, I could almost say, *Sit anima mea cum Langtono.*" I mentioned a very eminent friend as a virtuous man. JOHNSON. "Yes, Sir; but —— has not the evangelical virtue of Langton. ——, I am afraid, would not scruple to pick up a wench."

He however charged Mr. Langton with what he thought want of judgement upon an interesting occasion. "When I was ill, (said he) I desired he would tell me sincerely in what he thought my life was faulty. Sir, he brought me a sheet of paper, on which he had written down several texts of Scripture, recommending christian charity. And when I questioned him what occasion I had given for such an animadversion, all that he could say amounted to this,—that I sometimes contradicted people in conversation. Now what harm does it do to any man to be contradicted?" BOSWELL. "I suppose he meant the *manner* of doing it; 'roughly,—and harshly." JOHNSON. "And who is the worse for that?" BOSWELL. "It hurts people of weaker nerves." JOHNSON. "I know no such weak-nerved people." Mr. Burke, to whom I related this conference, said, "It is well, if when a man comes to die, he has nothing heavier upon his conscience than having been a little rough in conversation."

Johnson, at the time when the paper was presented to him, though at first pleased with the attention of his friend, whom he thanked in an earnest manner, soon exclaimed in a loud and angry tone, "What is your drift, Sir?" Sir Joshua Reynolds pleasantly observed, that it was a scene for a comedy, to see a penitent get into a violent passion and belabour his confessor.

He had now a great desire to go to Oxford, as his first jaunt after his illness; we talked of it for some days, and I had promised to accompany him. He was impatient and fretful to-night, because I did not at once agree to go with him on Thursday. When I considered how ill he had been, and what allowance should be made for the influence of sickness upon his temper, I resolved to indulge him, though with some inconvenience to myself, as I wished to attend the musical meeting in honour of Handel, in Westminster-Abbey, on the following Saturday.

On Thursday, June 3, the Oxford post-coach took us up in the morning at Bolt-court. The other two passengers were Mrs. Beresford and her daughter, two very agreeable ladies from America; they were going to Worcestershire, where they then resided. Frank had been sent by his master the day before to take places for us; and I found from the way-bill that Dr. Johnson had made our names be put down. Mrs. Beresford, who had read it, whispered me, "Is this the great Dr. Johnson?" I told her it was; so she was then prepared to listen. As she soon happened to mention in a voice so low that Johnson did not hear it, that her husband had been a member of the American Congress, I cautioned her to beware of introducing that subject, as she must know how very violent Johnson was against the people of that country. He talked a great deal. But I am sorry I have preserved little of the conversation. Miss Beresford was so much charmed, that she said to me aside, "How he does talk! Every sentence is an essay." She amused herself in the coach with knotting; he would scarcely allow this species of employment any merit. "Next to mere idleness (said he) I think knotting is to be reckoned in the scale of insignificance; though I once attempted to learn knotting. Dempster's sister (looking to me) endeavoured to teach me it; but I made no progress."

I was surprised at his talking without reserve in the publick post-coach of the state of his affairs; "I have (said he) about the world I think above a thousand pounds, which I intend shall afford Frank an annuity of seventy pounds a-year." Indeed his openness with people at a first interview was remarkable. He said once to Mr. Langton, "I think I am like Squire Richard in 'The Journey to London,' *'I'm never strange in a strange place.'* " He was truly *social*. He strongly censured what is much too common in England among persons of condition,—maintaining an absolute silence, when unknown to each other; as for instance, when occasionally brought together in a room before the master or mistress of the house has appeared. "Sir, that is being so uncivilised as not to understand the common rights of humanity."

At the inn where we stopped he was exceedingly dissatisfied with some roast mutton which he had for dinner. The ladies, I saw, wondered to see the great philosopher, whose wisdom and wit they had been admiring all the way, get into ill humour from such a cause. He scolded the waiter, saying, "It is as bad as bad can be: it is ill-fed, ill-killed, ill-kept, and ill-drest."

He bore the journey very well, and seemed to feel himself elevated as he approached Oxford, that magnificent and venerable seat of Learning, Orthodoxy, and Toryism. Frank came in the heavy coach, in readiness to attend him; and we were received with the most polite hospitality at the house of his old friend Dr. Adams, Master of Pembroke College, who had given us a kind invitation. Before we were set down, I communicated to Johnson, my having engaged to return to London directly, for the reason I have mentioned, but that I would hasten back to him again. He was pleased that I had made this journey merely to keep him company.

I fulfilled my intention by going to London, and returned to Oxford on Wednesday, the 9th of June, when I was happy to find myself again in the same agreeable circle at Pembroke College, with the comfortable prospect of making some stay. Johnson welcomed my return with more than ordinary glee.

After dinner, when one of us talked of there being a great enmity between Whig and Tory;—JOHNSON. "Why, not so much, I think, unless when they come into competition with each other. There is none when they are only common acquaintance, none when they are of different sexes. A Tory will marry into a Whig family, and a Whig into a Tory family, without any reluctance. But, indeed, in a matter of much more concern than political tenets, and that is religion, men and woman do not concern themselves much about difference of opinion; and ladies set no value on the moral character of men who pay their addresses to them; the greatest profligate will be as well received as the man of the greatest virtue, and this by a very good woman, by a woman who says her prayers three times a day." Our ladies endeavoured to defend their sex from this charge; but he roared them down! "No, no, a

342

lady will take Jonathan Wild as readily as St. Austin, if he has threepence more; and, what is worse, her parents will give her to him. Women have a perpetual envy of our vices; they are less vicious than we, not from choice, but because we restrict them; they are the slaves of order and fashion; their virtue is of more consequence to us than our own, so far as concerns this world."

Miss Adams mentioned a gentleman of licentious character, and said, "Suppose I had a mind to marry that gentleman, would my parents consent?" JOHNSON. "Yes, they'd consent, and you'd go. You'd go, though they did not consent." MISS ADAMS. "Perhaps their opposing might make me go." JOHNSON. "O, very well; you'd take one whom you think a bad man, to have the pleasure of vexing your parents. You put me in mind of Dr. Barroby, the physician, who was very fond of swine's flesh. One day, when he was eating it, he said, 'I wish I was a Jew.'—'Why so? (said somebody,) the Jews are not allowed to eat your favourite meat.'—'Because (said he,) I should then have the gust of eating it, with the pleasure of sinning.' "—Johnson then proceeded in his declamation.

Miss Adams soon afterwards made an observation that I do not recollect, which pleased him much; he said with a good-humoured smile, "That there should be so much excellence united with so much *depravity*, is strange."

Indeed, this lady's good qualities, merit, and accomplishments, and her constant attention to Dr. Johnson, were not lost upon him. She happened to tell him that a little coffee-pot, in which she had made him coffee, was the only thing she could call her own. He turned to her with a complacent gallantry, "Don't say so, my dear; I hope you don't reckon my heart as nothing."

On Friday, June 11, we talked at breakfast, of forms of prayer. JOHNSON. "I know of no good prayers but those in the 'Book of Common Prayer.' " DR. ADAMS. (in a very earnest manner,) "I wish, Sir, you would compose some family prayers." JOHNSON. "I will not compose prayers for you, Sir, because you can do it for yourself. But I have thought of getting together all the books of prayers which I could, selecting those which should appear to me the best, putting out some, inserting others, adding some prayers of my own, and prefixing a discourse on prayer." We all now gathered about him, and two or three of us at a time joined in pressing him to execute this plan. He seemed to be a little displeased at the manner of our importunity, and in great agitation called out, "Do not talk thus of what is so awful. I know not what time God will allow me in this world. There are many things which I wish to do." Some of us persisted, and Dr. Adams said, "I never was more serious about any thing in my life." JOHNSON. "Let me alone, let me alone; I am overpowered." And then he put his hands before his face, and reclined for some time upon the table.

I mentioned Jeremy Taylor's using, in his forms of prayer, "I am the chief of sinners," and other such self-condemning expressions. "Now, (said I) this cannot be said with truth by every man, and therefore is improper for a general printed form. I myself cannot say that I am the worst of men; I *will* not say so." JOHNSON. "A man may know, that physically, that is, in the real state of things, he is not the worst man; but that morally he may be so. Law observes, 'that every man knows something worse of himself, than he is sure of in others.' You may not have committed such crimes as some men have done; but you do not know against what degree of light they have sinned. Besides, Sir, 'the chief of sinners' is a mode of expression for 'I am a great sinner.' So St. Paul, speaking of our SAVIOUR'S having died to save sinners, says, 'of whom I am the chief;' yet he certainly did not think himself so bad as Judas Iscariot." BOSWELL. "But, Sir, Taylor means it literally, for he founds a conceit upon it. When praying for the conversion of sinners, and of himself in particular, he says, 'Lord, thou wilt not leave thy *chief* work undone.' " JOHNSON. "I do not approve of figurative expressions in addressing the Supreme Being; and I never use them. Taylor gives a very good advice: 'Never lie in your prayers; never confess more than you really believe; never promise more than you mean to perform.' "

Dr. Johnson and I went in Dr. Adams's coach to dine with Mr. Nowell, Principal of St. Mary Hall, at his beautiful villa at Iffley, on the banks of the Isis, about two miles from Oxford. While we were upon the road, I had the resolution to ask Johnson whether he thought that the roughness of his manner had been an advantage or not, and if he would not have done more good if he had been more gentle. I proceeded to answer myself thus: "Perhaps it has been of advantage, as it has given weight to what you said: you could not, perhaps, have talked with such authority without it." JOHNSON. "No, Sir; I have done more good as I am. Obscenity and Impiety have always been repressed in my company." BOSWELL. "True, Sir; and that is more than can be said of every Bishop. Greater liberties have been taken in the presence of a Bishop, though a very good man, from his being milder, and therefore not commanding such awe. Yet, Sir, many people who might have been benefited by your conversation, have been frightened away. A worthy friend of ours has told me, that he has often been afraid to talk to you." JOHNSON. "Sir, he need not have been afraid, if he had any thing rational to say. If he had not, it was better he did not talk."

Mr. Henderson, with whom I had sauntered in the venerable walks of Merton-College, and found him a very learned and pious man, supped with us. Dr. Johnson surprised him not a little, by acknowledging with a look of horrour, that he was much oppressed by the fear of death. The amiable Dr. Adams suggested that GOD was infinitely good. JOHNSON. "That he is infinitely good, as far as the perfection of his nature will allow, I certainly believe; but it is necessary for good upon the whole, that individuals should be punished. As to an *individual*, therefore, he is not infinitely good; and as I cannot be *sure* that I have fulfilled the conditions on which salvation is granted, I am afraid I may be one of those who shall be damned." (looking dismally.) DR. ADAMS. "What do you mean by damned!" JOHNSON. (passionately and loudly) "Sent to Hell, Sir, and punished everlastingly." DR. ADAMS. "I don't believe that doctrine." JOHNSON. "Hold, Sir, do you believe that some will be punished at all?" DR. ADAMS. "Being excluded from Heaven will be a punishment: yet there may be no great positive suffering." JOHNSON. "Well, Sir; but, if you admit any degree of punishment, there is an end of your argument for infinite goodness simply considered; for, infinite goodness would inflict no punishment whatever. There is no infinite goodness physically considered; morally there is." BOSWELL. "But may not a man attain to such a degree of hope as not to be uneasy from the fear of death?" JOHNSON. "A man may have such a degree of hope as to keep him quiet. You see I am not quiet, from the vehemency with which I talk; but I do not despair." MRS. ADAMS. "You seem, Sir, to forget the merits of our Redeemer." JOHNSON. "Madam, I do not forget the merits of my Redeemer; but my Redeemer has said that he will set some on his right hand and some on his left."—He was in gloomy agitation, and said, "I'll have no more on't."— If what has now been stated should be urged by the enemies of Christianity, as if its influence on the mind were not benignant, let it be remembered, that Johnson's temperament was melancholy, of which such direful apprehensions of futurity are often a common effect. We shall presently see, that when he approached nearer to his awful change, his mind became tranquil, and he exhibited as much fortitude as becomes a thinking man in that situation.

From the subject of death we passed to discourse of life whether it was upon the whole more happy or miserable. Johnson was decidedly for the balance of misery: in confirmation of which I maintained, that no man would choose to lead over again the life which he had experienced. Johnson acceded to that opinion in the strongest terms. This is an enquiry often made; and its being a subject of disquisition is a proof that much misery presses upon human feelings; for those who are conscious of a felicity of existence, would never hesitate to accept of a repetition of it. I have met with very few who would. I have heard Mr. Burke make use of a very ingenious and plausible argument on this subject; "Every man (said he,) would lead his life over again; for, every man is willing to go on and take an addition to his life, which, as he grows older, he has no reason to think will be better, or even so good as what has preceded." I imagine, however, the truth is, that there is a deceitful hope that the next part of life will be free from the pains, and anxieties, and sorrows, which we have already felt. We are for wise purposes "Condemn'd to Hope's delusive mine," as Johnson finely says.

It was observed to Dr. Johnson, that it seemed strange that he, who has so often delighted his company by his lively and brilliant conversation, should say he was miserable. JOHNSON. "Alas! it is all outside; I may be cracking my joke, and cursing the sun. *Sun, how I hate thy beams!*" I knew not well what to think of this declaration; whether to hold it as a genuine picture of his mind, or as the effect of his persuading himself contrary to fact, that the position which he had assumed as to human unhappiness, was true. We may apply to him a sentence in Mr. Greville's "Maxims, Characters, and Reflections;" a book which is entitled to much more praise than it has received: "ARISTARCHUS is charming: how full of knowledge, of sense, of sentiment. You get him with difficulty to your supper; and after having delighted every body and himself for a few hours, he is obliged to return home:—he is finishing his treatise, to prove that unhappiness is the portion of man."

On Sunday, June 13, our philosopher was calm at breakfast. There was something exceedingly pleasing in our leading a College life, without restraint, and with superiour elegance, in consequence of our living in the Master's House, and having the company of ladies. Mrs. Kennicot related, in his presence, a lively saying of Dr. Johnson's to Miss Hannah More, who had expressed a wonder that the poet who had written "Paradise Lost," should write such poor Sonnets:—"Milton, Madam, was a genius that could cut a Colossus from a rock, but could not carve heads upon cherrystones."

We talked of the casuistical question, "Whether it was allowable at any time to depart from *Truth?*" JOHNSON. "The general rule is, that Truth should never be violated, because it is of the utmost importance to the comfort of life, that we should have a full security by mutual faith; and occasional inconveniences should be willingly suffered, that we may preserve it. There must, however, be some exceptions. If, for instance, a murderer should ask you which way a man is gone, you may tell him what is not true, because you are under a previous obligation not to betray a man to a murderer." Boswell. "Supposing the person who wrote *Junius* were asked whether he was the authour, might he deny it?" Johnson. "I don't know what to say to this. If you were *sure* that he wrote *Junius,* would you, if he denied it, think as well of him afterwards? Yet it may be urged, that what a man has no right to ask, you may refuse to communicate; and there is no other effectual mode of preserving a secret and an important secret, the discovery of which may be very hurtful to you, but a flat denial; for if you are silent, or hesitate, or evade, it will be held equivalent to a confession. But stay, Sir, here is another case. Supposing the authour had told me confidentially that he had written *Junius,* and I were asked if he had, I should hold myself at liberty to deny it, as being under a previous promise, express or implied, to conceal it. Now what I ought to do for the authour, may I not do for myself? But I deny the lawfulness of telling a lie to a sick man, for fear of alarming him. You have no business with consequences; you are to tell the truth. Besides, you are not sure, what effect your telling him he is in danger may have. It may bring his distemper to a crisis, and that may cure him. Of all lying, I have the greatest abhorrence of this, because I believe it has been frequently practised on myself."

In the morning of Tuesday, June 15, while we sat at Dr. Adams's, we talked of a printed letter from the reverend Herbert Croft, to a young gentleman who had been his pupil, in which he advised him to read to the end of whatever books he should begin to read. Johnson. "This is surely a strange advice; you may as well resolve that whatever men you happen to get acquainted with, you are to keep to them for life. A book may be good for nothing; or there may be only one thing in it worth knowing; are we to read it all through? These Voyages, (pointing to the three large volumes of 'Voyages to the South Sea,' which were just come out) *who* will read them through? A man had better work his way before the mast, than read them through; they will be eaten by rats and mice, before they are read through. There can be little entertainment in such books; one set of Savages is like another." BOSWELL. "I do not think the people of Otaheité can be reckoned Savages." JOHNSON. "Don't cant in defence of Savages." BOSWELL. "They have the art of navigation." JOHNSON. "A dog or a cat can swim." BOSWELL. "They carve very ingeniously." JOHNSON. "A cat can scratch, and a child with a nail can scratch." I perceived this was none of the *mollia tempora fandi;* so desisted.

Upon his mentioning that when he came to College he wrote his first exercise twice over, but never did so afterwards; MISS ADAMS. "I suppose, Sir, you could not make them better?" JOHNSON. "Yes, Madam, to be sure I could make them better. Thought is better than no thought." MISS ADAMS. "Do you think, Sir, you could make your Ramblers better?" JOHNSON. "Certainly I could." BOSWELL. "I'll lay a bet, Sir, you cannot." JOHNSON. "But I will, Sir, if I choose. I shall make the best of them you shall pick out, better."—BOSWELL. "But you may add to them. I will not allow of that." JOHNSON. "Nay, Sir, there are three ways of making them better;—putting out,—adding,—or correcting."

On Wednesday, June 19, Dr. Johnson and I returned to London; he was not well to-day, and said very little, employing himself chiefly in reading Euripides. He expressed some displeasure at me, for not observing sufficiently the various objects upon the road. "If I had your eyes, Sir, (said he,) I should count the passengers." It was wonderful how accurate his observations of visual objects were, notwithstanding his imperfect eyesight, owing to a habit of attention.—That he was much satisfied with the respect paid to him at Dr. Adams's is thus attested by himself: "I returned last night from Oxford, after a fortnight's abode with Dr. Adams, who treated me as well as I could expect or wish; and he that contents a sick man, a man whom it is impossible to please, has surely done his part well."

After his return to London from this excursion, I saw him frequently, but have few memorandums; I shall therefore here insert some particulars which I collected at various times.

It having been mentioned to Dr. Johnson that a gentleman who had a son whom he imagined to have an extreme degree of timidity, resolved to send him to a publick school, that he might acquire confidence; "Sir, (said Johnson,) this is preposterous expedient for removing his infirmity; such a disposition should be cultivated in the shade. Placing him at a publick school is forcing an owl upon day."

Speaking of a gentleman whose house was much frequented by low company; "Rags, Sir, (said he,) will always make their appearance where they have a right to do it."

Of the same gentleman's mode of living, he said, "Sir, the servants instead of doing what they are bid, stand round the table in idle clusters, gaping upon the guests; and seem as unfit to attend a company, as to steer a man of war."

A dull country magistrate gave Johnson a long, tedious account of his exercising his criminal jurisdiction, the result of which was his having sentenced four convicts to transportation. Johnson, in an agony of impatience to get rid of such a companion, exclaimed, "I heartily wish, Sir, that I were a fifth."

Johnson was present when a tragedy was read, in which there occurred this line:

"Who rules o'er freemen should himself be free."

The company having admired it much, "I cannot agree with you (said Johnson:) It might as well be said,

"Who drives fat oxen should himself be fat."

Sir Joshua Reynolds having said that he took the altitude of a man's taste by his stories and his wit, and of his understanding by the remarks which he repeated; being always sure that he must be a weak man, who quotes common things with an emphasis as if they were oracles;— Johnson agreed with him; and Sir Joshua having also observed that the real character of a man was found out by his amusements,—Johnson added, "Yes, Sir; no man is a hypocrite in his pleasures."

Had Johnson treated at large *De Claris Oratoribus,* he might have given us an admirable work. When the Duke of Bedford attacked the ministry as vehemently as he could, for having taken upon them to extend the time for the importation of corn, Lord Chatham, in his first speech in the House of Lords, boldly avowed himself to be an adviser of that measure. "My colleagues, (said he,) as I was confined by indisposition, did me the signal honour of coming to the bedside of a sick man, to ask his opinion. But, had they not thus condescended, I should have *taken up my bed and walked,* in order to have delivered that opinion at the Council-Board." Mr. Langton, who was present, mentioned this to Johnson, who observed, "Now, Sir, we see that he took these words as he found them; without considering, that though the expression in Scripture, *take up thy bed and walk,* strictly suited the instance of the sick man restored to health and strength, who would of course be supposed to carry his bed with him, it could not be proper in the case of a man who was lying in a state of feebleness, and who certainly would not add to the difficulty of moving at all, that of carrying his bed."

When I pointed out to him in the news-paper one of Mr. Grattan's animated and glowing speeches, in favour of the freedom of Ireland, in which this expression occurred (I know not if accurately taken): "We will persevere, till there is not one link of the English chain left to clank upon the rags of the meanest beggar in Ireland;"—"Nay, Sir, (said Johnson,) don't you perceive that *one* link cannot clank?"

The difference, he observed, between a well-bred and an ill-bred man is this: "One immediately attracts your liking, the other your aversion. You love the one till you find reason to hate him; you hate the other till you find reason to love him."

The wife of one of his acquaintance had fraudulently made a purse for herself out of her husband's fortune. Feeling a proper compunction in her last moments, she confessed how much she had secreted; but before she could tell where it was placed, she was seized with a convulsive fit and expired. Her husband said, he was more hurt by her want of confidence in him, than by the loss of his money. "I told him, (said Johnson,) that he should console himself: for *perhaps* the money might be *found,* and he was *sure* that his wife was *gone."*

A foppish physician once reminded Johnson of his having been in company with him on a former occasion, "I do not remember it, Sir." The physician still insisted; adding that he that day wore so fine a coat that it must have attracted his notice. "Sir, (said Johnson,) had you been dipt in Pactolus, I should not have noticed you."

He seemed to take a pleasure in speaking in his own style; for when he had carelessly missed it, he would repeat the thought translated into it. Talking of the Comedy of "The Rehearsal," he said, "It has not wit enough to keep it sweet." This was easy;—he therefore caught himself, and pronounced a more round sentence; "It has not vitality enough to preserve it from putrefaction."

Though he had no taste for painting, he admired much the manner in which Sir Joshua Reynolds treated of his art, in his "Discourses to the Royal Academy." He observed one day of a passage in them, "I think I might as well have said this myself:" and once when Mr. Langton was sitting by him, he read one of them very eagerly, and expressed himself thus: "Very well, Master Reynolds; very well, indeed. But it will not be understood."

When I observed to him that Painting was so far inferiour to Poetry, that the story or even emblem which it communicates must be previously known, and mentioned as a natural and laughable instance of this, that a little Miss on seeing a picture of Justice with the scales, had exclaimed to me, "See, there's a woman selling sweetmeats;" he said, "Painting, Sir, can illustrate, but cannot inform."

No man was more ready to make an apology when he had censured unjustly, than Johnson. When a proof-sheet of one of his works was brought to him, he found fault with the mode in which a part of it was arranged, refused to

17
David Garrick, the famous actor, who as a youth attended
Johnson's school at Lichfield and was later a member of his
Literary Club.

read it, and in a passion desired that the compositor [1] might be sent to him. The compositor was Mr. Manning, a decent sensible man, who had composed about one half of his "Dictionary," when in Mr. Strahan's printing-house; and a great part of his "Lives of the Poets," when in that of Mr. Nichols; and who (in his seventy-seventh year) when in Mr. Baldwin's printing-house, composed a part of the first edition of this work concerning him. By producing the manuscript, he at once satisfied Dr. Johnson that he was not to blame. Upon which Johnson candidly and earnestly said to him, "Mr. Compositor, I ask your pardon; Mr. Compositor, I ask your pardon, again and again."

His generous humanity to the miserable was almost beyond example. The following instance is well attested: Coming home late one night, he found a poor woman lying in the street, so much exhausted that she could not walk; he took her upon his back, and carried her to his house, where he discovered that she was one of those wretched females who had fallen into the lowest state of vice, poverty, and disease. Instead of harshly upbraiding her, he had her taken care of with all tenderness for a long time, at a considerable expence, till she was restored to health, and endeavoured to put her into a virtuous way of living. [2]

He once in his life was known to have uttered what is called a *bull:* Sir Joshua Reynolds, when they were riding together in Devonshire, complained that he had a very bad horse, for that even when going down hill he moved slowly step by step. "Ay (said Johnson,) and when he *goes* up hill, he *stands still.*"

He had a great aversion to gesticulating in company. He called once to a gentleman who offended him in that point, "Don't *attitudenise.*" And when another gentleman thought he was giving additional force to what he uttered, by ex-

[1] Compositor in the Printing-house means, the person who adjusts the types in the order in which they are to stand for printing; and arranges what is called the *form,* from which an impression is taken.
[2] My informer was Mrs. Desmoulins, who lived many years in Dr. Johnson's house.

pressive movements of his hands, Johnson fairly seized them, and held them down.

On Tuesday, June 22, I dined with him at THE LITERARY CLUB, the last time of his being in that respectable society. The other members present were the Bishop of St. Asaph, Lord Eliot, Lord Palmerston, Dr. Fordyce, and Mr. Malone. He looked ill; but had such a manly fortitude, that he did not trouble the company with melancholy complaints. They all shewed evident marks of kind concern about him, with which he was much pleased, and he exerted himself to be as entertaining as his indisposition allowed him.

The anxiety of his friends to preserve so estimable a life, as long as human means might be supposed to have influence, made them plan for him a retreat from the severity of a British winter, to the mild climate of Italy. This scheme was at last brought to a serious resolution at General Paoli's, where I had often talked of it. One essential matter, however, I understood was necessary to be previously settled, which was obtaining such an addition to his income, as would be sufficient to enable him to defray the expence in a manner becoming the first literary character of a great nation, and, independent of all his other merits, the Authour of THE DICTIONARY OF THE ENGLISH LANGUAGE. The person to whom I above all others thought I should apply to negociate this business, was the Lord Chancellor, because I knew that he highly valued Johnson, and that Johnson highly valued his Lordship; so that it was no degradation of my illustrious friend to solicit for him the favour of such a man. I have mentioned what Johnson said of him to me when he was at the bar; and after his Lordship was advanced to the seals, he said of him, "I would prepare myself for no man in England but Lord Thurlow. When I am to meet with him, I should wish to know a day before." How he would have prepared himself, I cannot conjecture. Would he have selected certain topicks, and considered them in every view, so as to be in readiness to argue them at all points? and what may we suppose those topicks to have been? I once started the curious enquiry to the great man who was the subject of this compliment: he smiled, but did not pursue it.

354

I first consulted with Sir Joshua Reynolds, who perfectly coincided in opinion with me; and I therefore, though personally very little known to his Lordship, wrote to him, stating the case, and requesting his good offices for Dr. Johnson. I mentioned that I was obliged to set out for Scotland early in the following week, so that if his Lordship should have any commands for me as to this pious negociation, he would be pleased to send them before that time; otherwise Sir Joshua Reynolds would give all attention to it.

On Friday, June 25, I dined with him at General Paoli's, where, he says in one of his letters to Mrs. Thrale, "I love to dine." There was a variety of dishes much to his taste, of all which he seemed to me to eat so much, that I was afraid he might be hurt by it; and I whispered to the General my fear, and begged he might not press him. "Alas! (said the General,) see how very ill he looks; he can live but a very short time. Would you refuse any slight gratifications to a man under sentence of death? There is a humane custom in Italy, by which persons in that melancholy situation are indulged with having whatever they like best to eat and drink, even with expensive delicacies."

On Sunday, June 27, I found him rather better. I mentioned to him a young man who was going to Jamaica with his wife and children, in expectation of being provided for by two of her brothers settled in that island, one a clergyman, and the other a physician. JOHNSON. "It is a wild scheme, Sir, unless he has a positive and deliberate invitation. There was a poor girl, who used to come about me, who had a cousin in Barbadoes, that, in a letter to her, expressed a wish she should come out to that Island, and expatiated on the comforts and happiness of her situation. The poor girl went out: her cousin was much surprized, and asked her how she could think of coming. 'Because, (said she,) you invited me.'—'Not I,' answered the cousin. The letter was then produced. 'I see it is true, (said she,) that I did invite you: but I did not think you would come.' They lodged her in an outhouse, where she passed her time miserably; and as soon as she had an opportunity she returned to England. Always tell this, when you hear of people going abroad to relations, upon a notion of being well received. In the case which you mention, it is probable the clergyman spends all he gets, and the physician does not know how much he is to get."

We this day dined at Sir Joshua Reynolds's, with General Paoli, Lord Eliot, (formerly Mr. Eliot, of Port Eliot,) Dr. Beattie, and some other company. Talking of Lord Chesterfield;—JOHNSON. "His manner was exquisitely elegant, and he had more knowledge than I expected." BOSWELL. "Did you find, Sir, his conversation to be of a superiour style?" JOHNSON. "Sir, in the conversation which I had with him I had the best right to superiority, for it was upon philology and literature." Lord Eliot, who had travelled at the same time with Mr. Stanhope, Lord Chesterfield's natural son, justly observed, that it was strange that a man who shewed he had so much affection for his son as Lord Chesterfield did, by writing so many long and anxious letters to him, almost all of them when he was Secretary of State, which certainly was a proof of great goodness of disposition, should endeavour to make his son a rascal. His Lordship told us, that Foote had intended to bring on the stage a father who had thus tutored his son, and to shew the son an honest man to every one else, but practising his father's maxims upon him, and cheating him. JOHNSON. "I am much pleased with this design; but I think there was no occasion to make the son honest at all. No; he should be a consummate rogue: the contrast between honesty and knavery would be the stronger. It should be contrived so that the father should be the only sufferer by the son's villainy, and thus there would be poetical justice."

He entered upon a curious discussion of the difference between intuition and sagacity; one being immediate in its effect, the other requiring a circuitous process; one he observed was the *eye* of the mind, the other the *nose* of the mind.

A young gentleman present took up the argument against him and maintained that no man ever thinks of the *nose of the mind*, not adverting that though that figurative sense seems strange to us, as very unusual, it is truly not more forced than Hamlet's "In my *mind's eye,* Horatio." He persisted much too long, and appeared to Johnson as putting himself forward as his antagonist with too much presumption: upon which he called to him in a loud tone, "What is it you are contending for if you *be* contending?" —And afterwards imagining that the gentleman retorted upon him with a kind of smart drollery, he said, "Mr.*****, it does not become you to talk so to me. Besides, ridicule is not your talent; you have *there* neither intuition nor sagacity."—The gentleman protested that he had intended no improper freedom, but had the greatest respect for Dr. Johnson. After a short pause, during which we were somewhat uneasy.—JOHNSON. "Give me your hand, Sir. You were too tedious, and I was too short." Mr.*****. "Sir, I am honoured by your attention in any way." JOHNSON. "Come, Sir, let's have no more of it. We offended one another by our contention; let us not offend the company by our compliments."

He now said, "He wished much to go to Italy, and that he dreaded passing the winter in England." I said nothing; but enjoyed a secret satisfaction in thinking that I had taken the most effectual measures to make such a scheme practicable.

On Monday, June 28, I had the honour to receive from the Lord Chancellor the following letter:

"TO JAMES BOSWELL, ESQ.

"SIR,

"I should have answered your letter immediately; if, (being much engaged when I received it) I had not put it in my pocket, and forgot to open it till this morning.

"I am much obliged to you for the suggestion; and I will adopt and press it as far as I can. The best argument, I am sure, and I hope it is not likely to fail, is Dr. Johnson's merit.—But it will be necessary, if I should be so unfortunate as to miss seeing you, to converse with Sir Joshua on the sum it will be proper to ask,—in short, upon the means of setting him out. It would be a reflection on us all, if such a man should perish for want of the means to take care of his health.

"Yours, &c.
"THURLOW."

This letter gave me a very high satisfaction; I next day went and shewed it to Sir Joshua Reynolds, who was exceedingly pleased with it. He thought that I should now communicate the negociation to Dr. Johnson, who might afterwards complain if the attention with which he had been honoured, should be too long concealed from him. I intended to set out for Scotland next morning; but Sir Joshua cordially insisted that I should stay another day, that Johnson and I might dine with him, that we three might talk of his Italian Tour, and, as Sir Joshua expressed himself, "have it all out." I hastened to Johnson, and was told by him that he was rather better to-day. BOSWELL. "I am very anxious about you, Sir, and particularly that you should go to Italy for the winter, which I believe is your own wish." JOHNSON. "It is, Sir." BOSWELL. "You have no objections, I presume, but the money it would require." JOHNSON. "Why, no, Sir."—Upon which I gave him a particular account of what had been done, and read to him the Lord Chancellor's letter.—He listened with much attention; then warmly said, "This is taking prodigious pains about a man."—"O, Sir, (said I, with most sincere affection,) your friends would do everything for you." He paused,—grew more and more agitated,—till tears started into his eyes, and he exclaimed with fervent emotion, "GOD bless you all." I was so affected that I also shed tears.— After a short silence, he renewed and extended his grateful benediction, "GOD bless you all, for JESUS CHRIST's sake." We both remained for some time unable to speak.— He rose suddenly and quitted the room, quite melted in tenderness. He staid but a short time, till he had recovered his firmness; soon after he returned I left him, having first engaged him to dine at Sir Joshua Reynolds's next day.—I never was again under that roof which I had so long reverenced.

On Wednesday, June 30, the friendly confidential dinner with Sir Joshua Reynolds took place, no other company being present. Had I known that this was the last time that I should enjoy in this world, the conversation of a friend whom I so much respected, and from whom I derived so much instruction and entertainment, I should have been deeply affected. When I now look back to it, I am vexed that a single word should have been forgotten.

Both Sir Joshua and I were so sanguine in our expectations, that we expatiated with confidence on the liberal provision which we were sure would be made for him, conjecturing whether munificence would be displayed in one large donation, or in an ample increase of his pension. He himself catched so much of our enthusiasm, as to allow himself to suppose it not impossible that our hopes might in one way or other be realised. He said that he would rather have his pension doubled than a grant of a thousand pounds; "For, (said he,) though probably I may not live to receive as much as a thousand pounds, a man would have the consciousness that he should pass the remainder of his life in splendour, how long soever it might be." Considering what a moderate proportion an income of six hundred pounds a-year bears to innumerable fortunes in this country, it is worthy of remark, that a man so truly great should think it splendour.

As an instance of extraordinary liberality of friendship, he told us, that Dr. Brocklesby had upon this occasion offered him a hundred a-year for his life. A grateful tear started into his eye, as he spoke this in a faultering tone.

Sir Joshua and I endeavoured to flatter his imagination with agreeable prospects of happiness in Italy. "Nay, (said he,) I must not expect much of that; when a man goes to Italy merely to feel how he breathes the air, he can enjoy very little."

Our conversation turned upon living in the country, which Johnson, whose melancholy mind required the dissipation of quick successive variety, had habituated himself to consider as a kind of mental imprisonment. "Yet, Sir, (said I,) there are many people who are content to live in the country." JOHNSON. "Sir, it is in the intellectual world as in the physical world: we are told by natural philosophers that a body is at rest in the place that is fit for it; they who are content to live in the country, are *fit for* the country."

Talking of various enjoyments, I argued that a refinement of taste was a disadvantage, as they who have attained to it must be seldomer pleased than those who have no nice discrimination, and are therefore satisfied with every thing that comes in their way. JOHNSON. "Nay, Sir; that is a paltry notion. Endeavour to be as perfect as you can in every respect."

I accompanied him in Sir Joshua Reynolds's coach, to the entry of Bolt-court. He asked me whether I would not go with him to his house; I declined it, from an apprehension that my spirits would sink. We bade adieu to each other affectionately in the carriage. When he had got down upon the foot-pavement, he called out, "Fare you well;" and without looking back, sprung away with a kind of pathetick briskness, if I may use that expression, which seemed to indicate a struggle to conceal uneasiness, and impressed me with a foreboding of our long, long separation.

I remained one day more in town, to have the chance of talking over my negociation with the Lord Chancellor: but the multiplicity of his Lordship's important engagements did not allow of it; so I left the management of the business in the hands of Sir Joshua Reynolds.

Soon after this time Dr. Johnson had the mortification of being informed by Mrs. Thrale, that, "what she supposed he never believed," was true; namely, that she was actually going to marry Signor Piozzi, an Italian musick-master. He endeavoured to prevent it; but in vain. If she would publish the whole of the correspondence that passed between Dr. Johnson and her on the subject, we should have a full view of his real sentiments. As it is, our judgement must be biassed by that characteristick specimen which Sir John Hawkins has given us: "Poor Thrale, I thought that either her virtue or her vice would have restrained her from such a marriage. She has now become a subject for her enemies to exult over; and for her friends, if she has any left, to forget or pity."

It must be admitted that Johnson derived a considerable portion of happiness from the comforts and elegancies which he enjoyed in Mr. Thrale's family; but Mrs. Thrale assures us he was indebted for these to her husband alone, who certainly respected him sincerely. Her words are, *"Veneration for his virtue, reverence for his talents,* delight *in his conversation, and* habitual endurance of a yoke my husband first put upon me, *and of which he contentedly bore his share for sixteen or seventeen years, made me go on so long with* Mr. Johnson; *but the perpetual confinement I will own to have been* terrifying *in the first years of our friendship, and* irksome *in the last; nor could I pretend to* support *it without help, when my coadjutor was no more."* Alas! how different is this from the declarations which I have heard Mrs. Thrale make in his life-time, without a single murmur against any peculiarities, or against any one circumstance which attended their intimacy.

As a sincere friend of the great man whose Life I am writing, I think it necessary to guard my readers against the mistaken notion of Dr. Johnson's character, which this lady's "Anecdotes" of him suggest; for from the very nature and form of her book, "it lends deception lighter wings to fly."

"Let it be remembered, (says an eminent critick,) that she has comprised in a small volume all that she could recollect of Dr. Johnson in *twenty years,* during which period, doubtless, some severe things were said by him: and they who read the book in *two hours,* naturally enough suppose that his whole conversation was of this complexion. But the fact is, I have been often in his company, and never *once* heard him say a severe thing to any one; and many others can attest the same. When he did say a severe thing, it was generally extorted by ignorance pretending to knowledge, or by extreme vanity or affectation."

Having left the *pious negociation,* as I called it, in the best hands, I shall here insert what relates to it. Johnson wrote to Sir Joshua Reynolds on July 6, as follows; "I am going, I hope, in a few days, to try the air of Derbyshire, but hope to see you before I go. Let me, however, mention to you what I have much at heart.—If the Chancellor should continue his attention to Mr. Boswell's request, and confer with you on the means of relieving my languid state, I am very desirous to avoid the appearance of asking money upon false pretences. I desire you to represent to his Lordship, what, as soon as it is suggested, he will perceive to be reasonable,—That, if I grow much worse, I shall be afraid to leave my physicians, to suffer the inconveniences of travel, and pine in the solitude of a foreign country;—That, if I grow much better, of which indeed there is now little appearance, I shall not wish to leave my friends and my domestick comforts; for I do not travel for pleasure or curiosity; yet if I should recover, curiosity would revive.— In my present state, I am desirous to make a struggle for a little longer life, and hope to obtain some help from a softer climate. Do for me what you can." He wrote to me July 26: "I wish your affairs could have permitted a longer and continued exertion of your zeal and kindness. They that have your kindness may want your ardour. In the mean time I am very feeble, and very dejected."

By a letter from Sir Joshua Reynolds I was informed, that the Lord Chancellor had called on him, and acquainted him that the application had not been successful; but that his Lordship, after speaking highly in praise of Johnson, as a man who was an honour to his country, desired Sir Joshua to let him know, that on granting a mortgage of his pension, he should draw on his Lordship to the amount of five or six hundred pounds; and that his Lordship explained the meaning of the mortgage to be, that he wished the business to be conducted in such a manner, that Dr. Johnson should appear to be under the least possible obligation. Sir Joshua mentioned, that he had by the same post communicated all this to Dr. Johnson.

How Johnson was affected upon the occasion will appear from what he wrote to Sir Joshua Reynolds:

Ashburne, Sept. 9. "Many words I hope are not necessary between you and me, to convince you what gratitude is excited in my heart by the Chancellor's liberality, and your kind offices. * * * * * *

"I have enclosed a letter to the Chancellor, which, when you have read it, you will be pleased to seal with a head, or any other general seal, and convey it to him: had I sent it directly to him, I should have seemed to overlook the favour of your intervention."

"TO THE LORD HIGH CHANCELLOR.

"MY LORD,

"After a long and not inattentive observation of mankind, the generosity of your Lordship's offer raises in me not less wonder than gratitude. Bounty, so liberally bestowed, I should gladly receive, if my condition made it necessary; for, to such a mind, who would not be proud to own his obligations? But it has pleased GOD to restore me to so great a measure of health, that if I should now appropriate so much of a fortune destined to do good, I could not escape from myself the charge of advancing a false claim. My journey to the continent, though I once thought it necessary, was never much encouraged by my physicians; and I was very desirous that your Lordship should be told of it by Sir Joshua Reynolds, as an event very uncertain; for if I grew much better, I should not be willing, if much worse, not able, to migrate.—Your Lordship was first solicited without my knowledge; but, when I was told that you were pleased to honour me with your patronage, I did not expect to hear of a refusal; yet, as I have had no long time to brood hope, and have not rioted in imaginary opulence, this cold reception has been scarce a disappointment; and, from your Lordship's kindness, I have received a benefit, which only men like you are able to bestow. I shall not live *mihi carior*, with a higher opinion of my own merit.

"I am, my Lord,

"Your Lordship's most obliged,

"Most grateful, and

"Most humble servant,

"SAM. JOHNSON."

"September, 1784."

Upon this unexpected failure I abstain from presuming to make any remarks, or to offer any conjectures.

July 26, he wrote to me from Ashbourne: "On the 14th

I came to Lichfield, and found every body glad enough to see me. On the 20th, I came hither, and found a house half-built, of very uncomfortable appearance; but my own room has not been altered. That a man worn with diseases, in his seventy-second or third year, should condemn part of his remaining life to pass among ruins and rubbish, and that no inconsiderable part, appears to me very strange. —I know that your kindness makes you impatient to know the state of my health, in which I cannot boast of much improvement. I came through the journey without much inconvenience, but when I attempt self-motion I find my legs weak, and my breath very short; this day I have been much disordered. I have no company; the Doctor [1] is busy in his fields, and goes to bed at nine, and his whole system is so different from mine, that we seem formed for different elements; I have, therefore, all my amusement to seek within myself."

Having written to him in bad spirits, a letter filled with dejection and fretfulness, and at the same time expressing anxious apprehensions concerning him, on account of a dream which had disturbed me; his answer was chiefly in terms of reproach, for a supposed charge of "affecting discontent, and indulging the vanity of complaint." It, however, proceeded, "Write to me often, and write like a man. I consider your fidelity and tenderness as a great part of the comforts which are yet left me, and sincerely wish we could be nearer to each other.—* * * * * * * *.—My dear friend, life is very short, and very uncertain; let us spend it as well as we can. My worthy neighbour, Allen, is dead. Love me as well as you can. Pay my respects to dear Mrs. Boswell.—Nothing ailed me at that time; let your superstition at last have an end."

Feeling very soon, that the manner in which he had written might hurt me, he two days afterwards, July 28, wrote to me again, giving me an account of his sufferings; after which, he thus proceeds: "Before this letter, you will have had one which I hope you will not take amiss; for it contains only truth, and that truth kindly intended. * * * * * * *

[1] The Rev. Dr. Taylor.

Spartam quam nactus es orna; make the most and best of your lot, and compare yourself not with the few that are above you, but with the multitudes which are below you. * * * * * *. Go steadily forwards with lawful business or honest diversions. *'Be* (as Temple says of the Dutchmen,) *well when you are not ill, and pleased when you are not angry.'*—* * * * * *. This may seem but an ill return for your tenderness; but I mean it well, for I love you with great ardour and sincerity. Pay my respects to dear Mrs. Boswell, and teach the young ones to love me."

I unfortunately was so much indisposed during a considerable part of the year, that it was not, or at least I thought it was not, in my power to write to my illustrious friend as formerly, or without expressing such complaints as offended him. Having conjured him not to do me the injustice of charging me with affectation, I was with much regret long silent. His last letter to me then came, and affected me very tenderly·

"To James Boswell, Esq.

"DEAR SIR,

"I have this summer sometimes amended, and sometimes relapsed, but, upon the whole, have lost ground very much. My legs are extremely weak, and my breath very short, and the water is now encreasing upon me. In this uncomfortable state your letters used to relieve; what is the reason that I have them no longer? Are you sick, or are you sullen? Whatever be the reason, if it be less than necessity, drive it away; and of the short life that we have, make the best use for yourself and for your friends. * * * * * *. I am sometimes afraid that your omission to write has some real cause, and shall be glad to know that you are not sick, and that nothing ill has befallen dear Mrs. Boswell, or any of your family,

"I am, Sir, your, &c.
"Sam. Johnson."

"Lichfield, Nov. 5, 1784."

Yet it was not a little painful to me to find, that in a paragraph of this letter, which I have omitted, he still persevered in arraigning me as before, which was strange in him who had so much experience of what I suffered. I, however, wrote to him two as kind letters as I could; the last of which came too late to be read by him, for his illness encreased more rapidly upon him than I had apprehended; but I had the consolation of being informed that he spoke of me on his death-bed with affection, and I look forward with humble hope of renewing our friendship in a better world.

I now relieve the readers of this Work from any further personal notice of its authour; who, if he should be thought to have obtruded himself too much upon their attention, requests them to consider the peculiar plan of his biographical undertaking.

My readers are now, at last, to behold SAMUEL JOHNSON preparing himself for that doom, from which the most exalted powers afford no exemption to man. Death had always been to him an object of terrour; so that though by no means happy, he still clung to life with an eagerness at which many have wondered. At any time when he was ill, he was very pleased to be told that he looked better. An ingenious member of the *Eumelian Club* informs me, that upon one occasion, when he said to him that he saw health returning to his cheek, Johnson seized him by the hand and exclaimed, "Sir, you are one of the kindest friends I ever had."

His own state of his views of futurity will appear truly rational; and may, perhaps, impress the unthinking with seriousness.

"You know, (says he,) I never thought confidence with respect to futurity, any part of the character of a brave, a wise, or a good man. Bravery has no place where it can avail nothing; wisdom impresses strongly the consciousness of those faults, of which it is, perhaps, itself an aggravation; and goodness, always wishing to be better, and imputing every deficience to criminal negligence, and every fault to voluntary corruption, never dares to suppose the condition of forgiveness fulfilled, nor what is wanting in the crime supplied by penitence.

"This is the state of the best; but what must be the condition of him whose heart will not suffer him to rank himself among the best, or among the good? Such must be his dread of the approaching trial as will leave him little attention to the opinion of those whom he is leaving for ever; and the serenity that is not felt, it can be no virtue to feign."

His great fear of death, and the strange dark manner in which Sir John Hawkins imparts the uneasiness which he expressed on account of offences with which he charged himself, may give occasion to injurious suspicions, as if there had been something of more than ordinary criminality weighing upon his conscience. On that account, therefore, as well as from the regard to truth which he inculcated, I am to mention, (with all possible respect and delicacy, however,) that his conduct after he came to London, and had associated with Savage and others, was not so strictly virtuous, in one respect, as when he was a younger man. It was well known, that his amorous inclinations were uncommonly strong and impetuous. He owned to many of his friends, that he used to take women of the town to taverns, and hear them relate their history.—In short, it must not be concealed, that like many other good and pious men, among whom we may place the apostle Paul upon his own authority, Johnson was not free from propensities which were ever "warring against the law of his mind."—and that in his combats with them, he was sometimes overcome.

Here let the profane and licentious pause; let them not thoughtlessly say that Johnson was an *hypocrite,* or that his *principles* were not firm, because his *practice* was not uniformly conformable to what he professed.

Let the question be considered independent of moral and religious associations; and no man will deny that thousands, in many instances, act against conviction. Is a prodigal, for example, an *hypocrite,* when he owns he is satisfied that his extravagance will bring him to ruin and misery? We are *sure* he *believes* it; but immediate inclination, strengthened by indulgence, prevails over that belief in influencing his conduct. Why then shall credit be re-

367

fused to the *sincerity* of those who acknowledge their persuasion of moral and religious duty, yet sometimes fail of living as it requires? I heard Dr. Johnson once observe, "There is something noble in publishing truth, though it condemns one's self." And one who said in his presence, "he had no notion of people being in earnest in their good professions, whose practice was not suitable to them," was thus reprimanded by him:—"Sir, are you so grossly ignorant of human nature as not to know that a man may be very sincere in good principles, without having good practice?"

But let no man encourage or soothe himself in "presumptuous sin," from knowing that Johnson was sometimes hurried into indulgences which he thought criminal. I have exhibited this circumstance as a shade in so great a character, both from my sacred love of truth, and to shew that he was not so weakly scrupulous as he has been represented by those who imagine that the sins, of which a deep sense was upon his mind, were merely such little venial trifles as pouring milk into his tea on Good-Friday. His understanding will be defended by my statement, if his consistency of conduct be in some degree impaired.

I am conscious that this is the most difficult and dangerous part of my biographical work, and I cannot but be very anxious concerning it. I trust that I have got through it, preserving at once my regard to truth,—to my friend, —and to the interests of virtue and religion. Nor can I apprehend that more harm can ensue from the knowledge of the irregularities of Johnson, guarded as I have stated it, than from knowing that Addison and Parnell were intemperate in the use of wine; which he himself, in his Lives of those celebrated writers and pious men, has not forborne to record.

It is not my intention to give a very minute detail of the particulars of Johnson's remaining days, of whom it was now evident, that the crisis was fast approaching, when he must *"die like men, and fall like one of the Princes."* Yet it will be instructive, as well as gratifying to the curiosity of my readers, to record a few circumstances, on the authenticity of which they may perfectly rely, as I have been at the utmost pains to obtain an accurate account of his last illness, from the best authority.

Dr. Heberden, Dr. Brocklesby, Dr. Warren, and Dr. Butler, physicians, generously attended him, without accepting any fees, as did Mr. Cruickshank, surgeon; and all that could be done from professional skill and ability, was tried, to prolong a life so truly valuable. He himself, indeed, having, on account of his very bad constitution, been perpetually applying himself to medical inquiries, united his own efforts with those of the gentlemen who attended him; and imagining that the dropsical collection of water which oppressed him might be drawn off by making incisions in his body, he, with his usual resolute defiance of pain, cut deep, when he thought that his surgeon had done it too tenderly.

Having no other relations, it had been for some time Johnson's intention to make a liberal provision for his faithful servant, Mr. Francis Barber, whom he looked upon as particularly under his protection, and whom he had all along treated truly as an humble friend. Having asked Dr. Brocklesby what would be a proper annuity to a favourite servant, and being answered that it must depend on the circumstances of the master; and, that in the case of a nobleman, fifty pounds a-year was considered as an adequate reward for many years' faithful service;—"Then, (said Johnson,) shall I be *nobilissimus*, for I mean to leave Frank seventy pounds a-year, and I desire you to tell him so." It is strange, however, to think, that Johnson was not free from that general weakness of being averse to execute a will, so that he delayed it from time to time; and had it not been for Sir John Hawkins's repeatedly urging it, I think it is probable that his kind resolution would not have been fulfilled. After making one, which, as Sir John Hawkins informs us, extended no further than the promised annuity, Johnson's final disposition of his property was established by a Will and Codicil.

The consideration of numerous papers of which he was possessed, seems to have struck Johnson's mind, with a sudden anxiety, and as they were in great confusion, it is much to be lamented that he had not entrusted some faith-

369

ful and discreet person with the care and selection of them; instead of which, he, in a precipitate manner, burnt large masses of them, with little regard, as I apprehend, to discrimination. Not that I suppose we have thus been deprived of any compositions which he had ever intended for the publick eye; but from what escaped the flames, I judge that many curious circumstances relating both to himself and other literary characters, have perished.

Two very valuable articles, I am sure we have lost, which were two quarto volumes, containing a full, fair, and most particular account of his own life, from his earliest recollection. I owned to him, that having accidentally seen them, I had read a great deal in them; and apologising for the liberty I had taken, asked him if I could help it. He placidly answered, "Why, Sir, I do not think you could have helped it." I said that I had, for once in my life, felt half an inclination to commit theft. It had come into my mind to carry off those two volumes, and never see him more. Upon my enquiring how this would have affected him, "Sir, (said he,) I believe I should have gone mad."

During his last illness, Johnson experienced the steady and kind attachment of his numerous friends. Mr. Hoole has drawn up a narrative of what passed in the visits which he paid him during that time, from the 10th of November to the 13th of December, the day of his death, inclusive, and has favoured me with a perusal of it, with permission to make extracts, which I have done. Nobody was more attentive to him than Mr. Langton, to whom he tenderly said, *Te teneam moriens deficiente manu.* And I think it highly to the honour of Mr. Windham, that his important occupations as an active statesman did not prevent him from paying assiduous respect to the dying Sage whom he revered. Mr. Langton informs me, that, "one day he found Mr. Burke and four or five more friends sitting with Johnson. Mr. Burke said to him, 'I am afraid, Sir, such a number of us may be oppressive to you.'—'No, Sir, (said Johnson,) it is not so; and I must be in a wretched state, indeed, when your company would not be a delight to me.' Mr. Burke, in a tremulous voice, expressive of being very tenderly affected, replied, 'My dear Sir, you have always been too good to me.' Immediately afterwards he went away. This was the last circumstance in the acquaintance of these two eminent men."

Amidst the melancholy clouds which hung over the dying Johnson, his characteristical manner shewed itself on different occasions.

When Dr. Warren in the usual style, hoped that he was better; his answer was, "No, Sir; you cannot conceive with what acceleration I advance towards death."

Mr. Windham having placed a pillow conveniently to support him, he thanked him for his kindness, and said, "That will do,—all that a pillow can do."

As he opened a note which his servant brought to him, he said, "An odd thought strikes me:—we shall receive no letters in the grave."

He requested three things of Sir Joshua Reynolds:—To forgive him thirty pounds which he had borrowed of him; —to read the Bible;—and never to use his pencil on a Sunday. Sir Joshua readily acquiesced.

Johnson, with that native fortitude, which, amidst all his bodily distress and mental sufferings, never forsook him, asked Dr. Brocklesby, as a man in whom he had confidence, to tell him plainly whether he could recover. "Give me (said he) a direct answer." The Doctor having first asked him if he could bear the whole truth, which way soever it might lead, and being answered that he could, declared that, in his opinion, he could not recover without a miracle. "Then, (said Johnson,) I will take no more physick, not even my opiates: for I have prayed that I may render up my soul to GOD unclouded." In this resolution he persevered, and, at the same time, used only the weakest kinds of sustenance. Being pressed by Mr. Windham to take somewhat more generous nourishment, lest too low a diet should have the very effect which he dreaded, by debilitating his mind, he said, "I will take any thing but inebriating sustenance."

The Reverend Mr. Strahan, who was the son of his friend, and had been always one of his great favourites, had, during his last illness, the satisfaction of contributing to soothe and comfort him. That gentleman's house at Is-

lington, of which he is Vicar, afforded Johnson, occasionally and easily, an agreeable change of place and fresh
air; and he attended also upon him in town in the discharge of the sacred offices of his profession.

Mr. Strahan has given me the agreeable assurance, that,
after being in much agitation, Johnson became quite composed, and continued so till his death.

Dr. Brocklesby, who will not be suspected of fanaticism,
obliged me with the following accounts:

"For some time before his death, all his fears were
calmed and absorbed by the prevalence of his faith, and his
trust in the merits and *propitiation* of JESUS CHRIST.

"He talked often to me about the necessity of faith in the
sacrifice of Jesus, as necessary beyond all good works
whatever, for the salvation of mankind.

"He pressed me to study Dr. Clarke and to read his
sermons. I asked him why he pressed Dr. Clarke, an Arian.
'Because, (said he,) he is fullest on the *propitiatory sacrifice.*'"

Johnson having thus in his mind the true Christian
scheme, at once rational and consolatory, uniting justice
and mercy in the DIVINITY, with the improvement of human nature, previous to his receiving the Holy Sacrament,
in his apartment, composed and fervently uttered his
prayer:

"Almighty and most merciful Father, I am now as to
human eyes it seems, about to commemorate, for the last
time, the death of thy Son JESUS CHRIST, our Saviour and
Redeemer. Grant, O LORD, that my whole hope and confidence may be in his merits, and thy mercy; enforce and
accept my imperfect repentance; make this commemora-
tion available to the confirmation of my faith, the establishment of my hope, and the enlargement of my charity; and
make the death of thy Son JESUS CHRIST effectual to my
redemption. Have mercy upon me, and pardon the multi-
tude of my offences. Bless my friends; have mercy upon
all men. Support me, by thy Holy Spirit, in the days of
weakness, and at the hour of death; and receive me, at my

death, to everlasting happiness, for the sake of JESUS CHRIST. Amen."

Having, as has been already mentioned, made his will on the 8th and 9th of December, and settled all his worldly affairs, he languished till Monday, the 13th of that month, when he expired, about seven o'clock in the evening, with so little apparent pain that his attendants hardly perceived when his dissolution took place.

Of his last moments, my brother, Thomas David, has furnished me with the following particulars:

"The Doctor, from the time that he was certain his death was near, appeared to be perfectly resigned, was seldom or never fretful or out of temper, and often said to his faithful servant, who gave me this account, 'Attend, Francis, to the salvation of your soul, which is the object of greatest importance:' he also explained to him passages in the scripture, and seemed to have pleasure in talking upon religious subjects.

"On Monday, the 13th of December, the day on which he died, a Miss Morris, daughter to a particular friend of his, called, and said to Francis, that she begged to be permitted to see the Doctor, that she might earnestly request him to give her his blessing. Francis went into his room, followed by the young lady, and delivered the message. The Doctor turned himself in the bed, and said, 'GOD bless you, my dear!' These were the last words he spoke.—His difficulty of breathing increased till about seven o'clock in the evening, when Mr. Barber and Mrs. Desmoulins, who were sitting in the room, observing that the noise he made in breathing had ceased, went to the bed, and found he was dead."

About two days after his death, the following very agreeable account was communicated to Mr. Malone, in a letter by the Honourable John Byng, to whom I am much obliged for granting me permission to introduce it in my work.

373

"DEAR SIR,

"Since I saw you, I have had a long conversation with Cawston,[1] who sat up with Dr. Johnson, from nine o'clock on Sunday evening, till ten o'clock on Monday morning. And, from what I can gather from him, it should seem, that Dr. Johnson was perfectly composed, steady in hope, and resigned to death. At the interval of each hour, they assisted him to sit up in his bed, and moved his legs, which were in much pain; when he regularly addressed himself to fervent prayer; and though, sometimes, his voice failed him, his sense never did, during that time. The only sustenance he received, was cyder and water. He said his mind was prepared, and the time to his dissolution seemed long. At six in the morning, he enquired the hour, and, on being informed, said that all went on regularly, and he felt he had but a few hours to live.

"At ten o'clock in the morning, he parted from Cawston, saying, 'You should not detain Mr. Windham's servant:—I thank you; bear my remembrance to your master.' Cawston says, that no man could appear more collected, more devout, or less terrified at the thoughts of the approaching minute.

"This account, which is so much more agreeable than, and somewhat different from, yours, has given us the satisfaction of thinking that that great man died as he lived, full of resignation, strengthened in faith, and joyful in hope."

A few days before his death, he had asked Sir John Hawkins, as one of his executors, where he should be buried; and on being answered, "Doubtless, in Westminster-Abbey," seemed to feel a satisfaction, very natural to a Poet; and indeed in my opinion very natural to every man of any imagination, who has no family sepulchre in which he can be laid with his fathers. Accordingly, upon Monday, December 20, his remains were deposited in that noble and renowned edifice; and over his grave was placed a large blue flag-stone, with this inscription:

[1] Servant to the Right Honourable William Windham.

"SAMUEL JOHNSON, LL.D.
Obit XIII *die Decembris,*
Anno Domini
M.DCC.LXXXIV.
Ætatis suœ LXXV."

His funeral was attended by a respectable number of his friends, particularly such of the members of THE LITERARY CLUB as were then in town; and was also honoured with the presence of several of the Reverend Chapters of Westminster. Mr. Burke, Sir Joseph Banks, Mr. Windham, Mr. Langton, Sir Charles Bunbury, and Mr. Coleman, bore his pall. His school-fellow, Dr. Taylor, performed the mournful office of reading the burial service.

I trust, I shall not be accused of affectation, when I declare, that I find myself unable to express all that I felt upon the loss of such a "Guide, Philosopher, and Friend." I shall, therefore, not say one word of my own, but adopt those of an eminent friend, which he uttered with an abrupt felicity, superiour to all studied compositions:—"He has made a chasm, which not only nothing can fill up, but which nothing has a tendency to fill up.—Johnson is dead. —Let us go to the next best:—there is nobody; no man can be said to put you in mind of Johnson."

The character of SAMUEL JOHNSON has, I trust, been so developed in the course of this work, that they, who have honoured it with a perusal, may be considered as well acquainted with him. As, however, it may be expected that I should collect into one view the capital and distinguishing features of this extraordinary man, I shall endeavour to acquit myself of that part of my biographical undertaking,[1] however difficult it may be to do that which many of my readers will do better for themselves.

His figure was large and well formed, and his countenance of the cast of an ancient statue; yet his appearance was rendered strange and somewhat uncouth, by convulsive

---

[1] As I do not see any reason to give a different character of my illustrious friend now, from what I formerly gave, the greatest part of the sketch of him in my "Journal of a Tour to the Hebrides," is here adopted.

cramps, by the scars of that distemper which it was once imagined the royal touch could cure, and by a slovenly mode of dress. He had the use only of one eye; yet so much does mind govern, and even supply the deficiency of organs, that his visual perceptions, as far as they extended, were uncommonly quick and accurate. So morbid was his temperament, that he never knew the natural joy of a free and vigourous use of his limbs; when he walked, it was like the struggling gait of one in fetters; when he rode, he had no command or direction of his horse, but was carried as if in a balloon. That with his constitution and habits of life he should have lived seventy-five years, is a proof that an inherent *vivida vis* is a powerful preservative of the human frame.

Man is, in general, made up of contradictory qualities; and these will ever shew themselves in strange succession, where a consistency in appearance at least, if not reality, has not been attained by long habits of philosophical discipline. In proportion to the native vigour of the mind, the contradictory qualities will be the more prominent, and more difficult to be adjusted: and, therefore, we are not to wonder, that Johnson exhibited an eminent example of this remark which I have made upon human nature. At different times, he seemed a different man, in some respects; not, however, in any great or essential article, upon which he had fully employed his mind, and settled certain principles of duty, but only in his manners, and in the display of argument and fancy in his talk. He was prone to superstition, but not to credulity. Though his imagination might incline him to a belief of the marvellous and the mysterious, his vigorous reason examined the evidence with jealousy. He was a sincere and zealous Christian, of high Church-of-England and monarchical principles, which he would not tamely suffer to be questioned; and had, perhaps, at an early period, narrowed his mind somewhat too much, both as to religion and politicks. His being impressed with the danger of extreme latitude in either, though he was of a very independent spirit, occasioned his appearing somewhat unfavourable to the prevalance of that noble freedom of sentiment which is the best possession of man.

376

Nor can it be denied, that he had many prejudices; which, however, frequently suggested many of his pointed sayings, that rather shew a playfulness of fancy than any settled malignity. He was steady and inflexible in maintaining the obligations of religion and morality; both from a regard for the order of society, and from a veneration for the GREAT SOURCE of all order; correct, nay stern in his taste; hard to please, and easily offended; impetuous and irritable in his temper, but of a most humane and benevolent heart,[1] which shewed itself not only in a most liberal charity, as far as his circumstances would allow, but in a thousand instances of active benevolence. He was afflicted with a bodily disease, which made him often restless and fretful; and with a constitutional melancholy, the clouds of which darkened the brightness of his fancy, and gave a gloomy cast to his whole course of thinking: we, therefore, ought not to wonder at his sallies of impatience and passion at any time; especially when provoked by obtrusive ignorance, or presuming petulance; and allowance must be made for his uttering hasty and satirical sallies even against his best friends. And, surely, when it is considered, that, "amidst sickness and sorrow," he exerted his faculties in so many works for the benefit of mankind, and particularly that he achieved the great and admirable DICTIONARY of our language, we must be astonished at his resolution. The solemn text, "of him to whom much is given, much will be required," seems to have been ever present to his mind, in a rigourous sense, and to have made him dissatisfied with his labours and acts of goodness, however comparatively great; so that the unavoidable consciousness of his superiority was, in that respect, a cause of disquiet. He suffered so much from this, and from the gloom which perpetually haunted him, and made solitude frightful, that it may be said of him, "If in this life only he had hope,

---

[1] In the "OLLA PODRIDA," a collection of Essays published at Oxford, there is an admirable paper upon the character of Johnson written by the Reverend Dr. Horne, the late excellent Bishop of Norwich. The following passage is eminently happy: "To reject wisdom, because the person of him who communicates it is uncouth, and his manners are inelegant;—what is it, but to throw away a pine-apple, and assign for a reason the roughness of its coat?"

he was of all men most miserable." He loved praise, when it was brought to him; but was too proud to seek for it. He was somewhat susceptible of flattery. As he was general and unconfined in his studies, he cannot be considered as master of any one particular science; but he had accumulated a vast and various collection of learning and knowledge, which was so arranged in his mind, as to be ever in readiness to be brought forth. But his superiority over other learned men consisted chiefly in what may be called the art of thinking, the art of using his mind; a certain continual power of seizing the useful substance of all that he knew, and exhibiting it in a clear and forcible manner; so that knowledge, which we often see to be no better than lumber in men of dull understanding, was, in him, true, evident, and actual wisdom. His moral precepts are practical; for they are drawn from an intimate acquaintance with human nature. His maxims carry conviction; for they are founded on the basis of common sense, and a very attentive and minute survey of real life. His mind was so full of imagery, that he might have been perpetually a poet; yet it is remarkable, that, however rich his prose is in this respect, his poetical pieces, in general, have not much of that splendour, but are rather distinguished by strong sentiment, and acute observation, conveyed in harmonious and energetick verse, particularly in heroick couplets. Though usually grave, and even awful in his deportment, he possessed uncommon and peculiar powers of wit and humour; he frequently indulged himself in colloquial pleasantry; and the heartiest merriment was often enjoyed in his company; with this great advantage, that, as it was entirely free from any poisonous tincture of vice or impiety, it was salutary to those who shared in it. He had accustomed himself to such accuracy in his common conversation, that he at all times expressed his thoughts with great force, and an elegant choice of language, the effect of which was aided by his having a loud voice, and a slow deliberate utterance. In him were united a most logical head with a most fertile imagination, which gave him an extraordinary advantage in arguing: for he could reason close or wide, as he saw best for the moment. Exulting in his intellectual strength and

378

dexterity, he could, when he pleased, be the greatest sophist that ever contended in the lists of declamation; and, from a spirit of contradiction, and a delight in shewing his powers, he would often maintain the wrong side with equal warmth and ingenuity; so that, when there was an audience, his real opinions could seldom be gathered from his talk; though when he was in company with a single friend, he would discuss a subject with genuine fairness; but he was too conscientious to make errour permanent and pernicious, by deliberately writing it; and, in all his numerous works, he earnestly inculcated what appeared to him to be the truth; his piety being constant, and the ruling principle of all his conduct.

Such was SAMUEL JOHNSON, a man whose talents, acquirements, and virtues were so extraordinary, that the more his character is considered the more he will be regarded by the present age, and by posterity, with admiration and reverence.

APPRECIATION

by

COLIN BELL

The business of the biographer is often to pass slightly over those performances and incidents which produce vulgar greatness, to lead the thoughts to domestic privacies, to display the minute details of private life, where exterior appendages are cast aside, and men excel each other only by prudence and virtue.

SAMUEL JOHNSON, *The Rambler* (Number 60, 1751)

For the modern reader, the quotation above is an unexceptionable piece of Johnsonian dogma. We are accustomed both to the biographical form (newspapers always strive to personalize the news, television even more) and to the close-up view. None but the peculiarly devout buy, let alone read, the kind of dull, authorized life which we dismiss as " hagiography ". It is a commonplace that the reputable scholar, the honourable historian of today, should serve up his subject warts and all, and that his subject should be revealed in his dining-room, if not in his bedroom, rather than protected by a screen of pious omissions.

Nevertheless, at the time Johnson gave his opinion, it must have seemed startling and novel. The very word " biography " had not been in use for more than a century, and virtually every work published before Johnson's own *Life of Savage* (1744) we should now class as hagiography. There was good hagiography—Roper's *Life of More*—and bad —the great mass of the religious lives—but there certainly wasn't any tradition of intimacy, informality and total

383

honesty. In English at least, one great biographer had died virtually unpublished: John Aubrey's *Brief Lives* is today the only work of pre-Boswell biography that can be read for pleasure and illumination, with no spurring from a sense of duty. But in the main, Johnson's definition can best be classed as a work of prescience: for nothing existed to justify his assertion until after his own death—when Boswell undertook *The Life of Johnson* and displayed at length the minute details of a private life.

The place of Boswell's *Johnson* in the history of letters is secure. Almost before it was published (since Boswell's *Tour to the Hebrides* preceded it by six years) it was recognized for both its revolutionary novelty and its intrinsic merit. Even those who found either biographer or subject distasteful—or, like Macaulay, found it difficult to say a good word for either—had to confess the book itself magnificent. But not Boswell himself. Although Johnson's reputation has always been secure (thanks to Boswell), Boswell's own has been traduced consistently. Macaulay found himself—having called Boswell " servile, impertinent, shallow, pedantic, a bigot and a sot "—in the ludicrous position of explaining that " if he had not been a great fool, he would never have been a great writer."

Even if one allows for the fact that Boswell had immortalized Johnson's slighting opinion of Macaulay's great-uncle, and that Macaulay's own wealth and reputation were founded on exactly that sort of sanctimonious Cambridge whiggery which Johnson would have lacerated, and which could never rationalize the presence of genius in someone so alien as Boswell, Macaulay's judgement is nonsense. It has however survived, in some degree at least, until the present. For the mandarins of literature, for those embarrassed by excessive honesty and self-revelation, for the sexually prudish (and inadequate, a not uncommon coincidence), Boswell is a monstrous threat. One cannot patronize on social grounds a man whose family estates stretched for ten miles through Ayrshire: one cannot indulge with anachronistic psychology a man who drank to get drunk: one cannot dismiss an author who published in his lifetime three books to excellent reviews (*Corsica*, *Hebrides* and the *Life*), and since whose death we have discovered a fourth still greater (his private Journal). Boswell, even if Johnson thought him " a very clubable man," is not the sort of fellow that the great intellectual whigs of any generation since would have liked or understood. The fact that he got on well with Wilkes cannot excuse his Jacobite beliefs and religious piety, nor can his own genuine endeavours for the truly poor be understood by those whose charity is normally extended by committee.

It is only in our own generation that opinion has begun to change: no longer do we accept this strange phenomenon that Johnson, whose works we do not read, was a giant, upon whose mighty carcass climbed despicable Boswell, a scribbling jackal, the better to foist upon the decent world his one good work—and that, regrettably, inexplicably, not only still readable, but apparently immortal. That our views should begin to change is more remarkable than pure reason would suggest; it may be that the traditional view is insupportable by common sense, but such small obstacles have seldom interrupted the mindless flow of English cant.

The change has come about not because the old view has finally been seen as nonsense, but in part at least because of changing fashion. If Boswell now stands higher in the public fame, it may be but a reflection of a modern taste for anti-heroes. That is to say, we have not generally acquitted Boswell of impertinence, bigotry and sottishness—but we have reviewed our opinion of those qualities. No modern novel could be sold without its share of boozing insolence, few modern writers be reviewed unless their private lives amazed the bourgeoisie. From Verlaine to Scott Fitzgerald, we have come to expect the artist late for dinner, reeking of drink, and with attendant bawds and bailiffs.

This remains unfair to Boswell: to be dismissed by Macaulay because one honestly confesses to incontinence is bad enough, but to be embraced by his intellectual heirs precisely because they now approve what Boswell bitterly regretted is intolerable. Opinion may have changed, but the facts on

385

which it thinks to base itself remain inaccurate. Boswell has suffered bitterly for far too long from the endless repetition of unfounded slanders: no one ever wrote *his* life except from motives of inverted hagiography: not to canonize, but to condemn.

In part the fault for this is his family's. Boswell we now know to be one of history's best-documented men. He did not write a journal, file correspondence, conduct regular self-examinations, perform improving literary exercises, just to equip himself for Johnson's *Life*—it was the way he organized his own. But the vast collection of his papers that he left did not begin to come to light until the 1920's, since when, in attics, trunks and outhouses, more and more have been discovered. Their principal source was Malahide Castle, but others have been found in England, Scotland, Belgium and America.

Their origins are, however, less important than their present home; after a century and a half of oblivion, being read only to be bowdlerized from family piety, the overwhelming majority of Boswell's papers are now at Yale University. One can regret that their final home should be so far from Auchinleck, but since the great house itself, for which Boswell felt such feudal love, now stands empty and unkempt, and since Scotland long ago decided that Burns and Scott were more than enough of a literary heritage, it is probably better for Boswell's reputation that his work should be in the care of American scholars, and American endowments, than that it should be stored in some Edinburgh basement.

Yale has done, is doing, well by Boswell. To date, eight volumes have been produced of a " trade ," or reading edition, and a thirty-volume research edition is projected. When it is complete, Boswell's works will at last be available in something like their entirety. Already it is clear that Boswell was a lifelong literary artist—not a one-shot biographer—and that the style and technique of the *Life* were no happy accident, but the product of thirty years' practice as an autobiographer.

Yale's first volume, published in 1951, was the *London Journal, 1762-1763*: it was the first for the excellent reason that it was the first major journal to be kept by the author, and it had the additional importance of recording not only his proper introduction to London, but his celebrated introduction to Johnson. However, it had quite an amazing sale for a scholarly edition of a long-dead biographer's private letters and diary. Boswell retained both his naïvety and his lechery all his life, but that his first official trip as a young man to London (he was twenty-two) should be the most naïve and the most lecherous is hardly surprising. At any rate, it did not do much to redress the common view of Boswell, since it recounted with complete frankness both his social climbing and his social diseases.

Later volumes (Yale has got as far as 1776) have served him better, and with each new publication it becomes harder to maintain the old view, propagated by Mrs. Thrale, Fanny Burney, Macaulay, Vulliamy—and most of the public—of Boswell the scruffy eavesdropper. If he *had* been such a " great fool " he might, just possibly, have produced the great *Life*, but he could hardly have produced the Journal; and in any case it is quite clear from the Journal that he was neither a fool, nor thought by most of his contemporaries to be one.

On the basis of the Journal, one can examine, point by point, the charges so generally laid against him, and for the great majority, find no evidence. Boswell was in his life many more things than Johnson's biographer—and at some, at least, he was a success. When he sought an interview with the great French philosopher Rousseau, he first drew up a brief summary of his own life, in order, as he said, that " you shall see me completely, just as I am."

One might, in order to gain him an equally successful audience with posterity, draw up a similar biography. In doing so I am, as from henceforward all students of Boswell must be, totally indebted to the work of the Yale University " Boswell Office." So great is their scholarship, so lucid their presentation, that they have converted a lifetime's collection

387

of notebooks, diaries, letters and scraps of paper into an easy order, in which the footnotes illuminate, the indices guide, the additions assist. As anyone with any experience of definitive editions knows, such qualities are not rare—they are unique.

James Boswell was born, most probably in the family flat in Blair's Land, Edinburgh, on October 29, 1740. He told Rousseau " I am the eldest son of a Scots gentleman of ancient family " and this was both true and essential to Boswell's own vision of himself. His father was the eighth Boswell to be laird of Auchinleck, a substantial estate in Ayrshire, and was a successful lawyer. As such, he was appointed in 1754 to be one of the fifteen judges of Scotland's supreme civil court, the Court of Session. These judges were known as the " Lords of Session " and were accorded the title of Lord in common use. Boswell was then the heir to the estate of Auchinleck, and the son of Lord Auchinleck, without himself having any hereditary right to a title of nobility. His mother, Euphemia, who died while Boswell was in Paris in 1766, on his slow way home from the Grand Tour, was of slightly superior family, being related, albeit remotely, to Darnley, the father of King James VI & I (Sixth of Scotland, and First of England on the death of Queen Elizabeth.)

Boswell went to school at six: Mundell's—eighteenth-century Edinburgh's most progressive; it took both sexes, and offered not only Latin, but English, Writing and Arithmetic. At eight he left, and for the next four years was taught at home. At thirteen he entered the University of Edinburgh, where he remained for six years; neither the age at which he was admitted, nor the time he spent there, was unusual for the period.

Just before going to the University, he had, as the climax of a distinctly delicate and nervous childhood, suffered what was then considered to be a scorbutic illness. It was most probably not scurvy, but a nervous rash, particularly since with it was associated a mental condition known at the time

18
Samuel Johnson, LL.D., after a bust by Nollekens. " Though there was a roughness in his manner," Boswell reported on first meeting Johnson, " there was no ill-nature in his disposition."

19
James Boswell in 1793, two years before his death. He died at the early age of fifty-five.

THE
LIFE
OF
AMUEL JOHNSON, LL.D.

COMPREHENDING

AN ACCOUNT OF HIS STUDIES AND NUMEROUS WORKS,

IN CHRONOLOGICAL ORDER;

SERIES OF HIS EPISTOLARY CORRESPONDENCE
AND CONVERSATIONS WITH MANY EMINENT PERSONS;

AND

VARIOUS ORIGINAL PIECES OF HIS COMPOSITION,
NEVER BEFORE PUBLISHED.

HE WHOLE EXHIBITING A VIEW OF LITERATURE AND LITERARY MEN
IN GREAT-BRITAIN, FOR NEAR HALF A CENTURY,
DURING WHICH HE FLOURISHED.

IN TWO VOLUMES.

By JAMES BOSWELL, Esq.

——— *Quò fit ut OMNIS*
Votiva pateat veluti descripta tabella
VITA SENIS.——— HORAT.

VOLUME THE FIRST.

LONDON:
PRINTED BY HENRY BALDWIN,
FOR CHARLES DILLY, IN THE POULTRY.
M DCC XCI.

20
Title page of the first edition of Boswell's *Life of Johnson*, published in 1791. The book was an immediate success.

A PLAN of the *CITY'S* of LONDON, WESTMINSTER and Bo

A New Map of
LONDON

Most Humbly Inscrib'd to the Rt. Wor-
shipfull Sr. Peter Delme Knt. & Aldern.
of London 1700.

A Scale of Half a Mile

References to Westminster

Churches		Publick Buildings	
71	St. Clements Danes	D	Sommerset House
83	St. Pauls Covent Garden	E	New Exchange
84	St. Margaret Westminster	G	Westminster Hall
79	St. Martin in Fields	M	Berkeley House
80	St. Mary Savoy	N	Leicester House
86	St. James	O	Kings Play House
87	St. Anns	P	New Play House
		R	Exeter Exchange
		T	Burlington House
		V	Northumberland House

Referen

Parish Churches within the Walls.

1	St. Albans Woodstreet	17	St. Bennet Paulswharf	33	St. Margaret Lothbury
2	Alhallows Barking	18	Christ Church	34	St. Margaret Pattens
3	Alhallows Breadstreet	19	St. Christophers	35	St. Mary Abchurch
4	Alhallows Great	20	St. Clement Eastcheap	36	St. Mary Aldermanbury
5	Alhallows Lombardstreet	21	St. Dionis Backchurch	37	St. Mary Aldermary
6	Alhallows Steining	22	St. Dunstan East	38	St. Mary le bow
7	Alhallows the Wall	23	St. Edmond Lombard	39	St. Mary hill
8	St. Alphage	24	St. Ethelborough	40	St. Mary Oldstreet
9	St. Andrew Undershaft	25	St. George Botolphs Lane	41	St. Mary Somerset
10	St. Andrew Wardrobe	26	St. Hellen	42	St. Mary Woolnoth
11	St. Ann Aldersgate	27	St. James Dukes Place	43	St. Martin Ludgate
12	St. Antholins	28	St. James Garlick hill	44	St. Martin Outwich
13	St. Austins	29	St. Katherine Coleman	45	St. Mathew Fridaystreet
14	St. Bartholomew Exchange	30	St. Katherine Creechurch	46	St. Michael Bassishaw
15	St. Bennet Finch	31	St. Lawrence Jury	47	St. Michael Cornhill
16	St. Bennet Gracechurch	32	St. Magnus	48	St. Michael Crooked Lane

49	St. Mic
50	St. Mic
51	St. Mic
51	St. Mild
52	St. Mill
53	St. Mild
54	St. Nic
55	St. Ola
56	St. Ola
57	St. Pete
58	St. Pet
59	St. Ste
60	St. Ste
61	St. Sw
62	St. Vet

OUTHWARK; with the new Additional Buildings Anno, *1720*.

London

...thin and freedom		Out Parishes		Publick Build.ᵍˢ	The Names of the Several Wards into which this City is Divided	
Holborn		74	S.ᵗ Giles in Fields	A. Guild Hall	Aldgate	Cordwainers
..ldesgate		75	S.ᵗ James Clerkenwell	B. Royal Exchange	Aldgate	Cornhill
Aldgate		76	S.ᵗ Katherine Tower	C. Gresham Colledge	Baynard Castle	Cripplegate
Bishopsgate		77	S.ᵗ Leonard Shoreditch	F. London Hall mᵃˢ	Basishaw	Dowgate
..Wet		78	S.ᵗ Mary Whitechap	Q. New Bedlam	Billingsgate	Farrindon with.ᵃ
...pplegate		82	Wapping Chappel	S. Blackwell Hall	Bishopsgate	Farrindon wᵗ.out
..ru		85	Trinity Minories		Broadstreet	Langborn
...inew Great					Bridge within	Limestreet
...new Lesᵗ					Bridge without	Portsoken
Precinct					Broadstreet	Queenhith
					Candlewick	Tower
					Cheap	Vintry
					Coleman street	Wallbrock

References to Southwark
Churches

1	S.ᵗ Saviour	2	S.ᵗ Olave
3	S.ᵗ Thomas	4	S.ᵗ George
5	S.ᵗ Mary Magd.	6	Rotherhith
7	Christ Church	8	Lambeth

21
A plan of London in 1720. The city had not greatly changed when
Boswell first came to it some forty years later.

22-23
Boswell's London: a view of Whitehall by Canaletto, and (above)
Boswell's Scotland: the High Street, Edinburgh in the eighteenth
century.

as hypochondria. Boswell spent the rest of his life anxiously taking his mental pulse; and his Journal is at times concerned to the exclusion of all else with his "Hypochondriack" worries and fears. This did not then have its restricted modern meaning—exaggerated concern for one's health, readiness to believe that one is physically ill—but described a state of mind and spirit combining self-doubt and self-disgust, spiritual disquiet and intellectual torpor. It has been called the endemic disease of the Enlightenment, and did undoubtedly have some connection with the breakdown of accepted religious belief in the face of the industrial and scientific revolution.

At any rate, Boswell was a lifelong Hypochondriack, even using the term as the title for a series of essays he wrote. Whenever an opportunity presented itself, he sought the advice of others on his malady—and nothing seems to have given him greater satisfaction than to discover a fellow-sufferer. Johnson was of course one—as Boswell manages to establish very early in the *Life*—and Boswell on the Grand Tour seems to have been almost as intent on discovering Hypochondriacks as on meeting the great.

After Edinburgh, at which he took both an Arts and a Law course, Boswell, who had already at sixteen passed through a phase of martial fantasy when his father had to prevent him enlisting for the Seven Years' War, embarked on another adolescent passion: the stage. Since the theatre in Scotland was barely legal, let alone respectable, this caused his father great anxiety—and Boswell's departure from Edinburgh was in fact a parental device to remove him from the company of actors and actresses. He was sent to Glasgow where he fell under the influence of the great Adam Smith. It is not surprising that an intelligent, alert youth should have found Smith remarkable; the lectures that Boswell attended subsequently became famous as *The Theory of Moral Sentiments* and *The Wealth of Nations*. However, it is important for the defence of Boswell to note that Smith seems to have taken to the pupil as well, telling him that he had " a nice facility of manners "—which suggests that at nineteen he certainly was not Macaulay's boor.

It was at this moment that Boswell first published any of his writing—" A View of the Edinburgh Theatre during the Summer Season, 1759." A fifty-page pamphlet, it was published in London with the encouragement of Lord Somerville.

Apart from becoming stage-struck at Edinburgh, Boswell had also shown ominous signs of interest in the Roman Catholic religion, for Lord Auchinleck another good reason to remove his heir to Glasgow. A Catholic at that time could not have entered the Law, the Army, Navy, Church, or Universities, nor could he inherit the family estate, a spiritual luxury which his father had no intention of allowing. However, at Glasgow Boswell continued his inquiries into Catholicism, and wrote to his father in February 1760 that he was not only intent on conversion, but that he wished to become either a priest or a monk. Lord Auchinleck instantly summoned him home. Instead, Boswell ran away to London, where he embarked with great haste on his conversion, but also managed to lose his virginity to a prostitute called Sally Forrester. Having informed his father of his address, he was tracked down by a family friend, Lord Eglinton, and taken into Eglinton's town house in Mayfair. Professor Pottle assesses Eglinton's role neatly: " He rescued Boswell from religious error by making him a libertine." It was not a difficult transformation.

Eglinton introduced the young man to brilliant society; he met the Jockey Club, and the Duke of York, heir presumptive to the throne. He also met Laurence Sterne, at the height of his fame as author of *Tristram Shandy*, and Sterne praised some of his verses. Eglinton also persuaded Boswell that he would be happier as an officer of the Guards than as a lawyer, and so his father, relieved no doubt that his heir had abandoned Catholicism, suffered a new shock: James wished to be purchased a commission.

At this point, Lord Auchinleck broke away from his affairs at home and came to London. Opposed as he undoubtedly was to the idea, he seems to have played his hand with greater tact and delicacy than usual. As a result, when he returned to Scotland, he took Boswell with him, three months after the initial flight, on the understanding that the matter was to be given thought. The discussion that ensued reveals the reality of Boswell's martial ambition: offered a commission in a marching regiment (that is, one liable to be stationed abroad, and to fight) he dug in his heels and insisted on the Guards. The Guards carried not only social prestige, but a prospect of minimal duties, carried out in London.

At any rate, what happened was that Boswell spent the next two years at home, being coached for the Law by his father, a period of understandable family friction. He had returned from London with venereal disease, and he caught a worse dose in Edinburgh; it would be hopeless to maintain that Boswell was not at the very least a great deal randier than Macaulay, but on the other hand, the vast numbers of prostitutes available in every town, and the very mild censure (strongly tinged with sympathy) which most men at least extended to those who "catched a Tartar," indicates that Boswell's failing was more common than continence.

While cooped up in his father's household, ostensibly learning the law, Boswell began to write as a regular exercise: poems, pamphlets, criticism, journal, self-exhortation. Much of what he wrote then, like much of what he wrote for publication later (excluding the inimitable Journal) was poor; but it would nevertheless be unjust to conceal his life-long literary fecundity. He did not, one must emphasize again, stagger into the *Life* as a miraculous amateur—he was as much a professional writer as most men forced to earn a living have ever been.

By 1762, outraged by his son's devotion to publication, actresses, and the dream of a fashionable commission, Lord Auchinleck was prepared to disinherit Boswell. What he proposed, and James accepted, was to exchange an irrevocable allowance of £ 100 a year for James' signature on a document empowering Lord Auchinleck to appoint trustees of his estate. It now appears, indeed appeared to Boswell

391

later in life, that his father had no legal right to tamper with the succession to the estate in this fashion—but at the time, Lord Auchinleck held all the trumps, notably the marriage settlement drawn by Boswell's grandfather, and as a Lord of Session he could hardly be bested in a legal quibble.

At any rate in July, 1762 Boswell took, and passed with some distinction, the private examination in Civil Law, embarked on a tour of leave-taking, and in November, presumably feeling that he had complied with his part of the bargain, took off for London and the hoped-for commission.

Commissions in the eighteenth-century army, like seats in the Commons, or good livings in the Church, were not to be had by simple merit or ambition. They had to be bought —bought outright, by cash purchase, or bought by influence and the exchange of obligations. Boswell's influence existed only insofar as his father was prepared to pledge his social and political support—the " Auchinleck interest "—and, to a much lesser degree, insofar as he could win the favour of the influential. He had nowhere near enough to buy outright a commission in a decent regiment (then as now, the measure of decency was in inverse proportion to the risk of unceremonious soldiering).

In the circumstances—given that Boswell was not interested in the sort of commission he might have had, a marching regiment, and that his chances were low—he never came near the Guards, despite all his efforts to solicit the aid of the mighty. However, he spent his time in London enjoyably, and provoked his first literary scandal by the publication of his correspondence with the Honourable Andrew Erskine, a contemporary, a friend since the previous year, and a Lieutenant in the 71st of Foot. The letters made little attempt to disguise third persons, and were unflattering to most of Edinburgh society. The publication aroused interest, resentment, laughter and scorn—and Lord Auchinleck. He wrote, threatening to sell the entire estate so that Boswell should not inherit and bring further disgrace on the good name of the family: " it is better to snuff a candle out than leave it to stink in the socket."

24

Jean Jacques Rousseau, the great French philosopher. Young
Boswell tracked him down during his grand tour of the Continent
and spent five days recording Rousseau's conversation.

25
Voltaire, France's greatest man of letters, whom Boswell also interviewed in his home during his tour of the Continent.

26

John Wilkes, the radical politician, by Hogarth. Although Wilkes and Johnson were at opposite poles politically, Boswell stage-managed a meeting between the two which went off very well.

27
General Paoli, the Corsican leader. Boswell met him on Corsica,
became absorbed in Corsican affairs, wrote several books on the
subject and was soon recognized as *the* authority on Corsica.

The upshot of this latest family row was that Boswell was to abandon ambitions outside the Law, in exchange for which his father would send him to Holland for a year, and allow him a short tour abroad thereafter. Since Scots Law differs from the English, and is, like Dutch, strongly derivative of Roman Law, Holland was a common finishing-school for Scots lawyers. Auchinleck himself had, like his father before him, attended the University of Leyden. For Boswell, at the suggestion of Sir David Dalrymple, a family friend and also a personal friend of James, Auchinleck proposed Utrecht.

Boswell acquiesced in this plan: it was in the short run a great deal better than going back to Edinburgh, and it also carried once more the prospect of pleasing his father; for although father and son disagreed so strongly on so many counts, Boswell was at heart eager to win his father's love and respect.

Lord Auchinleck, and Boswell himself, may have been concerned for his career; but for posterity it is his vocation that counts. And while the family dispute wore on, Boswell in London had added more names we recognize to the list of those who had met him and thought him worthwhile. He had met Oliver Goldsmith, John Wilkes, Charles Churchill—and having once met them, was to see all of them again, on terms of equality. And finally, on Monday, May 16, 1763 he was introduced by the bookseller Tom Davies to Samuel Johnson.

Despite the prickly beginning to the relationship, within two months of the meeting Johnson so valued Boswell that the older man (fifty-three, painfully short-sighted, racked with physical ills and mental quirks) took the long coach journey to Harwich just to bid Boswell farewell on his departure for Holland. Dr. Johnson, like Adam Smith, Lord Kames, David Dalrymple and many another of the young Boswell's contemporaries, clearly shared neither Lord Auchinleck's hysterical delusion that his heir was a ninny, nor the nineteenth century's view that Boswell was wholly worthless.

Boswell's stay in Europe is marked once more with what his detractors may call social climbing—and what his friends may happily excuse by its success. There is no doubt that Boswell did want to meet the great, no matter how—and of his targets, only Frederick the Great was to elude him; but there is equally no doubt that, once trapped, most of his quarries enjoyed the experience. In Holland he began a long relationship with Belle de Zuylen—a relationship that on both sides came almost to the point of marriage; and Belle de Zuylen was one of the world's first and best-known bluestockings. He toured the German courts with the aid, and often the company, of Lord Marischal, the exiled Scot who had become one of Frederick's closest friends and advisers. The older man seems to have been happy to share a coach with Boswell, and so taken by his talk and his ambitions that he interceded for him with Lord Auchinleck.

The year in Holland, Belle apart, was a critical one in Boswell's development. The bouts of hypochondria were severe, the introspective passages in the Journal are often morbid; nevertheless, it is in this year that Boswell not only added a daily poem to his self-imposed literary tasks, but also formulated his " Inviolable Plan," which tells us fairly clearly the sort of man Boswell wanted to be: a serious, dutiful, religious man—but finally, his own man. Although Boswell's Journal continues to be studded with cryptic references to the desirable qualities of others, he abandoned in Holland the conflicting ambitions to emulate in detail those of his friends and acquaintances who had impressed him most, and resolved instead, as he put it in his Journal later, " to be Mr. Boswell of Auchinleck and no other."

In Germany, Boswell went from court to court (there were over sixty, ranging from Frederick's Prussia, a European Power, to Anhalt-Zerbst, whose entire Army totalled 180 men) until he reached Karlsruhe, seat of Karl Friedrich, Margrave of Baden-Durlach. The Margrave, an intelligent and literary man, talked to Boswell with great freedom and intimacy, and when Boswell left it was with the conviction that a Knighthood of the Order of Fidelity was bound to turn up in the post—for the Margrave had promised to correspond with him, and to think seriously of Boswell's request for the Order. Boswell, quite properly according to German usage, had spent the tour being addressed as " Baron, " and dearly wanted a glittering star to wear back home in Britain where he would revert to plain Mister.

No star ever came, but Boswell's tour continued in evermore impressive vein. No one now would count the favour of long-dead Princelings very high; but Boswell proceeded to collect two priceless intellectual distinctions. In fairly short order, he charmed his way into the homes and conversations of Jean-Jacques Rousseau and Voltaire. To Rousseau he addressed the sketch of his early life (" I present myself, Sir, as a man of singular merit ") , and within five days was granted six interviews by a man not only famous throughout Europe, but plagued with severe illness. The conversations, which Boswell naturally recorded with the fidelity and skill he had learned from four years' Journalising, show once more that when Boswell put himself out, he was neither a fool, a bore nor unduly vain. Undoubtedly he was engrossed by his own problems, but he was genuinely eager to hear the views of others, rather than to command their sullen audience.

Voltaire was not quite such a success; but nevertheless Boswell managed to augment a single brief reception into an invitation to stay for two nights. Voltaire's material circumstances were infinitely more grand than those of Rousseau, and his household large, but despite the competition for the philosopher's time, Boswell had a lengthy opportunity to attempt to convert Voltaire to his own religious view. And he gained once more some splendid conversation for his Journal.

From Switzerland, Boswell went into Italy, reaching Turin in January 1765. His Italian tour was of a more mundane sort than that of Switzerland, aiming as it did not at the living great, but at the sights of antiquity and, he hoped, the favours of a Countess. Any Countess would have done, but in the end he settled for the wife of the Mayor of Siena. In Italy he met Wilkes once more, and shared a coach for some time with Lord Mountstuart, son of Bute, the former Prime Minister—and the man responsible for Wilkes' being in exile. Yet again, we are left with a picture of Boswell that fits, in only one possible respect, the critical cartoon: he certainly did put himself out to know the famous and the powerful— but nothing save merit can explain why the famous and the powerful should have prolonged the acquaintanceship. Wilkes asked Boswell to dine, Mountstuart asked Boswell to share his coach.

By October, 1765 Boswell had done the obligatory sights of Italy, and set out on a side-trip that few travellers ever attempted; he went to Corsica, at that time a Genoese possession in armed revolt. The probable incentive was Rousseau, who was full of the Corsicans and their noble fight for liberty, and of Corsica itself, where it was a great deal easier to imagine the noble savage than in less rugged continental Europe.

Boswell landed, tramped over wild, unmapped country for eight days, and tracked down the Corsican patriot leader, General Paoli. Paoli soon joined the ranks of those whom Boswell charmed and won. William Pitt called Paoli a hero of the sort one only met in the pages of Plutarch.

From then on Boswell was wedded to the cause of Corsica —in newspaper paragraphs, pamphlets, and finally in an *Account of Corsica*. He was interviewed by Pitt on the subject, and although neither his efforts nor Paoli's could save the day for the islanders against the Genoese and their French allies, he was undoubtedly responsible for the climate of English opinion which welcomed the exiled Paoli after defeat, and caused him to be granted a pension of £ 1200 a year. Once more, here is evidence that neither Boswell's actions nor his writings were wholly without merit. Indeed, for many years, as Johnson was " Dictionary " Johnson, so Boswell was " Corsica " Boswell.

Returned from the Grand Tour, Boswell became the Scots lawyer his father intended, and he took it seriously enough.

28-29
James Boswell and his family, probably painted in the 1780's, and (above) Boswell taking tea with Dr. Johnson, a caricature by Rowlandson.

30
A sketch of Boswell in his last years, by the famous portraitist, Sir Thomas Lawrence.

Although he continued to visit London, it was always in the legal vacations, and his career as an advocate progressed. He never reached the heights of his profession, if for no other reason than that he willingly took briefs to defend the indefensible poor, thus gaining neither large fees nor the approval of the established powers. That he did not become a judge is as much a tribute to his genuine concern for the illiterate criminals as a criticism of his abilities. What his legal career proves is that he was capable of methodical and sustained work, and that when he took to heavier drinking than was wise, it was the product, not the cause, of his lack of professional success.

In 1769 Boswell finally married. For the previous ten years he had been in the habit of entertaining fantasies of marriage to virtually every eligible woman he met, ranging from the elderly and louche Duchess of Douglas, to " Zelide "—Belle de Zuylen. His final choice, for no other reason but love, was a cousin, Margaret Montgomerie. But although he settled in Edinburgh, had a legitimate family to add to his two certain bastards, and although for twenty years he pursued his career at the Scots bar, one cannot help feeling that from Corsica on, Boswell really lived fully only on his trips to London.

The *Life* itself records these, often in whole sections taken directly from his Journal, and to that extent one need not detail the evidence of his merit. He was elected to Johnson's Club, despite Burke's initial doubts, and was therefore accepted by Reynolds, Garrick, Goldsmith, Burke, just as he had been by Johnson. Johnson, who had begun their friendship by risking the trip to Harwich, valued it so over the years that at the age of sixty-three he allowed Boswell to persuade him away from London to the remote wildness of the Highlands and Islands. And when Johnson died, Boswell was the obvious person to be asked to provide a 400-page biography in six weeks—obvious not just because he loved Johnson, and Johnson him, but because he had a long record of publication, because he was the friend of Reynolds and the Johnson circle, because Adam Smith, David Hume,

Rousseau, Voltaire, Paoli, Wilkes had all considered him worthy of their time and their hospitality.

By the time of Johnson's death, Boswell's own affairs had struck bottom. He had finally succeeded to Auchinleck, in 1782, but debt and depression bore him down. In an effort to mend his fortunes, he entered the English Bar in 1786, and took up permanent residence in London in 1789—with his children, but not his wife. His attempts at a political career, and indeed at a legal career, failed, and although he pressed on with the *Life*, encouraged by Reynolds and assisted by Malone, drink and gaming took up more and more of his time. Four years after the *Life* appeared, on May 19, 1795, he died, fifty-five years old, poor, bloated and wretched. *The Gentleman's Magazine*, recording his death, said it would be " most sincerely regretted by all who really knew him." Unhappily, most of those who really knew, and loved, James Boswell had predeceased him.

Nevertheless, had it been generally thought that Boswell was a great fool, so much the prisoner of his weaknesses, no sensible man would have entrusted the biography to him; after all, before the *Life* was written his contemporaries could only judge him by his other work. Publishers are seldom rash enough to commission books from men without any reputation save for sottishness. The fact is that Boswell's unhappy, and unjust, reputation is posthumous in the main. It has roots in the rival biographies of Johnson—Sir John Hawkins' and Mrs. Piozzi's. Johnson said of Hawkins that he was " a very unclubable man, " a fundamental barrier to his rendering an accurate record of Johnson, and Mrs. Piozzi, who as Mrs. Thrale had been perfectly friendly with Boswell, turned against him as against most of her old friends when she remarried to their virtually unanimous disapproval.

And his reputation has the deepest roots of all in the *Life* itself. Like Rousseau's *Confessions*, Boswell's self-revelation is too honest for the respectable taste. Since his method is to illuminate by intimate recollection, and since he was, on

398

paper at least, transparently honest, he could not help but reveal altogether too much of his own weaknesses. All men have weaknesses, but there is nothing so generally despised as their admission—it simultaneously invites contempt and arouses discomfiting guilt. What is generally called a decent reticence is in fact a general agreement to suppress at large what most men strive to hide from themselves.

Boswell was accustomed over thirty years to write down in total detail everything about himself. He did not attempt to evade his own shortcomings, but chose instead both to record them and to seek advice about them. He was a hard man to snub, not because he was insensitive (the Journal records his hurt, and more often, his shame) but because he was prepared to take the snubs and evasions in his determination to get at the truth. The *Life* records many scathing remarks by Johnson to Boswell; but Johnson's conversational stock-in-trade was the well-turned insult. It is not important that Johnson was rude to Boswell, but that Boswell bore from him with devotion what most men got in any case, and had the honesty to publish transcripts of conversations in which he himself did not shine. No man is snubbed more often than he who persists in asking awkward questions; and given Johnson's customary treatment of bores, Boswell's testimonial is that Johnson willingly chose his company time and time again—for three months without interruption on the Tour to the Hebrides.

Nor is it the case that Boswell was Johnson's tame buffoon. Johnson's household was weighted down with social misfits and financial burdens, but Boswell was not another of the Doctor's weird charities. If Johnson, against opposition, pushed for Boswell's election to the Club, then he later reported " now you are in, none of them are sorry." Sir Joshua Reynolds, to whom the first edition of the *Life* was dedicated, made Boswell a present of his portrait when Boswell was unable to pay; Edmund Malone, whom Boswell called " Johnsonianissimus," laboured for many hours with Boswell to get the *Life* into shape for the press. And by now it should be plain that there were many men of great distinction who found time for Boswell before he knew Johnson, or who were well outside the Johnson circle.

The cartoon Boswell should by now be thoroughly despatched. He wrote, with merit, much besides the *Life*; his company, although sometimes unbidden, was widely valued; he drank in early years rather less than many of his friends, maintaining at all times a keen awareness of just how much he drank and what effect it had; he was capable of lengthy periods of chastity, and when he fell, did so with touching anxiety and admirable kindness towards his partners; he was an excellent husband and father, by the standards of his time; tried his best to please the incompatible demands of his father and of his vocation; gave genuine enthusiasm and effort to unpopular causes, in politics and before the law; and if he was a social snob, he was by the same token a good landlord to the people of Auchinleck. Even Fanny Burney's picture of him, notebook in hand, scribbling down the words of the great as they spoke, is inaccurate. He had an excellent memory, was a trained journalist, and both recorded and transmitted what was really said, no matter how well or ill he personally emerged: but he made his notes after the event, in private.

Finally, when Johnson died, although Boswell was poor, tormented by apparent failure, and shortly to be bereaved (his wife died at Auchinleck in 1789), he set to work and produced—not in six weeks, but in six years—a magnificent biography, drawn from his own extensive papers, from conversations with everyone he felt might have some memory to add, and from the kind of documented research that no sot, no fool could tackle—but would be familiar to a well-trained lawyer. Had he not been such an artist, he could never have been called a fool—and the *Life* would have told us infinitely less about its subject, and its author.

SOURCES OF THE ILLUSTRATIONS

Frontispiece : Boswell and Johnson setting off on their tour of Scotland. Detail from an illustration by Thomas Rowlandson, 1786. British Museum, London.

1 James Boswell, portrait by Sir Joshua Reynolds, 1786. National Portrait Gallery, London.

2 Samuel Johnson, after a portrait by Sir Joshua Reynolds. Radio Times Hulton Picture Library, London.

3 Edial Hall, c. 1736, engraving by Charles Smith. Mansell Collection, London.

4 Engraving of Lichfield. Mansell Collection, London.

5 Portrait of Dr. Johnson's wife, Tetty. Radio Times Hulton Picture Library, London.

6 Sketch of Bennet Langton by George Dance, 1789. British Museum, London.

7 The cover of the first edition of the *Dictionary*, published 1755. Mansell Collection, London.

8 Title page of the first edition of the *Dictionary*. British Museum, London.

9 Copy of Dr. Johnson's letter to the Earl of Chesterfield, 7th February, 1755. Mansell Collection, London.

10 Page from first edition of the *Dictionary*. Mansell Collection, London.

11 A letter from Dr. Johnson to Mrs. Thrale. Mansell Collection, London.

12 Hester Piozzi (Mrs. Thrale) by George Dance, 1793. National Portrait Gallery, London.

13 Dr. Johnson and Boswell in Scotland, engraving by T. Trotter, 1783, to illustrate Boswell's journal of their tour of Scotland. British Museum, London.

14 Oliver Goldsmith, portrait from the studio of Reynolds, 1769(?). National Portrait Gallery, London.

401

INDEX

This book, designed by
Werner Schelling
is a production of
Heron Books, London

Printed in England by
Hazell Watson and Viney Limited
Aylesbury, Bucks